THE BIG BOOK OF *Amazing* MAC FACTS

LON POOLE

UP-TO-DATE
TIPS ON ALL
MACINTOSH® MODELS,
INCLUDING THE MAC®
CLASSIC, LC AND IIsi

PUBLISHED BY
Microsoft Press
A Division of Microsoft Corporation
One Microsoft Way
Redmond, Washington 98052-6399

Library of Congress Cataloging-in-Publication Data
Poole, Lon.
The big book of amazing Mac facts / Lon Poole.
p. cm.
Includes index.
ISBN 1-55615-252-3
1. Macintosh (Computer)—Programming. I. Title.
QA76.8.M3P658 1990
005.265--dc20 90-6271
CIP

Printed and bound in the United States of America.

1 2 3 4 5 6 7 8 9 FGFG 4 3 2 1 0

Distributed to the book trade in Canada by General Publishing Company, Ltd.

Distributed to the book trade outside the United States and Canada by Penguin Books Ltd.

Penguin Books Ltd., Harmondsworth, Middlesex, England
Penguin Books Australia Ltd., Ringwood, Victoria, Australia
Penguin Books N.Z. Ltd., 182-190 Wairau Road, Auckland 10, New Zealand

British Cataloging-in-Publication Data available

Trademark information appears at the back of this book.

Project Editor: Ron Lamb and Nancy Siadek
Manuscript Editor: Rebecca Pepper
Technical Editors: Adrian Falla and Mark Dodge
Acquisitions Editor: Dean Holmes

In memory of my father.

In celebration of his grandsons.

CONTENTS

ACKNOWLEDGMENTS

This book wouldn't exist if it weren't for the thousands of readers who sent tips and questions to my *Macworld* magazine column "Quick Tips" (originally called "Get Info"). Their ideas are the backbone of the book. My sincere thanks to all who wrote and especially to those whose ideas appear in these pages.

I'd also like to thank Cathy Abes, Deborah Branscum, Jerry Borrell, and all the other editors and publishers of *Macworld* magazine who have encouraged and actually paid me to play with Macintosh products, read letters from the magazine's readers, and write about it all in my monthly column. It continues to be a real privilege.

Tony Reveaux deserves credit for the splendid work he did researching tip ideas for the last two chapters. He stepped in at the eleventh hour and kept the book going when it looked as though the project would grind to a halt for good.

I want to thank Freude Bartlett for generously offering valuable counsel, supplying endless terrific ideas, and being a vital wellspring of enthusiasm. Thanks also to Erfert Fenton and Diana Van Winkle for reviewing parts of the book and making valuable suggestions.

I'm indebted to Dean Holmes for continuing to believe in this book even when it dragged on far longer than either of us expected. For editorial assistance, my thanks to Rebecca Pepper, Nancy Siadek, Ron Lamb, and the proofreaders at Microsoft Press.

Thanks to Sue Nail of CE Software, Sarah Charf of Microsoft, Deb Lovig of Quark, Judy Marie Merrill of Ashton-Tate, and everyone else who collected and sent me tips about their companies' products.

Most of all, I want to thank my wife for urging me to keep writing even though she knew how tough it would be on her. I truly appreciate her indulgence of my compulsiveness and her (mostly) good humor despite my sometimes shameful neglect. You're the most, K.B.

INTRODUCTION

To use your Macintosh computer at a basic level, you don't have to read a book or manual. Pull down the menus, click the icons, manipulate text and graphics in a natural way, and you'll soon pick up your Mac's obvious features. However, you won't discover the mass of less-obvious features as easily. To tap the power lurking behind the veneer of simplicity, you can spend lots of time exploring and experimenting, or you can learn by using the experience of others. You'll find the ideas of hundreds of Macintosh users in this book. I won't say you can use every tip in this book, but I'm sure several dozen will make your Mac work faster, easier, and more fun.

For this book I've collected the best tips from seven years of my monthly *Macworld* column, "Quick Tips" (and its predecessor, "Get Info"). Don't worry; the book isn't larded with moldy tips from prehistory. I picked only the best ideas from my column.

To the material from my column, I added tips gleaned from software publishers and equipment manufacturers. This information either isn't in the manual or is buried there. In addition, this book contains tips suggested by a motley lot of individuals with whom I consort professionally, plus a few modest notions of my own.

ORGANIZATION

The tips are organized into chapters according to the type of software, hardware, or general topic to which they apply. Within each chapter the tips are grouped by specific topic.

The first six chapters cover system software and system hardware components. Chapter 1, "General Macintosh Operations," has tips related to Mac system software. The tips in Chapter 2, "Essential System Components," concern the hardware components present in every Macintosh system, whether it is a compact Mac, such as a 512K, Plus, SE, Classic, or SE/30; a modular Mac, such as an LC, II, IIx, IIcx, IIsi, IIci, or IIfx; or a portable Mac. Disks and disk drives warrant their own chapter, Chapter 3, "Disks and Disk Drives." Likewise, printers are covered separately in Chapter 4, "Printers and Printing." If your system isn't working properly and you want to diagnose the problem and attempt a cure, see Chapter 5, "Troubleshooting."

Chapters 6 through 11 cover application programs. Chapter 6, "Words," has tips on word processing programs. The tips in Chapter 7, "Graphics," concern painting and drawing software. Desktop publishing and desktop presentations are the subject of Chapter 8, "Publishing and Presentations." The hints in Chapter 9, "Spreadsheets and Charts," pertain to spreadsheet programs and chart programs. For tips on HyperCard, flat-file managers, and relational database managers, see Chapter 10, "Information Management." If you're looking for ideas on networking, telecommunications, or file transfer between computers, see Chapter 11, "Communications."

HOW TO USE THIS BOOK

This book is not meant to be read linearly, from beginning to end. Each tip is self-contained and doesn't rely on your having read previous tips or introductory text. Go ahead and browse haphazardly for new ideas. If you want to narrow your browsing to a particular topic, look for the topic in the table of contents, turn to the page where the discussion of the topic begins, and start scanning. You'll also find a summary of the topics covered in a chapter at the beginning of that chapter.

You can use the same procedure to locate a particular tip. Alternatively, you can look up the subject of the tip in the index.

When you're browsing, you can easily spot tips that apply to your software and hardware by looking at the icons in the page margins. Tips that apply to many programs or components, or to more than two programs or components, have generic icons with names such as "General Graphics." Specific, nongeneric icons identify a particular program or component to which a tip applies.

As you read a tip, you might encounter unfamiliar products. All but the best-known products are listed alphabetically in the Appendix, "Product Sources," along with the companies that publish or manufacture them.

General Information Management

THE ULTIMATE TIP

Here's a tip that will help you with anything you do with your Mac (and with most other gadgets, for that matter): Read the manual. You don't have to read all of it. Simply leaf through it and see how it's organized so that you know where to look later. The key to using a manual is not to memorize it from cover to cover but to know where to look when you need help.

Chapter 1

GENERAL MACINTOSH OPERATIONS

The tips in this chapter are related to tasks every Macintosh user performs, using the Macintosh system software that every user has. They cover the following:

- Pointing with the mouse and typing on the keyboard
- Manipulating windows
- Opening documents and applications
- Using standard commands from the File and Edit menus
- Using standard desk accessories, especially the Control Panel and the Chooser
- Working with fonts
- Customizing standard features

Tasks that involve working with disks and disk drives, using startup disks, and organizing disks are covered in Chapter 3, "Disks and Disk Drives." Another common task, printing, is discussed in Chapter 4, "Printers and Printing." And HyperCard, which is also part of the Macintosh system software, is covered in Chapter 10, "Information Management."

POINTING AND TYPING

HOUDINI'S KEYSTROKE

Keyboard

On occasion, a dialog box that has no buttons appears, such as the one that asks you to switch disks, as shown in Figure 1-1 on the following page. You can escape from most buttonless dialog boxes without restarting your Mac simply by pressing Command-period. You might need to press Command-period more than once because some application programs don't give up easily when a disk they want is not available. This trick doesn't work if you're using a version of the System file earlier than 3.2. Also, some older applications might crash when you try to escape from a disk-switch dialog box.

Please insert the disk:
Frequent Flyer

FIGURE 1-1. DISK-SWITCH ESCAPE.
Although this dialog box has no Cancel button, pressing Command-period (sometimes several times) usually has the same effect.

Keyboard

DIALOG-BOX NAVIGATION

In dialog boxes in which you must type several items, you can use the keyboard to advance from one item to the next. Press the Tab key. When you do so, the entire next item is usually selected, so you can replace it simply by typing the new text. Pressing the Tab key when you reach the last item in the box takes you back to the first item.

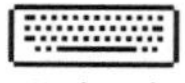
Keyboard

DIALOG-BOX CONFIRMATION

You can use the keyboard to click the OK button. If the OK button is surrounded by a thick-line border (as usual), press the Return key or the Enter key. If, however, the thick-line border surrounds a button other than OK, pressing Return or Enter has the effect of clicking that button instead.

In dialog boxes that have no OK button, pressing Return or Enter usually confirms the settings in the dialog box. Here again, a thick-line-bordered button takes precedence.

Keyboard

KEYBOARD MOUSE

Since April 1987, Macintosh system software has included a file named Easy Access, which provides a feature called "mouse keys." This feature lets you use the numeric keypad in place of the mouse. You can move the pointer, click, drag, and so forth—all from the keyboard.

You install Easy Access by dragging its icon into the System Folder on your startup disks. You must restart your computer before you can use the Easy Access feature. You can use it only with System file versions 4.1 and later.

To turn the "mouse keys" feature on, press Command-Shift-Clear. See Figure 1-2 for a diagram of keypad functions. To turn the "mouse keys" feature off, press the Clear key once.

With "mouse keys" on, the 5 key functions like the mouse button: Press it once to click, press it twice quickly to double-click, or press and hold it to drag. Pressing the 0 key once has the effect of pressing and holding the mouse button; pressing the period key once has the effect of releasing the mouse button. You can press the 5 key in combination with the Shift key, the Option key, or another modifier key to produce the same effect as pressing a modifier key and clicking the mouse button.

The number keys surrounding the 5 key move the pointer up, down, sideways, or diagonally. For very fine pointer movements, tap (quickly press and release) the corresponding number key for the direction in which you

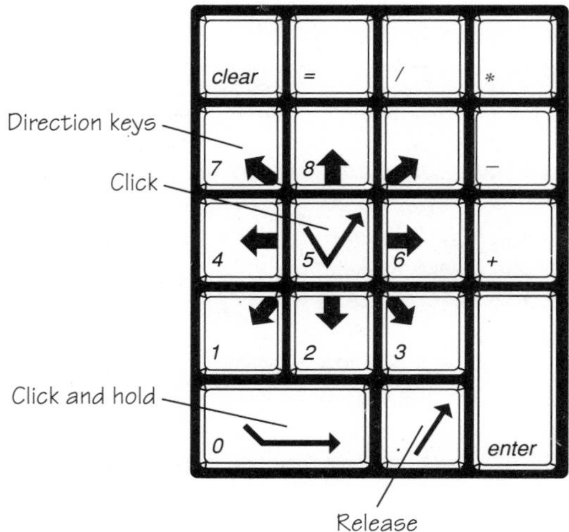

FIGURE 1-2. MOUSE KEYS.
The numeric keypad can double as a mouse.

want to move. To cover distance rapidly, press and hold the key. The pointer moves faster after you've held down the key for a second or more. You can adjust the cursor speed with the mouse speed control in the Control Panel.

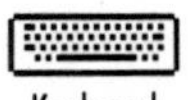

Keyboard

ONE-HANDED TYPING

After you restart with the Easy Access startup document in your System Folder, you can easily type anything with one hand. A feature called "sticky keys" lets you type combination keystrokes that include the modifier keys—Command, Option, Shift, and Control (if present)—without pressing several keys simultaneously. Instead, you press the keys sequentially.

To turn the "sticky keys" feature on, press the Shift key five times. Don't move or bump the mouse as you do so, or you'll need to begin again. When the "sticky keys" feature is on, an icon at the right edge of the menu bar shows its status. Figure 1-3 explains the meaning of each icon. To turn the "sticky keys" feature off, press Shift five times again, or press any two modifier keys simultaneously.

Icon	Meaning
	The "sticky keys" feature is on, but you have not begun a combination keystroke by pressing a modifier key such as Command, Option, Shift, or Control.
	You have begun a combination keystroke by pressing one or more modifier keys. Press another modifier key to continue the combination keystroke, or press a nonmodifier key to complete it.
	You have pressed the same modifier key twice in a row, effectively locking that modifier key. To unlock it, press it again.

FIGURE 1-3. STICKY KEYS.

Special icons at the right end of the menu bar indicate the status of the "sticky keys" feature, which lets you press the keys of a combination keystroke sequentially rather than simultaneously.

TAKING A SNAPSHOT OF THE SCREEN

Keyboard

You can record the current screen image as a MacPaint document by pressing Command-Shift-3. The result is called a screen snapshot, screen shot, or screen dump.

Screen snapshots are saved on the disk that contains the application program you're using, and each snapshot requires from 2 KB through 56 KB of disk space. The Mac beeps if you press Command-Shift-3 when not enough disk space is available to save a screen snapshot. You can take up to 10 snapshots, which will automatically be named Screen 0 through Screen 9. If you try to save an eleventh snapshot without first removing or renaming some of the Screen 0 through Screen 9 documents, the Mac will beep.

The Capture utility software from Mainstay replaces the standard snapshot feature. With Capture you can capture a menu and take a snapshot in color or in shades of gray as well as select a part of the screen to capture.

DESKTOP PATTERN FOR SCREEN SNAPSHOTS

Control Panel

The standard screen-snapshot feature described in the previous tip always captures the entire screen. If you plan to edit the screen snapshot later, temporarily set the desktop pattern to white before taking the screen snapshot. (Use the Control Panel desk accessory to do this.)

PRINTING SCREEN SNAPSHOTS

Keyboard

To print a screen image with an ImageWriter, press Command-Shift-4. If the Caps Lock key is turned on, you get a snapshot of the whole screen. If the Caps Lock key is turned off, only the active window is printed.

CONTROL-KEY CHARACTERS

Keyboard

The Control key on most Mac keyboards (not on the Mac Plus or 512K) lets you type special symbols. In the Chicago font, for example, press Control-Q to type the Command-key symbol, Control-R for a check mark, Control-P for a hollow Apple logo, and Control-T for a solid Apple logo. (See Figure 1-4 on the following page.)

Pressing these key combinations has no effect in MacWrite II, HyperCard, Cricket Draw, MacCalc, and some other applications.

Symbol	Key Combination
⌘	Control-Q
✓	Control-R
◆	Control-P
	Control-T

FIGURE 1-4. CONTROLLED CHARACTERS.
In the Chicago font, you can type the symbols shown here.

Keyboard

SECRET SYMBOLS

Judging by the Key Caps desk accessory, the Symbol font does not contain the symbols for subset and proper subset, $\subset$ and $\subseteq$. Key Caps does indicate that the converse symbols, $\supset$ and $\supseteq$, are available. There is a way to type the missing symbols, however. For the subset symbol, press Option-N followed by Shift-A in the Symbol font. Similarly, press Option-N and then Shift-O to type the proper subset symbol. Also available is $\not\subset$, which you type by pressing Option-accent (`) and then Shift-A.

Keyboard

TWO-HANDED CUT AND PASTE

By using the keyboard and the mouse to cut or copy and paste, you can avoid moving the pointer back and forth between the item you're working with and the menu bar. With one hand, simply select text or an object with the mouse, and use the other hand to press Command-Z, Command-X, Command-C, or Command-V to choose the Undo, Cut, Copy, or Paste command from the Edit menu.

MANIPULATING WINDOWS

General Operations

DRAGGING AN INACTIVE WINDOW

When several windows are displayed on the screen, dragging one window by its title bar normally places it on top of all others and makes it the active window. If you want to move an inactive window aside without activating it, press the Command key before you begin to drag. You can release the Command key after you begin dragging.

With more than one application open (when MultiFinder is active), you can move aside only windows belonging to the active application. Clicking on another application's window makes that application active and brings all its windows to the front.

FINDING A HIDDEN WINDOW

A quick way to bring the window of an open folder or disk to the front is to double-click the gray folder or disk icon, as shown in Figure 1-5.

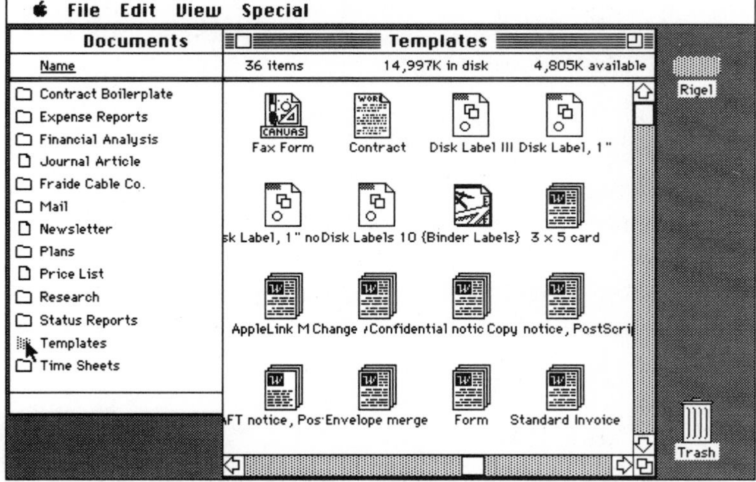

FIGURE 1-5. LOST WINDOW.
How would you find the hidden window for the already-open disk icon Rigel?

CLOSING WINDOWS WHEN QUITTING

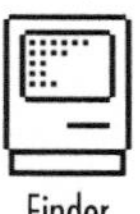

When quitting an application, you can close all previously open Finder windows (when MultiFinder is inactive). Hold down the Option key from the time you choose Quit from the File menu until the Finder menu bar appears. The desktop is displayed much more quickly with windows closed.

CLOSING ALL WINDOWS AT ONCE

To close all Finder windows at once, press the Option key while choosing Close from the File menu or while clicking the close box of any window. This shortcut works with Finder versions 5.1 and later and with MultiFinder.

PREVENTING WINDOWS FROM OPENING

When you start up the Mac, insert a disk, or quit an application, the Finder normally opens the same disk and folder windows that were open when you last shut down the Mac, ejected the disk, or started the application. How can you avoid this time-consuming operation?

Hold down the Option key until you see the Finder's menu bar or the icon of the disk you inserted. No windows open. This shortcut works with Finder versions 5.1 and later and with MultiFinder.

Another way to prevent a window from opening automatically later is to press the Option key while opening it; the Finder (versions 5.1 and later) does not remember the event. When you next start up the Mac, quit an application with the same disk inserted, or insert the same disk, the window does not reopen.

OPTIMAL USE OF WINDOWS

Optimize the use of windows in the Finder by placing seldom-used icons at the bottom of the window and then shrinking the window so that the icons are no longer visible. Keeping windows small makes it easier to work with more of them at one time. But don't make them so small that you spend more time hunting for icons with the scroll bars than you would spend moving windows around.

If you don't use MultiFinder, consider moving your most frequently used icons onto the desktop. Then you'll rarely need to open the windows they came from. For example, if you are a Microsoft Excel user, you could move the Resume Excel icon to the desktop and leave the Excel disk window closed. (When you use MultiFinder, desktop icons can be inaccessible behind the windows of inactive applications.) Be sure not to overlook the desktop icons when you back up your disk.

OPENING DOCUMENTS AND APPLICATIONS

CREATING AN ALIAS

To expedite the opening of frequently used applications, create aliases for them. Double-clicking an alias opens the corresponding application.

If you are using System 7, you can create an alias for an icon by selecting it and choosing Make Alias from the Finder's menu. If you are using system software earlier than System 7, you can use documents as application aliases. Simply save an empty document (or a template document) from each application for which you want an alias. Keep the aliases in one open folder not on the desktop, as shown in Figure 1-6. (If you don't use Multi-Finder, you can keep aliases on the desktop.)

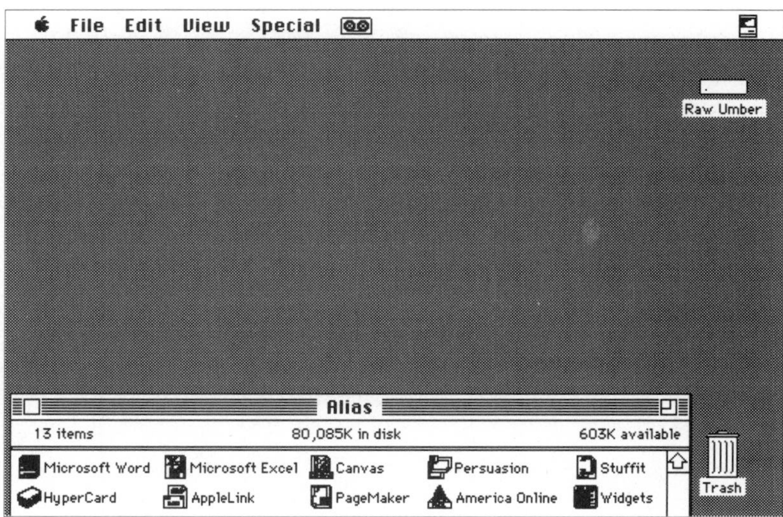

FIGURE 1-6. AKA.
This folder contains empty documents and template documents used to open often-used applications, which are buried in the folder hierarchy.

OPENING A BURIED APPLICATION

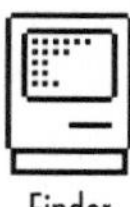

You can open an application or any other file that's buried in several layers of nested folders without opening the folders.

Use the Find File desk accessory to find the application or file. Then select it by name in the Find File window. Next choose the Move To Desktop command from the Find File menu. Doing so removes the application or file from its folder and places it on the desktop. If the application has support files, such as a help file or a spelling dictionary, that must be in the same folder as the application, then find and move the entire folder instead of only the application. You can easily return an icon on the desktop to its previous folder by selecting the icon and choosing Put Away from the Finder's File menu.

Finder

EZ OPEN

Moving through folders in search of an application you want to open can be cumbersome. You can open many applications by double-clicking their settings or preferences files, located in the System Folder. (These files usually remain in the System Folder to work with their applications, so don't drag them to an alias folder as described in the tip "Creating an Alias.")

Finder

OPENING MANY DOCUMENTS AT ONE TIME

You can open more than one document at a time by using the Finder to select the icons of all documents you want to open and then choosing Open from the Finder's File menu. (To select multiple icons, press Shift as you click each one, or drag a selection rectangle around a group of icons). You don't need to include the application in the selection; the Finder opens the appropriate application automatically. If MultiFinder is active, you can open documents created by more than one application.

All the icons you select must be in the same window or on the desktop, as shown in Figure 1-7. If you drag them to the desktop, you can return them to their folders later with the Put Away command (in the File menu).

Finder

OPENING A COMPATIBLE DOCUMENT

You can use the Finder to open a document in a compatible application different from the one that created it. For example, you might want to open a MacTerminal document with MacWrite.

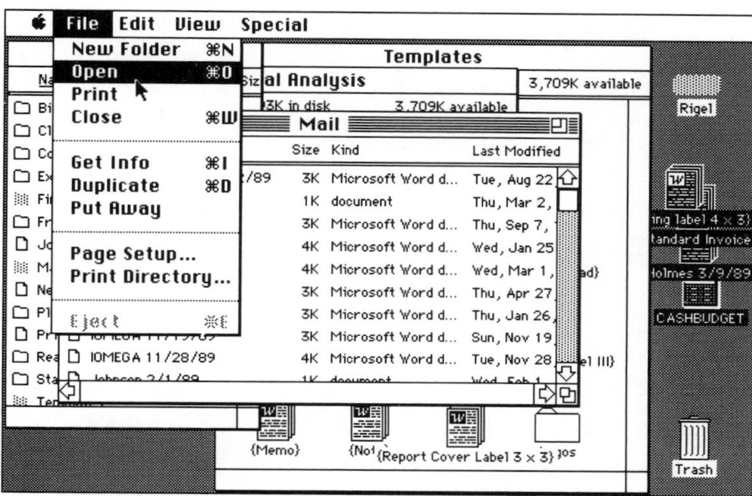

FIGURE 1-7. GROUP OPENING.

The selected documents were dragged to the desktop from various folders. You can open all of them at one time.

To do so, take the following steps:

1. Select the document and application icons. If they are not in the same window, drag them to the desktop, and select them there. Later, you can put them back in their respective folders by selecting them again and choosing the Put Away command from the Finder's File menu.
2. Choose *Open* from the Finder's File menu.

This method requires that the application you select is able to open the type of document you select. For example, MacDraw can open PICT documents saved by other applications but not documents saved by MacPaint.

DETERMINING VERSION NUMBERS

Finder

Nearly all software is updated periodically. How can you tell which version you have?

Using Finder version 6.0 or later, select the icon of the software you're curious about, and choose Get Info from the File menu. (See Figure 1-8 on the following page.)

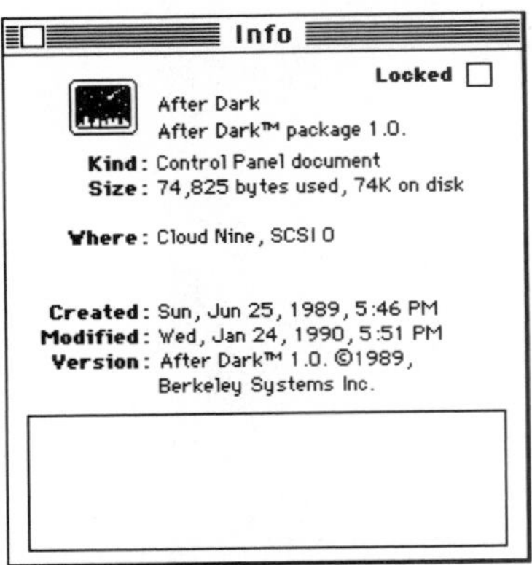

FIGURE 1-8. GET INFO VERSION.
The information window displayed by the Finder's Get Info command reports the version number of the selected item.

If you're using a version of Finder earlier than 6.0, you might be able to learn the version number of an application by choosing About from the Apple menu while you are using the application. Most versions of the Control Panel, Chooser, and some other desk accessories display their version numbers in very small print in the window that appears when you choose them. Similarly, recent versions of the ImageWriter and LaserWriter files show their version numbers in the dialog boxes that appear when you choose Print or Page Setup from any application program.

Multifinder

IS MULTIFINDER ACTIVE?

When MultiFinder is active, the Apple menu contains the command About MultiFinder. In addition, a small icon representing the current application appears at the right end of the menu bar. Figure 1-9 illustrates both clues. If any desk accessory is currently active, the icon at the right end of the menu bar looks like a suitcase with an Apple logo on it.

Multifinder

MULTIFINDER COMPATIBILITY

A few applications don't work properly with MultiFinder. To avoid accidentally opening an application that's incompatible with MultiFinder, set its application memory size to a value greater than the amount of available

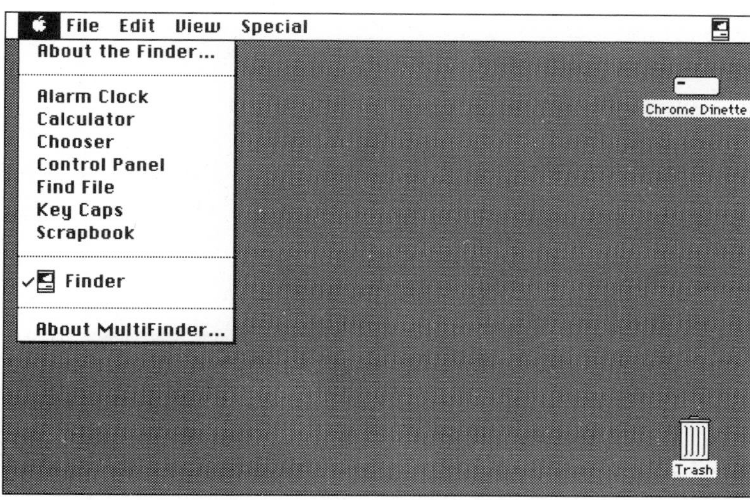

FIGURE 1-9. MULTIFINDER ON.
Which two elements on this screen show that MultiFinder is active?

memory when only the Finder is active. (You can find this out by choosing About The Finder from the Apple menu.) If you later try to use the application when MultiFinder is active, the system will remind you that there's too little memory. You can, however, open the application normally when MultiFinder is inactive.

To change the application memory size, be sure MultiFinder is active, select the application icon, and choose Get Info from the Finder's File menu. Type the desired size in the box at the bottom of the Get Info window.

MULTIFINDER IN 1 MB

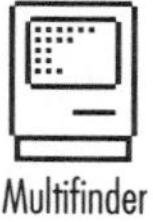

Very few applications can be opened concurrently when you are running MultiFinder with only 1 MB of memory. (See Figure 1-10.) The full megabyte is not available for applications because the Finder, which occupies 160 KB, remains open when you open an application with MultiFinder. In addition, system resources such as fonts and system software modules typically occupy at least 200 KB more. That leaves 640 KB available for applications—too little for running two of today's average-length applications concurrently. In fact, you might not be able to open even one complex application, such as HyperCard or FullWrite Professional, if you are running MultiFinder with less than 2 MB of RAM (random access memory).

MultiFinder does have its uses with 1 MB. It speeds switching from one application to another, even if you can't open both at once, by sharply reducing the time it takes to quit and return to the omnipresent Finder. And because the Finder is always open under MultiFinder, you can use it to copy disks and files, create new folders, and so on without quitting the application you're currently using. Of course, you can have all these advantages with less overhead by using a Finder replacement such as CE Software's DiskTop desk accessory.

About the Macintosh™ Finder

Finder: 6.1
System: 6.0.2

Larry, John, Steve, and Bruce
©Apple Computer, Inc. 1983-88

Total Memory: 1,024K
Largest Unused Block: 63K

Microsoft Word	512K	
Finder	160K	
System	289K	

FIGURE 1-10. WHO'S GOT MEMORY?

The About The Finder window shows that running MultiFinder on a 1-MB Mac doesn't leave enough memory in many cases for two applications; sometimes there is not enough to run even one program.

Multifinder

TURNING MULTIFINDER OFF TEMPORARILY

To deactivate MultiFinder temporarily, restart your Mac. Begin pressing the Command key from the time the *Welcome to Macintosh* message (or the last startup [INIT]) icon appears. Continue holding the key down until the Finder's menu bar appears. To reactivate MultiFinder, either restart your Mac normally or press Command-Option while double-clicking the MultiFinder icon in the System Folder.

USING STANDARD MENU COMMANDS

FORMATTED TEXT AND THE CLIPBOARD

General Operations

Have you ever wondered why formatted text you copy to the Clipboard loses its formatting and becomes plain text when you paste it into another document? This generally happens if, before pasting, you quit the current application or switch applications when using MultiFinder. When you leave an application, it must convert the Clipboard contents to a form that any other application can use. Since 1987, a convention has existed for retaining font, size, and style information between applications. But the convention doesn't provide for retaining paragraph and document formats. Unfortunately, very few applications follow this formatted-Clipboard convention.

TOO MUCH TO PASTE

General Operations

Is there a limit to the amount of information you can either cut and paste or copy and paste?

Yes. The limit is half the memory available to the application that's active when you use the Cut, Copy, or Paste command. Some applications impose a more restrictive limit. Thus, you might be able to copy a large graphic and successfully paste it into one application but be unable to paste it into another. If that happens, try working with smaller chunks of information.

USING KEYS TO SCROLL THROUGH FILES

Open & Save

The mouse is the standard tool for scrolling through the file and folder names listed in the Open, Save, and Save As dialog boxes and for opening folders and selecting a file by name. In addition, you can use the direction keys to navigate the list of file and folder names.

Pressing the Up or Down direction key selects the file or folder name listed above or below the currently selected name, scrolling the list if necessary. To open a selected folder or file, press Command-Down arrow key. To return to the previous folder, press Command-Up arrow key.

This keyboard navigation technique is not available on an unenhanced Mac 512K.

Open

SCROLL BY TYPING

When you choose the Open command from within an application, the Open dialog box appears, displaying a scrollable list of filenames from which you can choose the name of the file you want to open. Searching a long list can be tedious. To narrow the search, type the first part of the name you want. What you type doesn't appear anywhere. When you stop typing, however, the first name that matches your entry is selected and scrolled into view. The Delay Until Repeat setting in the Keyboard panel of the Control Panel desk accessory determines how long you can pause while typing before you initiate a new request.

Open & Save As

DISK CYCLE

When you're using more than one disk, the dialog boxes for disk commands such as Open and Save As contain a Drive button. You cycle through the names of the disks by clicking the Drive button or by pressing the Tab key.

Open & Save As

MOVING THROUGH NESTED FOLDERS

In an Open or Save dialog box, you can move upward through a hierarchy of nested folders one level at a time by clicking the disk name. The name appears to the right of the disk icon, which is commonly located near the Eject button, as shown in Figure 1-11. Each click takes you up one folder level until you finally arrive at the main disk directory (the root level).

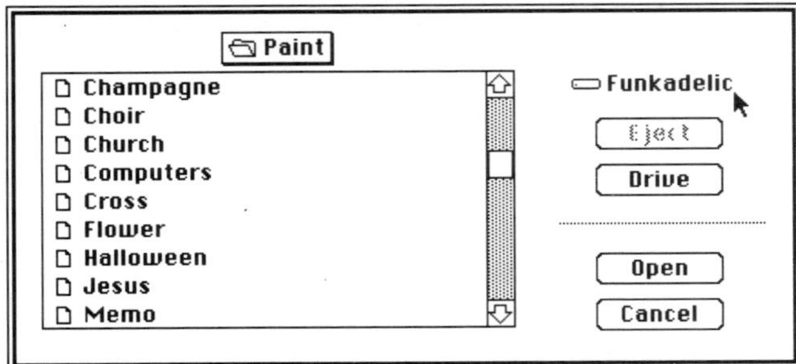

FIGURE 1-11. CLOSE FOLDER.

Click the disk name in the Open or the Save dialog box to close the current folder and move to the folder that contains it.

BOMB INSURANCE

Make a habit of the following to reduce the impact of a system error:

- Save whenever you pause to ponder.
- Save before switching applications with MultiFinder.

With most applications, pressing Command-S is all it takes to save the document you're working on.

TEXT-ONLY SAVES SPACE

General Operations

An unformatted, text-only document takes up less disk space than the same document with character-formatting and paragraph-formatting information. So if you can live without character, paragraph, and section formatting in your document, you can reduce your disk-space consumption by as much as 30 percent by turning on the Text Only option in the Save and Save As dialog boxes that offer it.

REMEMBERING TO MOVE

Finder

Save

When you save a document you know you'll want to move to another disk, prefix the document name with a special character, such as an asterisk. In the Finder, you'll see the prefix and remember to make the move.

DATES IN FILENAMES

Finder

You might want to include the date in the names of some correspondence and other documents, as shown in Figure 1-12. The Finder can list documents in order by date, but the Open dialog box cannot.

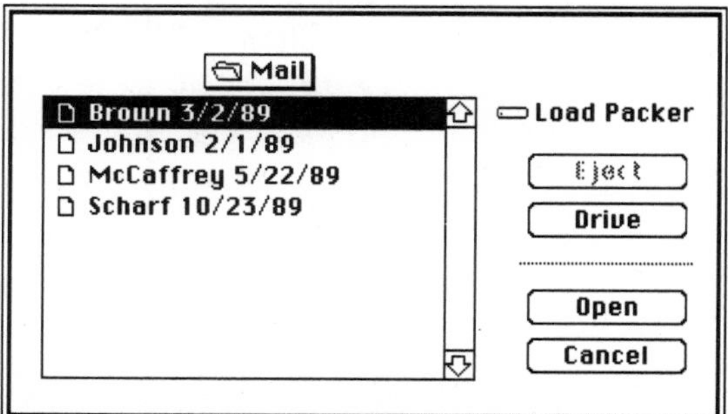

FIGURE 1-12. DATED NAMES.

You can include dates in names you give your documents.

USING STANDARD DESK ACCESSORIES

Control Panel

Chooser & Control Panel

ABOUT THE CHOOSER AND THE CONTROL PANEL

Have you ever wondered who did the programming on the Chooser and the Control Panel? To find out, click the version number that appears in each desk accessory's dialog box.

Control Panel

Desk Accessories

BACKING UP DESK ACCESSORIES

How do you back up information you created by using desk accessories but didn't save by using a Save command?

Desk accessories listed in the Apple menu store information in disk files, in the same way that regular application programs do. If you back up your entire disk by using any backup application, the desk accessory files will be backed up as well. Similarly, if you use such a program to back up only the files that have changed since the last backup and you have changed information in a desk accessory file, that file will be backed up.

To back up desk accessory files individually, you must know their names and locations. The Scrapbook, for example, uses a file named Scrapbook File in the System Folder. Filenames are often similar to the names of the desk accessories that use them, and the files are often located in the System Folder. Check the desk accessory documentation or call the publisher if you're not sure of a filename.

Control Panel

CHANGING THE DESKTOP PATTERN

The general Control Panel allows you to choose from among 38 predefined desktop patterns or to design your own. It displays a miniature desktop, complete with a miniature menu bar, where you can change the desktop pattern. (See Figure 1-13.) To see the predefined patterns, click the tiny right or left arrow in the miniature menu bar. When you see a pattern you like, make it the desktop pattern by clicking on the pattern displayed below the miniature menu bar.

To design your own pattern, use the magnified swatch next to the miniature desktop. Clicking on a white square in the swatch turns it black, and clicking on a black square turns it white. As you change the magnified pattern, watch the miniature desktop to the right. Click below the miniature menu bar when you've created the pattern you want.

You can edit in color or shades of gray if your monitor displays them. If so, a palette of eight colors or gray shades appears below the miniature desktop in the general Control Panel. Select the color or gray shade you want to use by clicking in the palette. Then apply that color or shade to the pattern by clicking the magnified swatch. You can change a color by double-clicking it in the palette and specifying a different color by using the standard color picker dialog box, which appears when you double-click a color.

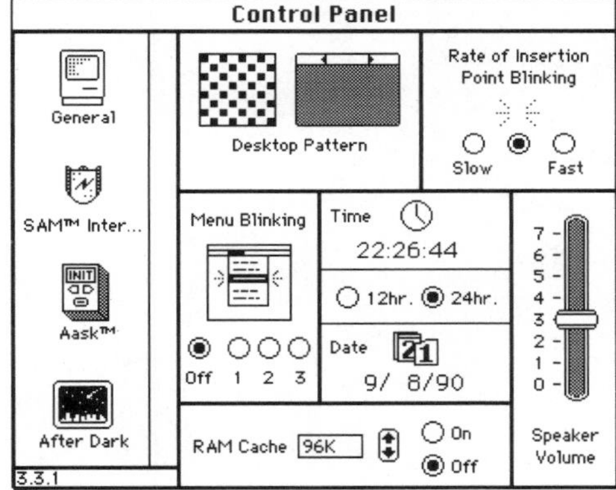

FIGURE 1-13. DESKTOP PATTERNS.
Use the general Control Panel to change the desktop pattern. Click the miniature menu bar to view pattern choices, and click the pattern below it to set that pattern for the desktop. You can also edit the magnified pattern by clicking the black or white squares.

CONTROL PANEL ORDER

You can arrange the icons in the Control Panel desk accessory in any order you want. (You must use a System version later than 4.0 but earlier than System 7.) The General icon appears first, and all other items follow in alphabetic order. To rearrange the icons, rename the files in the System Folder so that when the Control Panel alphabetizes them, they appear in the order you want. (See Figure 1-14 on the following page.) To rename some files—including General, Color, Keyboard, Monitors, Mouse, Sound, and Startup Device—you must first duplicate them (by using the Finder's Duplicate command), rename the copy, and then delete the original.

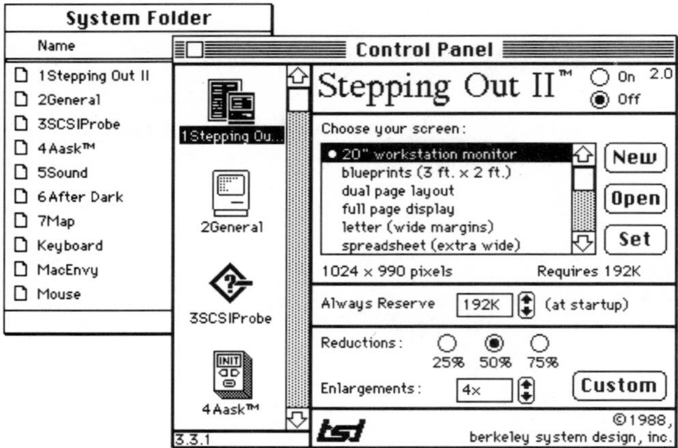

FIGURE 1-14. ORDER, PLEASE.
To change the order of the icons listed in the Control Panel, rename the files in the System Folder so that they appear in the order you want them when they are alphabetized.

For more information on the order of filenames, see the tips "Names at the Top," "Alphabetic Names," and "Numbered Names in Order," in Chapter 3, "Disks and Disk Drives."

DISK CACHING

You can put part of the Mac's memory to work as a disk cache for frequently used information. Use the RAM cache option on the General Control Panel to turn the cache on and off and to set the amount of memory it uses. If your system software is System 7, use the Memory Control Panel to set the cache size.

Here's how disk caching works: As information is transferred from a disk, a copy of it is kept in the area of memory set aside as the disk cache. When that information is needed again, it can be copied quickly from the disk cache instead of slowly from the disk. If the cache becomes full, the oldest or least-used information in it is discarded. Thus, if you switch applications, parts of the first application in the cache are eventually replaced by parts of the second application.

NEW BEEP

Most of the alert sounds you can choose by using the Sound Control Panel sound alike on all Macs. However, the Simple Beep does not sound the same on a Mac Plus or SE as it does on newer Mac models. (You must use System version 6.0 or later to select alert sounds on a Mac Plus or SE.)

You can use the newer, Mac II–style Simple Beep on a Mac Plus or SE, although it might sound distorted at times. To do this, you must copy, rename, and renumber the Simple Beep resource with Apple's ResEdit or ALSoft's FKey/Sound Mover.

To use ResEdit version 1.2 or later, take the following steps:

1. Make a copy of the System file. (Use the Finder's Duplicate command.) Start ResEdit and use it to open the copy of the System file.
2. Scroll through the list of resource types that appears until you find the 'snd ' type, and double-click on it to open it.
3. From the list of specific 'snd ' resources that appears, choose the resource named Simple Beep and choose Duplicate from ResEdit's Edit menu. ResEdit duplicates the selected resource, assigns the duplicate a new resource number, and selects the duplicate.
4. Choose Get Info from ResEdit's File menu. In the information window that appears for the selected resource, change the resource name to New Beep or to any name you like.
5. Quit ResEdit, clicking on the Yes button when the program asks whether you want to save changes.
6. Drag the original, unedited System file out of the System Folder. Then drag the edited System file into the System Folder. Be sure the edited System file is named *System*.
7. Restart your Mac. Use the Sound Control Panel to change the alert sound. As a precaution, make a backup copy of your original, unedited System file. Then drag the original System file to the Trashcan.

Chooser

THE CHOOSER'S USER NAME

The user name specified in the Chooser dialog box is the name by which you or, more accurately, your Mac is known on an AppleTalk network. The name can have up to 31 characters and for best results should be different from other names on the same AppleTalk network. Because the user name is stored in the System file, each startup disk can have a different name. To minimize confusion, make the user name the same on all your startup disks.

Key Caps

PRINTED KEY CAPS

The Key Caps desk accessory doesn't have a Print command, but you can print Key Caps with an ImageWriter by pressing Command-Shift-4. You can also make a MacPaint document, which you can print with any printer, by pressing Command-Shift-3.

To print Key Caps for one or more of the modifier keys—Command, Option, Shift, or Control—hold down the modifier key or key combination, place the pointer over the title bar of the Key Caps window, and hold down the mouse button. (You can also place the pointer at the extreme upper left corner of the screen.) Release the modifier key, but continue to hold down the mouse button, and then press Command-Shift-3 or Command-Shift-4. Before releasing the mouse button, again press the modifier key or key combination you want in the snapshot and, still pressing the key, release the mouse button.

Scrapbook

PURGING THE SCRAPBOOK

Old clippings in the Scrapbook waste disk space. Ideally, you should purge your Scrapbook file regularly, but if you can't bear to throw old clippings away, you can save the Scrapbook file under a different name, perhaps on another disk. Here's how:

1. Select the Scrapbook File icon, which is in the System Folder, and choose Duplicate from the File menu.
2. Change the name of the copy of the Scrapbook file and drag its icon to another disk.
3. Choose Scrapbook from the Apple menu and remove all the unnecessary clippings from the Scrapbook.

Later, if you want to retrieve a clipping from an old Scrapbook file, rename the Scrapbook file on the startup disk temporarily, change the name of the old Scrapbook icon back to Scrapbook File, and drag it to the current startup disk. Now, when you choose Scrapbook from the Apple menu, the Scrapbook window displays the contents of the old Scrapbook.

Alternatively, you can buy a replacement for the Scrapbook such as SmartScrap & The Clipper by Solutions International. SmartScrap lets you save multiple scrapbook files and open any of them from the Apple menu.

COLORIZING THE WORLD MAP

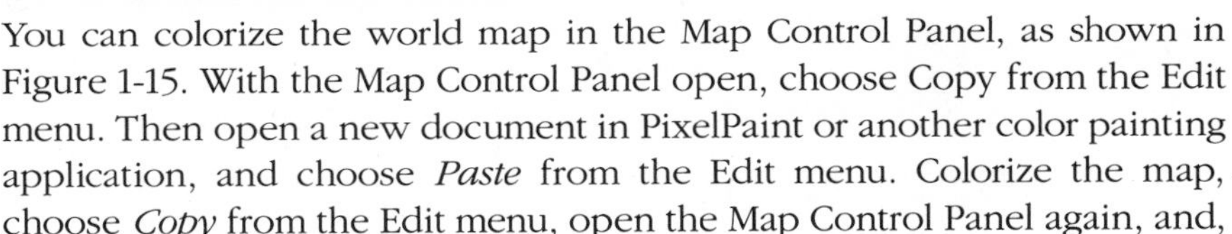

You can colorize the world map in the Map Control Panel, as shown in Figure 1-15. With the Map Control Panel open, choose Copy from the Edit menu. Then open a new document in PixelPaint or another color painting application, and choose *Paste* from the Edit menu. Colorize the map, choose *Copy* from the Edit menu, open the Map Control Panel again, and, finally, choose *Paste* from the Edit menu.

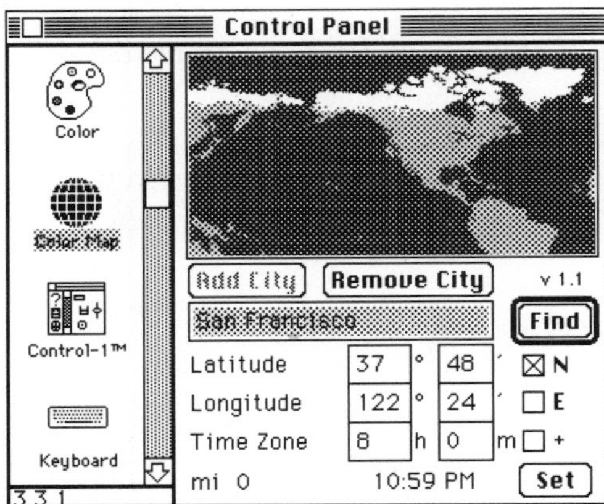

FIGURE 1-15. COLORIZED MAP.
Use a color painting application to colorize the world map in the Map Control Panel. Transfer the map to and from the painting application by using the Copy and Paste commands.

MAP VIEWS

In the Map Control Panel, you can scroll the world map by dragging the pointer beyond the map boundaries.

To enlarge the world map, press the Option key while opening the Map Control Panel. Figure 1-16 shows the result. To magnify the map further, press Shift-Option while opening the Map Control Panel.

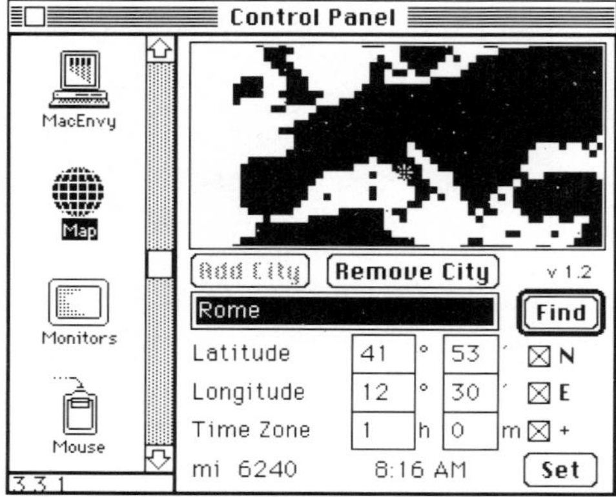

FIGURE 1-16. BIG MAP.
Pressing the Option key when you open the Map icon in the Control Panel displays a magnified world map.

MAP LOCATIONS

The Map Control Panel holds the name, latitude, and longitude of many locations. Tiny flashing dots on the map mark the known locations.

To find a location by name, type the name in the space provided and click the Find button. If Map holds the name, it scrolls the world map to display the location and marks it with a flashing star (not to be confused with the black, flashing cross). To cycle through the known locations alphabetically, press Option while clicking the Find button.

You can also click at or drag over a known location. Map displays its name, latitude, longitude, time zone, and distance from the location marked by the black, flashing cross. If you click at or drag over an unknown location, Map clears the name area but displays the other statistics.

To add a new location, specify its longitude and latitude by clicking, dragging, or typing the coordinates manually. Then type the name and click the Add City button.

CURRENT MAP LOCATION

Control Panel

The Map Control Panel lets you designate your current location. Map marks the current location with a black, flashing cross (not to be confused with the white, flashing star, which marks the last spot clicked). To designate a new current location, follow this procedure:

1. Specify the location. You can click the Find button, drag over or click the map, or type the longitude and latitude in the spaces provided. (For more information on specifying a location, see the previous tip.)
2. Click the Set button. The flashing cross appears in the new location, confirming the setting.

When you change the current location, Map automatically adjusts the time and date in your Mac's clock according to the time difference between the new and old current locations. The current location is stored in your Mac's battery-powered memory along with the time of day and other semipermanent Control Panel settings. These settings are retained while the Mac is turned off and when you restart with another startup disk.

MAP TIMES AND DISTANCES

Control Panel

The Map Control Panel normally shows the time zone of the location marked by the flashing star as a number of hours and minutes ahead of or behind Greenwich time. Clicking the words *Time Zone* prompts Map to show the time difference between the location marked by the flashing star and the location marked by the flashing cross, which is called the current location. If the current location is in the same time zone as Greenwich time, the time zone and time difference are the same.

Incidentally, Map estimates the time zone for a newly added location from the longitude of the location. Many time-zone boundaries are determined politically, however. You can enter the proper time difference between the location and Greenwich time manually and then click the Add City button. If the Add City button appears gray, click the Remove City button first.

WORKING WITH FONTS

System

FONT-SIZE FAKERY

Why aren't all fonts the same size when set at a 12-point size?

Point size measures maximum character height but says nothing about other character proportions. Fonts that have tall lowercase letters are larger overall than fonts that have short lowercase letters. Thick strokes appear heavier and take up more space than thin strokes do. Figure 1-17 illustrates the differences. If you change fonts, be prepared to adjust tabs, spacing, page breaks, and font size to compensate.

Times 10

This copy is set in 10-point type in a column 12 picas (72 points) wide. It is set solid, with no extra space inserted between the lines, to facilitate comparing its apparent size with the two adjacent examples. Every line is 10 points high, but the larger-bodied fonts take up more space on the page.

Palatino 10

This copy is set in 10-point type in a column 12 picas (72 points) wide. It is set solid, with no extra space inserted between the lines, to facilitate comparing its apparent size with the two adjacent examples. Every line is 10 points high, but the larger-bodied fonts take up more space on the page.

Bookman 10

This copy is set in 10-point type in a column 12 picas (72 points) wide. It is set solid, with no extra space inserted between the lines, to facilitate comparing its apparent size with the two adjacent examples. Every line is 10 points high, but the larger-bodied fonts take up more space on the page.

FIGURE 1-17. POINT DECEPTION.
Text size depends on more than point size. Other factors include the height of lowercase letters (called the x height) and stroke thickness.

System

FIXED-WIDTH SPACING

How can you get monospace text (text in which all letters are the same width) on a Mac?

Proportionally spaced fonts predominate on the Mac, and you cannot turn off proportional spacing. If you want nonproportional spacing, you must use a monospace font such as Monaco or Courier. If the monospace font of your choice is not available, use the Font/DA Mover to install it. (In System 7, you install fonts by dragging them onto the System file.)

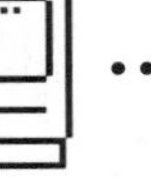

TEMPORARILY ENLARGED TEXT

Small type sizes can be difficult to read on the Mac screen. To avoid eyestrain, work in a large type size and change to a small size before printing. There's a quick and easy method for selecting an entire document in preparation for changing the type size, and it works with almost every Macintosh application that lets you change the type size of text. First move the pointer to the beginning of the document and click the mouse button. Then scroll to the end of the text (by dragging the scroll box to the bottom of the vertical scroll bar). Finally move the pointer to the end of the document, and press Shift while you click the mouse button.

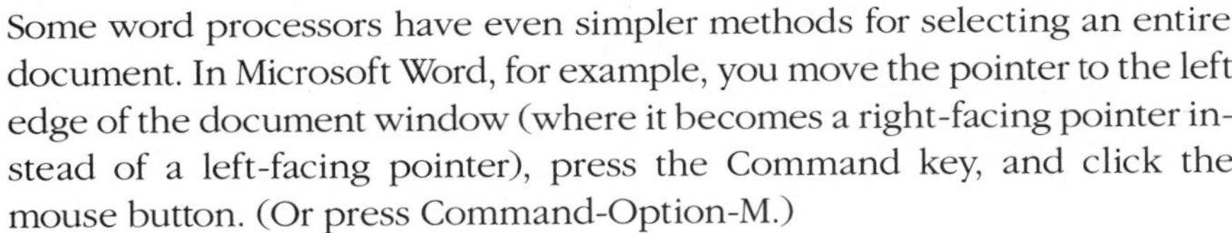

Some word processors have even simpler methods for selecting an entire document. In Microsoft Word, for example, you move the pointer to the left edge of the document window (where it becomes a right-facing pointer instead of a left-facing pointer), press the Command key, and click the mouse button. (Or press Command-Option-M.)

You might not always want to change an entire document to one type size, however. For example, you might want the headings to be larger than the body text. If your word processor has style sheets, you can use them to control the type sizes of different text elements. Word's Define Styles command lets you create style sheets.

A completely different approach is to use the utility software CloseView, which comes with System versions 6.0 and later. It provides a "magnifying glass" that can magnify from 2 to 16 times. The magnifying glass follows both mouse movement and movement of the insertion point as you type.

STYLED SCREEN FONTS

System

Many PostScript fonts (used on the LaserWriter IINT and other printers) come with separate screen fonts for stylistic variations such as bold, italic, and bold italic. For example, you can get B Times Bold, BI Times BoldItalic, and I Times Italic screen fonts in addition to plain Times from Adobe Systems. The styled fonts look better on the screen and provide better spacing with some applications than do the styles that QuickDraw derives from the plain font.

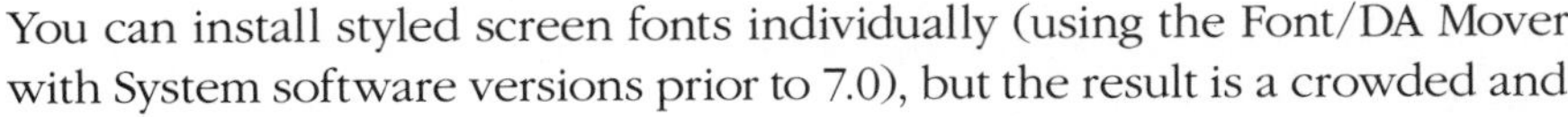

You can install styled screen fonts individually (using the Font/DA Mover with System software versions prior to 7.0), but the result is a crowded and confusing font menu. A better approach is to combine all styled screen fonts with the plain font of the same family, using the Font/DA Utility included with MasterJuggler from ALSoft.

If you decide not to combine styled and plain fonts of the same family, do not choose the styled screen fonts directly from your font menus, Character Format dialog boxes, Type Specification dialog boxes, and so on. Instead, choose the plain font and apply the desired styles to it separately. For example, choose Times and then choose the Bold format separately. The Mac will use the appropriate styled screen font if one is available. (If not, QuickDraw will derive the desired results from the plain font.) Choosing the styled screen font directly can make it harder to change fonts and styles later. Whatever you do, don't choose a styled screen font and then apply styles to it. For example, don't choose B Times Bold and then apply bold formatting to it.

System

LUMPY TEXT

With system software versions earlier than System 7, lumpy displayed text results when you choose an uninstalled type size for a font. You can improve the appearance by installing the missing type size (if you can find it) or by switching to a different font. Alternatively, you can upgrade to System 7. Versions prior to that use bit-mapped fonts, which define characters as patterns of dots, on the screen and with many printers. (See the tip "Best-Quality Font Requirements" in Chapter 4, "Printers and Printing.") System 7 uses outline fonts that look good in any size on any screen, printer, or other output device. Figure 1-18 illustrates the difference between a scaled, bit-mapped font and an outline font.

System

HOW OUTLINE FONTS WORK

Outline fonts store individual characters as a series of lines and curves rather than as a pattern of dots (a bit map). System software versions beginning with System 7 uses outline fonts. Earlier versions of the system software use bit-mapped fonts. When you choose a type size for a character, System 7 enlarges the outline to that size and fills it with dots.

At small sizes, however, simply scaling the font outlines results in unpleasant problems—for example, text that has unwanted dots on the edges of curves. These imperfections occur because the outline does not precisely

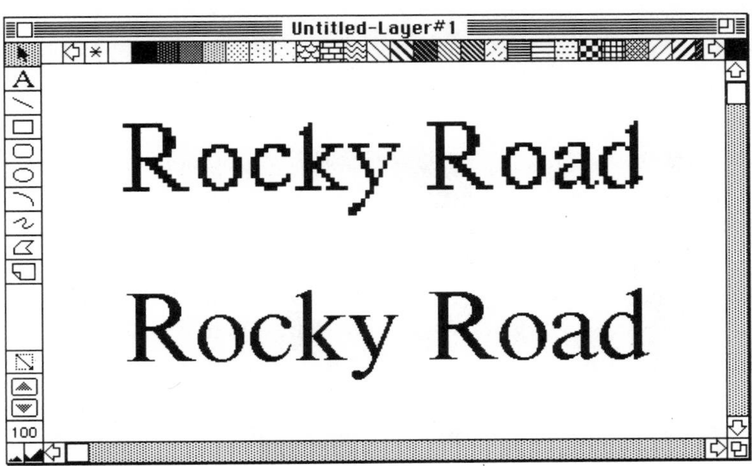

FIGURE 1-18. LUMPY AND SMOOTH.
The upper text is lumpy because it was scaled from a bit-mapped font. The smooth text below it was scaled from a System 7 outline font.

fit the grid of small point sizes, especially if the dots are relatively large (as they are on the Mac screen). The font designer provides a set of instructions, also known as hints, that tell the Macintosh how to modify character outlines so that they fit the grid. This process is called "grid fitting." Apple publishes the font format and instructions that can be used for grid fitting. Figure 1-19 on the following page illustrates how System 7 uses its outline fonts to display and print text in any size on any type of output device.

INVISIBLE TEXT

If you have the Adobe Type Manager (ATM) utility software installed in your System Folder, invisible text is a symptom of too little memory allocated to the ATM font cache. Try increasing the font cache size by using the ATM panel in the Control Panel desk accessory. You must then restart your Mac to get ATM to use the larger font cache.

DINGBAT VARIATIONS

How do you create an open ballot box symbol? Plain Zapf Dingbat characters become hollow when you apply the outline style. Press the N key (without pressing Command, Shift, or Option) to get a solid, square dingbat. Apply the outline style to it to get an open ballot box. The shadow and italic styles produce other useful effects. Figure 1-20 illustrates some possibilities.

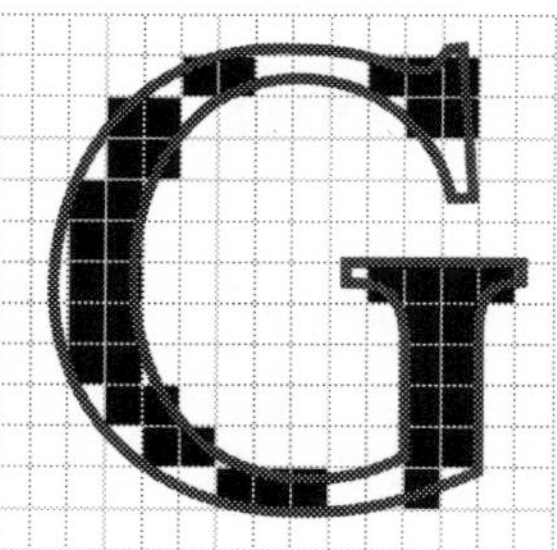

Before grid fitting

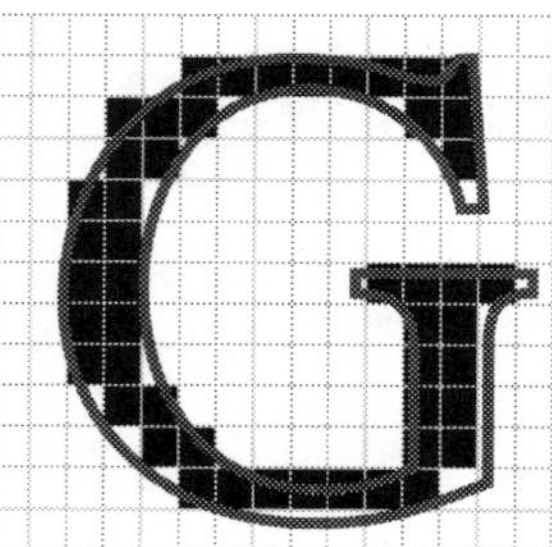

After grid fitting

FIGURE 1-19. GRID FIT.
Using one outline font for all sizes, the application tells the system at what size to display or print the character. Depending on the resolution and size of the character, the system applies grid-fitting instructions to make the best use of the available dots. The text is displayed in the chosen size. If no grid fitting is needed, the outline font is sent directly to any output device. When printing in a PostScript font, the application and the system software together generate a PostScript derivative of the document for output on a PostScript device.

Type style	H	*	Å	4	8	D	n	s	u	l
Regular	★	☛	)	✔	✘	✣	■	▲	◆	●
Outline	☆	☞	)	✓	✗	✤	□	△	◇	○
Shadow	★	☛	)	✔	✘	✣	■	▲	◆	●
Outline Italic	☆	☞	)	✓	✗	✤	□	△	◇	○

FIGURE 1-20. DINGBATS ON PARADE.
The outline, shadow, italic, and outline italic styles applied to the Zapf Dingbat font make useful variations of plain dingbats.

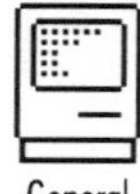

General Operations

SECRET SYMBOLS

Most fonts named after cities contain a hidden character that you can type by pressing Option-Shift-tilde (~). Different sizes of the same font might contain a different character, as shown in Figure 1-21.

New York 9	Geneva 9
New York 10	Geneva 10
New York 12	Geneva 12
New York 14	Geneva 14
New York 18	Geneva 18
New York 24	Geneva 24

FIGURE 1-21. COVERT CHARACTERS.
Many fonts have hidden symbols that you can type by pressing Option-Shift-tilde (~). In most PostScript fonts, the symbol is Ÿ.

SPOTTING LASERWRITER FONTS

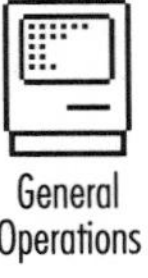

To make LaserWriter fonts easier to find in font menus, you can prefix their names with numbers or other symbols. The Mac groups prefixed font names together as it alphabetizes the font menu. You can change LaserWriter font names with the font-editor utility FONTastic from Altsys. As shown in Figure 1-22, you can also change font names and numbers by using the Font/DA Utility included with MasterJuggler from ALSoft.

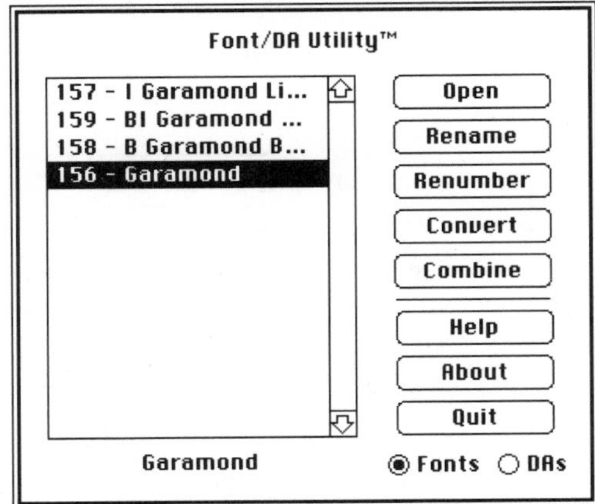

FIGURE 1-22. RENAME AND RENUMBER.
You can rename and renumber a font by using the Font/DA Utility software.

System

MULTILINGUAL MAC

Most Mac fonts include more than two dozen letters with various diacritical marks for international typing. If you need more, you can get two products from Linguists' Software that include the character sets of 79 languages plus the macron and other symbols needed to transliterate most of the languages of the world. MacPhonetics has two bit-mapped fonts for ImageWriter printing, one resembling Geneva and the other resembling Times Roman. LaserTransliterator has those fonts as well as PostScript fonts for the LaserWriter.

Font/DA Mover

FONTS IN APPLICATIONS AND DOCUMENTS

Fonts customarily reside in the System file, where they are available from any application for use in any document. But with system software versions earlier than System 7, fonts can also reside in application files. With some applications, notably HyperCard, fonts can also be installed in documents, such as HyperCard stacks.

Fonts placed in an application file appear on the font menu only when you use the application. Fonts installed in a document file are available only when that document is open. Transferring the burden of specialty fonts from the System file to an application or document file helps to reduce the size of the System file, leaving space for other items on an 800-KB disk.

You can install a font in an application or document file with Apple's Font/DA Mover utility. Normally, it lets you open only the System file and font files; they are the only files listed in the Open dialog box. But if you press the Option key while clicking the Open button, the Open dialog box lists all the files on the disk. (See Figure 1-23.) Even the names of invisible files, such as Desktop, appear. After opening an application file, you'll be able to copy fonts to it as if it were a System file. Don't forget to remove fonts from the System file after copying them to application files.

General Operations

OH, WHERE HAS MY FONT GONE?

No matter which sizes you install in the System file (in system software earlier than System 7), some old applications typically show only sizes 9, 10, 12, 14, 18, and 24. They ordinarily use the 20-point size only for best-quality printing of 10-point text on an ImageWriter I or ImageWriter II (as described in the tip "Best-Quality Font Requirements," in Chapter 4, "Printers and Printing.")

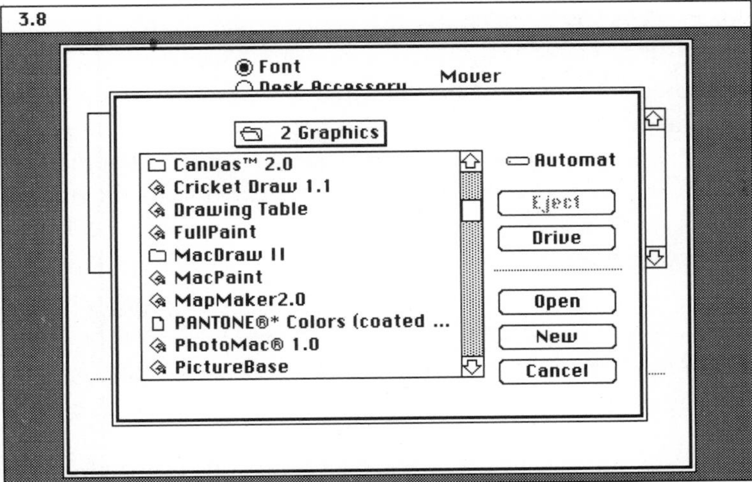

FIGURE 1-23. APPLICATION FONTS.

Pressing the Option key while clicking the Open button in the Font/DA Mover utility lets you open and copy fonts to and from any file, not only the System file and font files.

In most cases, upgrading to the latest version of the application solves the missing-type-size problem. Alternatively, you can copy and paste text in the size you want from another document. Then select the pasted text, change the font if necessary (but not the size), and begin typing. Your typing appears in the size you pasted. A public-domain MacWrite document called Fonts 4 to 48 contains text samples in every whole point size from 4 points through 48 points.

Another approach is to install the desk accessory WriteFontSize. It lets you type a character in any size, copy the character, and paste it into any document without losing the font or size.

THE STANDARD APPLICATION FONT

Most application programs use the Geneva font by default because the Mac's parameter RAM designates it as the standard application font. It has not always been so; longtime Mac users will remember that New York was the standard application font for the first five months of 1984. (Parameter RAM stores many of the settings made through the Control Panel and

Chooser desk accessories. A battery preserves the parameter RAM contents when the power is off.)

You can designate a different font as the standard application font by using the MasterJuggler utility from ALSoft. First choose Font List from the MasterJuggler submenu of the Apple menu. Then click on the name of the font you want as the standard application font, and press Return or Enter.

System

REMOVING SYSTEM FONTS

Because system software (earlier than System 7) uses certain fonts, you can't remove them by using the Font/DA Mover. Some of these fonts aren't needed in the System file, however, because the Mac's ROM (read-only or permanent memory) contains copies. All Macs except the Mac 512K have Chicago 12 in ROM. And except for the Mac Plus and 512K, all Mac ROMs contain Geneva 9, Geneva 12, and Monaco 9. You can free up some disk space by removing fonts from the System file that are duplicated in ROM. Using ResEdit version 1.2 or later, follow these steps:

1. Make a copy of the System file. (Use the Finder's Duplicate command.) Start ResEdit and use it to open the copy of the System file.
2. A list of resource types appears. Scroll through the list until you find the FONT type, and double-click it to open it. You'll see a list of sizes of every font in the System file.
3. Select each font size you want to remove, and then choose Clear from the Edit menu. In ResEdit versions 2.0 and later, a message appears advising you to remove a FOND (font family) resource. You can ignore this message for this tip. Click OK to dismiss it.
4. Quit ResEdit, clicking the Yes button when it asks whether you want to save changes.
5. Drag the original, unedited System file out of the System Folder. Then drag the edited System file into the System Folder. Be sure the edited System file is named System.
6. Restart your Mac and verify that all the text appears as you want it. As a precaution, make a backup copy of your original, unedited System file. Then drag the original System file into the Trash.

SUBSTITUTING SYSTEM FONTS

System

The Mac normally uses Chicago 12 for menus and dialog box text and Geneva 9 for icon names and other small text. It also uses Geneva 12 and Monaco 9. You can use ResEdit version 1.2 or later to replace the system fonts with other fonts as follows:

1. Make a copy of the System file. (Use the Finder's Duplicate command.) Start ResEdit and use it to open the copy of the System file.
2. A list of resource types appears. Scroll through the list until you find the FOND type, and double-click it to open it. You'll see a list of the font family names, such as Chicago and Geneva, with their ID numbers.
3. Find the name of a font family you want to replace, and note its ID number. (Chicago's is 0, Geneva's is 3, and Monaco's is 4.) Choose Clear from the Edit menu.
4. Select the name of the font family you want to use as a replacement, press Command-I to open the resource information window, and in the space provided, type the ID number of the font family you are replacing (the one you noted in the previous step). Figure 1-24 on the following page illustrates this process.
5. Repeat steps 3 and 4 for each font you want to replace. Then quit ResEdit, clicking the Yes button when it asks whether you want to save changes.
6. Drag the original, unedited System file out of the System Folder. Then drag the edited System file into the System Folder. Be sure the edited System file is named System.
7. Restart your Mac and verify that the new system fonts have replaced the old ones. As a precaution, make a backup copy of your original, unedited System file. Then drag the original System file into the Trash.

Remember that when the Mac changes startup disks it uses fonts from the System file on the new startup disk. (See the tip "System Folder Switching," in Chapter 3, "Disks and Disk Drives.") You might need to modify more than one System file.

FIGURE 1-24. NEW FOND ID.
Using ResEdit, you can change the FOND ID of a system font (Chicago, Geneva, or Monaco) to the ID of another font's FOND. The Mac will then use the second font as its system font.

Note: I don't recommend replacing Chicago. It is one of the few fonts that contain the Command-key and Apple symbols, which appear in menus. Other fonts display rectangles instead. Also, Chicago is used for button and menu text. When it is dimmed (grayed), you can still read it, whereas most other fonts are illegible when dimmed.

Warning: Some applications might not work correctly without Chicago, Geneva, or Monaco. Be sure to make changes initially to a copy of your System file, and use the modified copy to test your applications.

CUSTOM FONTS

Most system fonts displayed on the Mac are located on resource files contained in the System file. If you use a font utility such as MasterJuggler or Suitcase II, some fonts might be located in separate files. If you use a version of system software earlier than System 7, you can edit fonts to change the look of the letters, numbers, and symbols. The FONTastic utility software from Altsys makes font editing easy. Although it involves more work, you can also edit fonts by using ResEdit version 1.2 or later, as follows:

1. Make a copy of the System file or other file that contains the font you want to modify. (Use the Finder's Duplicate command.) Then start ResEdit and use it to open the copy of the file.
2. Scroll through the list of resource types that appears until you find the FONT type, and then double-click it to open it. You'll see a list of each size of every font in the file.
3. Double-click the font size you want to modify. A large font-editing window opens. (See Figure 1-25.) You might need to move the window to see all of it.
4. Select the character you want to change by typing it or by clicking it in the panel of three characters below the sample text. The character selected for editing is boxed in the center of this panel. Clicking at the left or right of the selected character steps through the range of ASCII numbers. You can move quickly through the range by clicking at the left or right and dragging the pointer outside the panel.

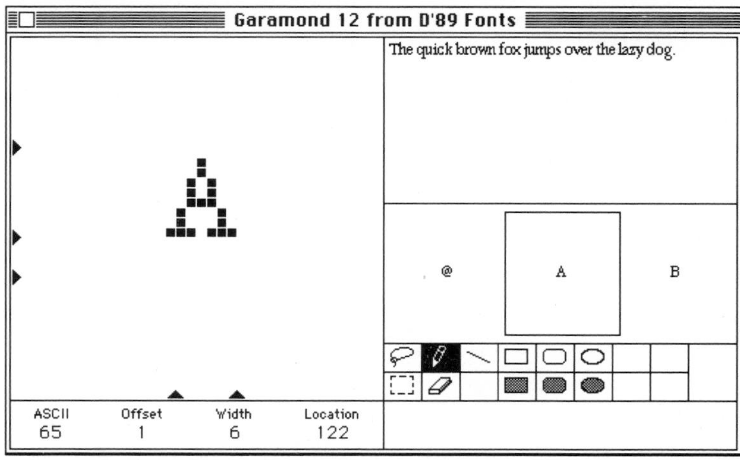

FIGURE 1-25. FONT-EDITING WINDOW.
Fonts displayed on the screen are FONT resources that you can edit in a ResEdit font-editing window.

5. Edit the enlarged image of the character using the familiar paint tools. (If you don't know how to use them, refer to the documentation that comes with HyperCard or MacPaint.)

6. You can change the horizontal space that the character occupies by dragging the black triangles at the bottom of the editing window. Watch the sample text on the right side of the editing window to see the results.

7. To adjust the vertical dimensions of the font as a whole, drag the top and bottom black triangles along the edge of the character-editing window. (The baseline marker cannot be moved.) Watch the effects of your changes in the sample text at the right side of the font-editing window.

8. Repeat steps 4 through 7 for each character you want to edit. Then quit ResEdit, clicking the Yes button when it displays a message that asks whether you want to save changes.

9. If you edited one of the fonts in the System file, drag the original, unedited System file out of the System Folder. Then drag the edited System file into the System Folder. Be sure the edited System file is named System.

10. Restart your Mac and verify that all the text appears as you want it. As a precaution, make a backup copy of your original, unedited System file. Then drag the original System file into the Trash.

The fonts Chicago 12, Geneva 9, Geneva 12, and Monaco 9 are included in the ROM of most Macintosh models. The FONT resource in the ROM overrides the same resource on a disk. If editing one character of a font has no effect on what is displayed, your Mac has the font in ROM.

There is no point in changing FONT resources for LaserWriter fonts, such as Times, Helvetica, and Courier. These resources are used only to display the fonts and to print on an ImageWriter. A LaserWriter or other PostScript output device uses separate font definitions, and they override any like-named FONT resources.

NAMING CUSTOM FONTS

If you want to use two versions of a font, you must give the versions different names; otherwise, you won't be able to distinguish between them in the Font menu. Renaming one of them is not enough, however, because most Mac applications identify a font by its number. For example, neither you nor MacWrite can tell the difference between a custom Geneva and a standard Geneva unless you change the name and number of one of them. Specialized font-editor programs, such as FONTastic, take care of this for you. You can also change font names and numbers by using the Font/DA Utility included with MasterJuggler from ALSoft.

ADDING CHARACTERS TO A FONT

More than 30 key combinations include the Option key, for which no particular character is produced. With most fonts, typing a nonexistent key combination produces a hollow rectangle, as shown in Figure 1-26. The exact set of undefined combinations varies from font to font. For example,

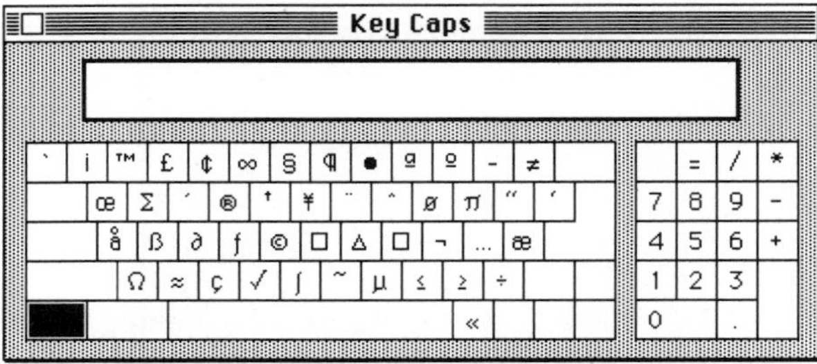

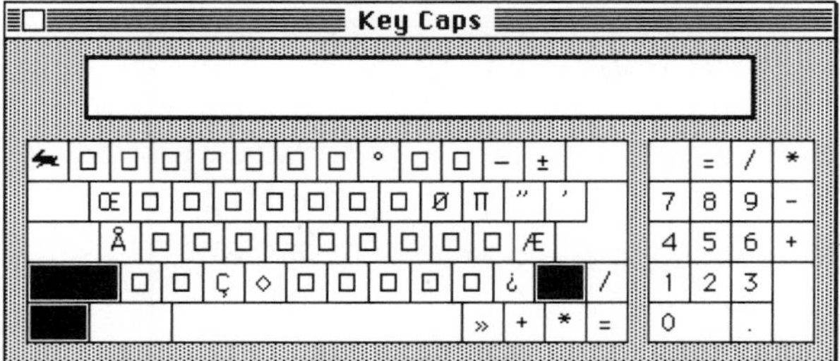

FIGURE 1-26. VACANT CHARACTERS.

Key combinations that include the Option key (top) or both the Option and Shift keys (bottom) produce hollow rectangles.

the character generated by pressing Option-Shift-tilde (~) is defined in some fonts but not in others. LaserWriter fonts generally have no undefined combinations. ASCII numbers 217 through 251 are usually undefined.

If you use a version of system software earlier than 7.0, you can assign your own characters to unused key combinations. For instructions, see the tip "Custom Fonts," earlier in this chapter.

CUSTOMIZING STANDARD FEATURES

Finder

DESKTOP LAYOUT

A number of Finder settings determine the standard appearance of icons and windows on the desktop. Other settings affect Finder behavior. Finder versions earlier than System 7 don't provide access to these settings. With these earlier versions of the Finder, you can change the settings to personalize the appearance of the desktop and change the way the Finder works by using Layout, a utility by Michael C. O'Connor.

Layout lets you set the following:

Windows: initial position, size, and view of new folder and disk windows

Icon view: spacing of rows and vertical offset (staggering) of alternate columns

Small icon view: spacing of rows and columns

Text views: column widths, text alignment (left or right) in each column, date format (long, medium, or short), and style of heading that identifies the type of text view

Icon grid: whether dragged icons always align to the invisible grid

Visual effect: zoom open

Trash warnings: displayed or skipped

Window navigation: whether clicking the title bar shows the parent window (moves to the next outer level of nested folders)

Watch-pointer animation: the time delay until the clock hands spin

Windows open: the maximum number

Color menu: which colors are available

Color style: normal or inverted

Text: font and font size of all icon names and similar text

QUITTING THE FINDER

Finder

Multifinder

Having trouble using MultiFinder on a 1-MB Mac, or want to gain 200 KB when using MultiFinder? It's easy—quit the Finder. The Finder doesn't have a Quit command, but if you're using a version of system software earlier than System 7, you can use ResEdit version 1.2 or later to add an FKey (function key) that acts like a Quit command. You use an FKey by pressing Command, Shift, and a number key. For example, Command-Shift-1 ejects the floppy disk in the internal drive.

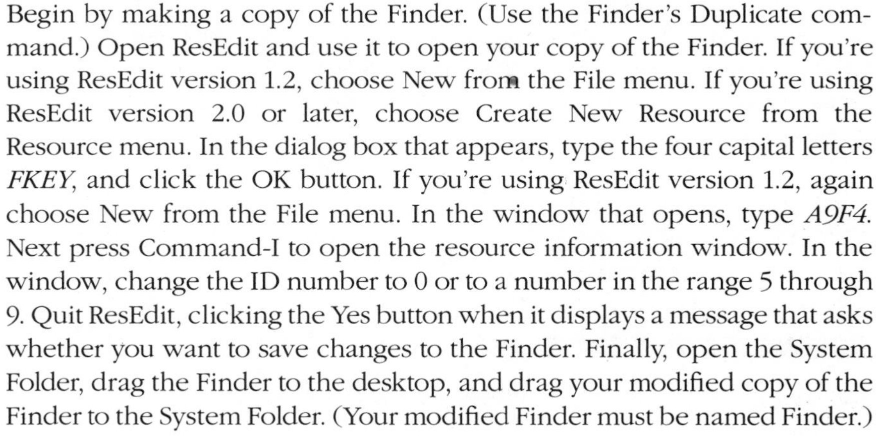

Begin by making a copy of the Finder. (Use the Finder's Duplicate command.) Open ResEdit and use it to open your copy of the Finder. If you're using ResEdit version 1.2, choose New from the File menu. If you're using ResEdit version 2.0 or later, choose Create New Resource from the Resource menu. In the dialog box that appears, type the four capital letters *FKEY*, and click the OK button. If you're using ResEdit version 1.2, again choose New from the File menu. In the window that opens, type *A9F4*. Next press Command-I to open the resource information window. In the window, change the ID number to 0 or to a number in the range 5 through 9. Quit ResEdit, clicking the Yes button when it displays a message that asks whether you want to save changes to the Finder. Finally, open the System Folder, drag the Finder to the desktop, and drag your modified copy of the Finder to the System Folder. (Your modified Finder must be named Finder.)

To use the FKey, activate MultiFinder by choosing the Finder's Set Startup command from the Special menu, and restart your Mac. Open any application or desk accessory, switch to the Finder, and press Command and Shift together with the one-digit number you assigned as the ID number in ResEdit. Notice that the disk and Trash icons disappear. Check the Apple menu—Finder is not open!

To make much use of the regained memory, you'll need to quit all open applications and desk accessories. (Then reopen them if you want.) The regained memory can be used only to open an application that needs no more memory than the Finder was using. Normally, the Finder uses 160 KB.

You can increase that amount by selecting the Finder icon, choosing Get Info from the Finder's File menu, changing the Application Memory Size option, and then restarting the Mac.

With no Finder, you'll need an alternative method of opening applications. On Cue from ICOM Simulations adds an application menu, which you can change, to either end of the menu bar. DiskTop from CE Software is a desk accessory that provides all the functionality of the Finder (and more) but with a different interface.

System

HEAP OVERFLOW

It's easy to expand and modify Macintosh system software with fonts, desk accessories, Control Panel add-ons, and startup documents (INITs). However, too many of these enhancements can make the Mac unreliable and more susceptible to crashing. They all contend for space in an area of the Mac's memory called the system heap. In addition, each SCSI device you connect requires space in the system heap for its controlling software, called a driver. Shortages in the system heap lead to ugly, scaled-font menus, system errors, and other antisocial behavior. If you're using a version of system software earlier than System 7, you can enlarge the system heap with CE Software's HeapFixer utility.

System

NUMBERS, SHORT DATES, AND TIMES

The standard formats for numbers, short (all-numeric) dates, and times are all kept in the System file. The number format specifies the symbols used for the decimal point, thousands separator, list separator, and currency. It also determines whether the currency symbol appears before or after the amount, how to display negative numbers (with a minus sign or parentheses), whether trailing zeros are used in fractions, and whether a zero is used before the decimal point in amounts between 0 and 1.

The short-date format specifies the punctuation used in the date and the order of the day, month, and year numbers. It also determines whether leading zeros are shown in day or month numbers less than 10 (as in *01/01/91*) and whether the century is specified.

The time format indicates the punctuation used in the time and whether a 12-hour or 24-hour clock is used. The format also defines the suffixes to be used for morning and afternoon time. In addition, it determines whether leading zeros are shown in hours, seconds, and minutes less than 10.

You can change the short-date and time formats by using the Control Panel add-ons Short Date and Time, both by Don Leeper. In addition, you can change the number, short-date, and time formats by using ResEdit version 1.2 or later as follows:

1. Make a copy of the System file. (Use the Finder's Duplicate command.) Then start ResEdit, and use it to open the copy of the System file.
2. Scroll through the list of resource types that appears until you find the itl0 type, and double-click it to open it.
3. In the list of specific itl0 resources that appears, double-click the resource with ID = 0.
4. In the dialog box that appears, change the formats as you want. (See Figure 1-27.) As you make changes, watch the effect on the examples at the left side of the dialog box.

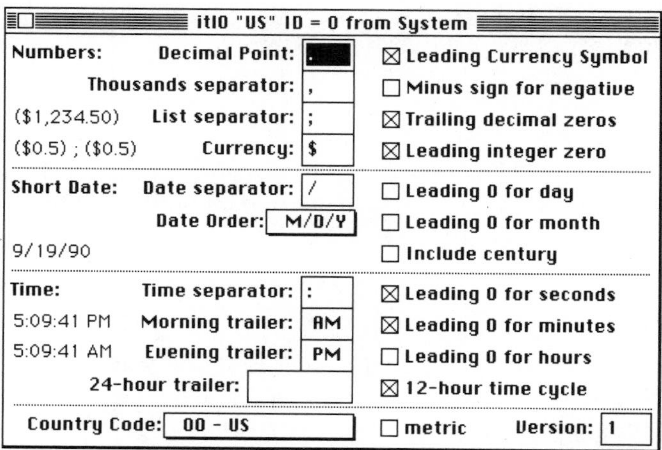

FIGURE 1-27. STANDARD FORMATS.

Change the standard formats for numbers, short (numeric) dates, and times using this ResEdit dialog box for itl0 resource ID = 0. The pop-up menu for Date Order lists the following choices: M/D/Y, D/M/Y, Y/M/D, M/Y/D, D/Y/M, *and* Y/D/M.

5. Quit ResEdit, clicking the Yes button when it displays a message that asks whether you want to save changes.
6. Drag the original, unedited System file out of the System Folder. Then drag the edited System file into the System Folder. Be sure the edited System file is named System.
7. Restart your Mac. As a precaution, make a backup copy of your original, unedited System file. Then drag the original System file into the Trash.

LONG DATE

The standard format for the long date, which names the day of the week and the month, is kept in the System file. The format specifies the spelling of the month and day names; the length of abbreviated month and day names; the punctuation used in the date; whether the day name is shown; whether a leading zero appears in day numbers less than 10; and the order of the date, day, month, and year.

You can change the long-date format by using the Control Panel add-on Long Date, by Don Leeper. You can also change the long-date format by using ResEdit version 1.2 or later. Take the following steps:

1. Make a copy of the System file. (Use the Finder's Duplicate command.) Then start ResEdit and use it to open the copy of the System file.
2. Scroll through the list of resource types that appears until you find the itl0 type, and double-click it to open it.
3. In the list of specific itl0 resources that appears, double-click the resource with ID = 1.
4. In the dialog box that appears, change the formats as you want. (See Figure 1-28.) As you make changes, watch the effect on the examples at the lower left corner of the dialog box.
5. Quit ResEdit, clicking on the Yes button when it displays a message that asks whether you want to save changes.
6. Drag the original, unedited System file out of the System Folder. Then drag the edited System file into the System Folder. Be sure the edited System file is named System.

7. Restart your Mac. As a precaution, make a backup copy of your original, unedited System file. Then drag the original System file into the Trash.

itl1 "US" ID = 0 from System

Names for months		Names for days
January	July	Sunday
February	August	Monday
March	September	Tuesday
April	October	Wednesday
May	November	Thursday
June	December	Friday
		Saturday

Day , Month Date , Year

Use 3 characters to abbreviate names

Country Code: 00 - US

Wed, Sep 19, 1990 Version: 1

Wednesday, September 19, 1990

☐ Leading 0 in Date
☐ Suppress Date
☐ Suppress Day
☐ Suppress Month
☐ Suppress Year

FIGURE 1-28. STANDARD DATE.
Change the standard format for long dates by using this ResEdit dialog box for itl resource ID = 0. The four pop-up menus that specify the various parts of the date list the following choices: Date, Day, Month, *and* Year.

COPYING AND EDITING ICONS

Tired of the same old icons? Want to use an icon as an illustration? Because most icons are resources in the System file or in an application file, you can copy or edit them with Apple's ResEdit utility. ResEdit can edit the types of icon resources listed in Figure 1-29 on the following page.

ResEdit has a different icon-editing window for each type of icon resource, as shown in Figure 1-30 on page 47. The editing window for ICON resources shows the icon both magnified and at actual size. The editing window for ICN# resources shows a magnified icon and a magnified, shadowlike mask of the icon. It also shows what the full-size icon looks like unselected, selected, and open, against both white and black backgrounds, as well as what the icon looks like in the Finder's small icon view. The editing window for SICN resources shows an icon magnified for editing and has a panel for selecting one icon from a group. (SICN icons usually

Resource Types	Uses	Where to Find Them
cicn	Ordinary color icons	System file Application files
ics4	Small, 16-color icons for applications and documents in Finder versions 7.0 and later	System file Finder
ics8	Small, 16-color icons for applications and documents in Finder versions 7.0 and later	System file Finder
icl4	Large, 10-color icons for applications and documents in Finder versions 7.0 and later	System file Finder
icl8	Large, 256-color icons for applications and documents in Finder versions 7.0 and later	System file Finder
ics#	Small, monochrome icons for applications and documents in Finder versions 7.0 and later	System file Finder
ICN#	Large, monochrome icons for applications and documents in the Finder	System file Application files DeskTop file
ICON	HyperCard button icons Dialog and alert box icons	Application files Document files HyperCard stacks System file
SICN	Small icons for Control Panels and dialog boxes	Application files Document files System file

FIGURE 1-29. ICON RESOURCE TYPES.
You can edit these types of icons by using the ResEdit utility.

appear in groups.) The editing window for cicn resources has a palette of editing tools, a palette of available colors, various representations of the icon, and a magnified view of the icon that you can use in editing.

Resource types ics4, ics8, icl4, icl8, and ics# exist only in System 7. All these resource types use the same editing window, the Icon family editing window (present only in ResEdit versions 2.0 and later). It has a palette of editing tools, a palette of available colors, various representations of the icon being edited, and a magnified view of the icon that you can use in editing.

(A)

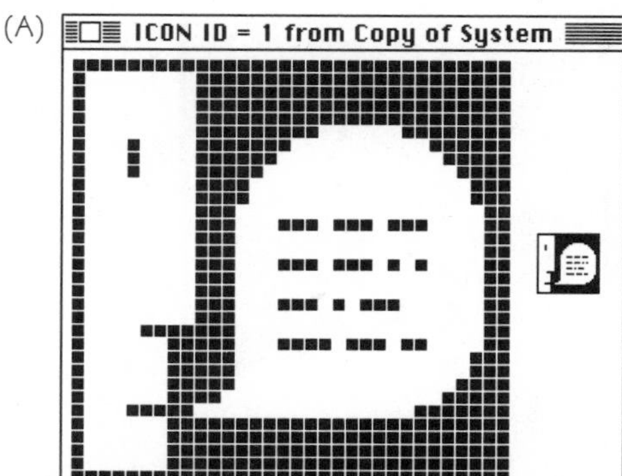

(B)

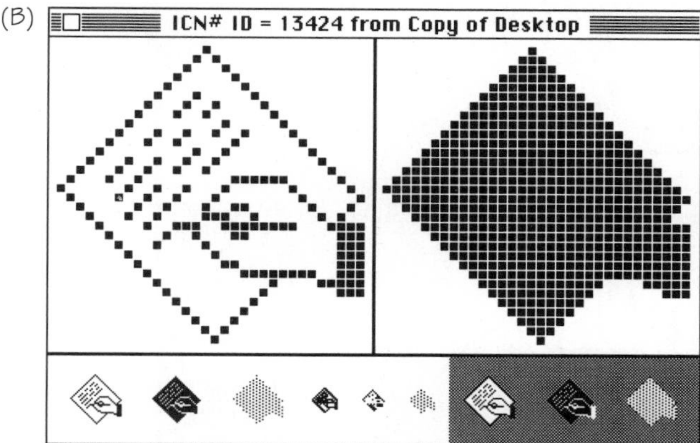

(C)

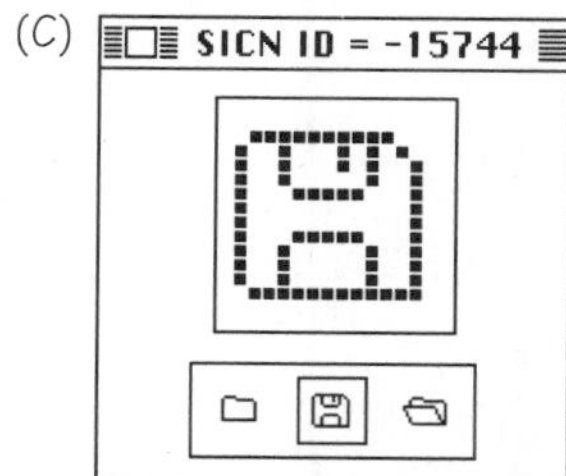

FIGURE 1-30. ICON EDITORS.

ResEdit has five icon-editing windows: one for ICON resources (A), one for ICN# resources (B), one for SICN resources (C), one for cicn resources (D), and one for ics4, ics8, icl4, icl8, and ics# resources (E).

(continued)

FIGURE 1-30. ICON EDITORS. *(continued)*

(D)

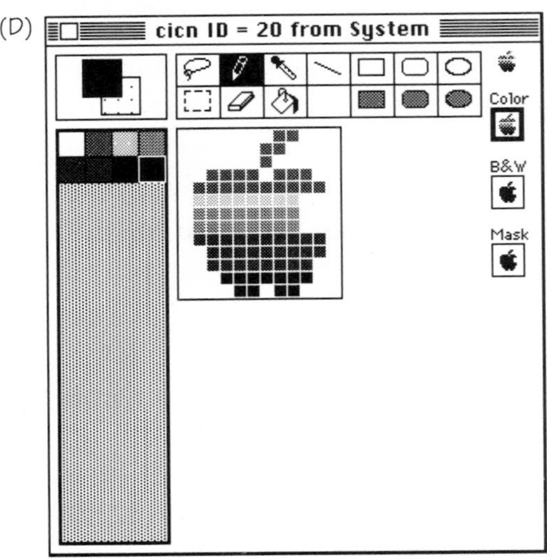

(E)

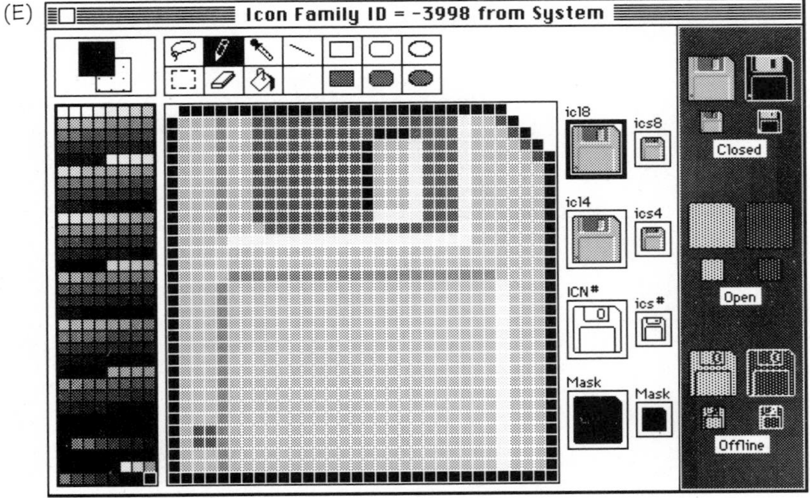

To locate an icon you want to copy or edit, use ResEdit version 1.2 or later as follows:

1. Use the Finder's Duplicate command to make a copy of each of the files that you want to check for icons. (You can copy the Desktop File by using the DiskTop utility.) Then start ResEdit.
2. Use ResEdit to open one of the copies you made. (You can't access the Desktop File from MultiFinder. Restart your Mac by using the Finder only.)
3. Scroll through the list of resource types that appears, and select all the icon resource types by pressing the Command key while clicking each one. Then choose Open from the File menu. You will see several windows of icons, one for each resource type.
4. Look through the icon windows for the icon you want. Double-click the icon to open an icon-editing window for it. If you don't find an icon you want, close all ResEdit windows except the disk windows and repeat from step 2.

To copy an icon after locating it, continue as follows:

5. Copy the entire icon by choosing the Copy command from the Edit menu. Or, before choosing the Copy command, copy part of the icon by pressing Shift while dragging a selection rectangle around the part you want.
6. If you want to copy more icons, open the Scrapbook (in the Apple menu) and paste the icon into it. If you want to copy more icons from the same file, repeat from step 4. If you want to look for icons in another file, repeat from step 2. When you have all the icons you want for the moment, quit ResEdit.

To edit an icon after locating it, continue from step 4 as follows:

5. Edit the magnified icon in the icon-editing window. Click to invert the color of a dot (black to white or white to black). To draw a line, point to a dot that is the inverse of the color in which you want to draw, press the mouse button, and drag. You can select all or part of the magnified icon by pressing the Shift key while you click and drag. After you make a selection, you can choose the Cut or Copy command from the Edit menu. You can move the selection by dragging it

while pressing the Shift key. In addition, you can paste in an icon-size image copied from a painting application such as MacPaint.

6. Close the icon-editing window. If you want to edit more icons from the same file, repeat from step 4. Otherwise, close all ResEdit windows except the disk windows; click the Yes button when ResEdit displays a message that asks whether you want to save your changes.
7. If you want to edit icons from other files, repeat from step 2. Otherwise, quit ResEdit.
8. As a precaution, make backup copies of the original, unedited files. Then replace the original files with the files that have edited icons. (Discard the originals.)
9. If you're using a version of system software earlier than System 7, rebuild the Desktop file on each disk that contains files with edited ICN# resources by holding down Command-Option during startup or during disk insertion. This lets the Finder know about the ICN# changes.

HyperCard

CONVERTING ICONS

The icons that represent application and document files in the Finder can't be used directly in HyperCard. Both are icon resources, but the file icons are of type ICN#, and the HyperCard-compatible icons are of type ICON. You can convert ICN# resources to ICON resources by using ResEdit version 1.2 or later. Beginning with System 7, a file icon can be type ics4, ics8, icl4, icl8, ics#, or ICN#. You must use ResEdit version 2.0 or later with them. To convert an icon, take the following steps:

1. Start ResEdit and use it to open the application that contains the file icon you want to convert.
2. Scroll through the list of resource types that appears and double-click the ICN# type or another type of file icon. You will see a windowful of file icons.
3. Double-click the icon you want to convert. An icon-editing window appears. (For a description of icon-editing windows, see the previous tip.)

4. Choose Copy from the Edit menu. Then close all ResEdit windows except its file windows. If ResEdit displays a message that asks whether you want to save changes, click the No button.
5. Use ResEdit to open the HyperCard stack in which you want to use the icon.
6. If you are using a version of ResEdit that is earlier than 2.0, choose New from the File menu. If you are using ResEdit version 2.0 or later, choose Create New Resource from the Resource menu. You see a dialog box in which you select a resource type.
7. Scroll through the types and double-click the ICON type. The dialog box closes, and you see the stack's ICON resources in a window. (If the stack has none, the window is empty.)
8. If you are using ResEdit version 1.2, choose New again from the File menu. An empty icon-editing window appears.
9. Choose Paste from the Edit menu. Then close all ResEdit windows except its file windows. Click the Yes button when ResEdit displays a message that asks whether you want to save changes.

ADDING COMMAND-KEY SHORTCUTS

Command-key shortcuts for menu choices are great time-savers, but some application programs don't have enough of them. In most applications, you can add your own Command-key shortcuts or change existing ones. Use ResEdit version 2.0 or later as follows:

1. Make a copy of the application whose menus you want to modify. (Use the Finder's Duplicate command.) Then start ResEdit and use it to open the copy of the application.
2. Scroll through the list of resource types that appears until you find the MENU type, and double-click it to open it. You'll see a list of menus identified by number. The number indicates the menu's location on the menu bar. The lowest number is the Apple menu, the next higher is usually a File menu, and so on. (You can't edit the menus of an application that has no MENU resources.)

3. Double-click the ID number of the menu for which you want to create Command-key shortcuts. You see a menu-editing window such as the one shown in Figure 1-31. You can identify the menu by its title, which is listed in the box labeled Title. If it is blank, the menu is probably a submenu.
4. At the left side of the menu-editing window, scroll to find the command you want. Click the command to select it.
5. In the box labeled Cmd-Key, enter the character that, in combination with the Command key, will be the shortcut for the selected command.
6. Repeat steps 4 and 5 for each Command-key shortcut you want to create or edit in the same menu.
7. If you want to work with another menu in the same application, go back to the MENU resource window, and repeat from step 3.
8. When you have finished editing menus in this application, quit ResEdit. Click the Yes button when it displays a message that asks whether you want to save changes.
9. Test the edited copy of the application. If it works, make a backup copy of the original, and replace the original with the edited copy.

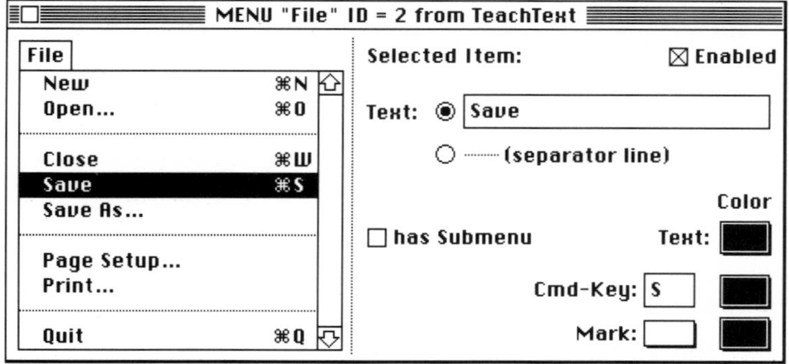

FIGURE 1-31. MENU-EDITING WINDOW.
Edit Command-key shortcuts and other aspects of menus in a ResEdit window.

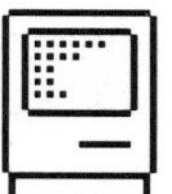

Menu commands that display submenus cannot have Command-key shortcuts. If ResEdit shows that a menu command has a solid triangle symbol (▶) as a key equivalent, do not change it.

Command-key shortcuts must be unique within an application. Do not try to use one Command-key shortcut for more than one menu command in the same program. (Be sure to check any submenus.) When used in combination with the Command key, shifted keys are considered the same as unshifted keys. Hence, *q* and *Q* are the same, and so are = and +. For consistency among applications, use uppercase letters in Command-key shortcuts.

It's best to avoid using numbers in Command-key combinations because Command-Shift-number combinations are reserved for ejecting disks, recording screen snapshots, and so on. If you run out of uppercase letters when creating your Command-key shortcuts, use Command-Option with uppercase letter or symbol keys.

CHANGING MENU WORDING

In most applications, the menu titles and menu commands are resources in the application files. You can edit the wording of menus. Using ResEdit version 2.0 or later, take the following steps:

1. Make a copy of the application whose menus you want to modify. (Use the Finder's Duplicate command.) Then start ResEdit and use it to open the copy of the application.
2. Scroll through the list of resource types that appears until you find the MENU type, and double-click it to open it. You'll see a list of menus identified by number. The number indicates the menu's location on the menu bar. The lowest number is the Apple menu, the next higher is usually a File menu, and so on. (You can't edit the menus of an application that has no MENU resources.)
3. Double-click the ID number of the menu whose wording you want to edit. You see a menu-editing window like the one shown in Figure 1-31, in the previous tip.
4. The menu title is listed in the box labeled Title. You can edit it using standard methods. However, if the menu title is blank, do not change it. It means the menu is probably a submenu.

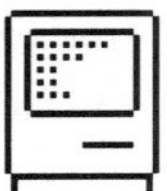

5. To change the wording of a menu item, select it in the replica of the menu at the left side of the menu-editing window and edit it in the box labeled Text. Repeat this step for each command you want to change in the same menu.
6. If you want to work with another menu in the same application, go back to the MENU resource window, and repeat from step 3.
7. When you have finished editing menus in this application, quit ResEdit. Click the Yes button when it displays a message that asks whether you want to save changes.
8. Test the edited copy of the application. If it works, make a backup copy of the original, and replace the original with the edited copy.

Sometimes an application has more than one MENU resource for a single menu. For example, Finder 6.0 has two resources for the File menu—one for a regular File menu and one for an AppleShare File menu. If you have changed the correct MENU resource, you should see the results the next time you use the application.

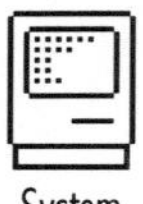

System

PERSONALIZING POINTERS

All pointers but one—the standard arrow—are CURS resources stored in the System file or in an application file. You can edit pointer shapes by using the ResEdit utility. (ResEdit calls each CURS resource a cursor.) You can also change a pointer's "hot spot," which aligns the pointer with the mouse location.

ResEdit's cursor-editing window has three editing panels, as shown in Figure 1-32 on page 56. The left panel shows a magnified version of the icon. The center panel shows the mask, which determines how the pointer looks against nonwhite backgrounds. The right panel shows the location of the hot spot. The window also shows the pointer against three background patterns.

The pointer mask is usually the pointer outline filled with black. However, a white mask dot under a white pointer dot makes the pointer transparent at that dot. A white mask dot under a black pointer dot makes the mask the inverse of the background color at that dot.

To edit a pointer in ResEdit version 1.2 or later, take the following steps:

1. Make a copy of the System file or another file that contains a pointer you want to change. (Use the Finder's Duplicate command.) Then start ResEdit and use it to open the copy of the file.
2. Scroll through the list of resource types that appears, and double-click the CURS type. You'll see a windowful of pointers.
3. Double-click the pointer you want. You'll see a cursor-editing window for it.
4. Edit the magnified pointer and mask. Click to invert the color of a dot (black to white or white to black). To draw a line, point to a dot that is the inverse of the color in which you want to draw, press the mouse button, and drag. To create a standard mask, use the Data->Mask command (on the Cursor menu).

   You can select all or part of the magnified pointer or mask by pressing the Shift key while you click and drag. After you have made a selection, you can choose the Cut command or the Copy command from the Edit menu. You can move the selection by dragging it while pressing the Shift key. In addition, you can paste a pointer-size image copied from a painting application such as MacPaint.
5. In the right panel of the editing window, click the place where you want the hot spot. A black dot appears there.
6. Try out the new pointer by choosing Try Cursor from the Cursor menu. See how it looks over various background patterns, and test the serviceability of the hot-spot location. If the pointer doesn't look right, edit it or its mask. If it doesn't have the right feel, change the location of the hot spot.
7. When you have finished editing, close the cursor-editing window. If you want to edit more pointers from the same file, repeat from step 3. Otherwise, quit ResEdit. Click the Yes button when it displays a message that asks whether you want to save changes.
8. If you edited a copy of the System file, drag the original, unedited System file out of the System Folder. Then drag the edited System file into the System Folder. Be sure the edited System file is named System. Then restart your Mac. As a precaution, make a backup copy of

your original, unedited System file before dragging the original System file into the Trash.

If you edited another file, replace the original with the copy that you edited.

Some applications don't use CURS resources to define their pointers. HyperCard, for example, uses a FONT or NFNT resource. You can change a pointer using the method described here only if it's a CURS resource.

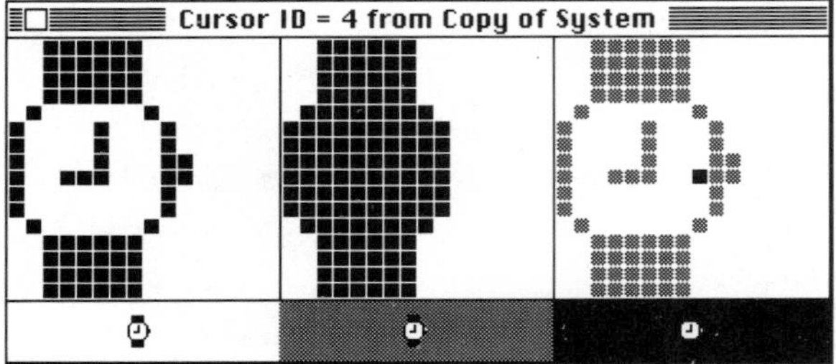

FIGURE 1-32. CURSOR-EDITING WINDOW.
All pointers except the standard arrow are resources that you can edit in a ResEdit cursor-editing window. You can change both the pointer shape and the hot spot that links it to the mouse location.

CHANGING DIALOG BOXES

You can change the size of a dialog box and the arrangement of items in it by using ResEdit version 1.2 or later. For example, if you are using system software earlier than System 7, you can enlarge the Finder's Get Info window to see more lines of text in the Comments area. Take the following steps:

1. Make a copy of the Finder. (Use the Finder's Duplicate command.) Then start ResEdit and use it to open the copy of the Finder.
2. Scroll through the list of resource types that appears until you find the DLOG type, and double-click it to open it.
3. In the list of specific DLOG resources that appears, double-click the resource with ID = 5120. A dialog-box-editing window opens, showing a miniature of the Get Info window. (See Figure 1-33.)

4. Double-click anywhere inside the dialog-box-editing window to open a window for editing the items in the dialog box. (See Figure 1-34.) Position this window so that you can see all of it.

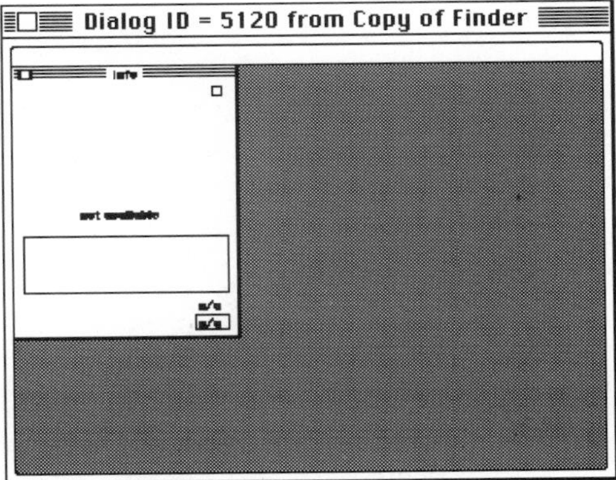

FIGURE 1-33. DIALOG-BOX EDITOR.
When editing a dialog box by using ResEdit, you can resize it by dragging its lower right corner. You can also drag the dialog box to a new location (although programs often ignore it).

DITL ID = 5120 from Copy of Fin

not available

n/a

n/a

FIGURE 1-34. DIALOG-BOX-ITEM EDITOR.
Using a ResEdit window like this, you can edit the items in a dialog box— buttons, text, text-editing areas, and so on.

5. Although you could resize the text-editing area by dragging the rectangle's lower right corner, it's easier and more accurate to specify a new size numerically. To do that, double-click inside the white text-editing rectangle near the bottom of the dialog-box-item-editing window. A dialog box appears in which you can change the characteristics of the dialog box item you double-clicked. (See Figure 1-35.)

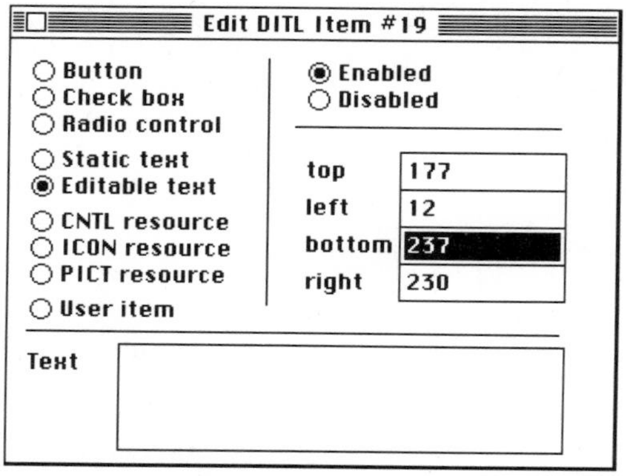

Edit DITL Item #19

○ Button
○ Check box
○ Radio control
○ Static text
◉ Editable text
○ CNTL resource
○ ICON resource
○ PICT resource
○ User item

◉ Enabled
○ Disabled

top 177
left 12
bottom 237
right 230

Text

FIGURE 1-35. CHARACTERISTICS OF DIALOG-BOX ITEMS.
A ResEdit dialog box like this lets you edit the characteristics of one dialog box item. You can select the type of item, specify its location and size, and edit any text it contains.

6. Change the number labeled *bottom* from 237 to 261. This will make the Comments rectangle 24 dots taller, which is the amount needed for two more lines of Geneva 9 text. Then close the dialog box and the dialog-box-item editing window.

7. Back in the dialog-box-editing window, lengthen the miniature Get Info dialog box by dragging its lower right corner straight down far enough to accommodate the newly lengthened Comments rectangle.

8. Quit ResEdit, clicking the Yes button when it displays a message that asks whether you want to save changes.

9. Drag the original, unedited Finder out of the System Folder. If your edited Finder is not already in the System Folder, drag it there and rename it Finder.

10. Restart your Mac and test the Get Info command. As a precaution, make a backup copy of your original, unedited Finder on another disk. Then drag the original Finder into the Trash.

DIALOG BOX CAVEATS

System

The appearance and contents of dialog boxes are defined by resources in an application program or the System file. You can change these resources by using ResEdit (as described in the previous tip). However, application programs can and do alter dialog boxes on the fly. If their alterations overlap changes you have made with ResEdit, "ugly" might be too polite a word to describe to the result. Hence, you should experiment on a copy of the application program or System file. Do not put a redesigned dialog box into service until you have thoroughly tested all aspects of it in action.

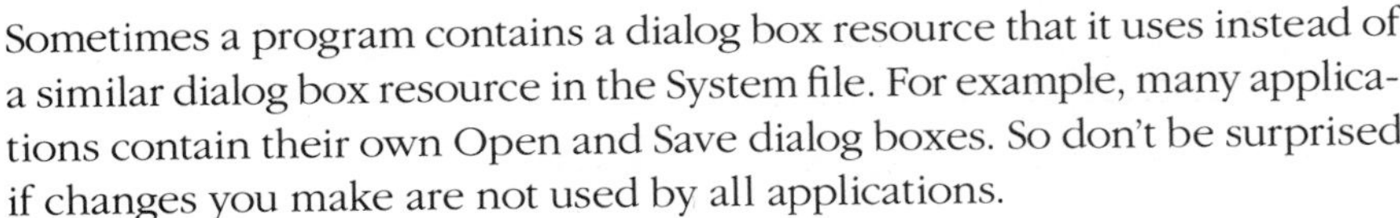

Sometimes a program contains a dialog box resource that it uses instead of a similar dialog box resource in the System file. For example, many applications contain their own Open and Save dialog boxes. So don't be surprised if changes you make are not used by all applications.

Some changes you can make to dialog boxes are almost sure to cause problems. Heed the following warnings:

- Never remove items from a dialog box.
- Never change the type of a dialog box item—button, check box, static text, CNTL resource, ICON resource, or PICT resource.
- Don't use the Send To Back or the Bring To Front command (on the DITL menu). Either can disrupt the way a dialog box works.
- Don't edit or remove text such as ^0 and ^1. When you use the application program, it replaces these markers with meaningful text.
- The Use Full Window command (on the DITL menu) might enlarge the dialog box considerably. You might find items at the edges of an enlarged dialog box. Such items are invisible when the dialog box is used unless the application program moves them while it is running. Don't move the "invisible" items at the edge of a full window.

Chapter 2

ESSENTIAL SYSTEM COMPONENTS

This chapter offers tips for working with the hardware components present in every Macintosh system, whether a compact Mac (512K, Plus, SE, or SE/30), a modular Mac (Classic, LC, II, IIx, IIcx, IIsi, IIci, or IIfx), or a Mac Portable. Every system includes the computer itself, a keyboard, a mouse, and a monitor. The tips in this chapter cover the following activities:

- Setting up
- Upgrading
- Maintaining
- Traveling

Disks and disk drives are covered in the next chapter, "Disks and Disk Drives." Likewise, printers are discussed in Chapter 4, "Printers and Printing." If your system isn't working properly and you want to diagnose the problem and find a cure, see Chapter 5, "Troubleshooting."

SETTING UP

CHANGING SCSI CONNECTIONS

It is important to turn off all SCSI devices before changing connections. The SCSI (Small Computer Systems Interface) port is actually a connection to an active bus, much like the NuBus slots in a Mac II or the slots in an Apple II. No one would think of adding or removing cards in those computers without first turning off the power. But many people believe that because you plug a cable into the SCSI port, it is simply another type of serial port.

In fact, plugging and unplugging SCSI devices while the power is turned on creates transient voltages that damage the delicate MOS (metal-oxide semiconductor) circuitry in the Mac and in many peripheral devices. It's not a question of whether damage occurs but one of how much damage occurs. SCSI etiquette demands that you perform a proper shutdown and switch off all devices before changing the cabling.

Cables

ADB DANGER

It's possible to damage the main logic board of a Mac simply by disconnecting or connecting a keyboard, mouse, or other ADB (Apple Desktop Bus) device while the power is turned on. A glitch in the design of the ADB connectors allows the connectors to flex as you make or break connections, shorting the power pin to the ground pin. This blows some fuses in the ADB circuitry and might damage the chip that controls the ADB functions. Always turn the power off before changing keyboard or mouse connections.

All Macs

AMPLIFIED SOUND

The audio-output jack lets you pipe the Mac's sound output to an external speaker, an audio amplifier, or even a tape recorder. The jack accepts a standard ⅛-inch miniature phone plug.

Electronics stores sell adapter cables that can send the monaural sound from the Mac to both channels of a stereo amplifier; one such cable is Radio Shack part number 42-2153. Connect the cable to high-level input jacks on the amplifier or tape recorder. The Mac's sound output signal will overload low-level input jacks, such as those intended for a magnetic phono cartridge or microphone, resulting in loud but distorted sound.

All Macs

SPEAKER PLACEMENT

If you attach an external speaker to your Mac, don't place it on or near an external disk drive or disk storage cabinets. The speaker contains a magnet that could destroy the information on your disks.

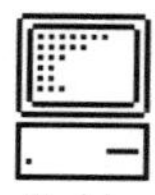
Modular Macs

STARTUP MONITOR

When you start a Mac, a number of icons and messages appear on the screen. You see the smiling Mac icon, the *Welcome To Macintosh* message, and icons for any startup documents you might have in your System Folder.

If your Mac has more than one monitor connected, the Mac chooses one as the startup monitor. On a modular Mac (the Mac II series) that has more than one monitor, the standard startup monitor is the one connected to the video card in the NuBus slot farthest from the disk drives.

You can select a different monitor as the startup monitor. Click the Monitors icon (in versions 4.0 and later) in the Control Panel desk accessory. Press the Option key; a miniature smiling Mac icon appears on one of the screens. (See Figure 2-1.) Drag the icon onto the screen that you want to be the startup monitor.

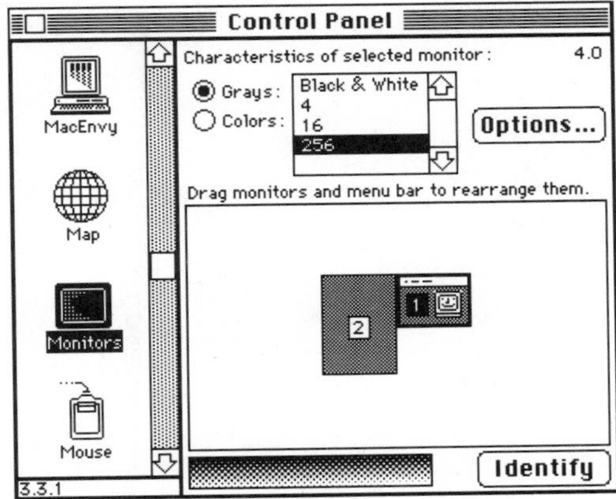

FIGURE 2-1. STARTUP MONITOR ICON.
On a Mac that has more than one monitor connected, you can choose the monitor you want to be the startup monitor.

AVOIDING SCREEN ETCHING

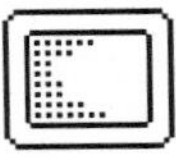

A stationary image, such as the Mac's menu bar, displayed continuously for weeks or months might etch the screen's phosphor, leaving a shadow. The Macintosh owner's manual suggests dimming the screen with the brightness control whenever you leave the machine on and unattended for a long time. On most compact Macs, the brightness control is located at the front of the machine on the overhang under the Apple logo. On a Mac Classic, use the Brightness Control Panel. On most external monitors, the brightness control is located on the right side or the front.

After Dark, a Control Panel add-on from Berkeley Systems, eliminates etching. It automatically darkens the entire screen after a period of no keyboard use or mouse-button activity and displays your choice of a dozen moving or dimmed visual novelties to remind you that the Mac is still turned on. (See Figure 2-2.) A click of the mouse or a tap on any key brings the screen back to life.

FIGURE 2-2. LIGHT SHOW.
Use screen-saver software such as After Dark to stop stationary images from burning into your Mac's screen.

Monitors

HIGH-TECH SUPPORT

You don't need to spend a lot of money on monitor support arms. Most arms cost between $150 and $400, but you can build your own for about $20. You need several lengths of 1½-inch galvanized iron water pipe and fittings. (Plastic pipe won't work.) For a diagram and complete parts list, see Figure 2-3.

When you connect the 6-inch pipe nipple to the two elbows, make the two joints as tight as possible by using a compound such as Loctite. Otherwise, the arm might dump your monitor on the floor. Tighten the other pipe-to-elbow joints as well, but leave the pipe-to-flange joints somewhat loose

to allow the arm to swivel. Be sure to use a flange on the underside of the desk to spread the load; washers are not enough.

You can change the reach of your support arm by using a different length of horizontal pipe. The 6-inch nipple specified provides an 8-inch reach from centerline to centerline. Similarly, to change the height of the plywood platform, use a different vertical pipe. A 2-inch nipple makes the platform 7½ inches above the desk. Using a close fitting instead would make the platform as low as possible, about 5½ inches.

The arm is plenty strong; it holds a 60-pound monitor easily. It is not as pretty or as flexible as an AnthroArm, but it doesn't cost $300 either.

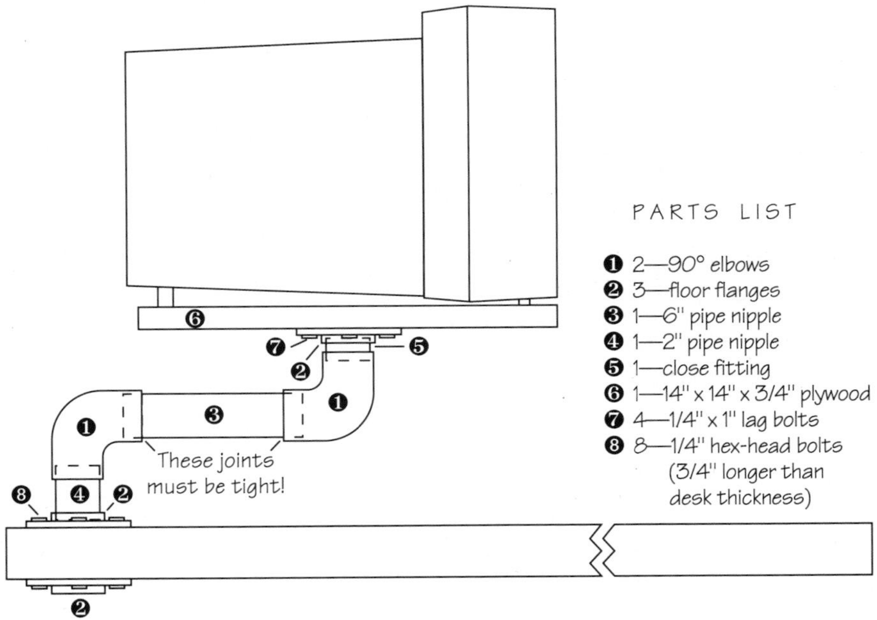

FIGURE 2-3. PIPE UP.

Construct your own swiveling monitor support arm from 1½-inch iron water pipe and fittings. Make the joints tight at the elbows, especially where the horizontal pipe connects. Leave the joints at the flanges somewhat loose.

Mac Plus or 512K

LONG KEYBOARD CABLE

If you need a long keyboard cable for a Mac Plus or 512K, you might be tempted to use a telephone handset cable. It won't work without modification, however, because the wiring is different. You *can* get a telephone handset cable to work by reversing the wires in the cable. To do so, cut the cable in the middle, strip the insulation from the cut ends, and connect black to yellow, and red to green. As an alternative, you can cut off one end of the phone cable and install a new modular connector upside down. You'll need a crimping tool, available at hardware stores and at Radio Shack, to install the new connector.

All Macs

SECURITY BLANKET

Instead of buying an expensive metal security clip that snaps into the Mac's security slot, you can make your own security system. A closed loop (about 1 inch in diameter) of 3⁄16-inch vinyl-coated steel cable (5⁄16-inch outer diameter) will slip neatly into the slot. After you insert it, the cable is difficult to remove—you have to open the case and pry the cable out. A loop at one end of the cable restrains the Mac and a loop at the other end lets you padlock the cable to the table. You form the loops by heavily crimping dual ferrules into place. (See Figure 2-4.)

All the parts cost less than $5 at a hardware store. The savings are remarkable if you must secure several Macs.

To handcuff lightweight accessories—power cord, mouse, external disk drive—simply lay their cords through the padlock just before closing it. If you need to secure components with removable cords, use a longer security cable with an extra crimped loop for each additional device. You can use an extra loop with a Mac Plus keyboard but not with the keyboards of later-model Macs.

Modular Macs

Mac SE/30

APPLICATION COMPATIBILITY

Some application programs do not work on a Mac II, IIx, IIcx, IIsi, IIci, IIfx, LC, SE/30, or any model upgraded with an accelerator card. An incompatible application might have trouble with the instruction cache feature built into the 68020 or 68030 microprocessor in those computers. The instruction cache saves recently executed instructions where the microprocessor can quickly reexecute them.

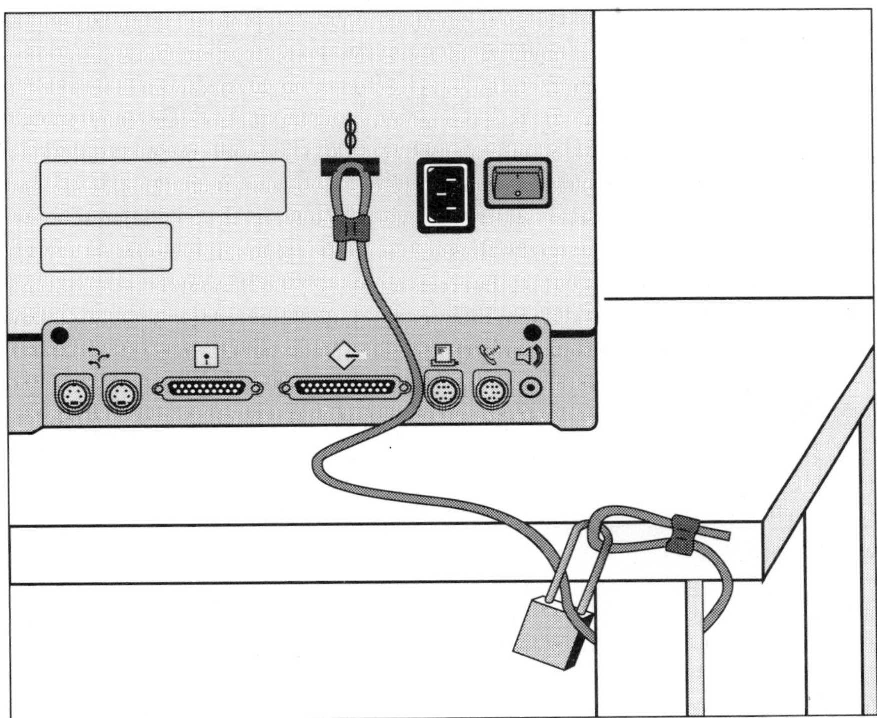

FIGURE 2-4. SECURE MAC.
Make an inexpensive security system for your Mac from steel cable, ferrules, and a padlock.

You might be able to get such applications to work if you disable the cache. A Control Panel add-on named CacheControl, created by Jim Hamilton, lets you turn the cache off or on. Note that CacheControl is not the RAM cache you set in the Control Panel.

HOT AIR

Mac Plus or 512K

Your standard Mac Plus or 512K shouldn't need a fan unless you do. If you keep its vents clear, convection will keep it cool enough, provided the air temperature is below about 100 degrees.

If the vents are blocked, the flow of air is stopped and the Mac will overheat and die. Hence, do not leave papers, books, cats, or other objects on top of the Mac, and do not stack anything against its sides.

You should strap a blower on your Mac Plus or 512K if you install an internal hard-disk drive, clip on an accelerator card, or add a memory expansion card. These internal modifications generate heat and block the normal convective airflow. Recognizing this, most add-on manufacturers include fans with their products. If you simply add or swap SIMMs (Single In-line Memory Modules) in a Mac Plus, however, you do not need a fan. (For more information on SIMMs, see the tip "Adding Memory," later in this chapter.)

Mac Plus or 512K

ADDING A FAN

Adding a fan to a Mac Plus or 512K won't shorten its life; actually, adding one might lengthen it. One model, the Fanny Mac QT from Mobius, fits into the handle recess at the top of the machine and increases the volume of air flowing through it. The fan includes an electrical surge suppressor and a power switch, which you use instead of the Mac's power switch.

Another model, the MacBreeze from Levco, clips inside the Mac. Instead of boosting the general airflow through the machine, the MacBreeze blows air directly at the power-supply components, which usually run much hotter and therefore tend to fail earlier than the Mac's other components.

Mac II

MAC II SILENCER

The standard fan inside the power supply of a Mac II or IIx is quite noisy. It's a Matsushita Panaflo DC fan measuring 3 inches square by 1 inch deep, drawing 0.45 amp, and blowing 31 cubic feet of air per minute. Two companies make Mac II power supplies—Astec and Sony—but they use the same fan.

You can replace the standard fan with a quieter fan, such as the Sea Breeze II from ComputerWare. It comes with instructions for replacing the fan in a Sony-built power supply. You can find instructions for the Astec-built power supply on CompuServe (file MACFAN.SIT in DL 11 of the MACPRO forum). You need sundry tools and supplies, including screwdrivers, a soldering iron, pliers, wire cutters, heat-shrink tubing, and wire ties.

Another quiet fan is Radio Shack part number 273-243A, a direct current (DC) brushless ball-bearing unit that draws 0.16 amp and blows 27 cubic feet per minute.

Warning: Replacing the fan voids the manufacturer's warranty and might void your AppleCare agreement if you have one. Apple dealers are not authorized to repair or replace any components that have been tampered with.

Because the replacement fans blow less air than the standard fan, you shouldn't use them in a Mac with an internal hard disk or more than two NuBus cards. You replace the fan entirely at your own risk.

AVOIDING ACCIDENTAL RESET

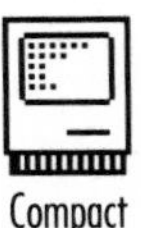

Compact Macs

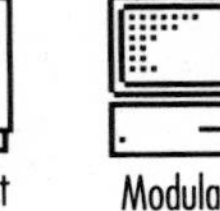

Modular Macs

The programmer's switch can be a real hazard. It is a plastic accessory that comes with the Mac and installs on the side of some Macs and the front of others. Someone might inadvertently lean against the programmer's switch and either reset your Mac or bring up what looks like a system-error alert. You might not even realize what's happening and simply chalk it up to another software bug.

You don't need the programmer's switch if, like most people, you use it only to restart after the Mac hangs or crashes. It's just as easy to restart under those conditions by switching the power off and then on, and you shouldn't have to do this often enough to wear out the power switch prematurely. (Premature aging of the switch was formerly a problem with Apple IIs.) If yours is an externally mounted, removable programmer's switch, simply pry it off carefully with a screwdriver or other flat-bladed tool.

THUMBSCREW WRENCH

Compact Macs

The overhang of the Jasmine BackPac hard-disk drive at the back of a Mac Plus, SE, or SE/30 makes it nearly impossible to tighten the thumbscrews of the mouse plug. You can manufacture a wrench by nipping the pocket clip off the cap of a ballpoint pen. This homemade wrench extends your reach 1½ inches into the cramped quarters beneath the BackPac. You might need to experiment to find a pen cap small enough to grip tightly yet large enough to break loose the thumbscrew when it is tight.

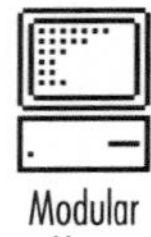

UNGROUNDED FEARS

Many older buildings have no electrical grounding available. You might be able to get around ungrounded outlets with adapter plugs, but they provide a true ground only if used properly. In some cases, connecting the small wire of the adapter to the screw on the outlet's cover plate is adequate. But often that cover-plate screw is not grounded.

You can ground the cover-plate screw by running a 14-gauge insulated wire from the screw to the nearest cold-water pipe, as shown in Figure 2-5. Use a cold-water pipe, not a hot-water pipe or radiator, because the water heater might interrupt the ground. A hardware store or electrical supply store should have a bracket that clamps to the pipe and that has a terminal to which you can attach the wire.

To be really secure, you should also ground the cold-water pipes by connecting them to a grounding rod on the house side of the water meter. Typically, the rod is 8 feet long, but to function properly, it ought to reach down into the water table.

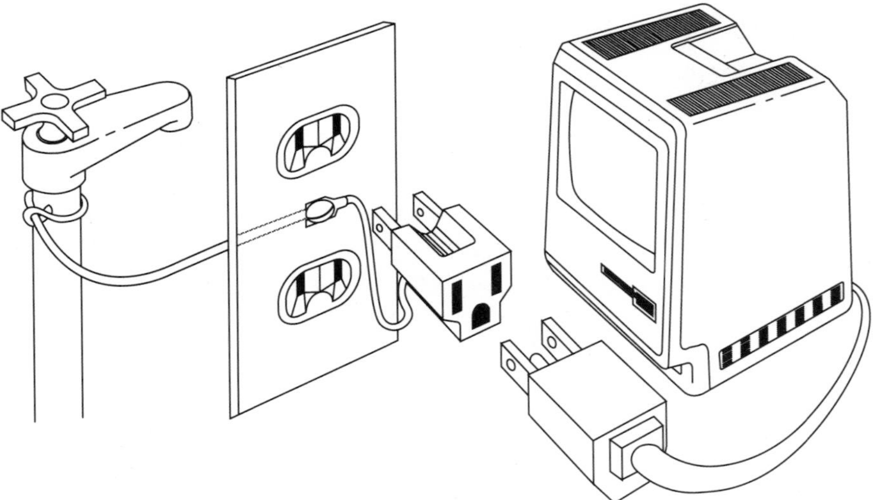

FIGURE 2-5. COLD GROUND.

To reliably ground your Mac in an older building, you might need to run a wire from the wire to the plug adapter at the electrical outlet to the nearest cold-water pipe.

12-VOLT BATTERY POWER

All Macs

Although the Macintosh is designed to use the 120-volt alternating current (AC) from most power outlets, it can also be powered by 12-volt direct current (DC) from car batteries. You'll need a device called an inverter, which transforms direct current to alternating current.

The two types of inverters are sine wave and square wave. Sine-wave inverters produce a smooth alternating current, but they are expensive. Square-wave inverters are inexpensive, but they alternate abruptly between the negative and positive flow of electrical current. If these transitions occur too quickly, the filter capacitors in the Mac's power supply could heat up. This situation is unlikely to cause a problem, however, because the inverter would probably fail before the capacitors did. Most inexpensive square-wave inverters contain transformers that produce comparatively slow voltage transitions.

The inverter must produce AC power between 95 and 120 volts under load—that is, when the Mac is plugged into it and turned on. Inexpensive inverters might produce peak voltages outside that range under no load, but the peaks usually smooth out when a load is applied. The frequency of the inverter's AC output is unimportant because the Mac controls the frequency internally as needed.

The inverter must also produce enough power for whatever you plug into it. A Mac Plus or 512K, for example, draws about 35 watts. Inverter output is usually given in amps, but you can convert the amps to watts by dividing watts by volts. Thus, the Mac Plus or 512K requires about 0.3 amp at 120 volts. Attaching an external floppy-disk drive does not increase the power requirement significantly, but plugging in a hard disk or printer does. For example, an Apple hard disk draws 20 watts (0.17 amp at 120 volts), and an ImageWriter II draws 20 watts on standby and 40 watts while printing (0.13 to 0.33 amps at 120 volts).

Here are some other maximum wattages: Apple color monitor, 105 watts; Apple monochrome monitor, 20 watts; Mac SE with two floppy-disk drives, 35 watts; Mac IIcx or IIci with an internal hard disk, 60 watts. The measured wattages listed here are lower than the manufacturers' rated wattages; manufacturers usually overstate wattages.

How long will a battery last? That depends on how much you plug into the inverter and on the capacity of the battery. Battery capacity is measured in amp-hours. If you divide the battery's amp-hour rating by the total amps drawn by the devices attached to it, you come up with the number of hours the battery will last. For example, a Mac Plus or 512K by itself draws about 3 amps at 12 volts DC (35 watts divided by 12 volts), so a 55-amp-hour battery will theoretically last about 18 hours.

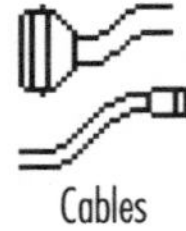

PINOUTS AND TECH NOTES

The pin assignments, or pinouts, for the serial port and SCSI port on all Macintosh models (except the Mac 512K) are shown in Figure 2-6 and Figure 2-7. Pinouts of other ports and of selected cables are printed in Apple's *Macintosh Technical Notes 10* and *65*. You can subscribe to the technical notes and buy sets of back numbers from APDA (Apple Programmers and Developers Association). Apple encourages the copying of the technical notes, so you might be able to photocopy a set from your local Mac user group's library. The notes are also available individually from online information services.

Macintosh
mini-circular 8 plug

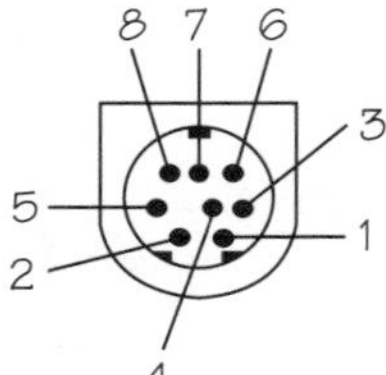

Handshake out → 1
Handshake in ← 2
Transmit data – → 3
Signal ground 4
Receive data – ← 5
Transmit data + → 6
No connection 7
Receive data + → 8

FIGURE 2-6. SERIAL PIN ASSIGNMENTS.
The modem port and printer port use a mini-circular 8 plug with the pin assignments shown here.

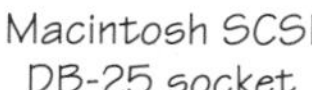

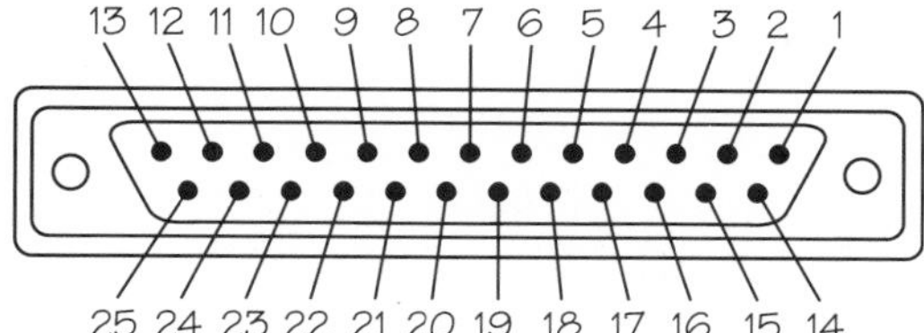

1 REQ–
2 MSG–
3 I/O–
4 RST–
5 ACK–
6 BSY–
7 Ground
8 DBO–
9 Ground
10 DB3–
11 DB5–
12 DB6–
13 DB7–
14 Ground
15 C/D–
16 Ground
17 ATN–
18 Ground
19 SEL–
20 DBP–
21 DB1–
22 DB2–
23 DB4–
24 Ground
25 Not connected

FIGURE 2-7. SCSI PIN ASSIGNMENTS.
The SCSI port uses a DB-25 socket with the pin assignments shown here.

UPGRADING

OPENING THE CASE

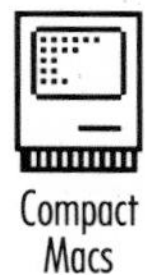

You might have wondered how difficult it would be to install more memory, a hard-disk drive, or another internal upgrade in a compact Mac. To see whether you want to tackle making internal modifications yourself, start by opening the Mac's case. (A word of warning: Opening the case does not void the warranty, but any damage you cause in the process is not covered under warranty.)

The four screws you must remove require a special screwdriver with a Torx T-15 tip and an 8-inch shaft. A Mac Plus or 512K has a fifth screw behind the clock-battery cover. After you remove the screws, a friction coating makes it very difficult to remove the back cover. Use a special case-spreader tool to avoid marring the Mac. (See Figure 2-8 on the following page.) The MacOpener from Central Products works well and has a built-in Torx T-15 screwdriver.

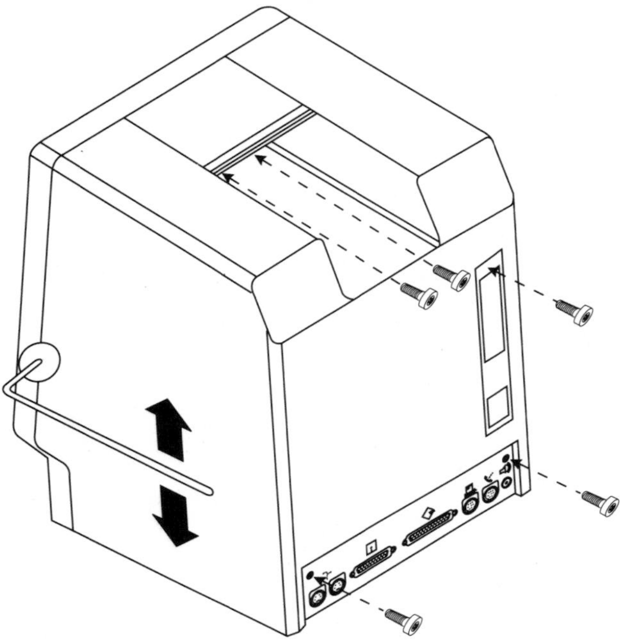

FIGURE 2-8. CASE CRACKING.
To open a Macintosh case, you must first remove four or five screws (on a Mac Plus or 512K, one from behind the battery cover) with a Torx T-15 screwdriver. Then use a case-spreader tool to pry the case apart.

As you open the case, a piece of foil might fall off the sockets at the back of Mac. Don't be alarmed. Save the foil so that you can slip it back over the sockets when you reassemble the machine.

Inside the case, you will see the following:

- A vertical circuit board called the analog, or power-supply, board
- A horizontal circuit board called the logic board
- The picture tube
- Beneath the picture tube, the disk drive or drives

Caution: Look, but don't touch unless you know what you're doing. The power-supply board and picture tube might contain dangerous residual high voltages.

ADDING MEMORY

With more memory, you can upgrade your system software or begin using upgraded features. MultiFinder, for example, lets you open multiple applications simultaneously. When you upgrade your system software (or start using upgraded features), you might also need to upgrade some of your applications. For example, DiskTop version 4.0 (from CE Software) opens files with MultiFinder active, whereas the previous version (3.0.4) did not.

Additional memory does generate more heat inside the Macintosh. Durability is not affected, however, because all models are designed to dissipate the heat created by the maximum amount of memory.

You add memory to all Macs except a Mac Portable or Mac 512K by adding or replacing small circuit boards called SIMMs (Single In-line Memory Modules). The Mac Portable uses a special memory-expansion board instead of SIMMs. Also, a Mac Classic requires a special memory-upgrade board, which is not present in all Classics.

The SIMMs snap into special sockets on a Mac logic board and are easily removed and replaced. They come in capacities of 256 KB, 1 MB, and 4 MB. You increase your Mac's total memory capacity by installing higher-capacity SIMMs and, in some cases, more SIMMs. The SIMMs must be installed in certain configurations, as shown in the diagrams in Figures 2-9 through 2-14 on the following pages.

A 1-MB Mac Plus or SE, for example, has four 256-KB SIMMs that can be replaced in pairs with 1-MB SIMMs of about the same size. Replacing one pair yields 2.5 MB and leaves two of the original 256-KB SIMMs unused. Replacing all the SIMMs yields 4 MB, with all four original 256-KB SIMMs left over. Note that you could remove all four 256-KB SIMMs and install only two 1-MB SIMMs, leaving all four original 256-KB SIMMs unused and two SIMM sockets empty. It makes no sense to do that, though. You might as well use two of the 256-KB SIMMs you already own.

SIMM LEFTOVERS

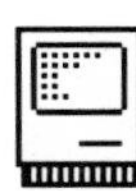

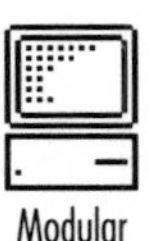

Goodwill Industries hasn't yet recognized the market for used and surplus Macintosh parts, but Pre-Owned Electronics Inc. has. They will buy the SIMMs you have left over from upgrading your Mac's memory. The price depends on current market conditions and on chip speed (150, 120, or 80 nanoseconds).

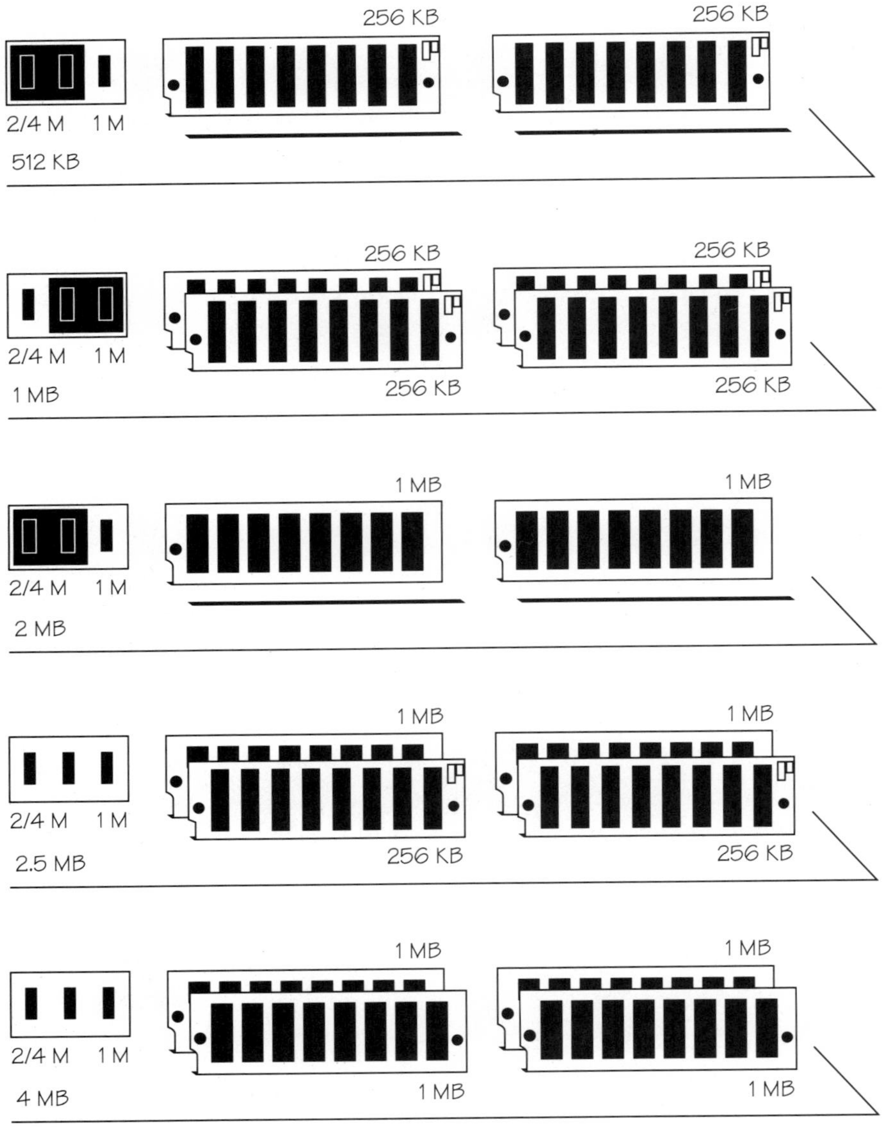

FIGURE 2-9. NEWER SE SIMMS.

To upgrade the memory on a newer Mac SE, add SIMMs in the configurations shown here. A newer SE has a jumper near the SIMM sockets. You must set it according to the SIMMs configuration. The SIMMs must be 150 nanoseconds or faster, and SIMMs of the same speed must be used within a row.

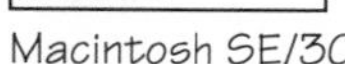

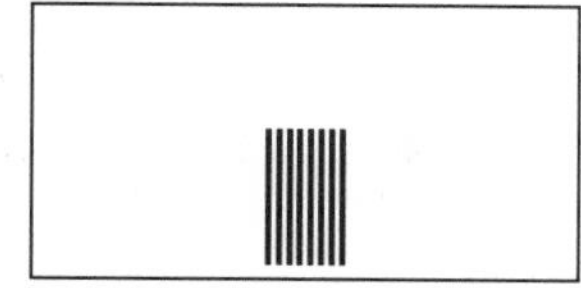

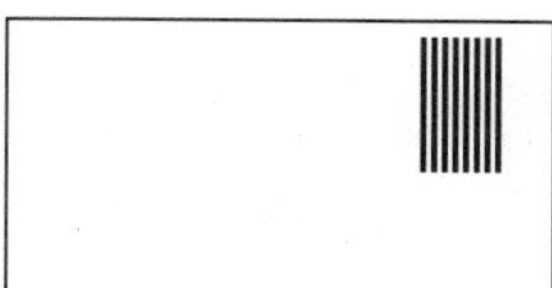

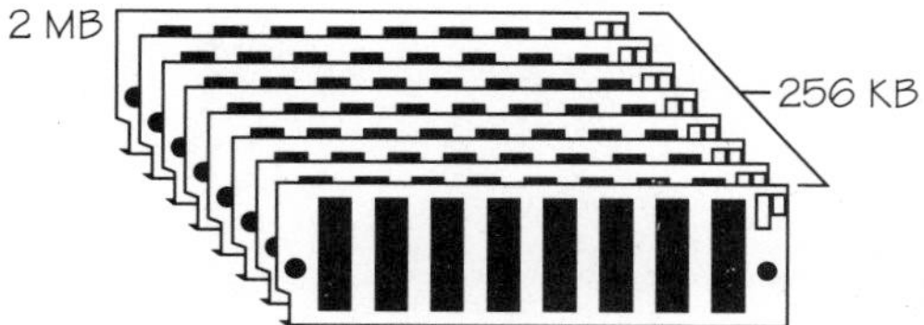

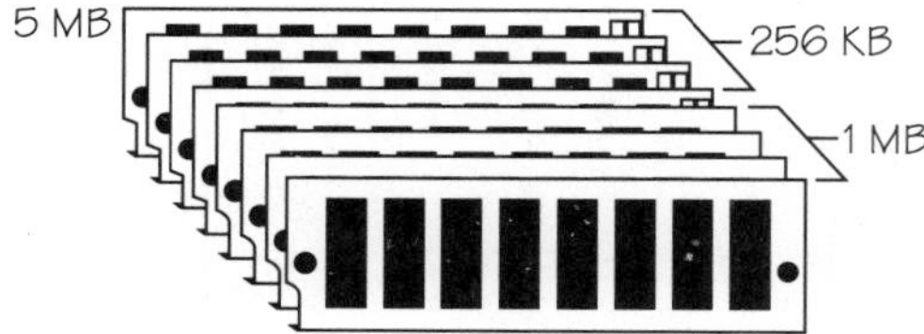

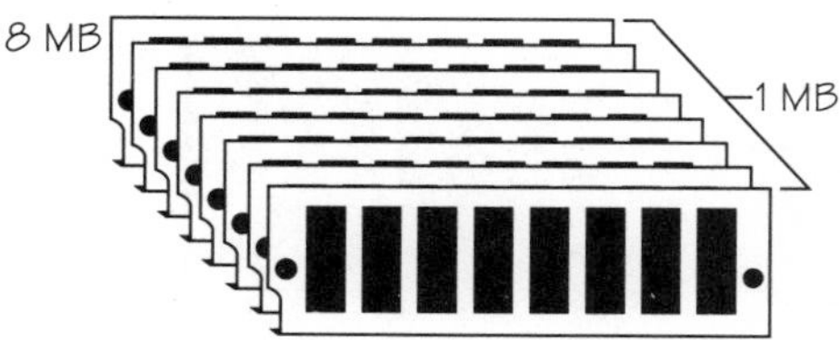

FIGURE 2-10. SE/30, IICX, II, and IIX SIMMS.

To upgrade the memory on a Mac SE/30, IIcx, II, or IIx, add SIMMs in the configurations shown here. The SIMMs must be 120 nanoseconds or faster, and SIMMs of the same speed must be used within a row.

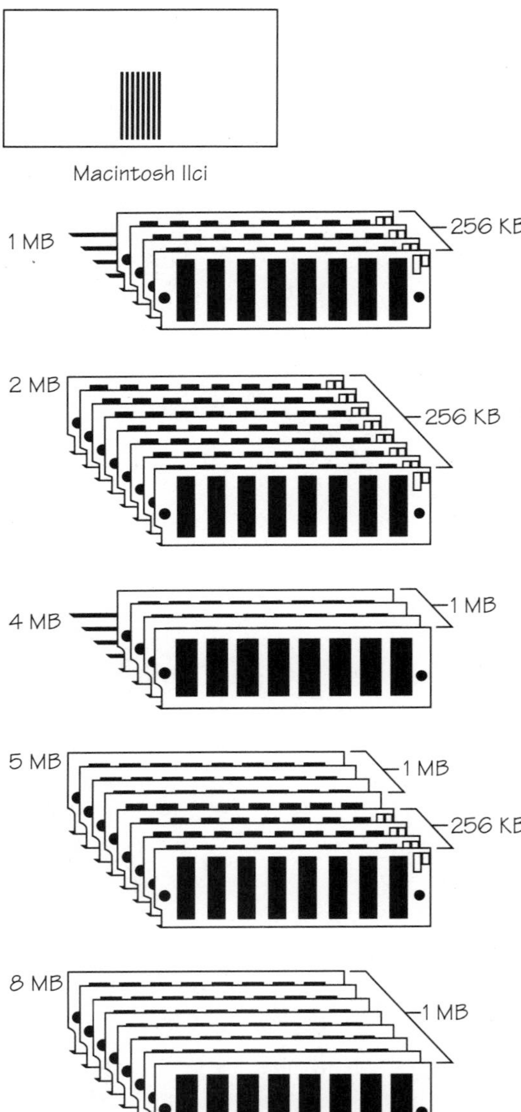

FIGURE 2-11. IICI SIMMS.

To upgrade Mac IIci memory, add SIMMs in the configurations shown here. The SIMMs must be 80 nanoseconds or faster, and SIMMs of the same speed must be used within a row.

FIGURE 2-12. CLASSIC SIMMS.

To upgrade the memory on a Mac Classic, you install a special memory-expansion card that contains 1 MB of memory and two SIMM sockets. Add SIMMs in the configurations shown here. The SIMMs must be 150 nanoseconds or faster.

FIGURE 2-13. LC SIMMS.

To upgrade the memory on a Mac LC, add SIMMs in the configurations shown here. The SIMMs must be 120 nanoseconds or faster.

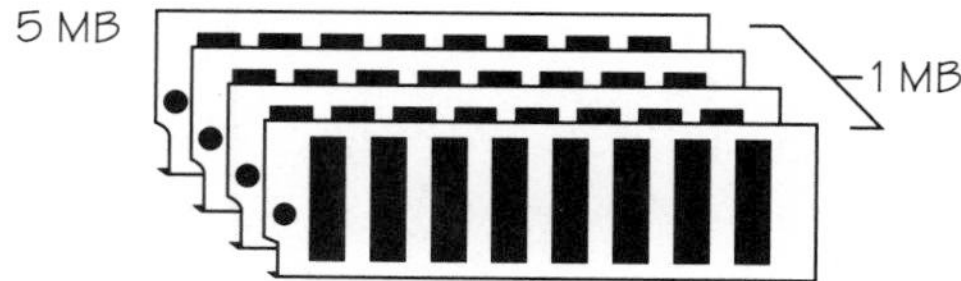

FIGURE 2-14. IISI SIMMS.

To upgrade the memory on a Mac IIsi, add SIMMs in the configurations shown here. The SIMMs must be 100 nanoseconds or faster.

Mac II

FASTER MATH

The Motorola 68881 coprocessor handles complex math functions on a Mac II. The Motorola 68882 is a newer, faster math coprocessor and is used in newer Mac models. You can replace the 68881 in a Mac II with a 68882. Expect a 25 to 40 percent improvement in tasks that involve lots of number processing, such as math calculations, statistics, and calculating new views of complex graphics. Applications written to take advantage of the 68882's features can achieve an increase in numeric processing speed of up to 100 percent. Installing a 68882 has no direct benefit aside from speeding up floating-point numeric calculations.

The 68882 is available from several sources, including Total Systems, Inc., and Tercom. Be sure to get 16-MHz chips for a Mac II.

Warning: The 68881 and 68882 have delicate pins and can sustain latent damage from static discharge during handling. Have a technician make the swap unless you know what you're doing.

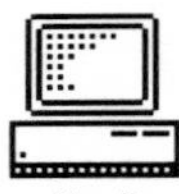
Mac II

VIRTUAL MEMORY UPGRADE

You can replace the Mac II's standard memory management coprocessor, which doesn't handle virtual memory, with a 68851 PMMU (paged memory management unit). You also need virtual memory software, either Virtual 2.0 from Connectix or System version 7 (or A/UX) from Apple. The Mac SE/30, IIx, IIcx, IIsi, IIci, and IIfx don't need a 68851 because the functions provided by a 68851 are built into the 68030 CPUs (central processing units) used in those models.

The 68851 is available from several sources, including Total Systems, Inc., Tercom, and Orvac Electronics. Be sure to get 16-MHz chips for a Mac II.

If you install a 68851 PMMU in your Mac II and the screen goes blank, the chip socket on the logic board is probably missing some pins. Take it to an Apple dealer for a free replacement logic board.

Warning: The 68851 has delicate pins and can sustain latent damage from static discharge during handling. Have a technician install it unless you know what you're doing.

MAC 512K HARD DISK

All Macs

Adding a hard-disk drive is the first step in upgrading the performance of any Macintosh, even a Mac 512K or 512Ke. To connect a SCSI hard disk to a Mac 512K or 512Ke, you need a SCSI adapter. However, a simple SCSI adapter freezes your Mac in time. Most simple SCSI adapters don't leave space inside the Mac for the addition of more memory. That might be fine if you use only one or two applications and are sure you'll never want to use software such as MultiFinder, HyperCard, and Adobe Illustrator. They, like more and more of today's software, demand 1 MB of memory at a minimum. To use System 7, you need at least 2 MB of memory.

You can start up directly from a SCSI hard disk connected to a Mac 512Ke. But to use a SCSI hard disk on an unenhanced Mac 512K, you'll need to start up with a 400-KB floppy disk that contains the System 3.2, Finder 5.3, and Hard Disk 20 1.1 files. After startup, you can make the SCSI disk the current startup disk provided it contains those same files in its System Folder. All you do is open an application that's on the hard disk.

The Hard Disk 20 file allows a Mac 512K to use the hierarchical file system (HFS), which is not included in its 64-KB read-only memory (ROM). It's HFS that makes folders for 800-KB floppy disks and hard disks appear in Open and Save dialog boxes instead of only in Finder windows.

Another way to upgrade the SCSI capabilities of your older Mac is to install an accelerator card such as the Gemini 20 or Gemini 30 from Total Systems, Inc. A highly recommended option that is available with these boards is the GemKit, which includes not only a faster SCSI port than that of the Mac Plus but also an upgraded power supply and a fan.

ENHANCING A MAC 512K

Mac 512K

Upgrading a Mac 512K to a Mac 512Ke improves its performance significantly. The upgrade replaces the 64-KB ROM and 400-KB (single-sided) disk drive with the Mac Plus 128-KB ROM and an 800-KB (double-sided) disk drive.

The 128-KB ROM displays text 50 percent faster and draws graphics an average of twice as fast as the 64-KB ROM. The larger ROM includes many of the most commonly used resources that formerly had to be transferred from disk, such as the 12-point Chicago font. The 800-KB disk drives are two to three times faster than 400-KB disk drives, not counting the speed improvements that result when you activate the disk caching included with the upgrade.

In addition, you can start up a 512Ke directly from a hard disk instead of having to start up from a floppy disk. Connecting a SCSI hard disk requires adding a SCSI port to your Mac 512Ke, however. (See the previous tip, "Mac 512K Hard Disk.")

Mac 512K

MAC 512K ALMOST-E

Technically, you need at least a Mac 512Ke to start directly from a hard disk. If you've ever had your Mac 512K's logic board replaced, you probably have half of the upgrade to a 512Ke. Apple supplies the 512-KB logic boards for service swaps with the enhanced 128-KB ROM (described in the previous tip). The 128-KB ROM lets you start up your unenhanced Mac 512K directly from a hard disk.

All Macs

RAM DISKS

If your Mac has more memory than you need, you can turn the extra memory into an electronic disk drive, called a RAM disk. You create a RAM disk with software such as RamDisk+, which lets you specify how much memory to allot to the RAM disk and designate which files you want copied onto the RAM disk when it is created.

Transferring information from an electronic RAM disk is much faster than from a mechanical disk. There are some drawbacks, however. When the Mac's power goes off, the RAM disk vanishes, and all the information on it is instantly erased. As a result, you must re-create the RAM disk every time you restart the Mac. Re-creating the disk and transferring information onto it adds about 30 seconds to startup time. Keep in mind that because the RAM disk is so volatile, it's a bad place to save documents on which you are working.

The best thing to keep on a RAM disk is your System Folder. A basic System Folder requires about 800 KB. If you have more memory available, you can add fonts and other items to the System Folder, or you can add an application to the RAM disk. If you have less than 800 KB available for a RAM disk (using system software prior to System 7) or want to use System 7, you should probably use the RAM Cache option, on the Control Panel.

MAINTAINING

ADB MATING CYCLES

Mac SE and SE/30 owners who regularly transport their systems might soon face some expensive repair bills. Apparently, the ADB connectors used in the keyboard and the Mac can wear out after only 500 mating cycles. Figure 2-15 shows which connectors are involved. If you disassemble and transport the Mac to and from work every day (two mating cycles per day), expect your keyboard and Mac ADB connectors to last less than one year! To help them last, leave the keyboard and mouse cables attached if you transport your Mac often.

If you have a problem with intermittent keyboard or mouse operation, press the various connectors to try to determine which one is bad. Connectors are fairly easy to replace. (Some soldering is required.) This route is far less costly than replacing the keyboard or logic board, which is likely to be your dealer's recommendation. The connector to buy is AMP part number 749264-1 or 749181-1. Do not use other connectors; some have a life rating of only 100 mating cycles.

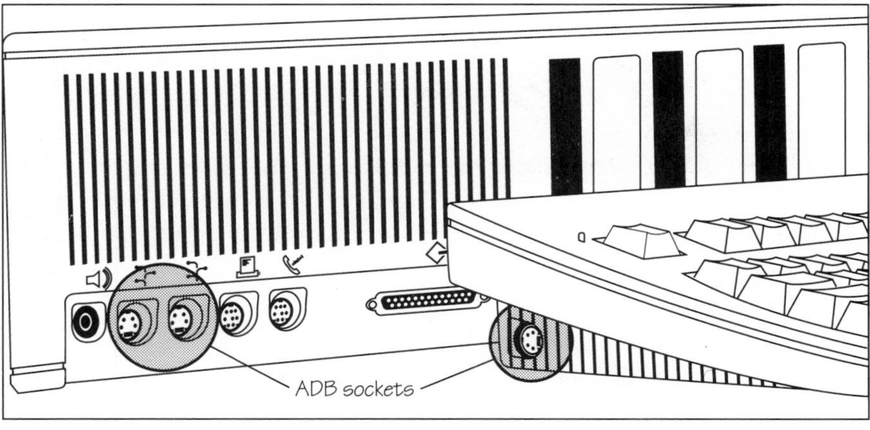

FIGURE 2-15. ADB FATIGUE.

The ADB connectors on the keyboard and the Mac can wear out after less than a year of daily unplugging.

You can replace the connectors in the Apple extended keyboard simply by removing the four screws on the bottom of the keyboard and then lifting off the top of the keyboard. The small printed circuit boards with the connectors mounted on them are then easily accessible.

Keyboard

SPILLING ON THE KEYBOARD

If you spill liquid on your keyboard and it stops working, unplug the keyboard, turn it upside down to drain out the liquid, and let it dry for a day. If that doesn't do the trick, you need to have it repaired.

Mac Plus or 512K

WORN-OUT MOUSE FEET

The two "feet" that support the front of the Mac Plus or 512K mouse can wear off after several months of continuous use on a hard surface. Without its front feet, the mouse wobbles and doesn't glide smoothly. To keep your mouse's feet from wearing out, you can buy or make a mouse pad.

To make a pad, you'll need a piece of the nylon-covered neoprene used for wet suits. Use the type called Nylon I, which has nylon on one side only. A 4-by-6-inch piece is adequate; 8 by 10 inches is ample. Place the fabric so that the nylon side is up and the rubber side is down.

If this advice comes too late and your mouse's feet are already worn out, buy a set of MouseEase self-stick Teflon pads. They replace worn mouse feet and give a smoother glide on almost any surface. Another alternative is to buy Magnum Software's Mouse Mover. It is a sort of three-wheeled, ball-bearing roller skate that clips to the base of your mouse, eliminating the worn-feet syndrome and making the mouse somewhat easier to move precisely. Its 90 ball bearings are a bit noisy, though, especially on hard surfaces.

Mac Plus or 512K

BATTERY REPLACEMENT

Look carefully at the polarity markings before replacing the Eveready 523 4.5-volt battery in your Mac Plus or 512K. Some time back Eveready interchanged the black and silver ends when they switched to a new logo. Don't trust the battery coloring—go by the + and – markings.

WORKING AROUND A BROKEN KEY

Keyboard

If a key on your keyboard breaks, you can work around it by copying the character it types from another place in the document and pasting it where you need it. If the character doesn't appear elsewhere, use the Key Caps desk accessory to generate it. In the Key Caps window, click the broken key (with the Shift and Option keys pressed, if necessary) to generate the needed character. Then copy the character from Key Caps, and paste it into your document. Use the MacroMaker utility to automate the process and assign it to an alternate keystroke. You can also use a utility such as MacKeymeleon by Avenue Software to reassign a broken key's characters to another keystroke.

FIXING A BROKEN MOUSE BUTTON

Mouse

Lots of clicking and double-clicking can wear out the switch on your mouse button. You can replace the switch yourself if you are mechanically inclined. If you're doing it yourself, you'll need a pair of needle-nose pliers, a small soldering iron (15 to 30 watts), and some 60/40 rosin-core solder.

You'll need to buy a subminiature single-pole, double-throw (SPDT) switch that measures ¾ by ¼ by ⅜ inch and is rated 0.1 amp at 250 volts or higher. Radio Shack has two switches that will work (part number 275-017 or 275-016). Figure 2-16 on the following page shows what's needed.

After you've collected these items, proceed as follows:

1. A metal lever is attached to the Radio Shack switch. Remove the lever with the needle-nose pliers.
2. Remove the screws that hold the mouse case together, and put them aside where they won't get lost.
3. Separate the two halves of the mouse case. When separating a Mac Plus or 512K mouse, be careful not to lose the plastic mouse button and its spring.
4. Remove the screws that hold the mouse circuit board to the case.
5. Desolder the old switch, and then solder the new switch in its place.
6. Reinstall the circuit board in the mouse.
7. Reassemble the mouse. Before screwing the case together, click the mouse button to be sure it feels right.

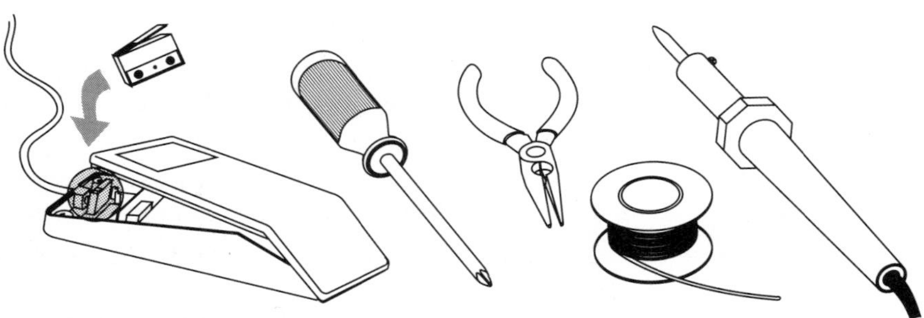

FIGURE 2-16. SWITCH SWITCH.
If your mouse button becomes erratic or stops working, you can replace the switch using the parts and tools shown here.

A+ Mouse

STATIC KO'S OPTICAL MOUSE

In a cold, dry winter climate there is lots of static electricity. Bedroom slippers on a nylon carpet are especially bad news. Static electricity is, in general, bad news for personal computers. It is particularly a bad idea to handle data disks or install SIMMs after walking about in bedroom slippers. The slightest zap to a Mouse Systems A+ optical mouse causes it to freeze and appear to be malfunctioning. To unfreeze the mouse, shut down the Mac, and unplug the mouse momentarily.

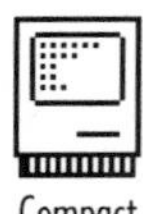
Compact Macs

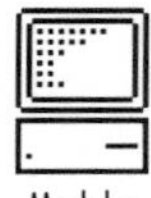
Modular Macs

AVOIDING SUNSTROKE

Heat builds up rapidly inside a car parked in the sun. The same is true inside a Mac if you leave it in the sun, and you can't cool it off by rolling down the windows! The electronic components inside your Mac are at least as sensitive to heat as you are, so find it a cool place in the shade.

Mac Plus or 512K

STOP SQUEALING

Don't let your Mac Plus or 512K torture you with high-pitched squealing. The squealer is part of the video circuitry, specifically the flyback transformer. It has two pieces that might vibrate against each other at a frequency of 15 kHz or so. You can usually quiet the transformer by removing it, disassembling it, placing a drop of oil in the gap of the armature, reassembling it, and reinstalling it. (See Figure 2-17.)

This service costs about $60 at CJS Systems in Berkeley, California, a company that does a lot of Mac repairs but is not an authorized Apple dealer.

The noise does not mean the flyback transformer is failing, according to John Sawyer of CJS Systems. When that happens, the screen goes black, the case gets very hot on the top left side, and you might see a puff of smoke. If you then switch your Mac off and back on, it might make a chirping sound every quarter of a second or half of a second. Replacing the transformer costs about $120 at CJS Systems. An Apple dealership would probably recommend you buy a reconditioned power-supply board that costs between $250 and $300.

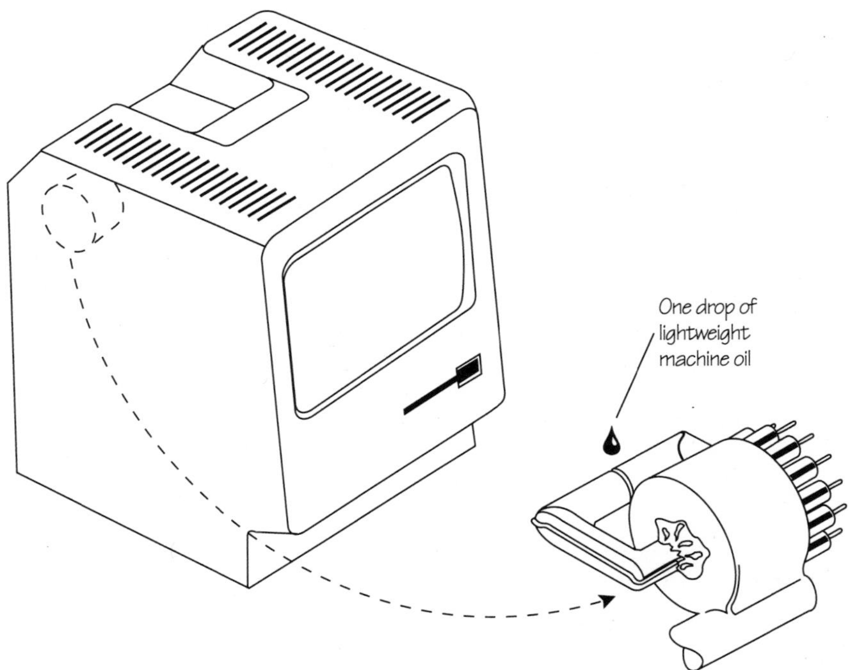

FIGURE 2-17. BAD VIBRATIONS.
A squealing Mac Plus or 512K can usually be silenced if you disassemble the flyback transformer and place a drop of oil in the spot shown here.

DANCING SCREEN

Does the picture on your Mac Plus or 512K periodically shrink a bit and then quickly return to normal? This common problem is usually caused by imperfect contact of the picture-tube signal cable connector at the analog board inside the Mac.

To fix it, first open the Mac as described in "Opening the Case," earlier in this chapter. Then unplug the picture tube signal cable, and use a jeweler's screwdriver to carefully compress the C-shaped metal sockets inside the cable connector so that they will make solid contact with the pins of the matching connector on the analog board. It's also a good idea to touch up the solder joints that connect the matching connector to the analog board. Figure 2-18 shows the location of the connector.

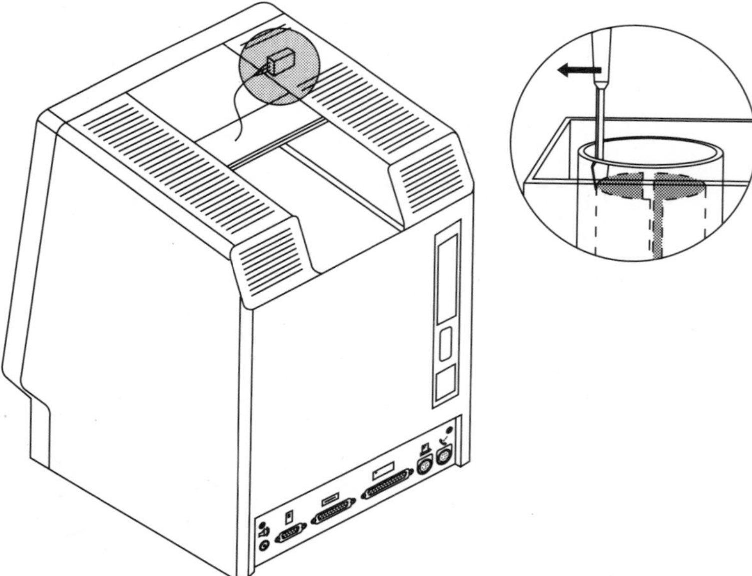

FIGURE 2-18. THE DANCE IS OVER.

Cure a sporadically shrinking screen by tightening the metal sockets inside the cable connector and resoldering the matching connector on the circuit board.

TRAVELING

WHEELS FOR THE MAC

Instead of lugging your Mac in the usual padded bag, why not wheel it along on a folding luggage cart? Bungee cords hold a complete Macintosh system securely. (See Figure 2-19.) Many department stores charge $25 to $80 for a rugged cart, but you can find them for $19.95. Larger, big-wheeled models are best at negotiating stairs.

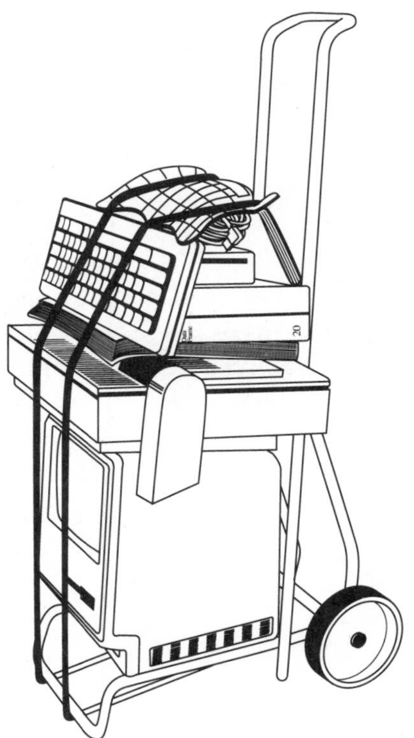

FIGURE 2-19. HAVE CART, WILL TRAVEL.
Use the latest modern invention, the wheel, and take a load off when you move your Mac.

MAC AND THE AIRLINES

All Mac models except the Mac Portable are too big to fit under most airline seats. (An LC, IIsi, IIcx, or IIci will fit sans monitor.) The compact Macs fit in the overhead bin on some planes; if yours doesn't fit in the bin, you might be able to get a flight attendant to put yours in a coat closet. If you decide to check your Mac, put it in its original shipping cartons. If you no longer have them, first put the equipment in padded carrying bags, and then pack them in cardboard boxes. You can also use expensive, hard-shell cases. Be prepared to pay an extra baggage charge.

Your disks might not survive the X-rays used to inspect checked and carry-on baggage in the United States. To be safe, put disks in a lead-lined pouch (available at photography stores). Have your hard-disk drive inspected by hand.

A MAC ABROAD

To get your Macintosh system into a foreign country, you might have to pay a stiff security deposit or import duty. Contact customs at your destination before leaving to see what documents you'll need, in order to avoid paying a deposit or duty. You might be able to avoid putting up the deposit by purchasing a carnet (pass) from the U.S. Council for International Business. The council has offices in New York, Los Angeles, San Francisco, and Schaumburg, Illinois.

To enter some countries outside the "free world" with your high-tech Macintosh, you'll need a special license from the U.S. Department of Commerce. Allow four months to get the license.

POWER STRIP TO GO

Headed overseas with your Macintosh system? Don't leave home without a multi-outlet power strip/surge protector. (See Figure 2-20.) Finding one won't be easy once you leave the United States.

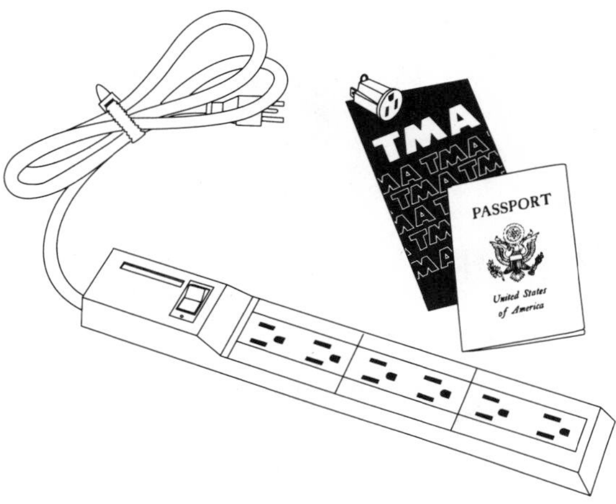

FIGURE 2-20. ESSENTIAL POWER.
Don't take your system out of the country without one of these devices—a multi-outlet power strip/surge protector.

UNIVERSAL POWER

Electrical power is only a minor concern with Apple products that have a universal, self-configuring power supply. To use any Mac (except a Mac Classic, Plus, or 512K), a Tape Backup 40SC, or any Apple external hard disk anywhere in the world, you need a plug adapter to match the wall socket. You can get adapters from Radio Shack and large hardware stores.

Devices that don't have power plugs, such as the mouse, keyboard, and external floppy-disk drives, take their power from the Mac. Therefore they work anywhere it works.

Some non-Apple products have power supplies that can be set manually for 220/240 or 110/120 volts. Look for a switch on the back panel. Failing that, ask the dealer or manufacturer whether there's a voltage-selector jumper inside the power supply.

POWER TRANSFORMER

Equipment that operates only on 110/120 volts requires a transformer to operate in Europe, Australia, and other locations with 220/240-volt, 50-Hz power. For a Mac Classic, Plus, or 512K, an ImageWriter I, and a LaserWriter

II, you can reduce the local voltage to 110/120 volts by using a good-quality grounded isolation step-down transformer. (Some equipment cannot handle 50-Hz power, however. See the next two tips for details.) The transformer should be rated to handle 50 percent greater wattage than the total of all equipment you attach to it. (See Figure 2-21.) For example, a transformer rated at 360 watts would handle a Mac 512 or Mac Plus and an ImageWriter I. Do not use a cheap voltage converter; it will ruin your computer equipment. Electronics Plus, Inc., has grounded step-down transformers in half a dozen wattage ratings, starting at 100 watts, for about $30.

Product	Voltage Range	Frequency Range	Maximum Watts
Isolation Step-Down Transformer Required for 220/240 Volts			
ImageWriter I	107–137	50/60	180
LaserWriter IISC, IINT, IINTX	90–126	50/60	900
Personal LaserWriter IISC, IINT	100–115	50/60	600
Macintosh 128, 512K, 512Ke, Plus, Classic	107–137	50/60	60
Isolation Step-Down Transformer Required for 220/240 Volts; Not Recommended for Use with 50-Hz Power			
AppleFax Modem	107–137	60	10
Apple Scanner	107–137	60	65
ImageWriter II	107–137	60	180
ImageWriter LQ	107–137	60	180
LaserWriter, LaserWriter Plus	104–127	60	760
Adapter Plug Required (No Transformer Required)			
Apple Hard Disk 20	85–270	47–64	35
Apple HD20SC	85–270	47–64	60
Apple HD40SC, 80SC, 160SC	85–270	47–64	60
AppleCD SC	85–270	47–64	40
Apple Tape Backup 40SC	85–270	47–64	15

FIGURE 2-21. VOLTS AND WATTS. *(continued)*
The total wattage of all equipment connected to a grounded step-down transformer should be about two-thirds of the transformer's rated capacity. The transformer permits the operation of 110/120-volt equipment from a 220/240-volt source, which is common in many countries.

FIGURE 2-21. VOLTS AND WATTS. *continued*

Product	Voltage Range	Frequency Range	Maximum Watts
Adapter Plug Required (No Transformer Required) *(continued)*			
AppleColor High-Resolution RGB Monitor	85–270	50/60	160
Apple High-Resolution Monochrome Monitor	85–270	50/60	40
Macintosh IIcx, IIci	100–240	48–62	90
Macintosh IIx, IIfx	100–240	48–62	230
Macintosh SE/30	120–240	48–62	75
Macintosh II, some IIx's	90–140 and 170–270	48–62	230
Macintosh SE	85–270	47–63	100

DOMESTIC POWER ONLY

Some equipment should be used only with 60-Hz power. If a device's nameplate or owner's manual lists only 60 Hz, assume it should not use 50-Hz power, which is standard in many foreign countries. Many non-Apple products have this restriction.

Apple products restricted to 60 Hz include the ImageWriter II, ImageWriter LQ, original LaserWriter, LaserWriter Plus, Apple Scanner, and AppleFax Modem. Apple's current advice is to get an international model if you want to use any of these products with 50-Hz power.

In the past, people have reported that U.S. ImageWriter IIs and LaserWriter Pluses work fine on 220/240-volt, 50-Hz European electricity (stepped down to 110/120 with a transformer). In 1987, Apple engineers did condone the use of an ImageWriter II on 50-Hz power, but that approval has apparently been rescinded. (See the next tip for another solution.) Apple has never blessed the U.S. LaserWriter for 50-Hz use. Its fuser/heater element is frequency dependent and might overheat after long sessions on 50-Hz power. A thermal sensor and a backup thermal sensor inside the LaserWriter detect overheating and shut the printer down if it gets too hot. You can probably get away with short-term, light-duty use of a U.S. LaserWriter on 50-Hz power, especially if you don't leave it on continuously. (Be sure to use a step-down transformer.)

GLOBAL PRINTER POWER

A U.S. ImageWriter II or ImageWriter LQ printer will work with an appropriate transformer in countries where the electrical power is other than 110 volts, 60 Hz. Apple doesn't recommend using 50-Hz power, however, because it adversely affects print registration and forces the printer's internal motors to run hotter and possibly wear out.

Instead, you can have the printer's power supply replaced with a universal model (Apple Service Part 915-0029 for the ImageWriter II or 915-0031 for the ImageWriter LQ). The universal power supply is not sold in the United States. You can ask a dealer in a foreign country to install one, however. After installing the universal power supply, you can use the printer anywhere in the world, without a transformer or other additional equipment.

FOREIGN POWER

If you're not sure of the voltage and frequency used at your destination, consult your travel agent or local library. Be specific about locale because power is not the same throughout all countries. For example, Japan has 100-volt power, but it has 50 Hz in some areas and 60 Hz elsewhere. The wrong line voltage and, in some cases, the wrong frequency could damage your equipment.

Keep in mind that the electricity in some countries might be less reliable than what you're used to. Protect your Mac against voltage spikes and noise by plugging it into a U.S. surge protector. Plug the surge protector into the step-down transformer if you use one. In some places, the actual voltage drops markedly below its nominal value during periods of heavy electrical use. To compensate, you should be able to buy a suitable step-up transformer after you arrive. Just ask how the local residents keep their TVs going. If power outages are common at your destination, you must decide between taking along an expensive, bulky, and heavy uninterruptible power supply and leaving your Mac behind.

MAC IN JAPAN

The Macs sold in Japan have the garden-variety U.S. power supplies. They work fine most of the time, but they can have a voltage problem. Japanese current is nominally 100 volts, 50 Hz or 60 Hz. Many areas suffer brownouts in the afternoons, especially the Tokyo region. Voltage usually drops into the 90-to-95-volt range and often goes as low as 85 volts. For some reason, this makes some Macs run hotter. Half the country uses 50 Hz, and the other half uses 60 Hz. The dividing line is somewhere between Tokyo and Osaka, with Tokyo being in the 60-Hz region.

If you are not going to use your Mac in the afternoons, then there will be no problem. Otherwise, you will need a step-up transformer. These are available in Japan in wattages ranging from 30 to 1500. Prices start at around $30.

Another point to remember is that most Japanese outlets are not grounded. So you need a grounded plug adapter, also available there. The transformers use two-prong plugs, but you can run a wire from the transformer base plate to a grounding point.

Buy your software in the United States. It's usually twice the price in Japan.

FOREIGN REPAIRS

When traveling outside the United States, you might encounter some difficulty should your computer need repairs. Apple dealers are not obliged to repair "foreign" equipment, even though most parts are the same regardless of nationality. A dealer should be able to order parts for any model, but then you have to wait for the parts to arrive.

Also, your Apple warranty or AppleCare service contract is valid only in the country of purchase. For warranty repairs or AppleCare service, you must return the malfunctioning equipment to the country where you bought it. Therefore, be sure you use new equipment thoroughly before exporting it so that any problems can be corrected on the warranty's home turf before you leave.

FOREIGN SHOPPING

If you're going to be overseas for a long time, you might want to buy equipment after you get there. Be aware, however, that the keyboard and software will be set up for the local language. So consider taking your own U.S. keyboard, system software, and applications to use instead of the ones that come with the local Mac. Also, expect to pay considerably more for hardware and software overseas.

Chapter 3

DISKS AND DISK DRIVES

Every Macintosh system has at least one floppy-disk drive; most systems also have a hard disk. The tips in this chapter are about the following disk-related subjects:

- Living with disks and disk drives
- Using startup disks
- Organizing disks, folders, and files

LIVING WITH DISKS AND DISK DRIVES

DISK FRAGMENTATION

Hard Disks

Hard disks slow down after long and frequent use. The fault lies in the organization of files, not in the disk mechanism. Your hard disk tends to become inefficiently organized when you frequently add and remove files. An individual file cannot be written in one area of an inefficiently organized disk. Instead, it must be scattered across the disk surface.

You can reorganize the disk by backing it up, erasing it, and restoring it from the backup. (The backup must be file by file, not a mirror image of the disk.) You can save time by using a disk reorganization utility such as Disk Express from ALSoft, although you must still make a complete backup in case a power interruption or an error wipes out your hard disk during reorganization.

MOUNTING AN SCSI HARD DISK

Hard Disks

Suppose you start up your Mac with your SCSI disk drive switched off. Later you turn on the drive, expecting to see its icon appear on the desktop. It doesn't.

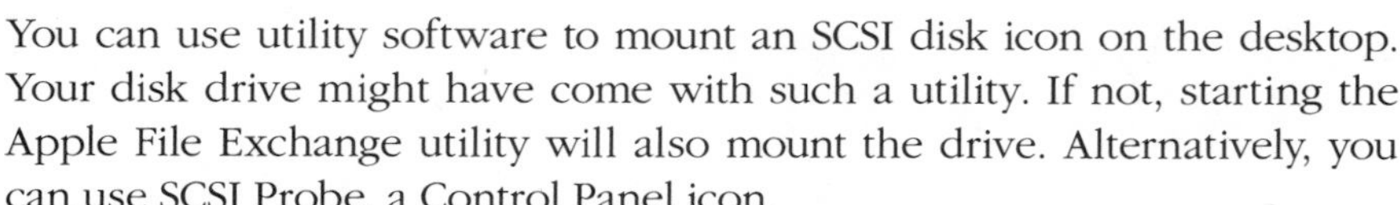

You can use utility software to mount an SCSI disk icon on the desktop. Your disk drive might have come with such a utility. If not, starting the Apple File Exchange utility will also mount the drive. Alternatively, you can use SCSI Probe, a Control Panel icon.

PARKING YOUR HARD DISK

Hard Disks

Hard disks can be damaged and data lost if the read/write heads contact the disk surface. Such an unfortunate event is most likely to occur if you bump or move the hard disk. Most hard-disk drives guard against damage by parking the heads in a safe area when you switch the drive off.

Some drives, however, do not park the heads automatically. Check your disk-drive manual for special parking instructions. If your drive came with parking utility software, use it before moving the drive.

UNTAPPED DISK POTENTIAL

Apple Hard Disks

Your Apple hard disk might have a megabyte or more of concealed disk space. To find out if your disk does, start the HD SC Setup utility. (It's on the System Tools disk that came with your Mac.) Click the Partition button. If you then see a dialog box listing several predefined partitioning schemes, click the Custom button. (If you see a message warning you that a volume is in use, click the Continue button instead.) Next you see a diagram of disk space allocation. The gray space in that diagram represents the amount of free space on the disk, as shown in Figure 3-1.

Free space usually exists on an Apple hard disk unless someone has used HD SC Setup to create a custom partition for the hard disk. Simply initializing an Apple hard disk creates a standard-size partition regardless of the disk's actual capacity. An Apple HD40SC, for example, always initializes at 40,000 KB, but the Quantum 40 disk mechanism used in many HD40SC drives has an actual capacity of over 41,000 KB. Mechanisms made by Sony and others, which Apple also has used in many HD40SC drives, might have different capacities.

Click Done and then click Quit to return to the Finder. Before you can recover the space, you must make a complete backup of your hard disk using a file-by-file backup rather than an image backup. Check your backup utility documentation for more information. When you are using an image backup, the partition size is fixed by the backup process. If you change the partition size, you will not be able to restore an image backup.

After backing up the disk, start the HD SC Setup utility. Click the Partition button and then click the Custom button. (As before, click Continue if you see a warning message saying that the volume is in use.) The disk allocation diagram appears. Click the white rectangle containing the name of your disk, and then click the Remove button. Move the pointer to near the top of the gray rectangle, which shows the amount of hidden disk space, and drag all the way to the bottom of the dialog box. When you release the mouse button, a list of partition types appears. Click Macintosh Volume to select it. You can adjust the size by typing in the box to the right of the list of partition types. The maximum size appears immediately below this box. Click the OK, Done, and Quit buttons in sequence to return to the Finder. Finally, restore your files from your backup.

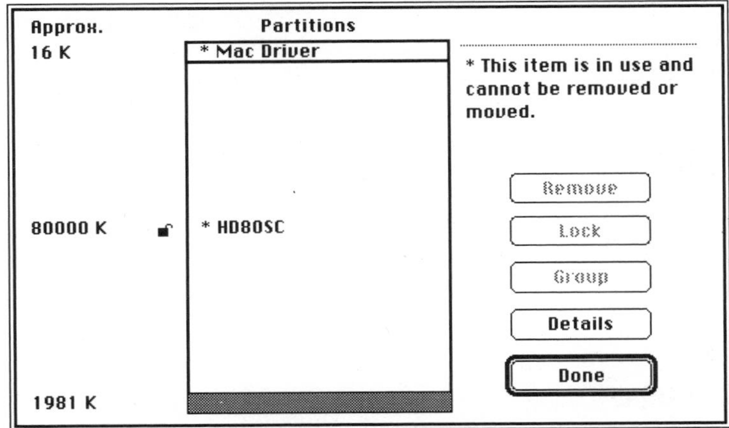

FIGURE 3-1. HIDDEN DISK SPACE.

Many Apple hard disks contain a substantial amount of unused disk space. Here, the HD SC Setup utility shows 1981 KB free on an 80-MB HDSC80. You can recover the free space by backing up the disk contents, setting up a custom partition with HD SC Setup, and then restoring the disk contents.

Apple Hard Disks

MACSSSH

If the noise of your HD20SC is driving you crazy, you can get a little more peace and quiet. Early HD20SC hard-disk drives had noisy fans, but in units built since late 1987 the chief noisemaker has been the disk drive mechanism itself. If the noise you loathe gets steadily louder for the first 8 to 10 seconds after you switch on the drive, you're hearing the drive mechanism, for which there is no remedy. If you have an early HD20SC with a fan that drowns out the disk mechanism, get a replacement fan from an authorized Apple dealer who sells service parts separately.

Floppy Disks

DISK LIFE

All floppy disks will fail some day. Their magnetic coating, which stores your documents and applications, gradually erodes in normal use because part of the disk drive (the read/write head) touches the disk surface while the disk rotates. Eventually the coating wears off. A floppy disk might last anywhere from 6 months to 10 years, with 2 years being about average. Disks wear out faster in smoky, dusty, or hot conditions. Because there is no guaranteed safe time limit, you should regularly copy your valuable documents onto backup disks.

Floppy disks do have an indefinite shelf life. Store them in a clean, dry area. The temperature should be between 39°F and 127°F (4°C and 53°C). Also, keep disks away from magnetic fields, which can erase the information on them. Magnetic fields are generated by electric motors, electric tools, telephones with traditional bell ringers, and the left side of a Mac Plus, 512K, or SE.

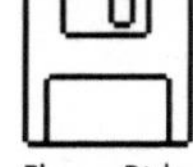
Floppy Disks

REMOVING FINGERPRINTS

A single fingerprint can render a disk unreadable. Fingers don't often find their way past the metal shutter on a 3½-inch disk, but they sometimes do. Young fingers, especially, have a way of circumventing the protective shutter. Should one of your disks suddenly become unreadable, you can check it for fingerprints by sliding open the shutter and looking at the disk surface under a strong light.

Remove any fingerprints you find by using a cotton swab moistened with alcohol. Twirl the swab to pick up any loose strands of cotton, and blow gently on the disk to dry the alcohol.

EZ LABELS

Floppy Disks

For easy disk relabeling, try Scotch brand Post-It Cover-Up Tape in the 1-inch width (item number 658). This removable white paper tape is intended for making corrections in documents before they are photocopied. It sticks as well as a permanent label and won't fall off by accident. But lift a corner, pull, and it comes off easily and cleanly.

Obviously, you can write on Cover-Up Tape with a pen or pencil. You can also print on it with an ImageWriter or a LaserWriter. Use a drawing application such as MacDraw to draw a rectangle slightly larger than the label, near the top of the page, and print the rectangle on plain paper. Then stick a length of Cover-Up Tape within the rectangle and reposition the paper for reprinting the same page. Finally, return to the drawing application, type your label contents inside the rectangle, and print again. Remove the label from the paper and place it on your disk.

EJECTING DISKS

Floppy Disks

How can you eject a floppy disk using the keyboard?

Press Command-Shift-1 to eject the disk in the internal drive. Press Command-Shift-2 to eject the disk in the external drive. (These keyboard shortcuts do not work when the disk-swapping alert box commands *Please insert the disk....*)

Don't switch off your Mac after you press Command-Shift-1 or Command-Shift-2 to eject a disk, especially if any documents are open at the time. You'll probably disrupt the Finder's desktop, and you might also corrupt the open documents.

HFS AND MFS EXPLAINED

Floppy Disks

Hard Disks

The Mac uses two systems for keeping track of disk files, folders, and disks. With disks 800 KB and larger, the Mac normally uses the hierarchical file system (HFS). With disks smaller than 800 KB, the Mac normally uses the Macintosh file system (MFS).

From the user's point of view, the major difference between HFS and MFS is the way in which they handle folders. HFS stores each disk's folder hierarchy on the disk. The Finder uses this hierarchy, and so do the Open and Save menu commands. In contrast, MFS folders are an illusion maintained solely by the Finder. When you use the Open and Save commands with an MFS disk, you don't see any of the folders that appear in the Finder.

The Finder identifies HFS disks by means of a tiny dot at the left edge of disk and folder windows, between the parallel lines located one-quarter inch below the title bar of the window. Figure 3-2 shows the difference between an HFS disk window and an MFS disk window.

Both HFS and MFS are built into every Macintosh except an original, unenhanced Mac 512K. To use HFS on a Mac 512K, the System Folder on the startup disk must contain Apple's Hard Disk 20 file.

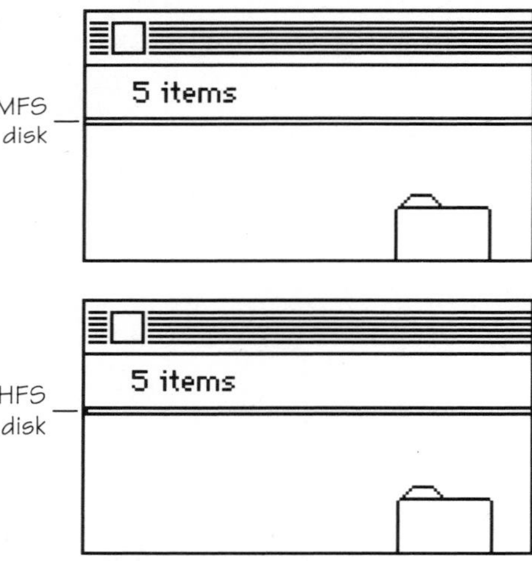

FIGURE 3-2. HFS DOT.
The Finder indicates an HFS disk by displaying a dot, as shown in the bottom window. No such dot appears in an MFS disk or folder window, as shown in the top window.

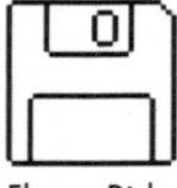

Hard Disks

DISAPPEARING DISK SPACE

Why doesn't an 800-KB disk ever have 800-KB available, as shown in Figure 3-3? Although the Finder reports zero items on a freshly initialized or erased disk, one or more files always take up space. The Finder doesn't count those files, and you can't see their icons, because the files are invisible. The files contain information the Finder uses for various purposes.

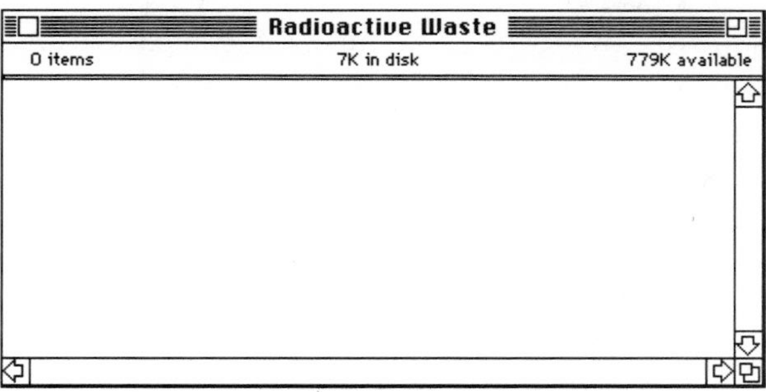

FIGURE 3-3. BLANK BUT NOT EMPTY.
After a disk is initialized or erased, it contains zero items, as you'd expect. However, something is taking up space (7 KB here). Also, the space used plus the space available doesn't equal 800 KB.

This information includes the Get Info comments, copies of icon images for most applications and documents on the disk, the whereabouts of applications on HFS disks, and folder contents on MFS disks. (For more information on HFS and MFS, see the previous tip, "HFS and MFS Explained.")

With Finder versions 5.0 and later, the space used plus the space available on any disk never adds up to the rated capacity of the disk. On an 800-KB disk, for example, you'll usually find 14 KB or 15 KB unaccounted for. The Mac file system uses this space for a disk directory, an allocation map, and the so-called "boot blocks" that contain information used at startup time.

ELEPHANTINE DESKTOP FILE

Hard Disks

Finder versions prior to 7.0 use an invisible file named Desktop to store various types of information. (See the previous tip, "Disappearing Disk Space," for details.) Each disk has its own Desktop file. A normal Desktop file on a 20-MB hard disk can easily be 80 KB to 100 KB, but the file can become enormous as you remove and add icons.

An overweight Desktop file wastes disk space and slows disk operations. For example, starting up and copying small files take longer than they normally would.

You can rebuild the Desktop file on a startup disk by holding down the Option and Command keys when you start up. A dialog box asks whether you want the desktop rebuilt. Click OK if you want to put the Desktop file on a crash diet. One warning: You lose Get Info comments if you rebuild the desktop.

The method of rebuilding the Desktop file on a non-startup disk is similar. Press Command-Option while inserting a floppy disk, mounting a hard disk, or quitting an application with MultiFinder inactive.

Floppy Disks

HD DISK INITIALIZED AS 800-KB DISK

The FDHD SuperDrive can store 1.4 MB on an HD (high-density) floppy disk. A hole in the disk shell, located across from the write-protect hole, informs the FDHD drive that it has an HD disk. If you initialize an HD disk in an 800-KB drive, which ignores the extra hole, you get an 800-KB disk that an FDHD drive can't read. By covering the hole in the HD disk with a piece of tape, as shown in Figure 3-4, you can make an FDHD drive treat the disk as an 800-KB disk.

The FDHD SuperDrive is standard on the Mac SE/30, IIx, IIcx, IIci, Portable, recent SE, and newer models. A Mac SE or Mac II without an FDHD SuperDrive can be upgraded by adding one. You can use 1.4-MB disks on a Mac 512Ke or later model by using the Rapport and Drive 2.4 products from Kennect Technology.

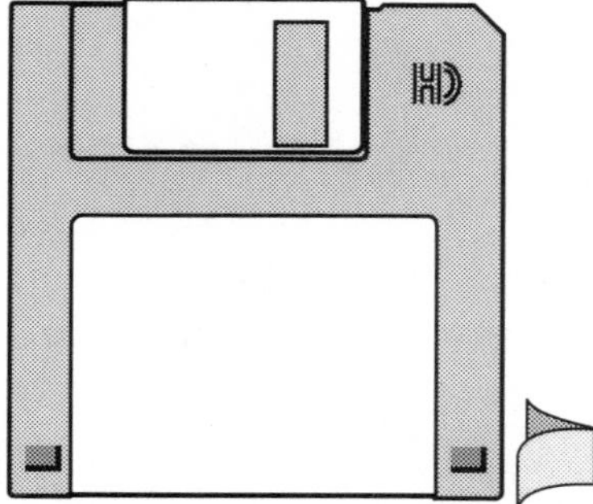

FIGURE 3-4. FLOPPY COVERUP.
An FDHD SuperDrive can access an HD disk that was accidentally initialized as an 800-KB disk if you place a piece of tape as shown here.

PUSHING SINGLE-SIDED DISK CAPACITY

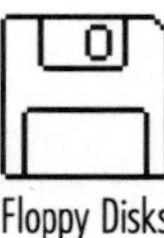
Floppy Disks

Are some single-sided disks sold with perfectly good, though untested, flip sides? Probably. But how can you tell which ones are good? Is initialization a sufficient test, or must you use a disk until it suddenly fails? You can take your chances at using both sides of single-sided disks, but I'm sticking with double-sided disks for valuable documents and applications—I'll do my gambling in a casino.

HIGH-DENSITY VS. DOUBLE-DENSITY DISKS

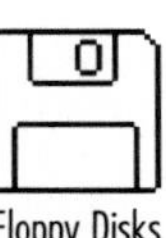
Floppy Disks

A 1.4-MB high-density (HD) disk that you can use in an FDHD SuperDrive looks like an 800-KB or 400-KB floppy disk with an additional hole. However, drilling another hole in an 800-KB or 400-KB disk won't convert it to a 1.4-MB HD disk. The HD disks have a special thin recording surface that allows the FDHD SuperDrive to use higher data rates. The recording surface of an 800-KB or 400-KB disk might not be sensitive enough to align its magnetic particles properly when the FDHD records at those higher rates. Errors can occur during the saving of documents that might not show up until later, after an apparently successful save.

SINGLE-SIDED HFS DISKS

Floppy Disks

Although the Mac does not normally use the hierarchical file system (HFS) on 400-KB disks, you can initialize a 400-KB disk to use HFS. To force HFS on a new 400-KB disk, insert the disk and click One-Sided in the dialog box that appears. At the end of the initialization process, when you finish typing the disk name, hold down the Option key as you press Return or click OK. (For more information on HFS, see the tip "HFS and MFS Explained," earlier in this chapter.)

Disks already in use must be erased before you convert them to HFS. Make a backup copy first; then choose Erase Disk from the Finder's Special menu, and hold down the Option key as you click One-Sided in the dialog box that appears. For best results, hold down the Option key until the erase process finishes. Finally, restore the disk's former contents by dragging all file and folder icons from the backup disk to the reinitialized 400-KB disk. If you drag the backup disk's icon over the reinitialized disk's icon, the reinitialized disk loses its HFS format during the disk copy operation.

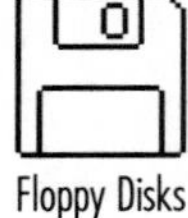
Floppy Disks

MAXIMUM NUMBER OF FILES

The Macintosh system software limits the number of files on a 400-KB (single-sided) disk. As a result, a 400-KB disk that contains only small documents (for example, 2-KB correspondence documents) might have up to 200 KB of disk space available when it reaches the number-of-files limit.

The number of files allowed on a disk depends on the length of the filenames, and the dependency is not linear, as you can see in Figure 3-5. You can have at most 84 files on a single-sided disk where the average filename has between 14 and 22 characters. If the filename averages 6 to 13 characters, you can put 96 files on the same disk. There's no point in making all names shorter than five characters, since you won't get more than 108 files on any single-sided disk by doing so.

The hierarchical file system (HFS) avoids the problem because it does not limit the number of filenames on a disk. The Mac automatically uses HFS on disks 800 KB and larger. (For more information on HFS and MFS, see the tip "HFS and MFS Explained," earlier in this chapter.)

Freedom from a limit on number of files is a good argument for initializing or converting 400-KB disks to use HFS. See the previous tip, "Single-sided HFS Disks," for details on how to do this.

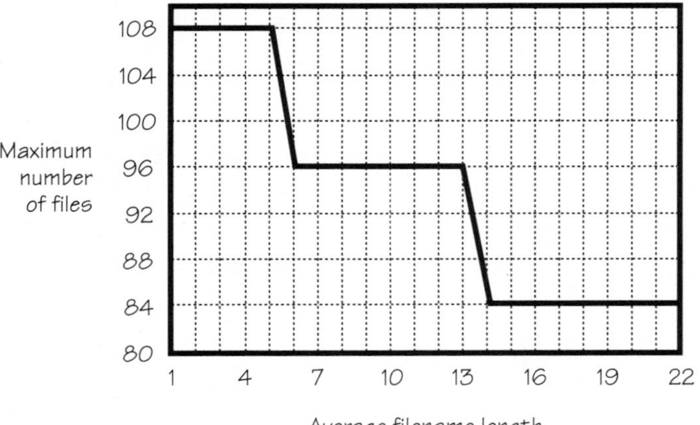

FIGURE 3-5. FILE LIMITS.
The number of files that can be stored on a 400-KB disk depends on the length of the filenames.

WORKING WITH ONE FLOPPY-DISK DRIVE

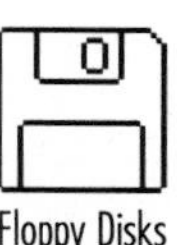

If your Mac has only one built-in floppy-disk drive—no external drive or hard disk—you must organize the contents of your disks carefully to avoid excessive disk swapping. First put every application program on its own startup disk. (For tips on startup disks, see "Using Startup Disks," later in this chapter.)

In whatever space that remains on each application's disk, put the documents you are still working on with that application. Most applications need some disk space for temporary work files, so be sure to leave 50 KB or more free on each disk. If all the documents in progress for a particular application won't fit on one disk, put the overflow on another startup disk, along with another copy of the application program. When you finish working on a document, copy it onto a disk that contains only documents and remove it from the application disk to make room for the next document you create. (Avoid keeping multiple copies of the same document on different disks; you can waste a lot of time figuring out which has the most recent changes.)

Disks multiply rapidly on one-drive Mac systems, so try to develop some compulsive habits with regard to labeling and storing your disks. Otherwise, finding a particular document may take 10 minutes or more. When your collection grows to more than 30 disks, seriously consider cataloging it with a program such as MDC II from New Canaan Microcode.

If your one-drive Mac has 1 MB or more of memory, you can use some memory as if it were a disk drive. (See the tip "RAM Disks," in Chapter 2, "Essential System Components.") The RamDisk+ utility software by Roger Bates can create a RAM disk, copy the System Folder to it, and make the RAM disk the startup disk. Your Mac then essentially becomes a two-drive system, and your floppy disks no longer need to carry the burden of a System file and Finder, leaving more room on them for documents. The RAM disk might even have enough room for an application, freeing up even more actual disk space.

WORKING WITH TWO DISK DRIVES

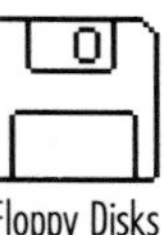

On a Mac with two or more floppy-disk drives, you'll probably want to reserve one drive for applications on startup disks and the other drive for documents on non-startup disks. If an application is particularly large and your startup disk does not have enough room for it, you can keep it, along with its documents, on a non-startup disk in the other drive. If the applications you want to work with are small, you might be able to fit more than one on the same startup disk, making switching between them faster. But be sure to leave 50 KB or so free on the startup disk. Most applications need work space on that disk even if the document you're working on is on another disk.

With some applications, certain files must be on the application disk. They often include help documents and preferences or settings files. You'll know an application requires special file arrangements if you can't open it or access some of its features.

You don't need as many startup disks with two drives as you do with one drive. This means you'll use fewer disks overall because they won't be filled with duplicates of the System Folder and the application programs.

USING STARTUP DISKS

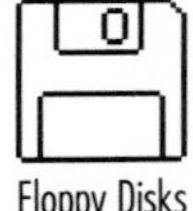

Floppy Disks

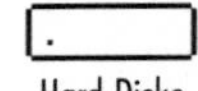

Hard Disks

WHAT MAKES A STARTUP DISK?

A startup disk contains a System file and a Finder in the same folder. By convention, that folder is named System Folder, although it can have any name. When the System Folder is closed, it's marked by a miniature system icon. The System Folder contains many other items as well, including the following:

- Startup documents (INITs), which modify or extend the system's general capabilities. Examples: Easy Access, MacroMaker.
- Control panel devices (CDEVs), which are modules that automatically (by their presence in the System Folder) plug into the Control Panel desk accessory. Examples: General, Mouse.
- Chooser documents, which permit the Mac to print on different printers and to select network services. Examples are ImageWriter, LaserWriter, and LaserPrep.
- Printer fonts for PostScript printers and output devices. Examples: GaramLig, GaramBol.
- Settings and preferences files for individual applications. Examples: MacWrite Options, Excel Settings.

Beginning with System 7, some of these items are inside folders within the System Folder. Because you're free to add items to and remove them from the System Folder, each startup disk can have a different configuration.

In addition, the startup disk determines which fonts and desk accessories are available. All fonts and desk accessories installed in the System file of the startup disk are available. The availability of other fonts and desk accessories might depend on utility software such as Suitcase II or MasterJuggler.

At startup time, the Mac uses the first startup disk it finds, looking for it in the following locations in the following order: internal floppy disk, external drive, the SCSI hard disk with the lowest ID number. You can also specify a particular SCSI hard disk with the Startup Device Control Panel.

UNDOING THE WRONG STARTUP DISK

If you mistakenly insert the wrong startup disk, you can eject it by pressing the mouse button before the smiling Mac icon appears. You have 10 to 40 seconds between the time you turn on your Mac and the time the icon appears.

During that time, the Mac is testing its RAM. The test takes longer on slower Macs and ones with more RAM than the standard amount. You can bypass the RAM test by pressing the mouse button as you switch on a Mac 512K, Mac Plus, or Mac SE.

CONVERTING A STARTUP DISK TO A NON-STARTUP DISK

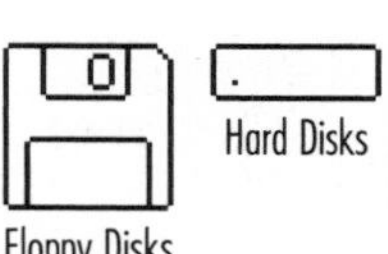

To make a startup disk a non-startup disk, remove the Finder or the System file from the System Folder of the startup disk. Drag the Finder or System file onto the desktop or into another folder. If you remove the Finder or System file from the current startup disk (represented by the icon that the Finder puts in the upper right corner of the desktop), you must restart the Mac for the procedure to take effect.

To make a 400-KB (single-sided) disk a non-startup disk, you must drag the Finder (or System file) to the Trash. This requirement also applies to any other disk that does not use the hierarchical file system (HFS). To learn how to tell whether a disk uses HFS, see the tip "HFS and MFS Explained," earlier in this chapter.

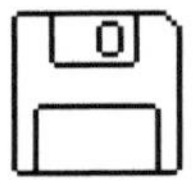
Floppy Disks

Hard Disks

SWITCHING SYSTEM FOLDERS

Initially, the Mac uses the System Folder on the startup disk. (See the tip "What Makes a Startup Disk?" earlier in this chapter.) If the startup disk is a hard disk, you can switch to the System Folder on a disk other than the startup disk by pressing the Option key while you open an application on the second disk. Alternatively, you can open the Finder on the second disk while pressing the Command-Option key combination. Some applications, such as Installer from Apple, force the Mac to switch System Folders.

If the startup disk is a floppy disk, the Mac switches System Folders when you open an application on another floppy disk that contains a System Folder. In this case, you keep the System Folder from being switched by pressing the Option key while opening the application. You can also prevent the switching by dragging the Finder out of the System Folder on the second disk.

The disk that contains the active System Folder is often called the startup disk, even if it wasn't used to start the Mac. It affects the set of fonts, desk accessories, certain Control Panels, and other system resources that are available. However, the availability of all startup documents (INITs) and some Control Panels (CDEVs) is fixed at startup time by the System Folder on the initial startup disk.

You can't switch System Folders if MultiFinder is active. The rules described in this tip apply only to versions 5.0 and later of the Finder.

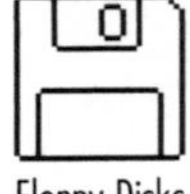
Floppy Disks

Hard Disks

USING PATTERNS TO IDENTIFY SYSTEM FOLDERS

Each startup disk keeps its own setting for the desktop pattern. If you use a different pattern for each startup disk, you can tell when the Mac has switched System Folders. Whenever you start up with or switch to a startup disk for the first time, use the Control Panel desk accessory to change the desktop pattern.

System Folder

DEALING WITH EXTRA SYSTEM FOLDERS

When you purchase an application program, the new disk has a System Folder on it. As a rule, you should not copy it onto your hard disk.

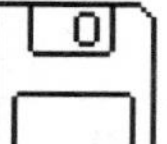

Never have more than one System Folder on a hard disk. If you do, your Mac might become confused, refuse to start up from the hard disk, restart unexpectedly, or worse.

When copying an application, don't drag the application's floppy-disk icon to the hard-disk icon. Instead, open the floppy-disk icon and choose Select All from the Finder's Edit menu to select the entire contents of the disk. Press the Shift key and click the System Folder icon, if present, to deselect it. Then drag the group of selected icons to the hard disk.

If you think you might have extra System Folders buried on your hard disk, use Apple's Find File desk accessory to locate them, and then drag them to the Trash.

Incidentally, the Mac treats any folder that has a copy of both the Finder and the System file as a system folder, regardless of its actual name. Conversely, a folder named System Folder that doesn't contain the Finder and System file is not a real system folder.

PERFORMING FASTER STARTUPS

Finder

From the Macintosh desktop, you can designate one application on each disk to be the "startup application." Then whenever you start the Mac with that disk, the startup application is opened, bypassing the Finder's desktop. Assuming you are using a floppy disk, this starts the application 5 to 20 seconds faster.

To designate the startup application, use the following steps:

1. Select the icon of the application you want started automatically.
2. Choose Set Startup from the Finder's Special menu.
3. In the dialog box that appears, select the Finder option and the option named after the application you selected. Then click OK.

This tip doesn't apply to System 7; when you use System 7, MultiFinder is always active. To designate startup applications with System 7, drag the icons for those applications into the Startup Folder in the System Folder.

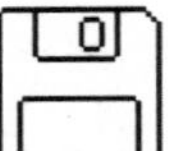

UNDOING THE STARTUP APPLICATION

To have a disk once again start up with the Finder instead of with an application such as MacWrite, make the Finder or the MultiFinder the startup application. Here's how:

1. Quit the current application.
2. Choose Set Startup from the Finder's Special menu.
3. In the dialog box that appears, select the options Finder and Finder Only. Or select the MultiFinder option and any of the three options below it. Then click OK.

This method doesn't work with System 7. If you are using System 7, empty the Startup Folder (located in the System Folder).

UPDATING THE SYSTEM

Use the Installer utility to update your startup disks with new versions of system software. By selecting the proper Installer scripts, as shown in Figure 3-6, you avoid getting useless files that waste space on your startup disks. If you simply drag the System Folder from the update disk to your startup disks, you might get more files than your system can use.

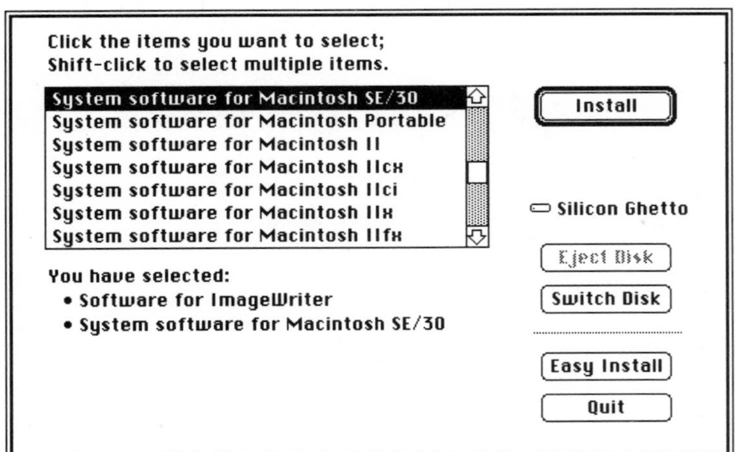

FIGURE 3-6. OPTIMAL UPDATE.

To install the correct set of files in the System Folder of a startup disk, choose the script appropriate for the system on which the disk will be used.

Not all the files the Installer puts in a System Folder are required. For example, you can discard Control Panels if you want to give up features to gain disk space.

You might have to juggle desk accessories before and after updating system software versions earlier than System 7 with the Installer. It puts a copy of the Find File desk accessory into your System file when you choose the Mac Plus, Mac SE, or Mac II option. So unless Find File is already installed, you can't have more than 14 desk accessories installed when you use the Installer.

The Installer also places copies of several optional fonts in the System file, including Helvetica, Times, and Courier. If you keep fonts outside the System file using a font organizer utility such as MasterJuggler or Suitcase II, you might need to remove some fonts from the System file after the update. Otherwise, any extra font sizes you have outside the System file won't be available.

REMOVING FONTS TO GAIN SPACE

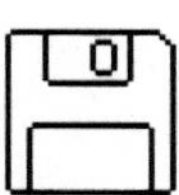

Floppy Disks

You can free up space on a startup disk by removing fonts you never use. With system software versions prior to 7.0, each size of every font is a separate entity that you can add to or remove from a System file with the Font/DA Mover utility. If you are using System 7 or later system software, you can remove fonts by opening the System file and dragging the font out. Removing all sizes of the New York font, for example, frees almost 27 KB.

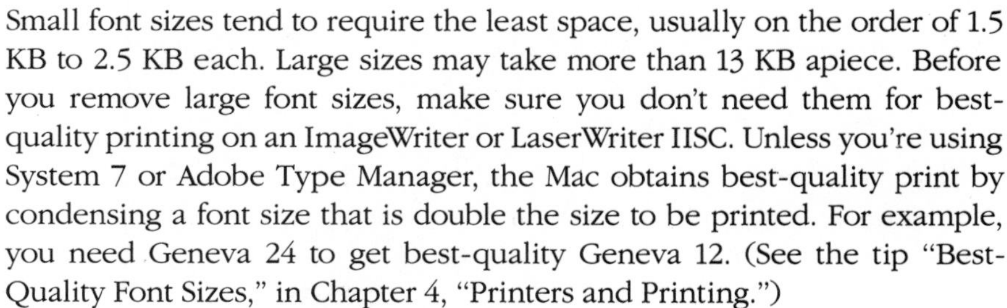

Small font sizes tend to require the least space, usually on the order of 1.5 KB to 2.5 KB each. Large sizes may take more than 13 KB apiece. Before you remove large font sizes, make sure you don't need them for best-quality printing on an ImageWriter or LaserWriter IISC. Unless you're using System 7 or Adobe Type Manager, the Mac obtains best-quality print by condensing a font size that is double the size to be printed. For example, you need Geneva 24 to get best-quality Geneva 12. (See the tip "Best-Quality Font Sizes," in Chapter 4, "Printers and Printing.")

Fonts you remove need not be lost forever. If you are using System 7, you simply keep them in any folder. In earlier versions of system software, the Font/DA Mover lets you save them in font files before removing them. Later you can copy them back to a System file from the font files.

Floppy Disks

REMOVING DESK ACCESSORIES TO GAIN SPACE

You can remove desk accessories from the System file (versions earlier than System 7) to save space on the startup disk using the Font/DA Mover utility. The amount of space required by an individual desk accessory might vary from less than 1 KB to more than 60 KB, although few are larger than 20 KB.

In addition to removing desk accessories you never use, you might want to consider removing ones you seldom use from most of your startup disks. For example, if you use only one printer, you don't really need the Chooser on every disk. The Control Panel and the Alarm Clock are two other desk accessories you might need on only one disk. When you need to change settings with one of those desk accessories, it's no great inconvenience to switch to the disk it's on.

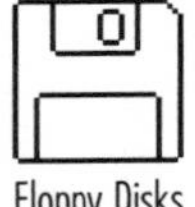
Floppy Disks

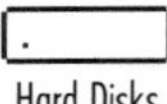
Hard Disks

REPAIRING DAMAGED STARTUP DISKS

Sometimes you can restore a damaged startup disk. Start up with another disk and copy the System file and Finder from the good disk to the damaged disk.

ORGANIZING DISKS, FOLDERS, AND FILES

Finder

SORTING ICONS

Have you wished the Finder (in versions earlier than System 7) would arrange icons in a window by name, date, size, kind, or color? The By Name, By Date, By Size, and By Kind commands in the View menu display sorted text information about the icons. Indirectly, you can make those commands sort the By Icon and By Small Icon views as well. Here's how:

1. Open the window whose icons you want to organize. Move the window if necessary so that you can see at least part of it as well as its folder icon.
2. Choose By Name, By Date, By Size, By Kind, or By Color from the View menu. Information about the icons is displayed in text format in the order you requested. (By Color is available only on a Mac that displays colors or gray shades.)
3. Choose Select All from the Edit menu, highlighting everything in the window.

4. Drag all the selected items to the folder icon, as shown in Figure 3-7. Nothing seems to happen.
5. Choose By Icon or By Small Icon from the View menu. The icons are displayed left to right and top to bottom in the same order as the text information they have replaced.

If you want fewer columns of icons, make the window narrower and repeat all the steps.

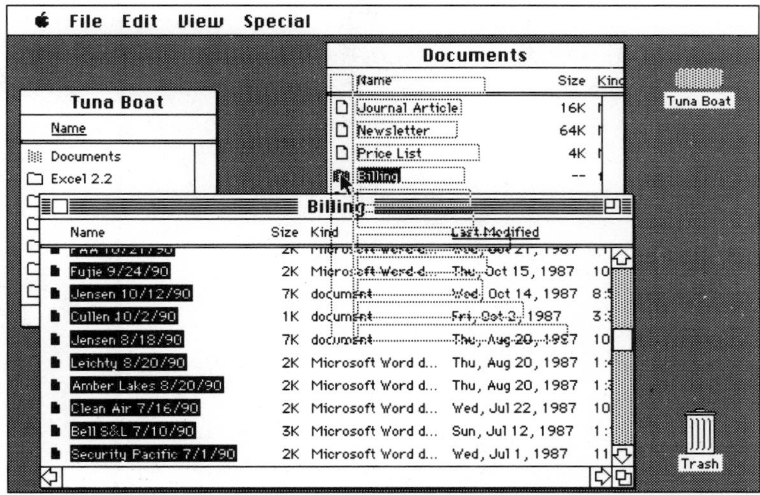

FIGURE 3-7. REARRANGE ICONS.
Starting with a window in a text view in the order you want, drag all items from the window to its folder, as shown here. Then choose an icon view, and the icons will be arranged as they were in the preceding text view.

NAMES AT THE TOP

File and folder names that begin with blank spaces appear at the top of a window viewed by name in the Finder. They also appear at the top of the list in the Open dialog box. Caution: Some INITs, notably QuickFolder 2.0 and Findswell, won't work properly if renamed.

However, the Finder won't let you simply insert a space in front of a name. To fool the Finder, press Option-Spacebar instead of the Spacebar alone.

Alternatively, type a non-space character followed by a space. Then delete the non-space character by, for example, pressing the Left arrow key and then the Backspace (or Delete) key.

ALPHABETIC NAMES

You can use letters, digits, and symbols as prefixes to folder and document names to determine where the folders and documents appear in the Open dialog box or the Finder's By Name view. The Finder orders capital letters, symbols, and foreign letters according to a different alphabetizing system than the Open dialog box does. Neither uses the ASCII code sequence. The Finder puts names beginning with a capital letter ahead of names beginning with the corresponding lowercase letter. In contrast, the Open dialog box considers capital and lowercase letters to be the same. For the correct order (with system software earlier than System 7), see Figure 3-8.

Finder's By Name view

! " « » " " # $ % ' ' ' ( ) * + , - . / 0 1 2 3 4 5 6 7 8

9 ; < = > ? @ A Ä Å á à â ã Æ B Ç C D E É è ê ë F G H I í

ì î ï J K L M Ñ N O Ö Ø ó ò ô õ Œ P Q R S ß T U Ü ú ù û V

W X Y ÿ Z [\ ] ^ _ ` { | } ~ † ° ¢ £ § • ¶ ® © ™ ´ ¨ ≠

∞ ± ≤ ≥ ¥ µ ∂ Σ Π π ∫ ª º Ω ¿ ¡ ¬ √ ƒ ≈ ∆ … – — ÷ ◊

Open dialog box

† ° ¢ £ § • ¶ ß ® © ™ ´ ¨ ≠ Æ ∞ ± ≤ ≥ ¥ µ

∂ Σ Π π ∫ Ω ¿ ¡ ¬ √ ƒ ≈ ∆ « » … Œ – — "

" ' ' ÷ ◊ ⌘ ✓ ◆ ! # $ % ' ( ) * + , - . /

0 1 2 3 4 5 6 7 8 9 ; < = > ? @ Ä ã A Å ª á

à â B C Ç D ë É è E ê F G H î ì í ï I J K L

M N Ñ ô ó ò O Ö õ Ø º P Q R S T ú Ü ù U û

V W X Y Z [\ ] ^ _ ` { | } ~

FIGURE 3-8. ORDERLY ARRANGEMENT.

The Finder alphabetizes words beginning with capital letters, symbols, and foreign letters according to a system different from that used by the Open dialog box. Lowercase letters are treated the same as capital letters.

NUMBERED NAMES IN ORDER

If you use numbers to differentiate similar file and folder names, those names might not be arranged as you'd like in the Finder's By Name view or in Open dialog boxes. For example, the name Q10 appears between Q1 and Q2, not following Q9. The Mac puts file and folder names in alphabetic order, not numerical order.

To get numbers in numerical order, put a space before the digit in names with single-digit numbers, and leave no space before the digits in names with two-digit numbers. This strategy makes Q10 follow Q 9, not Q1, for example. If some names have three-digit numbers, you must prefix single-digit numbers with two spaces, two-digit numbers with one space, and three-digit numbers with no space. You can also add leading zeros to your single-digit numbers. This way, Q09 will properly precede Q10 as well.

RULES FOR NAMES

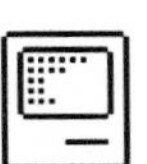

A disk name can contain up to 27 characters. A document, application, or folder name can contain up to 31 characters. On a 400-KB (single-sided) disk or any other disk that does not use the hierarchical file system (HFS), a document, application, or folder name can contain up to 63 characters. Do not use colons in names, and avoid putting a period at the beginning of a name. For more information on HFS, see the tip "HFS and MFS Explained," earlier in this chapter.

KEEPING ICON NAMES BRIEF

Keep document and folder names brief if you prefer By Icon to the other views available in the View menu. Names longer than about 12 characters tend to overlap when you arrange icons with the Clean Up command. If you are using System 7 or later system software, you can eliminate icon overlap in a window by using the Option key with the Finder's Clean Up command.

COMPACTING LONG NAMES

Use lowercase letters, which are narrower than uppercase letters, to squeeze longer filenames into less space.

Finder

ACCOMMODATING LONG NAMES

If you must use long icon names, you can arrange the icons so that their names do not overlap. The following method staggers alternate columns of icons quickly and neatly, as illustrated in Figure 3-9.

1. Arrange the icons into rows and columns by pressing the Option key while choosing Clean Up from the Finder's Special menu or by sorting the icons as described in the tip "Sorting Icons," earlier in this chapter.
2. Select every other column of icons by pressing the Shift key as you click each icon in the column or as you drag selection rectangles around the icons.
3. Drag the selected group of icons down one-half inch or so.

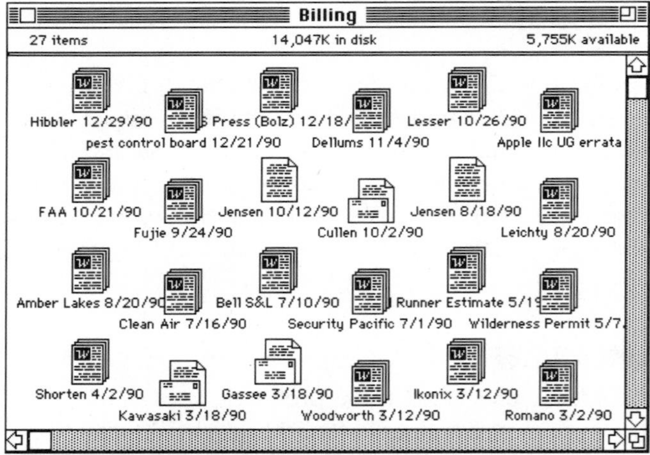

FIGURE 3-9. STAGGERED ICON NAMES.
If you stagger alternate columns of icons, you can keep long icon names from overlapping.

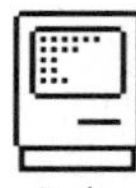
Finder

UNDOING A NAME CHANGE

If you rename an icon inadvertently, choosing Undo from the Edit menu or pressing Command-Z will restore the old name. Using another method, if you start to change the name of an icon and decide that you want the old name back, don't click anywhere outside that icon name. Instead, delete the icon name—for example, by pressing the Delete key until the name is empty—and then press Enter or click another icon. The Finder restores the icon's previous name. This tip works in all views.

ICONS ON THE DESKTOP

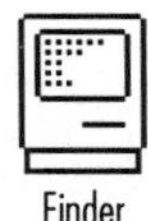

What happens to a file when you drag its icon onto the desktop? What folder is it in? Which disk is it on?

Icons on the desktop are much like icons that are not in any folder but are loose in the disk window, as shown in Figure 3-10. You can use all the same commands from the Finder's menus (except the View menu) on desktop icons. The corresponding icon names appear in an Open or Save dialog box along with files from the disk window.

You can have icons on the desktop from more than one disk. The Finder remembers the disk and folder from which each icon most recently came. To return a desktop icon to its previous folder, select the icon and choose Put Away from the Finder's File menu.

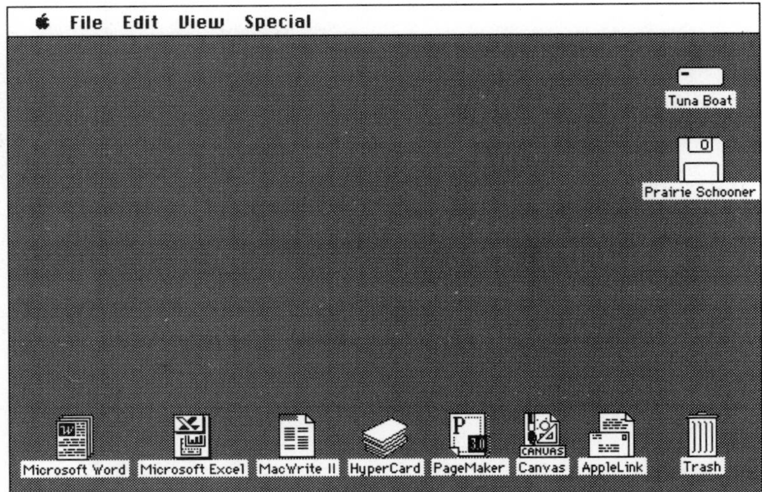

FIGURE 3-10. DESKTOP ICONS.
Make any icon more accessible by dragging it to the desktop. Keep desktop icons near the edges, where they're less likely to be covered by windows.

When you are using MultiFinder, however, desktop icons do not come to the front if you make the Finder active. They can be buried and inaccessible beneath the windows of other applications. And except when copying one 800-KB or 1.4-MB disk to another, the Finder does not copy icons on the desktop when you drag a disk or folder to another disk.

Finder

MOVING AN ICON BACK

You start to drag an icon in the Finder but change your mind. How can you quickly return the icon you're dragging to its previous location?

Setting the icon directly on the title bar returns the icon to its original spot in the window. Repositioning it by eye takes longer and might require the use of the Clean Up command to realign it.

Finder

ORGANIZED DRAGGING

Before dragging a number of items from several folders on one disk to another disk, drag the items to the desktop. There you can select them all at once for a one-drag copy. After copying, you can return them to their folders with the Put Away command (on the File menu) or you can drag them to the Trash if you want. This method expedites the process of copying and then discarding items that are scattered throughout one folder. (The Finder deselects items after copying them, and it's easier to reselect them if they're all on the desktop.)

You don't need much desktop space to use this technique. Simply pile icons on top of one another in a small area, and select them all by dragging a selection rectangle around them, as shown in Figure 3-11.

Finder

KNOWING THE DISK SPACE AVAILABLE

If you like to view your disk and folder windows in one of the text views, how can you see the amount of disk space available without switching to an icon view?

Create a new folder. Leave this empty folder open and in icon view, and position its window above and behind the disk window, as shown in Figure 3-12. It takes up little room there and always shows the amount of available disk space.

If you incorporate the disk name in the name of the empty folder, you'll always know on which disk the space is available.

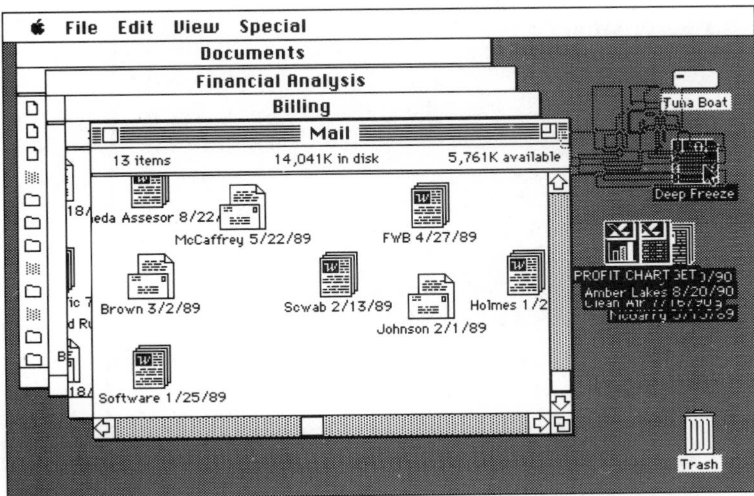

FIGURE 3-11. COPYING A PILE.
Piling icons on the desktop facilitates copying them to another disk together. Later you can easily reselect them and either drag them to the Trash or use the Put Away command (on the File menu) to return them to their folders.

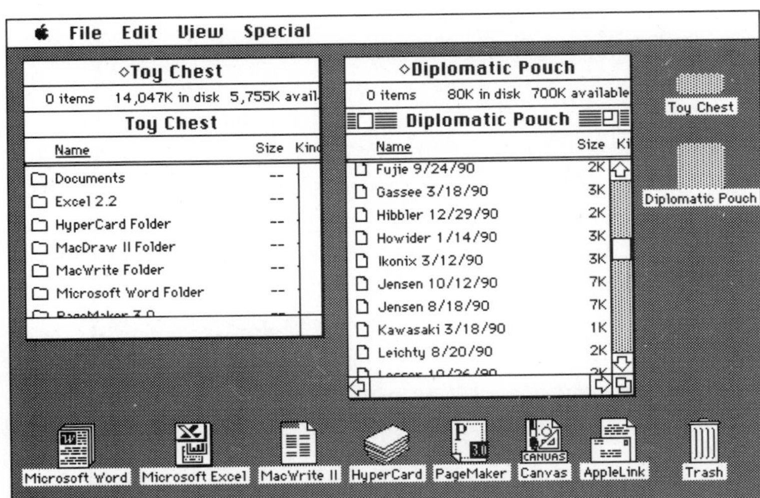

FIGURE 3-12. TELLTALE FOLDER.
Use a specially named empty folder set to view by icon as a way of seeing at a glance the amount of disk space available.

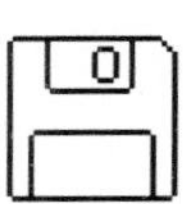
Floppy Disks

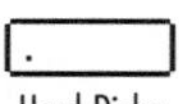
Hard Disks

WHEN YOU DON'T NEED HELP

Applications that provide built-in help information usually keep that information in a separate disk file. When you know a program well, you can remove the help file and free up a substantial amount of disk space. So if you are beyond help, look for an icon with the word "help" in its name, copy that icon to a backup disk, and then drag it from the working disk into the Trash.

Finder

GENERIC AND NAME-BRAND ICONS

A generic document icon usually appears when a document is saved on a disk that does not contain similar documents or when the disk does not contain the application that created the document.

You might be able to replace a generic document icon with a "name-brand" icon, as follows:

1. Drag the generic document icon to a disk that contains a name-brand icon for another document of the same type. The Finder then converts the generic icon to a name-brand icon.
2. Copy the newly converted name-brand icon back to its original disk.

Finder

STUBBORN COMMENTS

Rebuilding a disk's Desktop file (by holding down Command-Option during startup or during disk insertion) erases Get Info comments. But Finder versions 6.0 and later recover the comments for some applications. The Finder uses an application's creator (or signature) resource, whose type is the same as the application's four-character creator type and whose ID number is 0. For example, rebuilding a disk that contains MacWrite will put MACA resource ID = 0 into MacWrite's Get Info comments. Usually the creator resource contains the name of the application and its version number. (Unfortunately, the Finder doesn't restore Get Info comments for documents.)

Finder

LONG COMMENTS

The space for your comments in a Get Info window can hold more lines of text than it can display at once. The text scrolls as you type near the bottom of the comment space. You can see text that has scrolled out of view by placing the pointer near the middle of the box, pressing the mouse button, and dragging the pointer above the box.

This automatic scrolling doesn't work on an unenhanced Mac 512K. With that machine, you can bring unseen lines into view by temporarily cutting some of the visible lines. Be sure to paste them back before closing the Get Info window.

EXCLUDING ITEMS WHEN COPYING DISKS

When you drag one disk icon over another disk icon, the Finder completely replaces the contents of the destination disk with the contents of the source disk—assuming both disks are the same type and have the same storage capacity. If you want to keep some files from being copied, simply drag them to the desktop. The Finder does not copy any documents, applications, and folders whose icons you have previously dragged onto the desktop. After copying the disk, you can return the icons on the desktop to their former locations in the source-disk window by selecting the icons and choosing Put Away from the Finder's File menu.

REMOVING DISK ICONS

To eject a floppy disk and remove its icon in one move, drag the disk icon to the Trash, as shown in Figure 3-13. Doing this doesn't erase the disk, as you might think. If the icon of the disk remains dimmed on the desktop, it means documents or applications on the disk are in use. After closing them, you should be able to dispose of the icon by dragging it to the Trash. Because the System file is always in use, dragging the startup disk to the Trash ejects it, but its icon remains on the desktop, dimmed.

KEYBOARD DISMOUNT

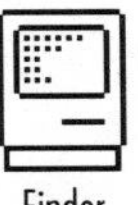

To eject a disk and dispose of its icon from the keyboard, press Command-Option-E. You must hold down the Option key until the disk has been ejected. Releasing the key too soon leaves the icon on the desktop. You can also press Option while choosing Eject from the Finder's File menu. If you're using MultiFinder, the Finder must be active for these shortcuts to work.

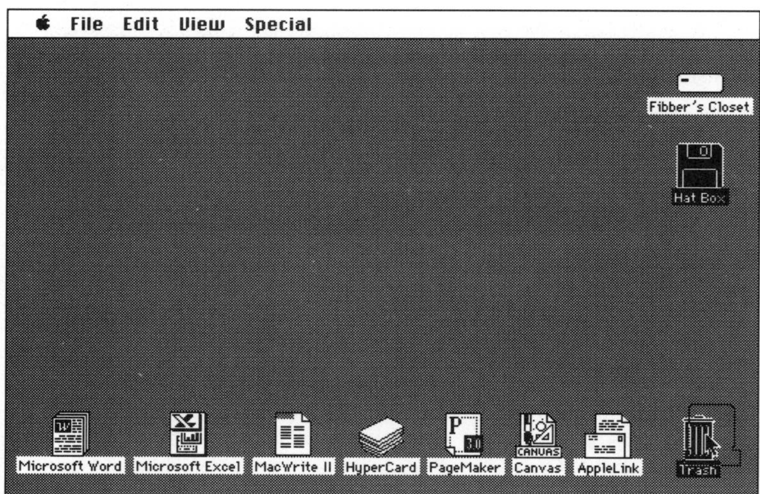

FIGURE 3-13. DISK TO TRASH.
What happens when you drag the icon of a floppy disk to the Trash?

Finder

TEMPORARY FILES

Many applications create temporary files with names like Paint1, Word Temp 1, and Undo File. Ordinarily, an application removes its temporary files when you choose Quit from the File menu. If you turn the Mac off without quitting, or if a system error or power failure precludes quitting, the temporary files remain.

Often you can tell which application created a temporary file by the filename. For example, the Word Temp prefix denotes a Microsoft Word file, and Paint1 is a MacPaint file. Other filenames don't give a clue as to which application created them. Undo File is created by MacWrite (for use with the Undo command), but you'd never guess that from the filename. You can always determine which application created a file by inspecting the file's normally invisible Creator attribute. To see Creator attributes, you must use utility software such as DiskTop.

Few temporary files contain useful information once the session during which they were created has ended. Unless you need temporary files for rescue efforts, go ahead and drag them to the Trash. Just be sure the files you remove are indeed temporary, that is, that they have generic icons and did not exist on the original program disk. If you're using MultiFinder or a desk accessory, don't delete temporary files belonging to an open application. Otherwise, you risk disrupting the application, causing a system error, and so forth.

To rescue a temporary file, try using DiskTop to change the file's Type attribute to match that of another file that has the same Creator attribute. If you find more than one Type for a particular Creator, try each alternative—setting the Type and then opening the file—to see which works best. Before experimenting, make a copy of the temporary file.

Microsoft Word versions 3 and 4 can open a temporary file (or any file, for that matter) as a text file. To do that, press the Shift key while choosing Open from Word's File menu.

THINK TWICE WHEN COPYING FOLDERS

When the Finder asks, "Replace items with same names with the selected items?" take a mental inventory of the destination disk before clicking OK. If you are copying a folder to a disk that contains a folder by the same name, the new folder will replace the old—and every last item in it. Unfortunately, the Finder doesn't warn you that it is about to replace the "entire contents" of one folder with those of another, as it does with disks. Until Apple makes this change (if ever), be alert when copying folders.

NAME TOO LONG FOR TRASH?

A long icon name might seem to interfere with the disposal of the icon. The name hits the right edge of the screen and keeps you from positioning the icon directly over the Trash. If this happens, keep pressing the mouse button and moving the pointer—ignore the icon outline. When the pointer is over the Trash, the Trash icon lights up, as shown in Figure 3-14 on the following page. Release the mouse button, and the icon you were dragging goes into the Trash.

TRASHING HARD-DISK ICONS

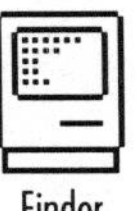

With most hard-disk drives, dragging the hard-disk icon to the Trash dismounts the disk. The icon disappears from the desktop and the disk is no longer available in Open and Save commands. The Finder won't let you dismount the startup disk.

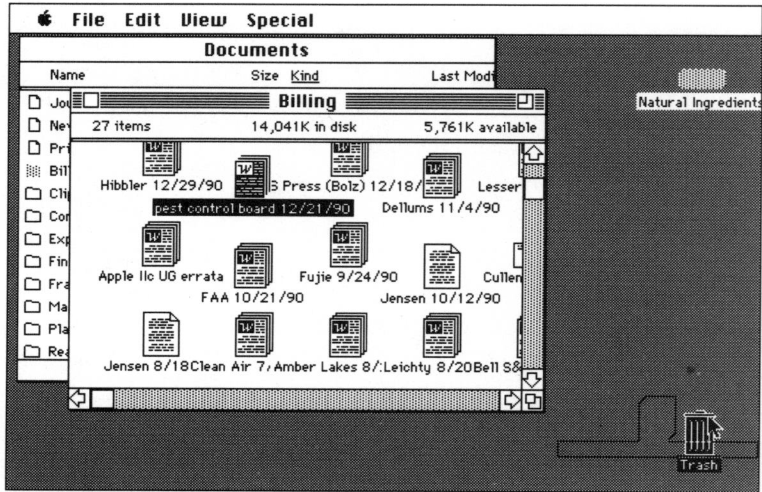

FIGURE 3-14. TRASHING LONG NAMES.
The right edge of the screen might stop an icon outline from approaching the Trash, but you can still discard the icon. Continue to drag until the pointer is over the Trash; then release the mouse button.

Some hard disks can't be dismounted. You'll know if your hard disk is one of these: Its icon will bounce out of the Trash.

DON'T ASK ME THAT AGAIN

Have you had enough of the Finder disrupting you with comments like "That item is locked or in use and cannot be removed" and "Are you sure you want to throw away the application _____?" You could haul out ResEdit and permanently silence those warnings. But you can also easily override the Finder's warnings about removing applications, system files, and locked items by pressing the Option key while you drag the icon to the Trash. Just remember to use this technique with caution.

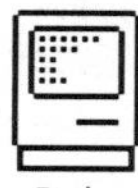

UNRELIABLE FILE LOCKING

The Finder's Get Info command includes an option for locking a document, application, or folder in order to keep you from erasing it or replacing it. Most applications respect this lock, but not all do. Before entrusting the safety of an important document to the Get Info lock, test the lock's efficacy on an unimportant document.

FOUND IN TRASH

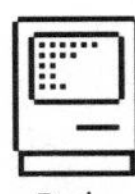

The Find File desk accessory thinks items in the Trash are still in their former locations. If you can't find a file or folder where Find File says it is, check the Trash.

ACCIDENTAL DISPOSAL

The Mac prevents you from saving a document directly into the Trash, but you can do it accidentally. Here's the scenario: You're using an application while MultiFinder is active. You switch to the Finder and drag a file to the Trash. Then you switch back to the application and use the Save As command to save a new document under the same filename as the file you just dragged to the Trash and in the same folder. The Mac doesn't know you have dragged the icon to the Trash. It asks whether you're sure you want to replace the existing file. You click Yes, and the Mac saves your new document in the Trash. The next time the Trash is emptied, the Finder disposes of your new document.

The moral: Don't save a new document using the same name as, and in the same folder as, a document you just dragged to the Trash.

Chapter 4

PRINTERS AND PRINTING

This chapter contains tips about printing that are relevant to any application with Page Setup and Print commands in its File menu. Included are general tips for printing on any printer and specific tips for the ImageWriter I, ImageWriter II, ImageWriter LQ, original LaserWriter, LaserWriter Plus, LaserWriter IISC, LaserWriter IINT, LaserWriter IINTX, Personal LaserWriter SC, Personal LaserWriter NT, and PostScript imagesetters. The tips are arranged by type of printing activity, as follows:

- Selecting paper and supplies
- Formatting documents
- Handling paper
- Controlling print jobs
- Adjusting print quality
- Maintaining printers

SELECTING PAPER AND SUPPLIES

HEAVY QUALITY

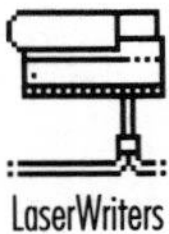

You can get better results from a LaserWriter or LaserWriter Plus if you print on a heavier paper than normal, such as Xerox 4024 (a 28-pound paper). Also, copying LaserWriter output with a good photocopier improves contrast.

FROZEN INK

Buying printer ribbons in large numbers is convenient because you always have one when you need it. But after a while, unused ribbons dry out. You can avoid this problem by freezing them. Wrap them tightly in zipper-style plastic bags, and then put them in the freezer. Be sure to thaw a frozen ribbon for at least 30 minutes before using it. Never, never, never put a frozen ribbon into your printer.

ODD-SIZE PAPER

If you have trouble getting 6-by-9-inch paper to track evenly in an ImageWriter, try this. Manually feed a sheet of standard-size paper along with the small piece of paper, as shown in Figure 4-1. Before inserting the two pieces of paper, align their top and left edges. Feed the two sheets into the printer with the large sheet nearer the platen. You might have to adjust the paper-thickness lever to avoid streaking.

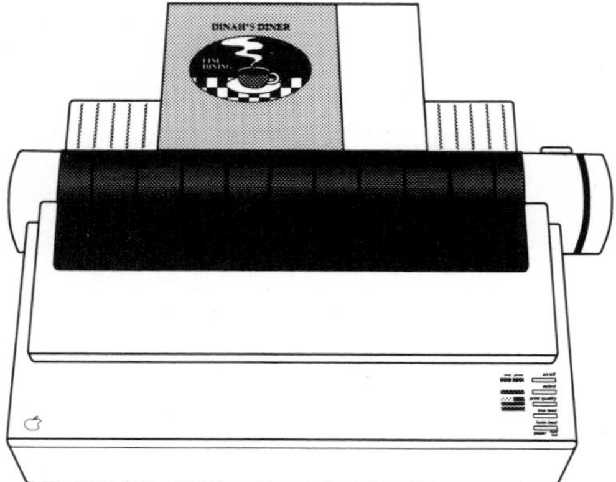

FIGURE 4-1. BIG BACKER.
Small paper travels through an ImageWriter better when backed by letter-size paper.

REGULAR STENCIL BLANKS

An ImageWriter does a good job of creating mimeograph stencils. The standard AB Dick F-1960 stencils work fine and are cheaper than the AB Dick 2060 stencils designed specifically for dot-matrix printers. For best results, remove the plastic cover sheet, and print directly on the stencil. If you remove the plastic sheet, you must use a ribbon to protect the print head from mimeo wax. Keep an old, dried-out ribbon around for this purpose.

STENCIL TRAPS

When creating a stencil to be printed on an ImageWriter, keep in mind the limitations of the stencil duplication process. For example, you can minimize tearing when you run the stencil by using dotted lines in place of solid lines. Also, use light patterns, not solids, for filling in illustrations. Heavy black areas cause ink buildup to which copies stick instead of ejecting freely from the mimeo machine.

QUICK COLOR OVERHEAD

Have you ever needed an overhead transparency in a hurry—and in color? Hewlett-Packard PaintJet transparency film in an ImageWriter II with a color ribbon produces good results. Although the ink smears a little, it adheres well enough to take fine patterns. If you can't find the film, call (800) 752-0900 for the name of a Hewlett-Packard dealer near you. To order directly from Hewlett-Packard, call (800) 538-8787.

FORMATTING DOCUMENTS

FORMATTING IN ADVANCE

You don't have to own a LaserWriter to use one. Many copy shops, computer stores, and desktop publishing service bureaus offer LaserWriter printing, charging by the page or by the hour. But you must plan ahead; otherwise, your first attempt to use this service might be disappointing. Documents formatted for an ImageWriter have different fonts, letterspacing, margins, and page breaks than documents formatted for a LaserWriter.

To format a document accurately for printing on the LaserWriter, you must use only LaserWriter fonts in it. The minimal set of fonts includes Times, Helvetica, Courier, and Symbol in 10-point and 12-point sizes. The LaserWriter Plus, LaserWriter IINT, Personal LaserWriter NT, and LaserWriter IINTX have additional fonts built in. If you'll be using one of those printers, you might also want to install Avant Garde, Bookman, Helvetica Narrow, New Century Schoolbook, Palatino, Zapf Chancery, and Zapf Dingbats. You should be able to get copies of these standard screen fonts from the service bureau you use.

You can install the fonts in your System file (using the Font/DA Mover utility with a system software version prior to 7.0). Alternatively, you can install the fonts in separate files with the MasterJuggler or Suitcase II utility. To save disk space, install only the fonts you plan to use.

The LaserWriter fonts look crowded on the screen, and with system software versions prior to 7.0, the fonts might look blotchy if the sizes you use aren't installed in the System file. Don't let screen appearances bother you. The LaserWriter uses built-in PostScript fonts for printing, and they always print beautifully in any size.

There are two ways to get the proper letterspacing, margins, and page breaks for a LaserWriter. You can put the LaserWriter and LaserPrep files in your System Folder and then use the Chooser desk accessory to select the LaserWriter as your printer. You don't have to have a LaserWriter connected to do that. Alternatively, you can leave the ImageWriter selected in the Chooser and set the Tall Adjusted option, using the Page Setup command (in the File menu). Figure 4-2 shows how to do this. You must set the Tall Adjusted option separately for every document.

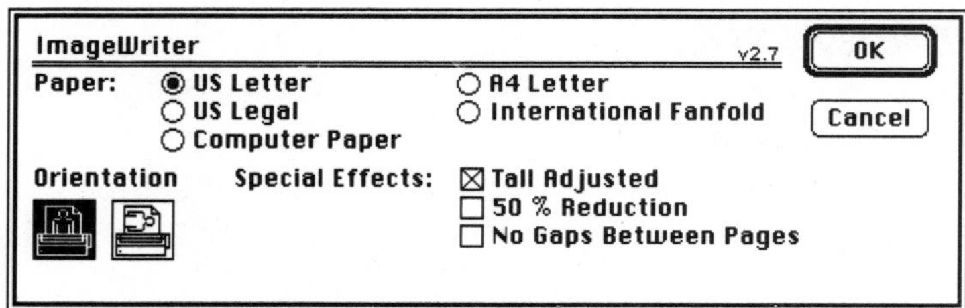

FIGURE 4-2. LASERWRITER EQUIVALENT.
If you don't have a LaserWriter but want to format your document for one, select the Page Setup command's Tall Adjusted option.

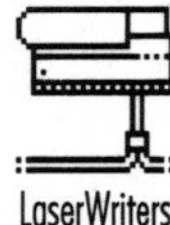

LINE LAYOUT DIFFERENCES

The layout of a line of text in a given font and font size might not be the same on all printers. For example, about 10 percent more text fits on a LaserWriter line than on an ImageWriter line of the same length. To make ImageWriter line layout match LaserWriter line layout, set the Tall Adjusted option by using the Page Setup command (in the File menu).

When you change printers with the Chooser desk accessory and subsequently choose Page Setup for a document, the application must adjust the line layout. Many applications, including Microsoft Word and WriteNow, change the amount of text on a line and leave the printed line length unchanged. When switching from an ImageWriter to a LaserWriter, for example, these applications effectively reduce the font size by 10 percent.

Other applications, notably MacWrite, adjust the printed line length and leave the amount of text on a line unchanged. When switching from an ImageWriter to a LaserWriter, for example, MacWrite reduces the font size by 10 percent and shortens the line length by 10 percent. To get full-width lines again, you must either set the Tall Adjusted option or manually change the document's right margin.

KEEPING ITALICS FROM COLLIDING

Italic text might collide with plain text that follows it, especially on an ImageWriter. Fonts commonly used on an ImageWriter have no special italic versions, so the Mac fabricates italics by slanting the plain versions of the fonts. To prevent collisions when using most ImageWriter fonts, type an extra blank space between the last italic word and the following nonitalic word, as shown in Figure 4-3. Do not add extra space after italics if you plan to print the document in a font that includes a special italics version, such as most LaserWriter fonts.

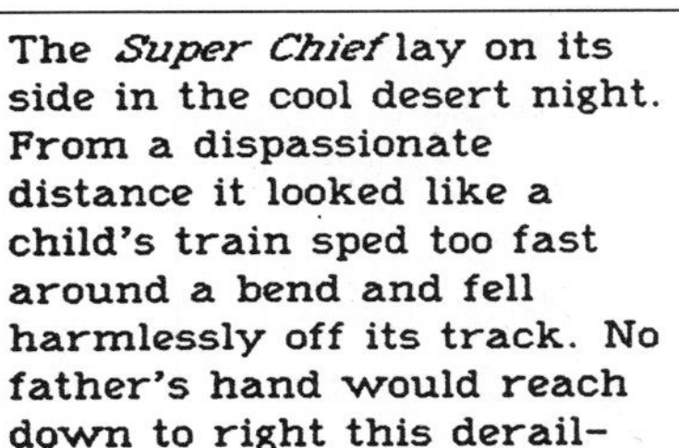
The *Super Chief*lay on its side in the cool desert night. From a dispassionate distance it looked like a child's train sped too fast around a bend and fell harmlessly off its track. No father's hand would reach down to right this derail-

The *Super Chief* lay on its side in the cool desert night. From a dispassionate distance it looked like a child's train sped too fast around a bend and fell harmlessly off its track. No father's hand would reach down to right this derail-

FIGURE 4-3. TOUCHY TEXT.

If italic text leans into plain text that follows it (left), add an extra space after the italic text (right).

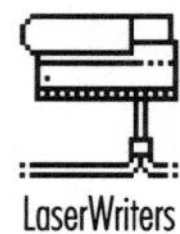

LINING UP

You can rely on displayed line breaks when you are fitting copy on a page. The Mac maintains the line breaks when printing on an ImageWriter in any print quality or on a LaserWriter with or without font substitution. Due to the difference in resolution between the printer and the screen, however, word and character spacing might change slightly on the printed page to maintain line breaks.

Although you can't do anything about these spacing changes (except to use fractional character widths in the applications that support them), they are usually noticeable only when you're trying to align text with graphics. Gaps between words become wider with LaserWriter font substitution because LaserWriter fonts are narrower than the screen fonts they replace. Compose in LaserWriter fonts to avoid "gaposis."

Because the Mac doesn't maintain exact word spacing when printing, words aligned with spaces on the screen might not stay aligned on paper. Font substitution worsens the misalignment because the width of a space character in a screen font differs from its width in the substitute LaserWriter font. Use tabs, not spaces, for reliable alignment.

REMOVING BLANK PAGES

Blank lines at the end of a text document sometimes cause the printer to print a blank page after the last page of the document. A manually inserted page break at the end of a text document has the same effect. You can avoid blank spaces at the end of a document by removing all unnecessary white space or page breaks. Simply drag across the white space to select it, and press the Delete (or Backspace) key.

Other types of documents might also have useless page breaks that cause blank pages. If you enlarge or move objects in a MacDraw document, for example, MacDraw might expand the size of a drawing so that it covers more pages. If you later shrink the objects, MacDraw will not automatically reduce the size of the drawing. To eliminate the resulting blank pages, use the Drawing Size command on the Layout menu.

Spreadsheet documents might also have useless page breaks. Most spreadsheet programs let you set page breaks manually by selecting a cell and choosing a command. Microsoft Excel, for example, creates a page boundary above and to the left of the selected cell when you choose Set Page Break from the Options menu. If you have too many manually set horizontal page breaks, you can remove some by selecting any cell in the row below the page-boundary line and choosing Remove Page Break from the Options menu. Similarly, you can remove a manually set vertical page break by selecting any cell in the column to the right of the page-boundary line and choosing Remove Page Break from the Options menu.

LASERWRITER ENVELOPES

You can feed and print envelopes manually one at a time on any LaserWriter. Create a new document by using any word processor. Use the Page Setup command (in the File menu) to set the sideways orientation. Leave the paper size set for US Letter. If you want to print a return address, click the Options button and set the Larger Print Area option.

Margin settings vary depending on the model of LaserWriter and on whether you want to print a return address. Figure 4-4 shows the details. If you include a return address, leave about seven blank lines between it and the recipient's address, and indent the recipient's address about 4 inches.

You might want to create a standard envelope template into which you can paste the address from your letter. After printing, close the template document, but do not save changes because pasting the address is only a temporary change to the template.

When you use the Print command (in the File menu), be sure to select the Manual Feed option. On a LaserWriter II, place the envelope face up

Printer	Top	Bottom	Left	Right
LaserWriter II, no return address	4 in.	2.75 in.	4 in.	1 in.
LaserWriter II, return address	2.5 in.	2.75 in.	0.5 in.	1 in.
LaserWriter Plus, no return address	2 in.	4.75 in.	4 in.	1 in.
LaserWriter Plus, return address	0.5 in.	4.75 in.	0.5 in.	1 in.

FIGURE 4-4. ENVELOPE MARGINS.
Use the margin settings shown in this table to print number 10 envelopes on a LaserWriter.

between the self-centering manual-feed guides. On a LaserWriter Plus, which has no centering guide, place the envelope face up at the top of the LaserWriter's manual-feed tray so that it is just under the roller inside the printer. During printing, the heat inside the LaserWriter might partially seal the envelope, but you should be able to reopen it.

ImageWriters

IMAGEWRITER ENVELOPES

Here's an easy method for printing number 10 business envelopes on an ImageWriter. Create a new document using any word processor. Use the Page Setup command (in the File menu) to set the No Gaps Between Pages option. Leave the orientation set for portrait printing (not sideways printing) and the paper size set for US Letter.

The margin settings you use depend on whether you want to print a return address. If you want a return address, make the top margin 0.375 inch and the left margin 0.5 inch. Leave about five blank lines between the return address and the recipient's address, and indent the recipient's address about 4 inches. If you don't want to include a return address, make the top margin 2 inches and the left margin 4 inches. Either way, make the right margin 1 inch. The bottom margin doesn't really matter.

You might want to create a standard envelope template into which you can paste the address from your letter. After printing, close the template document, but do not save changes because pasting the address is only a temporary change to the template.

When you use the Print command (in the File menu), be sure to select the Hand Feed option. Adjust the paper-thickness lever inside the printer's front cover to accommodate the envelope, which is two or three times thicker than a sheet of paper.

Instead of using the platen knob to crank an envelope into an ImageWriter II, use the printer's Form Feed/Paper Load button, as shown in Figure 4-5. First press the printer's Select button to turn off the Select light. Place the envelope in the printer so that its left edge aligns with the mark on the back cover of the ImageWriter II. Then press the Form Feed/Paper Load button to feed the envelope into the printer. Press the Select button again to turn on the Select light, and you're ready to print.

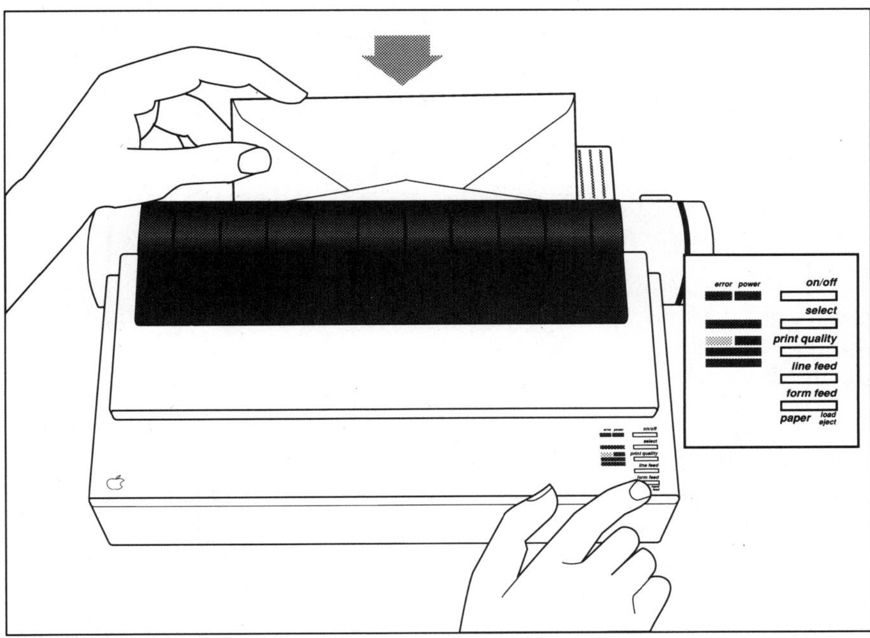

FIGURE 4-5. ENVELOPE FEEDING.
Use the Form Feed/Paper Load button to feed an envelope into an ImageWriter II. You might have to rest your hand lightly on the edge of the envelope to get it started.

INDIVIDUAL LABELS

You don't need a typewriter to prepare individual mailing or shipping labels. Use any word processor to create a new document. Position the text and graphics you want printed—your return address and logo along with the recipient's address—so that they'll print on a label when you manually feed it through the printer. On any type of LaserWriter II, position the information at the top center of a portrait-oriented letter-size page. If you are printing on a LaserWriter Plus, place the information in the upper left corner of a landscape-oriented letter-size page.

Choose Page Setup from the File menu, click the Options button, and set the Larger Print Area option. Set the orientation for either portrait or landscape printing (depending on your printer type) and set the paper size for US Letter.

Margin settings depend on the label dimensions, on the model of Laser-Writer, and on whether you want to print a return address. The table in Figure 4-6 lists some margins for printing labels one-at-a-time that are 4 by 3 inches and come two to a backing sheet, such as Avery S-6448. (These labels are meant to be addressed with a pen or a typewriter but they work fine in a LaserWriter.) If you include a return address, leave about an inch between it and the recipient's address, and indent the recipient's address about 0.75 inch.

You might want to create a standard label template into which you can paste the address from your letter. After printing, close the template document, but do not save changes because pasting the address is only a temporary change to the template.

When you use the Print command (in the File menu), be sure to select the Manual Feed option. On a LaserWriter II, place the label face up between the self-centering manual-feed guides. On a LaserWriter Plus, which has no centering guide, place the label face up and wide edge first at the top of the LaserWriter's manual-feed tray so that it is under the roller inside the printer.

Printer	Top	Bottom	Left	Right
LaserWriter II, no return address	1.625 in.	7.875 in.	2.375 in.	2.375 in.
LaserWriter II, return address	0.125 in.	7.875 in.	2.375 in.	2.375 in.
LaserWriter Plus, no return address	1.625 in.	7.875 in.	4.375 in.	0.375 in.
LaserWriter Plus, return address	0.125 in.	7.875 in.	4.375 in.	0.375 in.

FIGURE 4-6. LABEL MARGINS.
Use the margins settings shown in this table to print 4 by 3 shipping labels (Avery S-6448) on a LaserWriter.

HANDLING PAPER

TEST BAN

Many people complain that the LaserWriter wastes paper by printing a test page every time it's turned on. To prevent the waste, simply put a piece of scrap paper in the manual-feed guide before switching on the printer. The LaserWriter uses the manual-feed paper for the test page (if there is a piece of paper in the manual-feed guide).

If you don't have a piece of scrap paper to sacrifice for the LaserWriter test page, simply pull the paper cassette tray out far enough to disengage the feed mechanism—approximately 1 inch. Then turn the LaserWriter on. Wait until the green light ceases to flash and remains constant, indicating that it is warmed up, and shove the tray back in.

You can also use a utility called Widgets to halt the flood of test pages pouring out of your LaserWriter. Widgets, from CE Software, has commands to turn the test page on and off semipermanently—either command stays in effect until you choose its opposite.

EASY LEGAL PAGES

Normally, LaserWriter software versions 4.0 through 6.0 don't permit you to print a legal-size page on manual-feed paper without a legal-size paper tray in the printer. You can fool the printer into thinking it has a legal-size paper tray. Use the Page Setup command (on the File menu) to set the US Legal page size. Before clicking the OK button, click the Options button and set the Larger Print Area option, as shown in Figure 4-7. Now when you select the Manual Feed option in the Print dialog box, the LaserWriter prints a legal-size page on manual-feed legal paper.

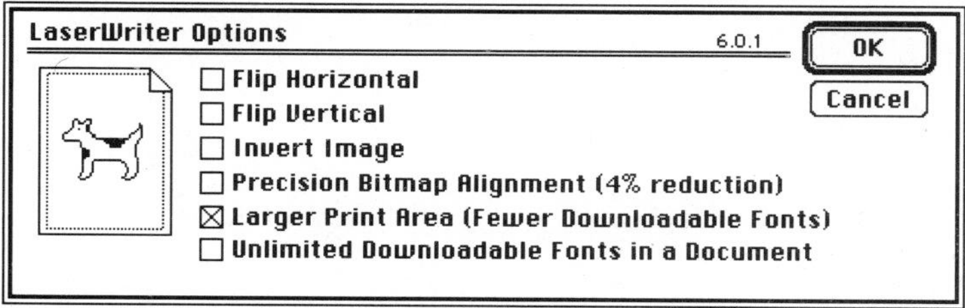

FIGURE 4-7. LEGAL FOOLERY.
To print hand-fed legal pages on a LaserWriter with a letter-size paper tray, set the Page Setup command's Larger Print Area option.

PRINTING BOTH SIDES NOW

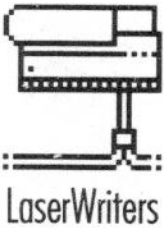

Few applications help you to print on both sides of the page by printing odd-numbered pages in one batch and, after you flip that batch, printing even-numbered pages in a separate batch. (MacWrite II is one that does.) However, here's a method for printing any document on both sides of the page without sitting at the Mac and producing one double-sided page at a time:

1. Print one complete copy of your entire document.
2. Arrange the pages consecutively with page 1 on top. Place the stack face up.
3. Take the first two pages (1 and 2) together from the stack, and lay the stacked pair face up in a new pile. Then take the next two pages (3 and 4), and place them face up on top of the new pile. The new pile now contains, from the top down, pages 3, 4, 1, and 2. Continue placing pairs of pages face up on top of the new pile. If the last page is odd numbered, do not place it on the new pile; put it aside for now.
4. Put the rearranged pages face down in the printer's paper tray, with the top of the page toward the printer. Remember not to put the last page back into the printer if it is odd numbered.
5. Print another copy of the complete document. You end up with two complete double-sided copies of your document, which you have only to separate. Figure 4-8 shows what you have after the second printing.

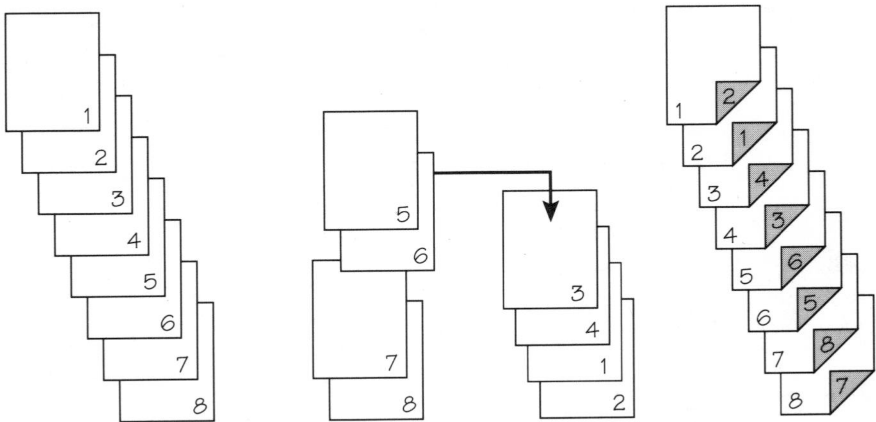

FIGURE 4-8. TWO-FACED.
You can print any document on both sides of the page. You print it once, rearrange the pages in the order shown in the middle diagram, and then print it again. You end up with two double-sided copies.

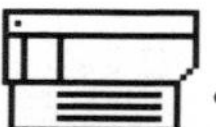

This method works for any even number of finished copies on a LaserWriter II, Personal LaserWriter, LaserWriter Plus, or ImageWriter II or LQ with a cut-sheet feeder.

ANOTHER TWO-SIDED APPROACH

Print Monitor

Super LaserSpool

You can use a print spooler to print double-sided pages from any application. First you print the odd-numbered pages and then, on their backs, you print the even-numbered pages. With any LaserWriter, you can use Apple's PrintMonitor spooler or SuperMac's SuperLaserSpool. With an ImageWriter, use SuperMac's SuperSpool or SuperLaserSpool. Proceed as follows:

1. If you're using a LaserWriter II, open its side exit door. This causes printed pages to be collated in reverse order. (An original LaserWriter, a LaserWriter Plus, and an ImageWriter using continuous paper or a cut-sheet feeder all naturally collate in reverse order.)
2. Use the Print command to print only page 1. After a few seconds, the Mac will have spooled the page to disk. Use the Print command again to print only page 3. Continue printing the odd-numbered pages one at a time, in sequence, until you reach the end of the document. Then go ahead with another task while the printing continues in the background.
3. When the odd-numbered pages are printed, be sure they are in reverse order (page 1 on the bottom, the last page on top). Then turn the stack over and put it in the printer's input paper tray.
4. Print the even-numbered pages one at a time in sequence. If you're using a LaserWriter II, you can close its side exit door so that the pages end up collated in proper sequence.
5. If the document ends with an odd-numbered page, that last page will still be in the printer's paper tray. Add it to the stack of printed pages.

TWO-SIDED PRINTING IN PAGEMAKER

PageMaker

You can easily print double-sided documents on any printer with PageMaker version 3.0 or later. First you print the even-numbered pages in reverse order, and then, on their backs, you print the odd-numbered pages in normal order. The result is collated correctly. Follow these steps:

1. Choose Page Setup from the File menu, and select the Double-Sided and Facing Pages options.
2. On the master pages, set the ruler origin to the top left corner of the left page.
3. Choose Print from the File menu. Select the Manual Tile option. If you're using a LaserWriter II or another printer that normally arranges printed pages in correct sequence, also select the Reverse Order option. Click OK; all the even-numbered pages are printed, with the highest-numbered page on top.
4. Still on the master pages, move the ruler origin to the upper left corner of the right page.
5. Place the stack of even-numbered pages face down in the paper tray, with the top edge nearest the printer. If the document has more odd-numbered pages than even-numbered pages, add a blank sheet of paper to the top of the paper tray.
6. Choose Print again, turn the Reverse Order option off, but leave the Manual Tile option on, and click OK.

ImageWriters

ALL TORN UP

Here's a method for quickly tearing off the perforated edges of pin-feed paper. First fanfold the printed paper into a stack as it came from the box. Then loosely fold it in half lengthwise so that the tear-off strips are together. Now you can tear all the edges off together, as shown in Figure 4-9, and—lickety-split—you're off doing something better with your time.

If you have a thick stack of printed pages, separate it into smaller stacks before applying this method.

LaserWriter Plus

LASERWRITER PAPER FLIPPER

The LaserWriter and LaserWriter Plus stack the first page they print on the bottom and the last page on the top. You then usually have to rearrange the pile by hand. To eliminate the manual collating, remove the paper output tray, and place a small box next to the printer. As paper comes out of the LaserWriter, it will fall into the box upside down. When you turn the stack of paper over, the first page is first and the last page is last. (MacWrite prints the last page first, so use the standard output tray for documents.)

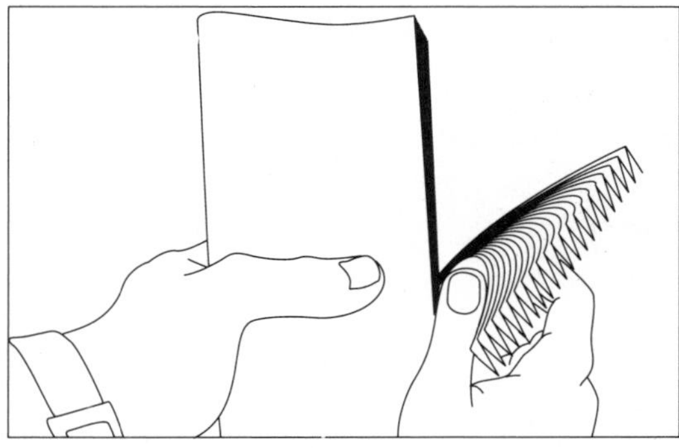

FIGURE 4-9. PAPER TEARER.
Holding a stack of continuous paper so that the right and left edges are together lets you tear off all the tractor-feed strips at once.

AVOIDING PAPER CURL

Paper that sits in the ImageWriter for a couple of hours acquires a permanent curl from being wound around the platen. To avoid the curl, roll the paper back just far enough to turn on the ImageWriter's red Paper Error light. At that point, the paper clears the platen but is still engaged in the pin-feed sprockets. Remember to roll the paper forward again before printing.

UNAVOIDABLE PAGE GAPS

With some odd sizes of paper, it's impossible to completely eliminate breaks between pages on an ImageWriter. Selecting the No Gaps Between Pages option in the Page Setup dialog box forces the vertical length of the page image to be a multiple of eight dots. (Eight dots equal ⅑ inch.)

If the vertical length of the paper size selected in the Page Setup dialog box is not a multiple of eight dots, the paper size and page size cannot match. A mismatch causes a very thin gap (less than eight dots) at the bottom of every page. All of the standard paper sizes—US Letter, US Legal, A4, Computer Paper, and International Fanfold—are an even multiple of eight dots in length.

PRINTING NEAR THE TOP OF THE PAGE

Ordinarily, you load paper into the ImageWriter so that the top edge of the paper is about half an inch above the print head, putting the top edge of the paper immediately above the place where the pressure rollers contact the platen.

Application programs normally consider the top ½ inch of every page an unprintable area. Selecting the No Gaps Between Pages option in the Page Setup dialog box allows printing in the top ½ inch of the page but requires you to handle the paper somewhat differently.

On an ImageWriter I, load manual-feed paper with the pressure rollers pulled back and the top edge of the paper even with the top of the print head. The entire page is then printed with the pressure rollers back.

On an ImageWriter II, use the Form Feed/Paper Load button to load manual-feed paper. The Select light must be off to use that button.

Load continuous (pin-feed) paper as usual, with the top edge nearly even with the top of the pressure rollers. Then, if the first page of the document contains something to be printed in the top ½ inch of the page, the Mac rolls the first sheet of paper forward until the print head is even with the perforation between sheets and prints the first page of the document on the second sheet of continuous paper. The first sheet of paper is wasted. However, if there is nothing to be printed in the top ½ inch of the first page, printing begins immediately, and the first sheet is not wasted.

IMAGEWRITER II COMMOTION

Before an ImageWriter II starts printing a document on pin-feed paper, it rolls the paper back and forth. This commotion is required because standard paper-loading practice puts the top of the paper just under the pressure rollers. That leaves the print head ½ inch below the top of the printable area. So the ImageWriter rolls the paper backward to reach the top of the printable area and then rolls the paper forward to the printed image's starting point on the page.

This might jam the paper unless the print head is in the center of the platen. With the head off-center, the clear plastic paper guides on either

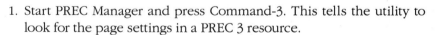

side of the head might have trouble routing the paper under the pressure rollers during the down-and-up movement. You can manually center the print head by lifting the ribbon cover to create an error condition, replacing the cover, and pushing the Select button on the printer. Switching the printer's power off and on also centers the print head.

To avoid these paper jams without centering the print head, you can start printing on the second sheet of pin-feed paper. If you prefer to start on the first sheet, use the printer's Form Feed/Paper Load button to load the pin-feed paper, and then select the Manual Feed option in the Print dialog box. (This method requires you to click an OK button to start each page.) Alternatively, you can forsake pin-feed paper and get a sheet feeder.

CUSTOM PAGE SIZES

Two or three of the five paper sizes that the Page Setup command offers for an ImageWriter are of no use to most Mac users. Few people use both US Letter and A4 Letter, for example. The five standard paper sizes are part of the ImageWriter file in the System Folder. You can change the standard sizes and add a sixth size with the PREC Manager utility by Bill Steinberg or the Widgets utility from CE Software. Figure 4-10 on the following page shows what PREC Manager's ImageWriter window looks like. Proceed as follows:

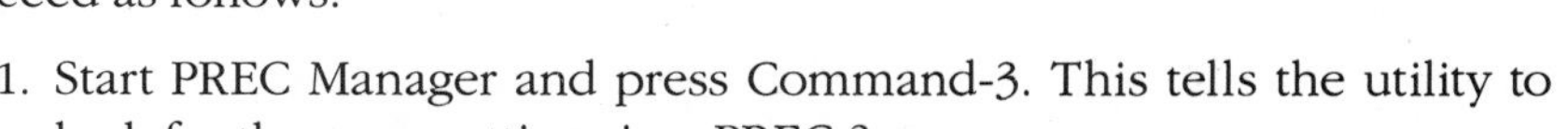

1. Start PREC Manager and press Command-3. This tells the utility to look for the page settings in a PREC 3 resource.
2. Use the Open Resource command in PREC Manager's File menu to open the ImageWriter file in the System Folder. You see a window in which you can change the standard sizes and add a sixth size.
3. Change paper sizes and add a size if you want. If you add a sixth size, enter *6* in the space provided at the bottom of the window. You can preview the new Page Setup dialog box settings by clicking the Show Me button.
4. Quit PREC Manager, answering Yes when it asks whether you want to save changes.

File Edit Special

ImageWriter

Paper Type		Width	Height
US Letter	[1]	8.500	11.000
A4 Letter	[2]	8.250	11.667
US Legal	[3]	8.500	14.000
International Fanfold	[4]	8.250	12.000
Computer Paper	[5]	14.000	11.000
Envelope	[6]	8.500	4.125

Number of Active Types = 6 Show Me

FIGURE 4-10. PAGE-SIZE EDITOR.
The PREC Manager utility lets you change the paper sizes available for the ImageWriter.

SPECIAL PAGE SIZES

When you print on an ImageWriter, the Page Setup command normally offers paper-size options specified by the ImageWriter file in the System Folder. However, an application can have the Page Setup command offer a different set of paper sizes. You can add a set of special paper sizes to any application with the PREC Manager utility by Bill Steinberg or the Widgets utility from CE Software. Follow these steps:

1. Start PREC Manager and press Command-4. This sets the utility to put the page settings in a PREC 4 resource.
2. Use the New command in PREC Manager's File menu to create a new set of paper sizes. You see a window in which you can edit the paper sizes. PREC Manager presets these to the standard paper sizes.
3. Change the paper sizes if you want. If you change the number of sizes, enter the new number in the space provided at the bottom of the window. You can preview the new Page Setup dialog box by clicking the Show Me button.

4. Use the Save In command (on the File menu) to put the set of paper sizes in the application of your choice. Then quit PREC Manager.

CONTROLLING PRINT JOBS

IMAGEWRITER AND THE PC

ImageWriters

An ImageWriter can be connected to an IBM PC–compatible computer equipped with a serial port. (The ImageWriter can't be connected to a parallel printer port.) You can buy the necessary cable, or you can make one using the wiring diagram shown in Figure 4-11 or Figure 4-12 on the following pages.

Every time you turn on the PC or reboot it by pressing Ctrl-Alt-Del, you must configure its serial port and tell it to send printer output there instead of to the parallel printer port. The following two DOS commands do the job:

```
MODE COM1:9600,N,8,1,P
MODE LPT1:=COM1:
```

The first MODE command sets the transfer rate, parity, word length, number of stop bits, and continuous-retry settings. The second MODE command redirects output destined for the printer from the parallel port to the serial port. In both MODE commands, use COM2: instead of COM1: if the IBM PC has two serial ports and you attach the ImageWriter to the second IBM serial port. You can also put the two MODE commands in a batch file. If you include them in the special batch file AUTOEXEC.BAT, they will be executed automatically whenever the PC is started or rebooted. Batch files are discussed in the DOS manual that comes with the PC.

Before starting a PC application, you can test the ImageWriter by pressing Shift-PrtSc, which dumps the text on the screen to the printer. If nothing happens, switch the ImageWriter off and back on again. Try retyping the two MODE commands. Be sure you're using the correct cable and that the cable connections are tight. The settings of the two banks of small switches under the ImageWriter's cover should be the same as for printing from the Macintosh: All the switches in SW1 should be open except SW1-6; SW2-1 and SW2-2 should be closed; and SW2-3 and SW2-4 should be open.

In addition, each PC application you print from must be set up to use the ImageWriter. An application that directly supports the ImageWriter will be able to take advantage of its special features such as character pitch selection, boldface, underlining, headline type, custom characters, and graphics printing. Otherwise, you'll have to settle for the plain text you get when you instruct the application to treat the ImageWriter as a teletype or TTY-type printer.

ImageWriter I DB-25 plug

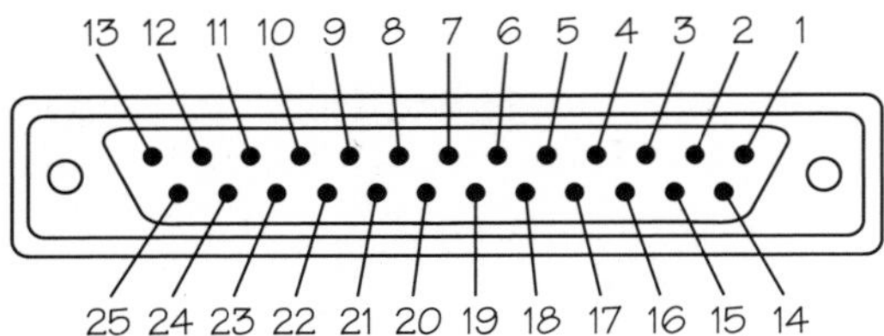

IBM PC DB-25 socket

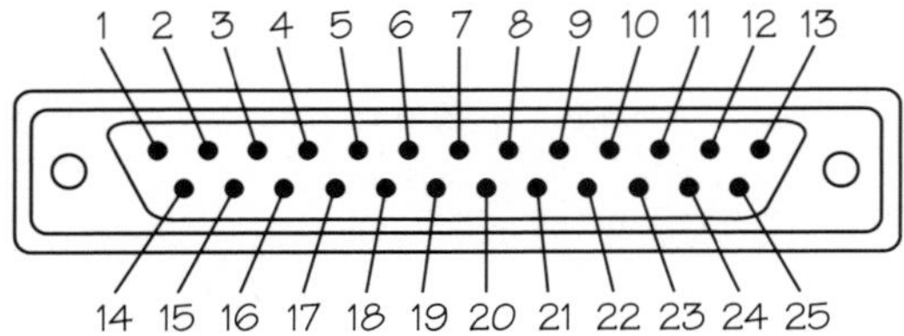

ImageWriter I	IBM PC
Frame ground 1	1 Frame ground
Transmit data → 2	2 ← Transmit data
Receive data ← 3	3 → Receive data
Request to send → 4	4 ← Request to send
Clear to send ← 5	5 → Clear to send
Data set ready ← 6	6 → Data set ready
Signal ground 7	7 Signal ground
Data terminal ready → 20	

FIGURE 4-11. IMAGEWRITER I TO PC.

A cable wired according to this diagram connects an ImageWriter I to an IBM PC–compatible computer. (Connectors are viewed from the back, where the connections are made.)

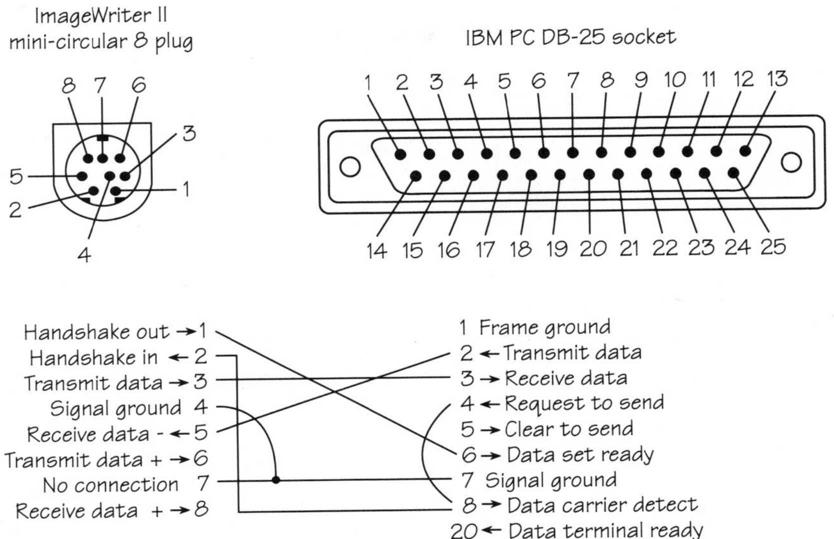

FIGURE 4-12. IMAGEWRITER II OR LQ TO PC.

A cable wired according to this diagram connects an ImageWriter II or LQ to an IBM PC–compatible computer. (Connectors are viewed from the back, where the connections are made.)

PRINT SPOOLERS

When printing, the Macintosh stands idle much of the time because it outputs information much faster than the printer can print it. For more efficient use of your Mac, you can use print-spooler software. The spooler stores printer-bound information on an unused part of the hard disk and sends the information to the printer on demand. With a spooler, you can print documents while you work on other documents. Spooled printing is temporarily suspended while you actively use the Mac. Therefore, a document might take longer to print with a spooler than without one, but you can use the Mac while the spooled printing proceeds.

PrintMonitor, which comes with the Macintosh system software, can spool LaserWriter printing while MultiFinder is active. SuperLaserSpool, a utility created by SuperMac, works with or without MultiFinder and with an ImageWriter, AppleTalk ImageWriter, or LaserWriter.

Print Monitor

Super LaserSpool

REPRINTING A SPOOLED PRINT JOB

Have you ever wanted to intercept a spooled print job to increase the number of copies or perhaps to reprint the job? Such flexibility is especially desirable with reports that take a long time to generate. The SuperMac print spoolers, SuperSpool and SuperLaserSpool, don't let you reprint or change the number of copies. Neither does Apple's PrintMonitor spooler. However, you can get equivalent results by duplicating the spool folder immediately after a job begins printing. To do that in the Finder, select the spool folder and choose the Duplicate command from the File menu. The SuperMac spool folder appears in the disk window and is customarily named SS Spool Files or SLS Spool Files. The PrintMonitor spool folder appears in the System Folder and is usually named Spool Folder.

To reprint the job, simply copy the icons from the duplicate spool folder into the real spool folder. (Press the Option key while dragging the icons if the folders are on the same disk.) Reprinting begins. Sometimes the spooling software gets confused by the sudden appearance of icons in the spool folder and displays a spurious message describing an imaginary problem. Dismiss the message to continue the reprinting. You can reprint any number of times by copying the icons again. You can park duplicate spooled print jobs for as long as necessary—days, weeks, months, or forever.

ImageWriters

Print Monitor

POKY PRINTING

How can you speed up printing on an ImageWriter?

The quality setting you make in the Print dialog box has a decided effect on print time. For example, the chart in Figure 4-13 compares the time Microsoft Works took to print 100 four-line labels two-up using Best, Faster, and three variations of Draft qualities. You select a Draft variation with the Print Quality switch on the ImageWriter II, as described in the tip "Native Printing," later in this chapter.

The chart in Figure 4-13 also shows that you can regain use of your Mac very quickly if you use a print spooler such as SuperSpool or SuperLaserSpool from SuperMac Technology. For more information on print spooling, see the tip "Print Spoolers," earlier in this chapter.

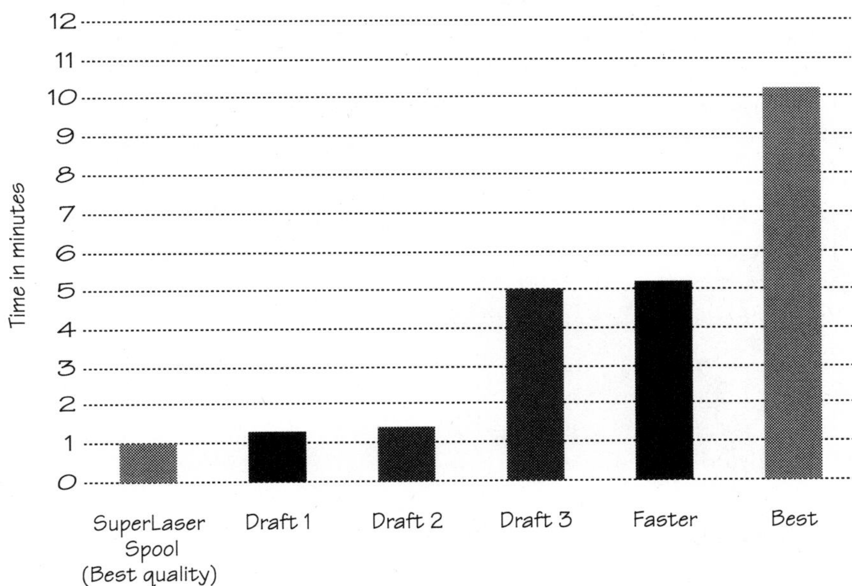

FIGURE 4-13. IMAGEWRITER TIME TRIALS.
The Quality setting in the ImageWriter Print dialog box affects printing time as well as appearance. With Draft quality, the printer's Print Quality switch also affects printing time and appearance—good looks take longer. Using a print spooler frees up the Mac quickly.

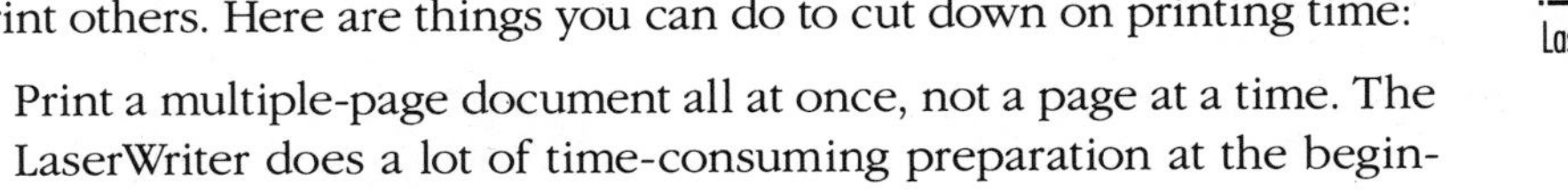

AVOIDING SLOW PRINTING

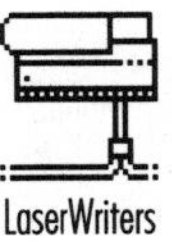

The LaserWriter takes much longer to print some documents than it does to print others. Here are things you can do to cut down on printing time:

- Print a multiple-page document all at once, not a page at a time. The LaserWriter does a lot of time-consuming preparation at the beginning of every print run.
- Use LaserWriter fonts rather than screen fonts. The Mac has to create PostScript versions of screen fonts, but LaserWriter fonts are defined as PostScript fonts.
- If you do use screen fonts, avoid large, heavy ones such as Athens, London, and Venice. The LaserWriter takes much longer to print a page that contains these fonts.

- Download (transfer) to the printer fonts you will be using that aren't built into the printer. The printer then treats them like built-in fonts until you turn the printer off or reset it with utility software. To download fonts, use a utility such as Widgets from CE Software, Font Downloader from Adobe Systems, or Apple's LaserWriter Font Utility.
- Don't change fonts frequently in the document. The LaserWriter builds each character to be printed. It keeps characters it builds in its memory for reuse. When the font changes, it must clear its memory and build each character in the new font from scratch.
- In object-oriented graphics applications, such as MacDraw, avoid patterns other than black, white, and the standard grays. The LaserWriter has built-in definitions for those patterns, but others must be constructed from scratch.

PRINTING NONADJACENT PAGES

In any spreadsheet application, you can print several nonadjacent pages with one Print command. Your spreadsheet must be organized so that the pages are in a horizontal row, with none stacked vertically. To suppress printing of a particular page, you temporarily set all the column widths in that section to 0.

Finder

UNATTENDED CHAIN PRINTING

How can you print several documents in succession without having to choose the Print command for each one?

Use the Finder to select the icons of all documents you want to open, and then choose Print from the Finder's File menu. The icons you select must all be either in the same window or on the desktop, as shown in Figure 4-14. If you drag them to the desktop, you can return them to their folders later with the Put Away command (on the File menu).

The Finder starts with the selected icon nearest the upper left corner of the window or desktop and continues from left to right and top to bottom. For each selected icon, the Finder opens the appropriate application and tells it to print the document. The documents you select for printing can be from different applications. If the Finder can't find an application for a selected document, however, it stops printing.

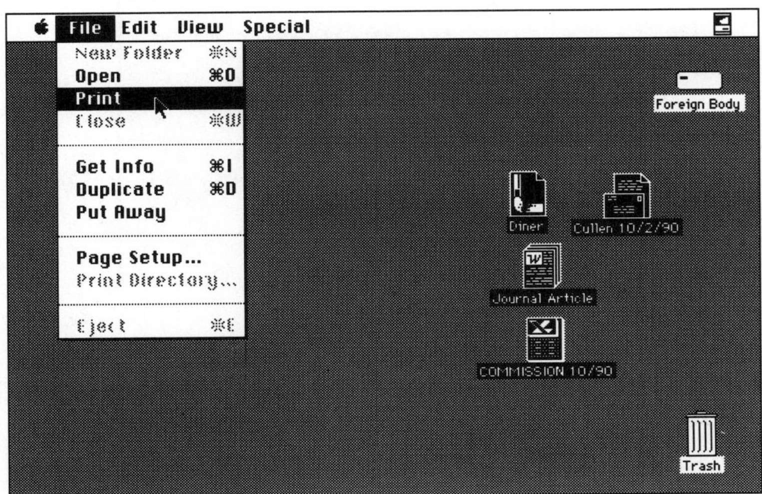

FIGURE 4-14. GROUP PRINTING.
The selected documents have been dragged to the desktop from various folders and are about to be printed all at once.

DEALING WITH A FULL DISK WHILE PRINTING

With some applications, printing an entire document in standard or high quality on an ImageWriter might require as much as twice the amount of disk space needed to save the document. The extra disk space is used to store an image of every printed page. Other applications prepare and print one page image at a time and therefore require only enough disk space to save the entire document and store the image of the page about to be printed. If not enough disk space is available, a message appears during preparation of the page images advising you that the disk is full.

Draft-quality printing on the ImageWriter does not require extra disk space because the preparation of page images is not necessary for printing. Likewise, printing on the LaserWriter does not require extra disk space because each page image is prepared in the LaserWriter's memory.

If the disk becomes full while printing, try printing a few pages—or even one page—at a time. Alternatively, make more disk space available. The amount of space you need depends on the application doing the printing and on the complexity of the document being printed. MacWrite and

Microsoft Word, for example, need about 6 KB per page for pages that contain only text. With graphics, the sky's the limit.

ImageWriters

IMAGEWRITER AS TYPEWRITER

An ImageWriter can't print one character at a time, as a typewriter can, because its print head cannot stop and start as it moves across the page. Subject to that limitation, the desk accessory TypeNow from Mainstay turns a Mac and ImageWriter into a memory typewriter. It's great for typing envelopes and mailing labels, but because of the printer's insistence on line-by-line printing, TypeNow is harder to use for airbills and other forms that require you to fill in several boxes on a single line. You use the program by typing a line in a window on the Mac screen. TypeNow uses native ImageWriter fonts, not screen fonts such as Geneva or New York. (See the next tip.)

ImageWriters

NATIVE PRINTING

An ImageWriter II or LQ can print several fonts that aren't listed in any Font menu. They are built into the printer, and they include Pica, Elite, Pica Proportional, Elite Proportional, Semicondensed, Condensed, and Ultracondensed. The ImageWriter can print these fonts in three qualities and in a variety of styles. Figure 4-15 shows samples of the built-in fonts.

The ImageWriter normally uses its Pica font only when you select the Print command's Draft option. Various utility software bypasses the normal Print command, however, to give you broader access to the built-in ImageWriter fonts. For example, the desk accessory miniWRITER from Maitreya Design is a text editor that lets you choose among Pica Proportional, Pica, Elite, and Compressed.

You determine the quality of the native font by pressing the ImageWriter II's Print Quality button while the printer's Select light is off. The Print Quality light indicates which quality is selected. If the left half of the light is on, the printer's draft quality is selected (not to be confused with the Draft option of the Print dialog box). If the right half of the light is on, the printer's medium quality is selected. If both halves are on, the printer's best quality is selected.

Here is a supplemental bulletin from the Office of Fluctuation Control, Bureau of Edible Condiments, Soluble and Indigestible Fats and Glutinous Derivatives, Washington, D.C., Correction of Directive 943456201, issued a while back, concerning the fixed price of groundhog meat. In the directive above named, the quotation on groundhog meat should read ground hogmeat. --Bob and Ray

Here is a supplemental bulletin from the Office of Fluctuation Control, Bureau of Edible Condiments, Soluble and Indigestible Fats and Glutinous Derivatives, Washington, D.C., Correction of Directive 943456201, issued a while back, concerning the fixed price of groundhog meat. In the directive above named, the quotation on groundhog meat should read ground hogmeat. --Bob and Ray

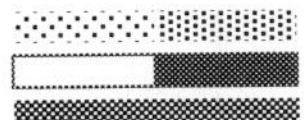

FIGURE 4-15. IMAGEWRITER NATIVES. *(continued)*
The Print Quality lights on an ImageWriter II show which of three print qualities the printer uses when you have selected the Draft quality option by using the Print command.

FIGURE 4-15. *continued*

```
Here is a supplemental bulletin from the
Office of Fluctuation Control, Bureau of
Edible Condiments, Soluble and Indigestible
Fats and Glutinous Derivatives, Washington,
D.C., Correction of Directive 943456201,
issued a while back, concerning the fixed
price of groundhog meat. In the directive
above named, the quotation on groundhog meat
should read ground hogmeat. --Bob and Ray
```

ADJUSTING PRINT QUALITY

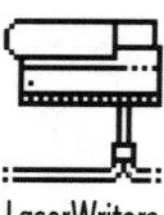

LASERWRITER BLACKS

The grayish blacks from LaserWriters can be turned as black as black should be with a little help from an artist's friend. Large black blocks of graphics, large black lettering, and even smaller lettering can have sharp edges, high contrast, and black blacks.

Go to an art supply store and purchase a can of Blair spray clear matte finish no. 201, Krylon matte finish no. 1311, or the equivalent. Spray it on your LaserWriter output. Be sure to use it in a well-ventilated place—it has a strong odor. Also, don't touch your paper until it is completely dry. (These coatings seem to be toner solvents, and your "ink" will smear if you touch it.) You will be amazed. The treatment improves your print 100 percent.

These coatings also help prevent the toner from chipping off the paper, as it sometimes does. If you saturate the paper with the spray or spray it several times on both sides, you will create a water-resistant page.

BEST DRAFT QUALITY

Why does an ImageWriter leave wide gaps between words when you select the Print command's Draft option? What can you do about it?

The ImageWriter uses its own nonproportional font when you select the Print command's Draft option. To match the word spacing of the Mac's proportional fonts, the printer (actually the ImageWriter driver software) inserts unsightly gaps between the draft-quality words. Figure 4-16 illustrates the effect. You eliminate the gaps by changing the entire document to a fixed-width font, such as Courier 12 or Monaco 12, before printing it in draft quality.

To eliminate the gaps in a Microsoft Works document printed in draft quality, you must also choose Page Setup and deselect the Tall Adjusted option. You have to do this only once for each document. Works selects the Tall Adjusted option for each new document. Most other word processors—including Word, MacWrite, and WriteNow—do the opposite.

```
Computers   are useless.  They  can  only  give  you
answers.   -- Pablo  Picasso
```

```
Computers are useless. They can only give you
answers. -- Pablo Picasso
```

FIGURE 4-16. GAPOSIS.
When you select the Print command's Draft option, the ImageWriter inserts gaps between words (top) unless you use a fixed-width font in the document (bottom).

BEST-QUALITY FONT REQUIREMENTS

When printing in best quality on a LaserWriter IISC, ImageWriter LQ, or ImageWriter I or II, you might need fonts in large sizes. With these printers, system software versions earlier than 7.0 use bit-mapped fonts, which define characters as patterns of dots.

The system software achieves the best resolution with these printers by compressing large fonts by factors of four, three, or two, depending on the printer. The result is more dots per inch. Printing best-quality 24-point text, for example, requires a 96-point font for a LaserWriter IISC, a 72-point font for an ImageWriter LQ, and a 48-point font for an ImageWriter I or II. The table in Figure 4-17 on the page after next shows the system font size needed with the three Apple printers for various printed font sizes.

The large sizes of a font must be installed in the same file as all other sizes of the same font. The Mac will not look in multiple files for a single font. An ImageWriter or LaserWriter IISC can't print in best quality properly unless the Mac can find the necessary large font sizes. If you use a utility such as Suitcase II, Font/DA Juggler, or MasterJuggler to keep some of your fonts in files other than the System file, be sure the System file doesn't contain any sizes of those fonts. New York and other basic fonts can sneak back into the System file when you upgrade or replace system software.

Several companies make fonts in a full range of sizes from 9 through 96 points. SoftFonts from Bitstream are bit-mapped versions of all 35 PostScript fonts—11 font families—that come standard on a LaserWriter IINT. They come in sizes for best-quality printing on the LaserWriter IISC and ImageWriter LQ. You can get a FluentFonts bit-mapped version of Garamond in large sizes from Casady & Greene.

Also, the application FontSizer from U.S. Microlabs can create large bit-mapped fonts from PostScript fonts. FontSizer uses the PostScript processor in a LaserWriter to generate the bit-mapped images. The application is meant to be used to create supplemental screen fonts that eliminate ugly scaled fonts and to enable precise kerning and spacing of headlines and other display type in any font size on the screen. Using it to create bit-mapped fonts for use in another printer might violate the font publisher's license agreement, however. Single-user license agreements typically restrict the use of the font to one printer (the PostScript LaserWriter that created the bit map, in this case).

ImageWriter II

FASTER FASTER, BEST BEST

When you select the Print command's Faster option, the bidirectional printing capability of the ImageWriter II is normally suppressed to improve quality. You can sacrifice some quality for bidirectional speed by pressing the Caps Lock, Shift, and Option keys while you click the OK button in the Print dialog box. Some ImageWriter IIs are adjusted well enough for satisfactory bidirectional faster-quality printing. Bidirectional printing stays in effect until you change startup disks, restart, or press the Command key while clicking the OK button in the Print dialog box. Other ImageWriter models continue to print bidirectionally when you select the Best option. Suppressing bidirectional printing would not improve the quality; it would only slow down printing.

Printed Font Sizes			
LaserWriter IISC Personal LaserWriter SC	**ImageWriter LQ**	**ImageWriter I and II**	**Font Size Needed**
(4:1)	**(3:1)**	**(2:1)**	
	6	**9**	18
5		**10**	20
6	8	**12**	24
7		**14**	28
	9		27
	10	15	30
9	**12**	**18**	36
10		20	40
	14	21	42
	15		45
12	16	**24**	48
	18	27	54
14		28	56
15	20	30	60
18	**24**	36	72
24	32	48	96

FIGURE 4-17. FONT REDUCTION.
This table shows which size of a bit-mapped font must be installed to print a particular font size in best quality on any of three Apple printers. The most commonly used sizes appear in boldface print. Fractional sizes are omitted.

BETTER BIT MAPS

Bit-mapped graphics (also called paint graphics) don't always look their best when printed on a LaserWriter. They're created by HyperCard and by paint-style graphics applications, such as MacPaint, at 72 dots per inch. Those dots are 4.1666667 times larger than the dots a LaserWriter uses to print the bit-mapped graphics at 300 dots per inch. Because that ratio is not a whole number, bit-mapped graphics can look lumpy on a LaserWriter. However, reducing the printed image by 4 percent makes the screen dots exactly 4 times larger than LaserWriter dots and eliminates the lumps. Figure 4-18 on the following page shows the difference a 4 percent reduction can make.

So when using a LaserWriter to print any document that includes bit-mapped graphics, choose Page Setup from the File menu, click the Options button, and set the Precision Bitmap Alignment option. Alternatively, you can enter *96* as the Reduce or Enlarge option of the Page Setup command.

Instead of reducing the whole document, you might be able to reduce only the bit-mapped graphics. You can reduce a graphic pasted into Microsoft Word, for example, by pressing the Shift key and dragging the handle in the lower right corner of the graphic. The percentage of reduction is reported in the lower left corner of the document window as you drag.

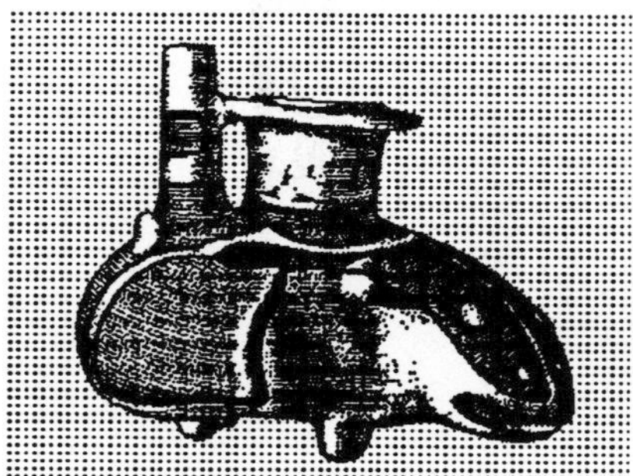

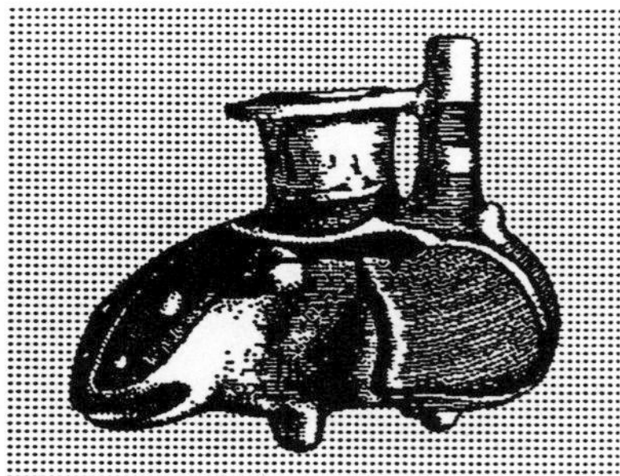

FIGURE 4-18. FOUR PERCENT SOLUTION.
More patterns and lumps might appear in bit-mapped graphics printed on a LaserWriter (left) unless you reduce them by 4 percent (right).

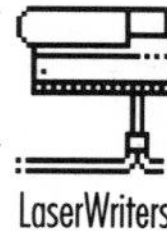

BEST BIT MAPS

Reducing bit-mapped graphics by one-fourth, one-half, or three-fourths makes them progressively sharper when printed on a LaserWriter. At these greater reductions, none of the dots that make up the bit-mapped graphics are lost. The dots are merely condensed into a smaller area. For example, a reduction by one-half effectively increases the resolution of bit-mapped graphics from 72 dots per inch to 144 dots per inch. The more dots per inch, the finer the detail of the printed image. Figure 4-19 shows the kind of improvement you can get.

To reduce an entire document by one-fourth, one-half, or three-fourths, enter *75*, *50*, or *25* as the Reduce or Enlarge option of the Page Setup command. Be sure to set the Precision Bitmap Alignment option as well. (Click

the Options button in the Page Setup dialog box to display this option.) If you don't set Precision Bitmap Alignment, then enter *72*, *48*, or *24* as the Reduce or Enlarge option.

Use the same percentages if you reduce only the bit-mapped graphics in a document and not the whole document. Reduce the graphics to 75, 50, or 25 percent if you set the Precision Bitmap Alignment option or to 72, 48, or 24 percent if you don't set that option.

FIGURE 4-19. REDUCED BIT MAPS.
Get sharper bit-mapped graphics on a LaserWriter by reducing them to 75 percent (left), 50 percent (middle), or 25 percent (right) with the Precision Bitmap Alignment option set.

PAINT TEXT

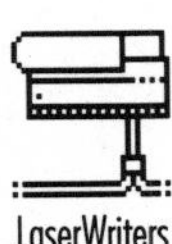

Why does text printed by a paint-style graphics application such as MacPaint look different from text in the same font and size printed by a word processor?

MacPaint can't tell the difference between text and a taco. Text created with the Text tool in paint-style graphics applications or with HyperCard becomes part of the bit-mapped graphic—simply a pattern of dots. In that form, a printer can't apply its techniques for improving text resolution. A LaserWriter can't use PostScript fonts. An ImageWriter, printing in best quality, can't use large-size fonts (as described in the tip "Best-Quality Font Requirements," earlier in this chapter). Figure 4-20, on the following page, shows the difference between paint text and true text printed on a LaserWriter.

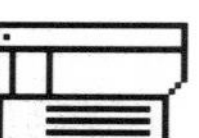

He can compress the most words into the smallest idea of any man I ever met. —Abraham Lincoln	He can compress the most words into the smallest idea of any man I ever met. —*Abraham Lincoln*

FIGURE 4-20. GRAPHIC OR TEXT.
Text printed by a paint-style graphics application such as MacPaint (left) looks different from text in the same font and size printed by a word processing application (right).

ImageWriters

PATTERN QUALITY

An ImageWriter I has trouble evenly printing certain patterns—especially the standard gray desktop pattern. An ImageWriter II or LQ has less trouble printing evenly.

A number of factors contribute to the problem, including the type of paper you use, the method of paper feed, and the alignment of the print head. If you are having problems, see if any of the following suggestions help: Try a heavy paper with a rough finish. Move the pin-feed sprockets off to the side and try pin-feed paper with the paper-feed lever in the friction-feed position. Or try a combination: Feed pin-feed paper through the sprockets, and put the paper-feed lever in the friction-feed position. But print only two or three pages at a time this way because the friction-feed and pin-feed mechanisms get out of sync after about three pages, and the paper might wrinkle.

Unfortunately, there's little you can do about print-head alignment. Sometimes removing and reinstalling the printhead helps; the procedure for doing this for the ImageWriter I is described on page 28 of the ImageWriter user's manual.

ImageWriters

PICTURE PROPORTIONS

What can you do about MacPaint pictures and other bit-mapped graphics that seem elongated when printed as part of other types of documents on an ImageWriter?

You can print correctly proportioned bit-mapped images on an ImageWriter by selecting the Tall Adjusted option of the Page Setup command (in the File menu). With that option off, an ImageWriter prints 80 dots per inch. With the Tall Adjusted option on, printing matches the screen's 72 dots per inch. The Tall Adjusted option also affects the layout of text lines. (See the tip "Line Layout Differences," earlier in this chapter.) Figure 4-21 compares a sample printed with the Tall Adjusted option off to one printed with the option on. The Tall Adjusted option is not available with the Orientation option set for sideways printing. Sideways printing on an ImageWriter always matches the screen resolution, as if Tall Adjusted were selected.

Traffic signals in
New York are just
rough guidelines.
David Letterman

Traffic signals in
New York are just
rough guidelines.
David Letterman

FIGURE 4-21. EL GRECO.
An ImageWriter prints elongated bit-mapped graphics (top) unless you select the Page Setup command's Tall Adjusted option (bottom).

FAINT GRAPHICS

ImageWriters

Once upon a time, bit-mapped graphics created with MacPaint or another paint-type graphics application looked gray when pasted into a word processor document and then printed on an ImageWriter. This complaint vanishes if you use ImageWriter software version 2.3 or later. The version number appears in small type in the dialog boxes you see when you choose Print or Page Setup from most File menus. The ImageWriter software is part of the Macintosh system software, which you can get from an Apple dealer or a user group.

ImageWriters

IMAGEWRITER RAINBOWS

An ImageWriter II with an out-of-alignment multicolor ribbon prints rainbows where it should print solid colors. For example, an underscore might appear in a different color from the text directly above it. This condition might be caused by a loose ribbon cartridge. To check, press down firmly on the ribbon cartridge. If you hear the cartridge click into place, turn the printer off and on, and try printing again.

If the ribbon cartridge is secure and the problem remains, the ribbon and print head might be misaligned. Remove the ImageWriter's front cover, and look for a knob and a red adjusting ring to the right of the ribbon cartridge, as shown in Figure 4-22. Note the position of the marks on the knob, in case you want to revert to the standard setting. Push the red ring down to unlock it. If the wrong color appears at the bottom of a character, turn the ring clockwise. If the wrong color appears at the top of a character, turn the ring counter-clockwise. Never turn the ring more than 180 degrees in either direction. When you release the ring, it snaps back into place. Replace the front cover. Check the adjustment by performing a printer self-test. (Hold down the Form Feed button as you switch on the printer.)

Some ImageWriter IIs don't have a knob for adjusting the ribbon. And with some ribbons, the adjusting knob can't make adequate adjustment. The solution is to make a shim of masking tape or tiny self-adhesive labels.

Build the shim by layering tape or labels on the underside of the ribbon cartridge in a solid, flat area so that it will lie against a flat part of the ribbon deck. Figure 4-23 illustrates this technique. Don't let the shim touch holes, depressions, or protrusions. If the print head is hitting too low on the ribbon—for example, yellow text is red at the bottom—apply the shim to the end of the ribbon cartridge nearest the front of the printer. If the print head is hitting too high on the ribbon—red text is yellow at the top, for example—apply the shim to the end of the cartridge nearest the print head.

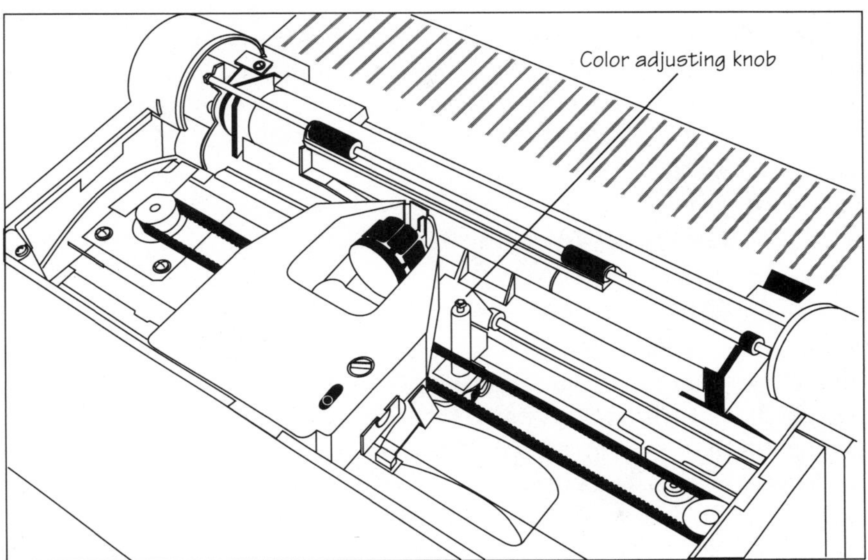

FIGURE 4-22. COLOR ADJUSTING KNOB.
If your ImageWriter II prints two colors where there should be one, you might be able to fix it by adjusting the ring around this knob. (Older ImageWriters have a lock nut and knurled shaft instead of an adjusting knob.)

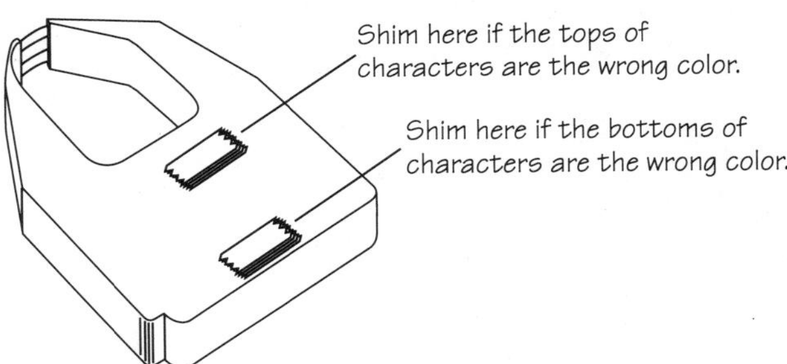

FIGURE 4-23. SHIM FOR A COLOR RIBBON.
Another remedy for problems with a color ribbon is to make a shim of tape or labels applied to the underside of the ribbon cartridge.

Test your shim by using the printer's self-test feature. Adjust the thickness of the shim by adding or removing layers of masking tape or tiny labels to get the best results. Don't make the shim so thick that you can't snap the cartridge into place easily, however. I used 22 labels (about 3⁄16 inch thick overall) to correct one of my ribbons, and it still snapped into place easily. If you have to make the shim so thick that the cartridge won't snap into place, give up and get another ribbon.

NO CURE FOR NO-GAPS GLITCH

When you print without gaps between pages on an ImageWriter, a slight imperfection might appear about ½ inch below the top of some pages. This glitch occurs if pin-feed paper buckles slightly as the perforation rolls through the pressure rollers. The design of the ImageWriter's paper-feed mechanism causes the problem, so there's not much you can do about it except try different weights and kinds of paper or use single sheets of paper. (See the tip "Compressed Line at Top of Page," in Chapter 5, "Troubleshooting," for more about this problem.)

MAINTAINING PRINTERS

SQUEAKY IMAGEWRITER

The ImageWriter I user's manual suggests lubricating the shaft on which the head mechanism travels with a light machine oil once a year. However, it cautions that you should not use electric-motor oil or any lubricant that contains rust inhibitors. The problem is that it's almost impossible to find a machine oil without rust inhibitors. Apple recommends sewing-machine oil—even if it contains a rust inhibitor—for lubricating the ImageWriter I.

The ImageWriter II and ImageWriter LQ do not require lubrication.

HEAD BREAKDOWN

If you print large pictures containing many solid black areas, the print head of an ImageWriter I might overheat and fail, requiring a new head. To avoid this expense, design your pages so that they are no more than 25 to 30 percent solid black. Allowing the head to cool off between pages also helps prevent overheating. Incidentally, the ImageWriter II and LQ have built-in protection against overheating in the print head.

UNEVEN PRINTING

If a LaserWriter prints darker or lighter on one part of every page, the toner might be distributed unevenly. Remove the toner cartridge, and rock it gently to redistribute the toner. Figure 4-24 shows the correct motion.

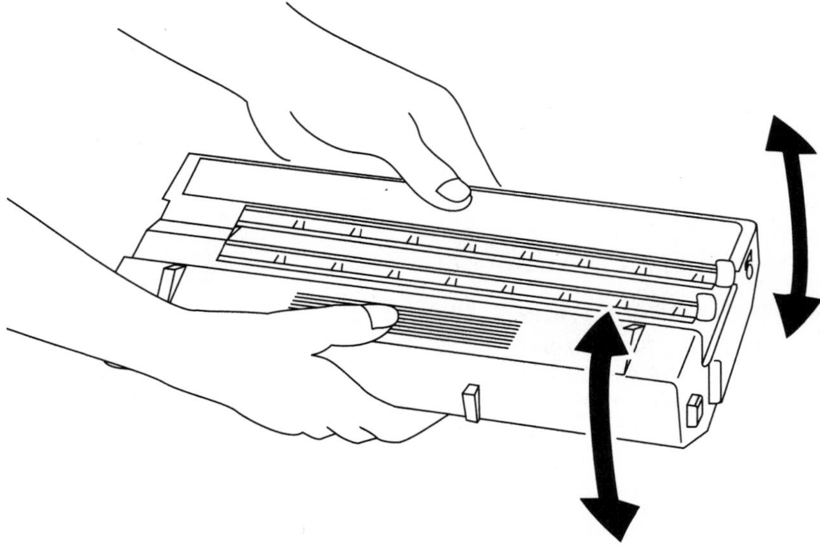

FIGURE 4-24. ROCK AND ROLL.
If a LaserWriter prints unevenly, rock its toner cartridge to redistribute the toner.

TONER CARTRIDGE LIFE

LaserWriter toner cartridges have a shelf life of 2½ years from the date of production. A coded form of the production date is stamped on Apple-brand cartridges. Figure 4-25 shows how to decode the date.

A	January	G	July
B	February	H	August
C	March	I	September
D	April	J	October
E	May	K	November
F	June	L	December

FIGURE 4-25. CARTRIDGE BIRTHDAY.

You can decipher the code on a LaserWriter toner cartridge to determine its production date. The cartridge will be good for 2½ years after that date.

Chapter 5

TROUBLESHOOTING

When something goes wrong with the Macintosh, it displays a message or exhibits more overt symptoms. This chapter contains tips for diagnosing and, where possible, dealing with the following:

- Error messages
- Startup trouble
- Keyboard or mouse trouble
- Disk trouble
- Printer trouble
- Other trouble

ERROR MESSAGES

SYSTEM ERROR DIAGNOSIS

The message "Sorry, a system error occurred" tells you the Mac has gone out of control and has quit working; it has crashed. (See Figure 5-1.) In most cases, all you can do is restart the computer. (However, see the next tip.) The ID number reported with a system error message has little practical meaning unless you are a programmer and know the context in which the error message appeared. See the table in Figure 5-2 on the following page for possible enlightenment.

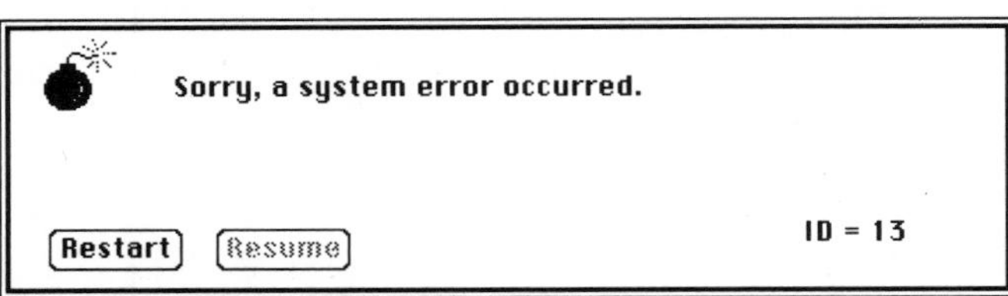

FIGURE 5-1. BOMB.
The dreaded system error message often means you must restart your Mac.

ID	Definition	Likely Cause
01	Bus error	Macintosh malfunction
02	Address error	Application error or software incompatibility
03	Illegal instruction	Application error or software incompatibility
04	Divide by zero	Application error
05	Check exception	Application error
06	TrapV exception	Application error or software incompatibility
07	Privilege violation	Application error or software incompatibility
08	Trace exception	Trouble occurred with programming tools or an unusual hardware accessory
09	Line 1010 exception	Application error
10	Line 1111 exception	Application error
11	Miscellaneous exception	Application error or software incompatibility
12	Unimplemented core routine	Application error or software incompatibility
13	Spurious interrupt	Interrupt part of programmer's switch was pressed, or trouble occurred with programming tools or an unusual hardware accessory
14	I/O system error	Trouble occurred with programming tools or an unusual hardware accessory
15	Segment loader error	The System file is probably corrupted
16	Floating-point error	The System file is probably corrupted
17–24	Can't load package	The System file is probably corrupted
25	Memory full	The application suddenly ran out of memory
26	Segment loader error	Trouble opening an application, or the System file is corrupted
27	File map destroyed	The System file is probably corrupted
28	Stack overflow error	The application suddenly ran out of memory
29	AppleShare error	Problem with AppleShare file server

FIGURE 5-2. SYSTEM ERROR ID.
When a Mac gets out of control, it usually stops working and reports one of these error codes.

Here are some common causes of system error messages and their cures:

Application software error: Restart and check for damage to your document. If the problem persists, try to avoid the sequence of events that causes the problem. Call the software publisher for help.

Software damaged: Replace the System file, the Finder, and the program.

Printing trouble: Try printing smaller sections by specifying page ranges in the Print dialog box.

Hard disk switched off: Switch it on and restart the Mac.

Hard-disk cable disconnected: Switch all power off and reconnect the cable.

Disk damaged: Restart with another disk. Repair or replace the broken disk.

Although you can't do much about system errors and you can't do much to prevent them, you can do something to minimize their impact: Save often. Don't wait until the end of a session to save. Whenever you pause to think about what to do next, use the Save command. You can do this from the keyboard in many applications by pressing Command-S.

SYSTEM ERROR RECOVERY

The System Error dialog box always has a Resume button, but the button is rarely enabled. Instead of clicking the Restart button, try pressing the Interrupt part of the programmer's switch (not the Reset part). With luck, you'll get a dialog box containing a greater-than symbol (>) in the upper left corner. (See Figure 5-3.) Typing *G FINDER* and pressing Return might

```
>G FINDER
```

FIGURE 5-3. BOMB DISPOSAL.
Sometimes you can recover from a system error by pressing the Interrupt switch, typing this command, and pressing Return.

take you back to the Finder without restarting. If you were using MultiFinder, you can then save all your open documents and restart properly by using the Finder's Restart command.

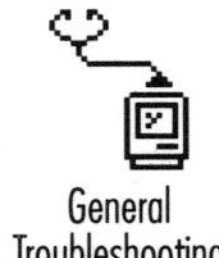

TOO LITTLE MEMORY

Applications might notify you from time to time that they're out of memory. Figure 5-4 shows a typical message. If you're using MultiFinder, quit the application and use the Finder's Get Info command (on the File menu) to increase the application memory size. If you don't want to increase the memory size or aren't using MultiFinder, consider the following problems and cures:

Too many windows open: Close desk accessories. If the application allows you to open more than one document at once, close some.

Document too large or complex: With applications that keep the entire document you're working on in memory, such as MacDraw, MacProject, ThinkTank, and most spreadsheet programs, split the document by cutting and pasting several pages of it to new documents.

Large Clipboard: Select one letter or a similar small object, choose Copy from the Edit menu, and then choose Copy again.

Memory cluttered: Save the document you're working on. Quit, reopen the application, and reopen the document.

Memory fragmented (with MultiFinder active): Quit all open applications, including DAs (the desk accessory layer), and then open the applications you want.

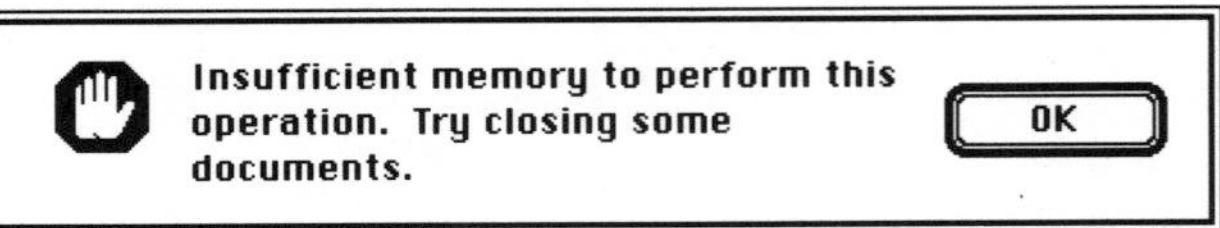

FIGURE 5-4. MEMORY SHORTAGE.
A message such as this means the application has run out of memory.

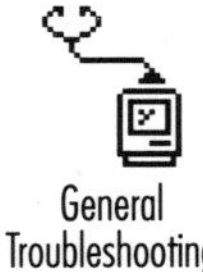

OTHER ALERT WITH ERROR CODE

Applications display many different messages and warnings, most of which are self-explanatory. Occasionally, however, you might create a situation that the software author did not anticipate. Write down the message and

the circumstances that led up to its appearance. Contact the software publisher to see whether it's a known problem with a cure. See Figure 5-5 for some possibilities.

ID	Meaning
Input/output device errors	
−17	Can't perform requested control procedure
−18	Can't perform requested status procedure
−19	Can't read
−20	Can't write
−21	Device or driver unknown (reference number doesn't match unit table)
−22	Device or driver unknown (reference number specifies NIL handle in unit table)
−23	Driver not opened for requested read or write; attempt to open RAM serial driver failed
−25	Attempt to remove open drive
−26	Driver resource missing
−27	Input or output request aborted, or error while aborting print operation
−28	Driver not open
File errors	
−33	Directory full
−34	Disk full (all allocation blocks on volume full)
−35	No such volume
−36	I/O error
−37	Bad name (perhaps zero length)
−38	File not open
−39	End of file reached while reading
−40	Attempt to position before start of file
−42	Too many files open
−43	File not found
−44	Volume physically locked
−45	File locked
−46	Volume locked by software flag
−47	File busy; attempt to delete open file(s)
−48	Duplicate filename

FIGURE 5-5. MISCELLANEOUS ERROR IDS. *(continued)*

If a message appears citing one of these error codes, you did something that surprised the application software. Inform the application publisher.

FIGURE 5-5. *continued*

ID	Meaning
File errors, *continued*	
–49	File already open for writing; multiple paths for writing not allowed
–50	Error in file specification; parameters don't specify existing volume, and no default volume; bad disk-drive positioning information; bad disk-drive number
–51	Attempt to use nonexistent access path
–52	Error getting file position
–53	Disk ejected or volume offline
–54	Attempt to open locked file for writing
–55	Volume already mounted and online
–56	No such drive
–57	Not Macintosh disk; volume lacks directory in Macintosh format
–58	External file system; file-system identifier is nonzero, or path reference number is greater than 1024
–59	Problem during renaming
–60	Bad block on master directory; must reinitialize volume
–61	Writing not allowed
Disk errors	
–64	Drive disconnected
–65	No disk inserted
–66	Disk seems blank
–67	Can't find address mark
–68	Verification of read failed
–69	Bad address mark
–70	Bad address mark
–71	Missing data mark
–72	Bad data mark
–73	Bad data mark
–74	Write underrun occurred
–75	Drive error
–76	Can't find track 0
–77	Can't initialize disk controller chip
–78	Tried to read side 2 of disk in single-sided disk drive
–79	Can't correctly adjust disk speed
–80	Drive error
–81	Can't find sector

(continued)

FIGURE 5-5. *continued*

ID	Meaning
Clock-chip errors	
−85	Can't read clock
−86	Verification of time change failed
−87	Verification of parameter RAM failed
−88	Validity status not $A8
AppleTalk errors	
−91	Socket already active; socket not known; no room for more sockets
−92	Data-size error
−93	Bridge between two AppleTalk networks missing
−94	Protocol error
−95	Can't get clear signal to send
−97	Can't open driver because port already in use
−98	Can't open driver because port not configured for this connection
Scrap errors	
−100	Desk scrap (Clipboard) not initialized
−102	Scrap doesn't contain data of type requested
Memory errors	
−108	Not enough room in heap zone
−109	NIL master pointer
−111	Attempt to use free block
−112	Attempt to purge locked block
−117	Block is locked
Resource errors	
−192	Resource not found
−193	Resource file not found
−194	Unable to add resource
−195	Unable to remove resource
More AppleTalk errors	
−1024	Buffer overflow (Name-Binding Protocol—NBP)
−1025	Name not confirmed (NBP)
−1026	Name confirmed for different socket (NBP)

(continued)

FIGURE 5-5. *continued*

ID	Meaning
More AppleTalk errors, *continued*	
−1027	Duplicate name (NBP)
−1028	Name not found (NBP)
−1029	Names information socket error (NBP)
−1096	Send request failed (AppleTalk-Transaction Protocol—ATP)
−1097	Too many concurrent requests (ATP)
−1098	Too many responding sockets (ATP)
−1099	Bad responding socket (ATP)
−1100	Bad sequence number (ATP)
−1101	No release received (ATP)
−1102	Control block not found (ATP)
−1103	Additional response packet sent before first response packet (ATP)
−1104	Too many outstanding calls (ATP)
−1105	Request aborted
−3101	Too much data for buffer
−3102	MPP driver not installed
−3103	Bad checksum (Datagram-Delivery Protocol—DDP)
−3104	Can't find name-address pair in buffer (NBP)
−3105	Socket or protocol type invalid or not in table
−3106	Response message too large (ATP)
−3107	Bad response from ATPRequest function
−3108	AB Record not found
−3109	Asynchronous call aborted because socket closed before call completed

STARTUP TROUBLE

All Macs

SCREEN DARK, NO BEEP OR CHIME

A display screen that stays completely black when you try to start up your Mac suggests a power problem. Check all power switches, cords, and circuit breakers or fuses. Pay particular attention to devices that you don't normally turn off. Someone else might have turned them off, or you might have done it yourself unthinkingly.

Try switching on all SCSI devices, especially if you have an old Mac Plus. (See the tip "Startup Hangup," at the end of this section of the chapter.)

MAC CLICKS OR CHIRPS

Mac Plus or 512K

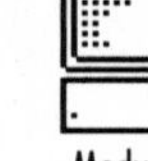

Modular Macs

A Mac Plus or 512K that clicks or chirps when you switch it on has a power-supply problem. Its voltage levels might need adjusting, or its flyback transformer might need replacing.

When a Mac with internal expansion cards clicks and won't start up, one or more cards is drawing too much power. The power supply is designed to handle one internal hard disk with all expansion slots filled. However, some expansion cards use more electrical current than allowed by Apple specifications. Switch off the Mac and remove one of the expansion cards.

DISK DRIVE DOESN'T OPERATE

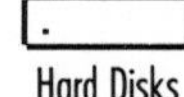

Hard Disks

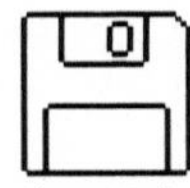

Floppy Disks

You start up the Mac and see a flashing question mark in a disk icon at the center of the screen, and there's no sign of disk activity. The following are likely causes and their remedies:

No startup inserted: Insert a startup disk (or turn on your hard disk).

Command key pressed: Wait until disk activity begins before pressing the Command key to bypass startup documents (INITs) or to bypass Multi-Finder.

Some SCSI devices switched off: Switch them on and restart. Also see the tip "Multiple SCSI Devices," later in this chapter.

Bad cable connection: Turn off the power and check all cables for tightness. Then restart the Mac.

Disk damaged: If you can start up from another disk, repair or replace the damaged disk.

Mac broken: If you can't start up from any drive, have the Mac repaired.

CAN'T START FROM HARD DISK

Hard Disks

Startup proceeds normally. You see a smiling Mac icon and hear hard-disk activity. Suddenly the disk activity stops and a flashing question mark appears in a disk icon. Check the following causes and cures:

Hard disk not ready: Turn on the hard disk, wait a minute or so, and try restarting the Mac. If you have more than one SCSI device connected, try turning them all on. (Also see the tip "Multiple SCSI Devices," later in this chapter.)

Hard-disk cable loose: Turn off all power switches, check cable tightness, turn on the power, and try again. With an internal hard disk, have the internal connections checked.

System file missing or damaged: Try restarting with a different disk. If that's successful, replace the System file on the problem disk.

Normal with some old hard disks: You might have to start up with a special floppy disk.

Hard disk needs reformatting: Start up with a floppy disk and reformat according to the instructions in the hard-disk manual.

Hard disk broken: If all else fails, have the hard disk repaired. Some Apple 40-MB and 80-MB hard disks sold in 1989 develop a problem when starting up. An Apple dealer will repair such a drive free through the end of 1991.

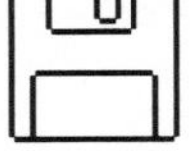
Floppy Disks

PROBLEMS WITH STARTUP FLOPPY DISKS

If the Mac ejects a floppy disk before startup is complete or if a flashing X is displayed on the disk icon at the center of the screen during startup, the disk is not a startup disk or is damaged. Insert a startup disk. (A startup disk contains the System file and Finder in the same folder.) If the Mac rejects all disks, check the causes and cures listed in the tip "Disk Drive Doesn't Operate," earlier in this chapter.

0F0003

SAD MAC ICON

A black screen with a sad-looking Mac icon in the center tells you that the Mac has failed its startup tests. Sometimes a System file that has gone bad is the culprit. Try restarting with a different disk. If all disks fail, have the Mac repaired.

System Error

STARTUP SYSTEM ERROR

When a system error occurs during startup, suspect a bad System file. Try restarting with a different disk. If that's successful, replace the System file on the problem disk.

Incompatible startup documents (INITs) in the System Folder can also cause a system error during startup. Start up with a different disk and experiment with different combinations of startup documents.

CAN'T LOAD FINDER

System Error

The message "Can't load the Finder" appearing during startup means that the Finder is damaged on the startup disk. Start up with a disk that contains a good Finder, and then copy the Finder to the problem disk.

MULTIPLE SCSI DEVICES

All Macs

In theory, you should be able to start up a Mac that has multiple SCSI devices connected even if some SCSI devices are off. Switching off devices you're not using saves wear and tear on them. In practice, however, you might find that all SCSI devices must be on.

It might be possible to solve startup problems with multiple SCSI devices by changing their cabling and termination. Try standard termination first: Terminate the first device in the chain. If the Mac has an internal hard-disk drive, that drive is the first device in the chain and has built-in termination. Also terminate the last device in the chain. Do not terminate devices between the first and last. Be aware that many external hard-disk drives—but not Apple-brand drives—have built-in termination that you should remove if the drive is not the first or last SCSI device connected to the Mac. For specific instructions on terminating or removing termination from a SCSI device, see the owner's manual for the device.

If standard termination doesn't solve startup problems, try using shorter or longer cables, or change the order of the devices in the SCSI chain. However, some SCSI devices, especially ones made in 1986 or early 1987, simply have to be on; otherwise, none of the other devices in the SCSI chain will work.

By the way, be sure you switch off all SCSI devices—including the Mac—before connecting or disconnecting any SCSI cables or terminators. Otherwise, you will probably damage the SCSI electronics in the Mac and the SCSI peripheral devices. The damage won't result in immediate failure, but it will add up to a costly repair bill in the future.

STARTUP HANGUP

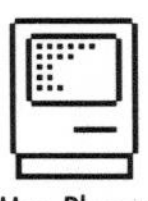

Mac Plus or 512K

An error in the ROM of early Mac Pluses causes them to hang at startup unless all SCSI devices are switched on. Apple fixed the error and installed a corrected ROM in all Mac Plus computers built after the last week of November 1985.

You can determine the age of a Mac Plus, and hence the version of the ROM originally installed in it, by inspecting the serial number. A Mac Plus with a serial number that begins F609 or lower was built with the original ROM. The Mac Plus serial number starts with a letter that identifies the factory where it was made; either F for Fremont, California, or C for Cork, Ireland. The next digit corresponds to the last calendar year of the fiscal year of manufacture, such as 6 for fiscal year 1986. (Apple's fiscal year begins October 1.) The next two digits specify in which week of the fiscal year the Mac Plus was made. The next three characters are the serial number. The rest, starting with the letter M, is the model number. The serial-number test is not infallible because the ROM might have been replaced.

For the final word on the ROM version, you can check the ROM signature by using the programmer's switch. (This is a plastic accessory that comes with the Mac Plus and that you install on the left side of the machine near the lower rear corner.) With the Mac Plus switched on, press the rearmost half of the programmer's switch—the part labeled Interrupt. Be careful not to press the frontmost part—labeled Reset—or you'll restart the Mac. Pressing the Interrupt switch brings up a dialog box containing a greater-than symbol (>) in the upper left corner. Type *DM 400000* and press Return. If the third pair of characters that appears is EE, as shown in Figure 5-6, you have an original ROM. If the third pair of characters is EA or anything else, you have a revised ROM. To return the Mac to what it was doing before you pressed the Interrupt switch, type *G* and press Return.

```
>
400000   4D1E  EEE1  0040  002A  0075  6000  0056  6000
400010   0750  6000  0044  6000  0016  0001  76F8  4EFA
400020   2BFC  0000  0000  0000  0000  6000  0016  1080
400030   4DFA  0006  6000  0D40  6600  00FC  538F  200F
400040   66EE  4CF9  0101  00F8  0000  0C80  55AA  AA55
400050   6610  43FA  000E  4ED0  4CB9  0007  00F0  0000
```

FIGURE 5-6. ROM AGE

The original Mac Plus ROM won't let the computer start up unless all SCSI devices are switched on. You can check the ROM vintage by pressing the Interrupt half of the programmer's switch and typing the command DM 400000. *If the Mac's response has EE in the beginning of the third column, as shown here, it has the original ROM.*

KEYBOARD OR MOUSE TROUBLE

KEYBOARD OR MOUSE DIES

Keyboard

Mouse

The next time your keyboard and mouse "go dead," try pressing the Interrupt part of the programmer's switch (not the Reset part). With luck, you'll get a dialog box containing a greater-than symbol (>) in the upper left corner. Typing *G FINDER* and pressing Return should take you back to the Finder without restarting. If you were using MultiFinder, you can then save all your open documents and restart properly by using the Finder's Restart command.

Instead of going to the Finder, you can restart the Mac with the built-in ShutDown Manager. It properly unmounts your volumes so that restarting doesn't take extra time to reconstruct the volume directories. To do this, press the Interrupt part of the programmer's switch and, in the empty dialog box, type *SM 0 3F3C 0002 A895* and press Return. Then type *G 0* (zero) and press Return.

KEYBOARD DEAD

Keyboard

If nothing appears on the screen when you type, check for the following conditions:

No typing expected: Use the mouse.

Program crashed: Restart the Mac.

Cable loose: Ensure that the cable is securely inserted into the Mac and the keyboard.

Keyboard or cable broken: Repair or replace the keyboard or the cable.

Mac broken: Have the Mac repaired.

KEYBOARD ERRATIC

Keyboard

When one or more keys don't work or all keys generate the wrong characters, investigate the following possibilities:

Debris inside keyboard: Repeatedly tap faulty keys to dislodge debris. Open the keyboard case, vacuum out or blow out dust and debris, and reassemble the keyboard.

Key broken: Work around the broken key by copying and pasting from the Key Caps desk accessory. (See the tip "Working Around a Broken Key," in Chapter 2, "Essential System Components.") Have the keyboard repaired.

Inadvertent switch to old system software: The Mac switched System Folders. (See the tip "System Folder Switching," in Chapter 3, "Disks and Disk Drives.") Drag the Finder out of the current System folder and restart the Mac. Update that disk or remove its System Folder.

Mouse

MOUSE DOESN'T MOVE POINTER

A pointer that doesn't move when you move the mouse might be the result of one of the following situations:

Program crashed: Restart the Mac.

Mouse cable loose: Plug the mouse cable firmly into the Mac or the keyboard. (You can't plug the mouse cable into the keyboard of a Mac Plus or 512K.)

ADB port broken: If the mouse is plugged into the keyboard, try plugging it into the Mac. Have the keyboard's mouse port repaired. (See the tip "ADB Mating Cycles," in Chapter 2, "Essential System Components.")

Mouse broken: Repair or replace the mouse.

Mac broken: Have the Mac repaired.

Mouse

MOUSE POINTER MOVES ERRATICALLY

Uneven pointer movement occurs for the following reasons:

Mac busy: Jerky pointer movement is normal during disk access. Background tasks such as print spooling might also make the pointer unsteady. The pointer might also hesitate on a Mac whose disk is being shared on a network.

Mouse dirty: Remove the mouse ball, clean it and the metal rollers inside the mouse, and reassemble the mouse.

Mouse rolling on an uneven surface: Provide a flat, smooth surface.

Mouse feet worn off: Install replacement mouse feet. (See the tip "Worn-Out Mouse Feet," in Chapter 2, "Essential System Components.") Alternatively, replace the mouse.

Optical mouse not aligned: Align the mouse squarely with its pad.

DOUBLE-CLICKING IS UNRELIABLE

Mouse

When you find yourself triple-clicking, quadruple-clicking, or pounding the mouse button frequently, you know the mouse button is worn out. Replace the mouse-button switch or replace the whole mouse. (See the tip "Fixing a Broken Mouse Button," in Chapter 2, "Essential System Components.")

DISK TROUBLE

HARD DISK SLUGGISH

A hard-disk drive that seems slower than when it was new might have too many fragmented files. A fragmented file is saved in pieces all over the disk instead of whole, in one space. The disk drive can access a whole file faster than it can a fragmented file.

Fragmentation occurs inevitably over time as you remove files, add new files, or change file sizes. The only way to prevent it is never to delete or change anything. The prevention is worse than the disease.

You can cure fragmentation, however, by using a utility application such as Disk Express or the SUM Tuneup feature of the Symantec Utilities for Macintosh (SUM).

CAN'T OPEN A DOCUMENT

Hard Disks

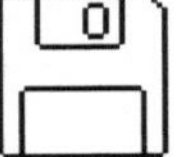
Floppy Disks

An application, including the Finder, might refuse to open a document for any of the following reasons:

Application unknown: Open the application icon instead of the document icon, and then use the Open command in the application's File menu. Sometimes the Finder can't tell which application to use with a document.

Finder can't open document directly: Open the application icon instead of the document icon, and then use the Open command in the application's File menu. Some applications don't cooperate with the Finder.

Too many files open: Close some documents or, if you're using MultiFinder, some applications. Remove unneeded disk icons from the desktop.

Disk damaged: Make a copy of the disk and try to open the document from the copy. (See the tip "Text Files Damaged," later in this chapter.)

Disk too cold: Leave the disk partially inserted or lying on top of your Mac until it warms up.

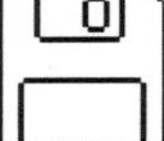

CAN'T SAVE A DOCUMENT

If you can't save a document, check for the following conditions:

File locked: Use the Save As command to save it under a different name.

Disk locked: Slide the disk-locking tab so that no hole shows in the corner of the disk. Alternatively, save on another disk.

Disk full or nearly full: Save on another disk for now. Later, reorganize disks.

Disk, drive, or cable not functioning: See the tip "Not a Macintosh Disk," below.

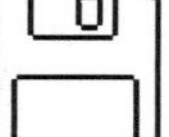

FOLDERS OR FILES MISSING

If you open a disk icon and discover that it seems to have lost all its folders, the startup disk has an old version of the system software. Restart the Mac using a startup disk with the current version. One of your application disks might have an old version of the System file and Finder. Replace them with current versions.

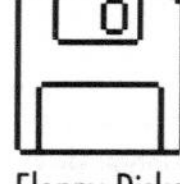

CAN'T EJECT DISK

If the Mac crashes with a floppy disk inserted, you can eject the disk by holding down the mouse button while you restart. As a last resort, push a straightened paper clip into the small hole near the disk-insertion slot. On a Mac II, IIfx, or Mac IIx, be sure the top cover is down all the way.

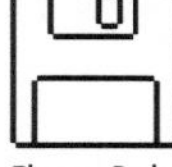

NOT A MACINTOSH DISK

The message "This is not a Macintosh Disk: Do you want to initialize it?" can appear by mistake. Click the Eject button unless you're sure you want to completely erase the disk's contents. Investigate the following possibilities:

High-density disk in an 800-KB drive: Use 1.4-MB disks only in a FDHD Super-Drive, the Drive 2.4 from Kennect, or an equivalent.

High-density disk initialized as an 800-KB disk: Cover the hole opposite the write-protect tab with tape and insert the disk again. Alternatively, insert

the disk into an 800-KB drive and copy it to an 800-KB disk. An FDHD SuperDrive can't access a high-density disk that was formatted in an 800-KB drive.

800-KB or 1.4-MB disk in a 400-KB drive: A 400-KB drive can access only 400-KB (single-sided) disks.

Disk foreign: You inserted a disk formatted for a different computer, such as an Apple II or an IBM PC. To access foreign disks, use the Apple File Exchange utility or Dayna Comunications' DOS Mounter utility.

Disk askew in drive: Eject the disk and reinsert it.

Disk bad or flaky: Insert the disk several times. Try fixing it with Apple's Disk First Aid utility software. See the tip "Disk Life," in Chapter 3, "Disks and Disk Drives."

External-drive cable loose: Use the internal drive. Then quit, shut down, turn off the power, and check the external drive cable for tightness.

Drive dirty: Clean the drive mechanism with a disk-cleaning kit.

Drive broken: Try a different drive. Have the broken drive repaired.

CAN'T INITIALIZE DISK

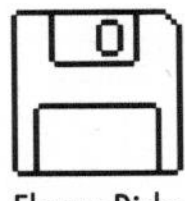
Floppy Disks

The message "Initialization failed!" might indicate one of the following conditions:

Disk bad: Retire the disk and use a different one. (See the tip "Disk Life," in Chapter 3, "Disks and Disk Drives.")

Quirk: Try again.

Drive broken: Try a different drive and have the problem drive repaired. A drive that needs repairs might be able to read disks but not initialize them. An FDHD SuperDrive that needs repairs might work fine with 800-KB disks but not with 1.4-MB disks.

CAN'T FULLY INSERT DISK

Floppy Disks

If a floppy disk won't go in all the way, don't force it. Check for the following problems:

Disk held upside down: Insert disk with the metal hub facing down.

Disk label stuck inside drive: Try to remove the label with a bent paper clip or needle-nose pliers (carefully!). If necessary, have the drive repaired.

Cracker in drive: Admonish child. Try removing crumbs with a low-powered vacuum cleaner, such as a small, hand-held model. If necessary, open the Mac and clean the drive, or have this done by a repair person.

Drive broken: Have drive repaired.

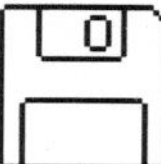

Floppy Disks

DRIVE DOESN'T SPIN

A disk drive should make noises for a few seconds after you insert a disk. If it doesn't, check for the following conditions:

Mac busy: Wait a minute. If MultiFinder is active, try switching to the Finder.

Mac confused: Press Command-Shift-1 or Command-Shift-2 to eject the disk, and then reinsert the disk. Try restarting the Mac.

Disk, drive, or cable not functioning: Try the cures listed in the tip "Not a Macintosh Disk," earlier in this chapter.

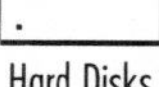

Hard Disks

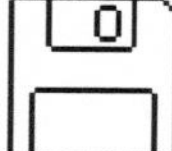

Floppy Disks

DISK DAMAGED

If you're unable to start up with a disk that contains a valuable document, you might be able to retrieve the document by treating the damaged disk as a non-startup disk. This technique works—sometimes—because the Finder is more finicky than most applications with regard to damaged disks. Here are the steps to follow:

1. Start the Mac with a good startup disk, preferably one that contains the application that created the documents you want to retrieve.
2. Start the application.
3. Open the document from the damaged disk by using the application's Open command, and save the document on a good disk by using the Save As command.

You might be able to reuse a damaged disk if you erase it. Use the Finder's Erase Disk command (on the Special menu) or hold down the Option, Command, and Tab keys while you insert the troublesome disk. The Mac asks whether you're sure you want to completely erase the disk; click Yes.

TEXT FILES DAMAGED

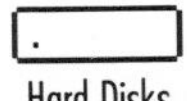
Hard Disks

Floppy Disks

All is not lost when an application tells you it encountered an unrecoverable disk error while trying to open a document. If the document contains text, you might be able to recover most of it. First, make an exact copy of the problem disk. If the Finder fails to make a copy, try making a sector copy using a utility such as the FastCopy feature of Central Point Software's PC Tools Deluxe. Then use Microsoft Word to open the document from the duplicate disk as plain text. Word's Open Any File command, which you display by pressing the Shift key while pulling down the File menu, interprets everything in the document as text. Some text might be missing, the formatting will be gone, and there might be some garbage to clean up, but that beats retyping a long document.

DISK CAUSES SYSTEM ERROR

Finder

If a system error message (with the bomb icon) appears when you insert a disk, it's possible that the Finder's invisible Desktop file has become corrupted. The Desktop file keeps track of which documents, applications, and folders are present on a disk, what their icons look like, where the icons are located on the desktop, and so on. (For more information on the Desktop file, see the tip "Disappearing Disk Space," in Chapter 3, "Disks and Disk Drives.")

The Finder usually recognizes a corrupt Desktop file and rebuilds it. Occasionally, however, the Finder falls down on the job. To force the Finder to rebuild the Desktop file for a disk, start up with another disk and then press the Option and Command keys while you insert the troublesome disk. The Finder asks whether you're sure you want to rebuild the desktop; click Yes.

Rebuilding the Desktop file erases any comments you might have entered in Get Info windows and, on 400-KB disks, erases the names of folders. You can forestall about 90 percent of the problems you're likely to encounter with the Desktop file if you always eject your disks before switching off the Mac.

Beginning with System 7, the Finder does not use the Desktop file, so it can't become corrupted and cause a system error.

PRINTER TROUBLE

PRINTER NOT AVAILABLE

Trouble choosing the Print or Page Setup commands often stems from having too many applications and documents open simultaneously. Each open application and document means one or more open files, and printing requires the opening of one or more additional files. The Macintosh has a standard limit of 40 files open at one time. It's easy to exceed this limit when MultiFinder is active.

The exact symptoms vary widely, depending on the application you try to print from. You might get a vague message such as "Can't open printer" or "Error printing on LaserWriter." You might get a message reporting error number 42 (which means there are too many files open). Some applications simply do nothing when you choose Print or Page Setup.

To verify the diagnosis regardless of the exact symptoms, try opening another document or two. If the Mac refuses, you have reached its limit on the number of files that can be open.

You can work around this problem by closing a couple of documents or applications. If you have the problem often, you can use the Suitcase II utility to increase the number of suitcase files that can be open, as described in the Suitcase II manual. You can also increase the number of files open by using the Set File Count utility, which comes with MasterJuggler.

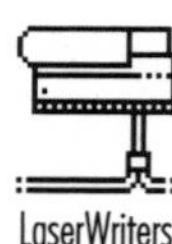

LASERWRITER DOESN'T PRINT

If a LaserWriter doesn't print your document, check for the following conditions:

Still preparing page image: Wait until the light on the printer stops blinking. On some LaserWriter models, a complex page might take 20 minutes or more to prepare.

Printer disconnected or power off: If you're using a print spooler, it stores page images on disk and sends them to the printer when the printer is ready. Turn on the printer and then use the controls in the print-spooler software to resume printing.

Out of paper: Add paper.

Paper jam: Remove the printed pages from the output tray. Clear the paper path.

Program malfunction: Quit, restart the program, and try printing again.

Mac confused: Use the Chooser desk accessory to verify your printer and port choices and to make sure AppleTalk is active. Recopy the LaserWriter and Laser Prep icons from the system software disk to the startup disk.

IMAGEWRITER DOESN'T PRINT

If an ImageWriter doesn't print your document, check the following conditions:

Power off: Turn it on.

Select lamp unlit: Press the Select switch once.

Cable loose: Plug the cable securely into the ImageWriter and the Mac.

Covers off or loose: Place the covers securely on the ImageWriter.

Out of paper: Put more paper in the printer and be sure the Select lamp is lit.

Transparency lacks backing: Use transparent film with a white backing paper. Newer ImageWriter IIs and ImageWriter LQs use an optical paper-out sensor that "sees" through unbacked transparencies.

Program malfunction: Quit, restart the program, and try printing again.

Disk full: Print the document a few pages, or even one page, at a time. Alternatively, copy the document, the application, or both to a blank disk. Remove the document from the original disk after copying.

Mac confused: Verify your printer and port choices with the Chooser desk accessory. If you're using an AppleTalk ImageWriter, make sure AppleTalk is active. Recopy the ImageWriter or the AppleTalk ImageWriter icon from the system software disk to the startup disk.

Internal switches set incorrectly: For the correct switch settings, see the tip "Printed Gibberish," later in this chapter.

ImageWriter broken: Test the ImageWriter by turning it off and holding down the Form Feed button while turning the printer back on. It should repeatedly print a line of letters, numbers, and symbols. If it doesn't, have it repaired.

ImageWriters

PRINTS WITHOUT PAPER

An ImageWriter is supposed to stop printing when it runs out of paper. However, the optical paper-out sensor used on newer ImageWriter IIs and on ImageWriter LQs might not work properly if the platen has become shiny from accumulated ink and paper deposits. A dirty platen can reflect light (as paper does), whereas a clean platen does not. If your ImageWriter keeps printing after the paper runs out, replace the platen or clean it with a solvent such as Fedrol.

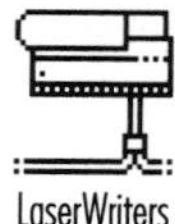
LaserWriters

EXCESS SPACE BETWEEN WORDS

The LaserWriter usually puts extra space between letters and words where font substitution takes place, as shown in Figure 5-7. This is a necessary side effect because the substitution fonts—Times, Helvetica, and Courier—are smaller than the fonts they replace—New York, Geneva, Monaco, and others that have no matching printer font. The extra space maintains the line breaks and the overall line width displayed on screen.

To eliminate the gaps, use the Page Setup command (on the File menu) to turn off the Font Substitution option. Then manually change all the text in

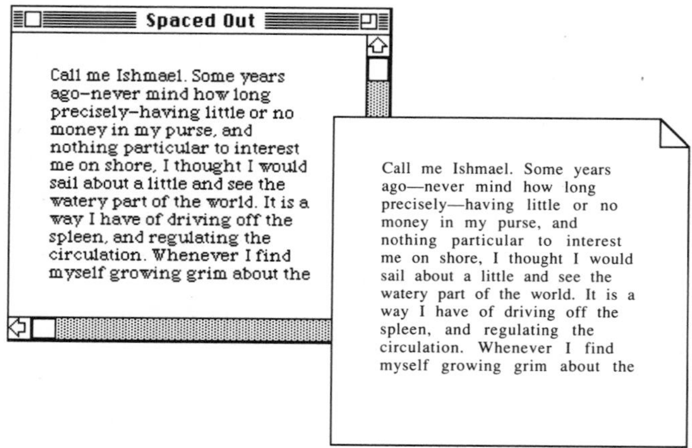

FIGURE 5-7. SPACED OUT.

The Font Substitution option in the LaserWriter Print dialog box automatically replaces a screen font such as New York with an equivalent LaserWriter font such as Times. Font Substitution adjusts the spacing between letters, words, and lines to maintain fidelity with the screen.

the document to a LaserWriter font. All LaserWriters except the IISC and Personal SC have the Times, Helvetica, Courier, and Symbol fonts built in. The LaserWriter Plus, IINT, Personal NT, and IINTX also have Avant Garde, Bookman, Helvetica Narrow, New Century Schoolbook, Palatino, Zapf Chancery, and Zapf Dingbats. Other downloadable LaserWriter fonts are also available.

NO BEST OR FASTER QUALITY

An ImageWriter can't print in best or faster quality if the startup disk is locked. Either eject the startup disk and slide the disk-locking tab so that no hole shows in the corner of the disk, or select the Draft quality option. Draft printing on an ImageWriter does not require images of the printed pages to be saved on disk, so you can usually print in draft quality when all disks are locked.

PAPER MISFEED

If paper wrinkles, tears, or jams in an ImageWriter, look for the following conditions:

Paper supply obstructed: Clear the paper path. Be sure the paper exiting the printer doesn't pile up on incoming paper. If you've been printing labels, check for a label that's come off in the paper path.

Paper-feed lever set incorrectly: Set the lever for the type of paper you're using: pin-feed or pressure-feed.

Paper curled: On an ImageWriter I, stick a Post-it note on the front cover to bridge the gap where incoming paper enters the machine, as shown in Figure 5-8 on the following page. Incoming paper feeds under the Post-it. Outgoing paper glides across the Post-it bridge rather than curling back into the machine. Also see the tip "Avoiding Paper Curl," in Chapter 4, "Printers and Printing."

Paper-out sensor: If your older ImageWriter II has a mechanical paper-out sensor, have it replaced with an optical sensor such as the ones used on newer ImageWriters. The mechanical sensor requires a small, black plastic device that fits around the left end of your ImageWriter platen and can cause paper jams.

FIGURE 5-8. FOIL FEEDBACK.

A Post-it note on the front cover of an ImageWriter I, directly behind the platen, keeps paper from curling back into the printer and doesn't interfere with normal printer operation.

ImageWriters

COMPRESSED LINE AT TOP OF PAGE

An ImageWriter might vertically compress the first line on a page of pin-feed paper when the perforation at the top of the page passes under the pressure rollers. The glitch occurs about 1 inch from the top of the page on an ImageWriter II. The paper-feed path is different on an ImageWriter I, where the glitch occurs about ½ inch from the top of the page. The compressed line is more likely to occur under one of the following conditions:

Narrow top margin: On an ImageWriter II, use a top margin of 1 inch or more. On an ImageWriter I, use a top margin of ½ inch or more, and do not set the No Breaks Between Pages option of the Page Setup dialog box.

Paper started too low: The perforation should be immediately above the pressure rollers.

Lightweight pin-feed paper: Try 20-pound paper.

Insufficient tension: Advance one sheet of paper through and let it hang there. Attach a clothespin or binder clip to the exiting paper. Let the exiting paper fall to the floor.

Paper-feed lever set wrong: Set the lever for the type of paper you're using: pin-feed or pressure-feed.

Slack in gears: Press the Line Feed button on the printer. Or turn the printer off and on just before printing.

Paper binding on cover: Leave the clear plastic cover of an ImageWriter I open, or at least prop it partway open with a pencil.

To eliminate the problem, switch to single-sheet paper. I highly recommend the use of a cut-sheet feeder on an ImageWriter II. It works well, but be careful when removing and reinstalling it not to break the plastic hinges that hold the two halves together.

LINE HEIGHT UNEVEN

ImageWriters

On an ImageWriter I, variations in line height with small font sizes are normal. The situation might improve if you raise the clear plastic cover and blow air across the print head with a table fan. The only sure cure is to use a larger font size or get an ImageWriter II.

PRINTED GIBBERISH

ImageWriters

If an ImageWriter prints random letters and symbols, check for the following problems:

Internal switches set wrong: For the correct switch settings, see Figures 5-9 through 5-11 on the following pages.

Cable bad: Try a different cable.

Print spooler malfunction: Disconnect, turn off, or deactivate the spooler and try again.

HEX ON THE IMAGEWRITER

ImageWriters

An ImageWriter that prints nothing but hexadecimal codes (pairs of numbers and the capital letters A through F) is in a special test mode. It goes into that mode if you press its Select button while switching it on. It's easy to inadvertently press the Select button on an ImageWriter II. To get out of test mode, turn the printer off and turn it back on. Then reprint your documents.

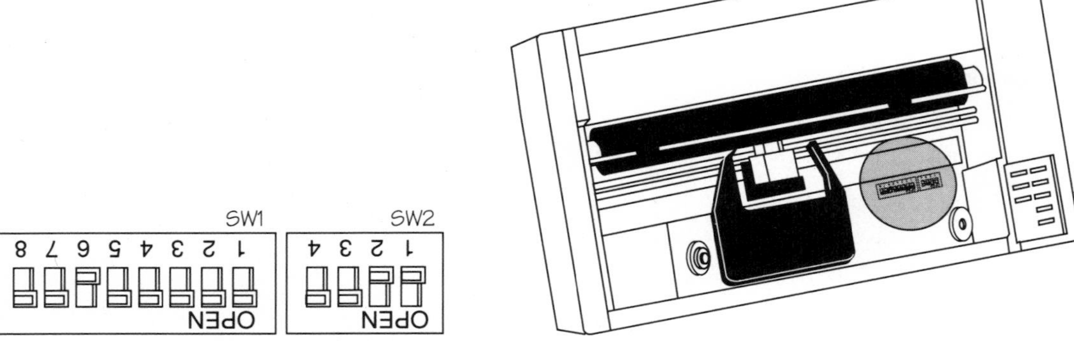

FIGURE 5-9. IMAGEWRITER I SWITCHES.

The switches at the right under the front cover of an ImageWriter I should be set as shown here.

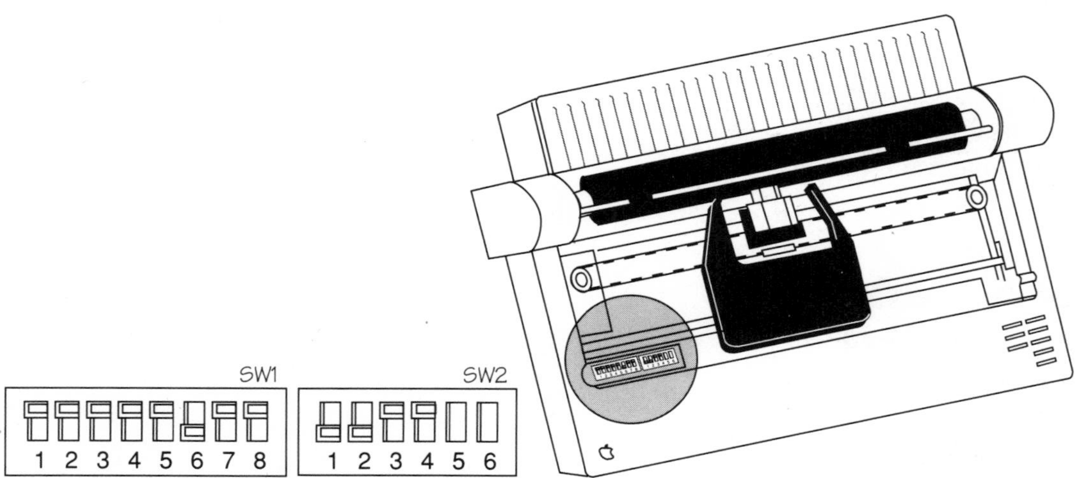

FIGURE 5-10. IMAGEWRITER II SWITCHES.

The switches located at the left under the front cover of an ImageWriter II should be set as shown here. Switches 5 and 6 of SW2 should not be changed from the factory settings.

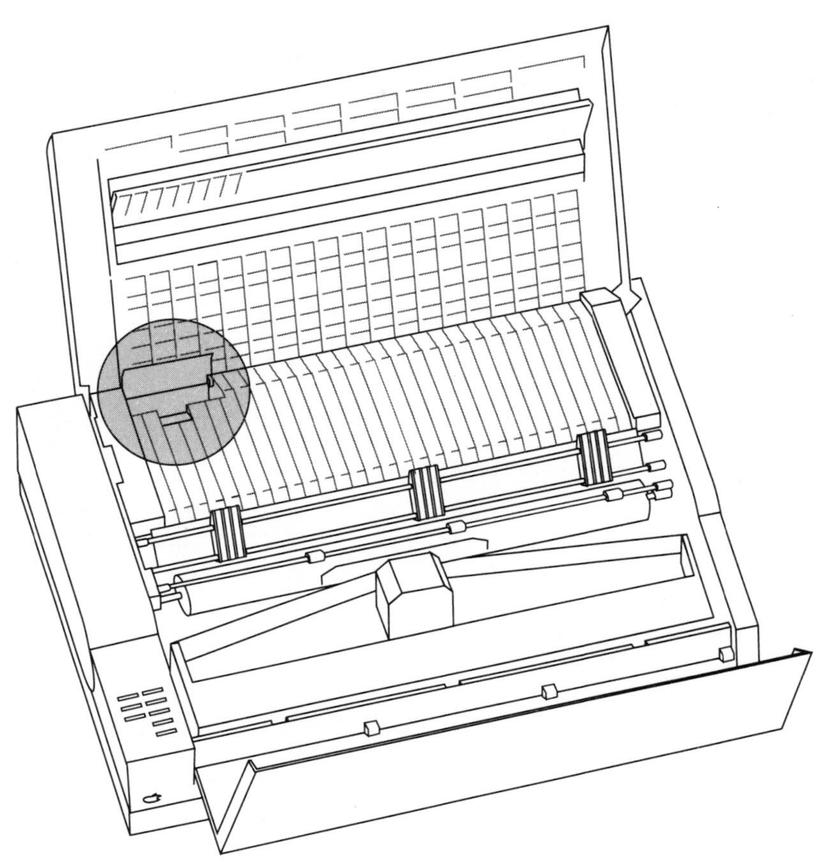

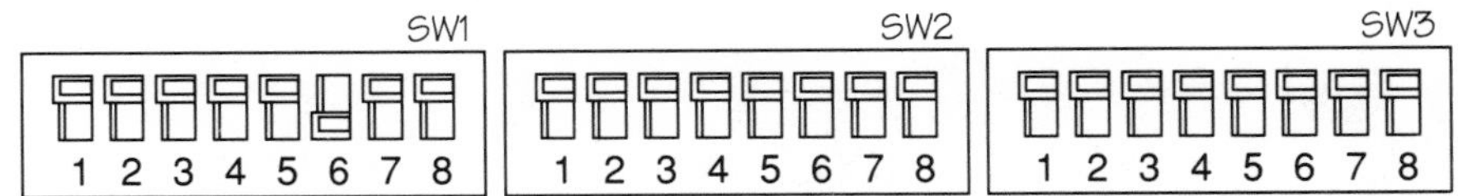

FIGURE 5-11. IMAGEWRITER LQ SWITCHES.

The switches located at the left under the front cover of an ImageWriter LQ should be set as shown here. Settings for switches 4 through 8 of SW2 vary according to which options are in use (option card, cut-sheet feeders, pull tractor). Don't change the switches of SW3 from the factory settings.

ImageWriters

PRINT TOO LIGHT OR TOO DARK

The most common cause of light print on an ImageWriter is a worn-out or dried-out ribbon. You can often rejuvenate a dried-out ribbon with WD-40 spray lubricant. First pry off the top of the ribbon cartridge. (Be careful, or you'll spill the ribbon and create a useless, spaghettilike mess.) Spray a little WD-40 on the top of the ribbon. Close the cartridge, put it in a plastic bag, and leave it for an hour or so.

An ImageWriter that prints sparse dots or streaks and smudges may be set for the wrong paper thickness. Set the thickness lever (located under the printer cover) all the way up for one-part paper; move it down one notch for each additional copy.

ImageWriters

THIN LINES ACROSS PATTERNS

ImageWriters can't print some patterns as well as others, especially on lightweight paper. Try heavy paper and experiment with different settings of the paper-feed and paper-thickness levers. See also the tip "Pattern Quality," in Chapter 4, "Printers and Printing."

ImageWriter II or LQ

COLORS MUDDY

An ImageWriter II or LQ that prints dingy colors probably needs a new ribbon. The print head has picked up color from one band and deposited it on another. To minimize color mixing, use color sparingly (white background and sparse patterns).

OTHER TROUBLE

All Macs

SCREEN DARK

When the computer is working but the display screen is dark, investigate the following possibilities:

Brightness turned down: Turn the brightness control clockwise.

Screen power off (external monitor): Be sure the monitor is plugged in and switched on.

Nothing to display: On a Mac with multiple monitors, only one has a menu bar. Other monitors display only the desktop pattern unless you drag windows to them. The desktop pattern appears black on a monochrome monitor if it's set to a dark solid color (in the General Control Panel).

Screen-saver active: Tap any key, or move the mouse to deactivate screen-saver software.

Mac broken: Have the Mac repaired.

NO SOUND

All Macs

If your Mac is mute when you should be hearing music or sound effects, check the following conditions:

Volume set too low: Use the Control Panel to adjust the volume level.

Audio port in use: Unplug the cable connected to the Mac's audio port to use the built-in speaker while you find out what's wrong with the external sound system.

FLASHING APPLE MENU

All Macs

A flashing icon at the left end of the menu bar indicates that something needs your attention outside the application you're currently using. Switch to any application whose name is marked with a diamond in the Apple menu. If the Apple icon itself is flashing, then the Alarm Clock desk accessory is "ringing."

BROKEN LINES AND STATIC

All Macs

A screen full of broken lines and visual static usually means a software error has occurred. Restart your Mac. Usually the only harm is a loss of all work done since you last saved. However, there is a remote danger of a disk becoming corrupted, particularly if the crash occurs while you are saving to disk. The risk is a bit greater if you were saving to a 400-KB disk drive when the Mac went haywire.

CLOCK INACCURATE

If your Mac can't keep accurate time anymore, its battery might be low or dead. The battery on a Mac Plus or 512K is designed to last two years. Replace it with an Eveready number 523, Duracell PX-21, or equivalent.

The batteries in other Mac models (except the Mac Portable) are designed to last seven years. You can replace them on a Mac SE/30, IIcx, IIci, and all newer models. Replacing the battery on a Mac SE, II, or IIx requires the services of a technician.

All Macs

FONT CORRUPTION

Sometimes a system error occurs when you try to use a particular font. You might be able to cure the problem by removing the font from your System file. (Use the Font/DA Mover with system software versions prior to 7.0.) However, attempts to remove it might also result in system errors.

If you're unable to remove a troublesome font, something might be wrong with the System file. To eliminate this possibility, replace the System file and other items in the System Folder with like-named items from a clean copy of the latest system software disks. Before replacing your current System Folder, be sure to make a copy of it in case something goes wrong. After replacing your System file, you must reinstall fonts, desk accessories, and any other enhancements you had added to your old System file.

Finder

WRONG FONT

Text displayed in the wrong font usually means that the Mac's parameter RAM settings have become garbled. Figure 5-12 illustrates the problem. The parameter RAM preserves many of the settings made with the Control Panel and Chooser desk accessories. A battery preserves the contents of the parameter RAM when the power is off.

Another parameter RAM setting determines which font the Mac uses as the application font. Most applications use this application font by default, and the standard setting for it is Geneva. If the parameter RAM somehow becomes scrambled, it might specify a nonexistent font instead of Geneva. The Mac, unable to find the nonexistent font, substitutes Chicago. It must scale down Chicago 12, the only size of Chicago available, to get the 9-point size the application wants.

To reset the parameter RAM, press Command-Option-Shift while choosing the Control Panel. On a Mac Plus or 512K, unplug the computer and remove the battery for a few minutes. After resetting the parameter RAM, check all settings in the Control Panel and Chooser.

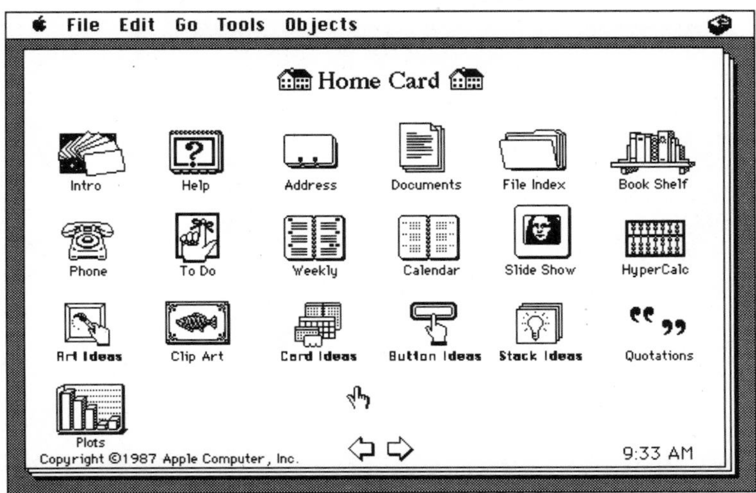

FIGURE 5-12. IMPROPER FONT.
If an application displays text in the wrong font—particularly Chicago instead of Geneva—the Mac's parameter RAM probably needs resetting. Here, HyperCard displays button icon names in 9-point Chicago (scaled down from Chicago 12). What appear to be icon names in the correct font are actually instances of paint text that were typed onto the card picture using the Text painting tool.

STRANGE SCALING

All Macs

Ugly menu text is often an indication of a temporary memory shortage, especially if you're using MultiFinder. To fix it, try quitting an application or restarting the Mac. If it happens frequently, you might need to allocate more memory to the area of the Mac's memory called the system heap. You can do that with CE Software's HeapFixer utility.

Chapter 6

WORDS

If you're like most Mac users, you do some writing with your Mac. You probably use a word processing application such as MacWrite or Microsoft Word to write at least an occasional letter. On the surface, word processing applications are almost as easy to use as an electric typewriter.

Beneath the surface, however, are dozens of powerful features that let you work more efficiently. This chapter can help you make use of these features, with tips on the following aspects of word processing:

- Environment
- Selecting
- Editing
- Characters and words
- Lines and paragraphs
- Pages and documents
- Illustrations and special effects

ENVIRONMENT

LOST AND FOUND

When you scroll up and down in a large word processing document to review your work, it's easy to get lost. To bring back into view the area in which you were working, press the Left arrow key and then the Right arrow key (or vice versa). Alternatively (if your keyboard has no arrow keys), type any letter and then press Delete to delete the letter.

FINDING THE INSERTION POINT

After scrolling a MacWrite document so that the insertion point is no longer in view, you can quickly scroll back to the vicinity of the insertion point by pressing the Enter key.

CREATING BOOKMARKS

Some word processors have a built-in "bookmark" feature that lets you mark various locations in your document so that you can go to them quickly. If your word processor does not have this feature, you can make your own bookmarks. Here's what you do:

1. Type unique character combinations, such as §*1*, §*2*, and so on, at the points in the document that you want to mark. (See Figure 6-1.)
2. Locate the markers later, using the Find command or the Search command. Don't forget to remove the markers when you finish editing the document.

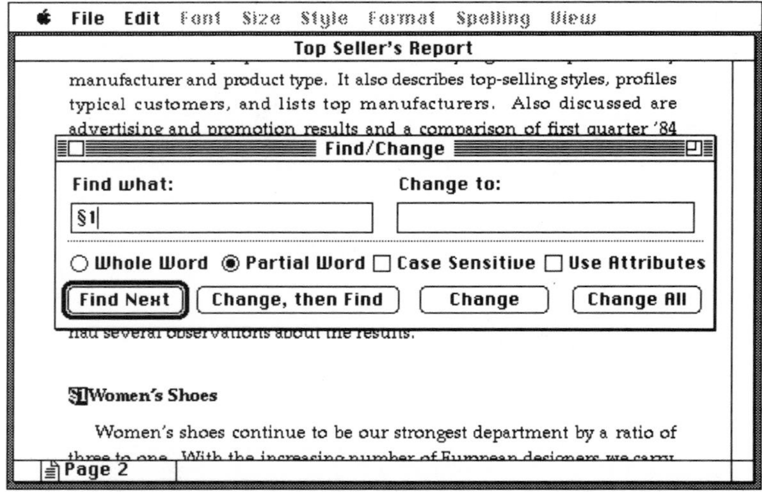

FIGURE 6-1. PLACING BOOKMARKS.
Use unique symbols as place markers in long documents, and then locate them quickly with the Find command.

NONTEXT FIND

You can search for a graphic or other nontext item in a Microsoft Word or Microsoft Write document by typing a caret (Shift-6) followed by the appropriate numeric code in the Find What box of the Find or Change dialog box. For example, type *^1* to find either a graphic pasted from another

application or an empty graphics frame placed with Word's Insert Graphics command. Similarly, *^6* finds formula prefixes, which appear as .\ in text.

To determine which numeric code to use, select an instance of what you want to search for and then press Command-Option-Q. You'll see the numeric code in the lower left corner of the screen.

These numeric codes supplement the regular search codes, such as *^t* for a tab, *^p* for a paragraph mark, *^n* for a newline mark, and *^d* for a page or section mark. (For a list of the regular codes, look under the Find topic in the Word or Write online help.)

FAST FIND TEXT

Word Perfect

When searching forward to find multiple occurrences of a word or phrase in a WordPerfect document, you must repeatedly use the Forward command (in the Search menu). After you have used the Forward command once, bringing up the dialog box to enter the text you want to search for, there is an easy way to repeat the search. To keep WordPerfect from redrawing the Forward command's dialog box each time, and thus go faster, quickly press the F key twice while pressing the Command key.

WORD'S PAGE NUMBER AREA

Microsoft Word

Have you ever seen the word *Code* suddenly appear in inverse type in the lower left corner of the Microsoft Word document window, where the page number usually appears? Word uses the page number area of the document window to get information from you to complete actions begun by the following keyboard shortcuts:

Command-Option-Q: Insert a special character.

Command-Shift-S: Apply a style to a paragraph.

Command-Shift-E: Change the font.

Command-Delete: Insert a glossary entry.

When you type any of these combination keystrokes, Word displays a word in the page number area that prompts you to enter additional information. For example, the word *Code* means you should enter the code number of a character you want to insert. Pressing Command-period or clicking anywhere outside the page number area cancels the keyboard shortcut.

You can repeat the most recently used of these four keyboard shortcuts by clicking in the page number area. The prompt word appears again, cuing you to type the needed information.

JUMPING TO A PAGE

You can jump quickly to any page in a FullWrite Professional document by double-clicking the page number at the lower left corner of the document window. The dialog box shown in Figure 6-2 appears, allowing you to type the page number to which you want to go. Optionally, you can jump to the first or last paragraph of the document or chapter.

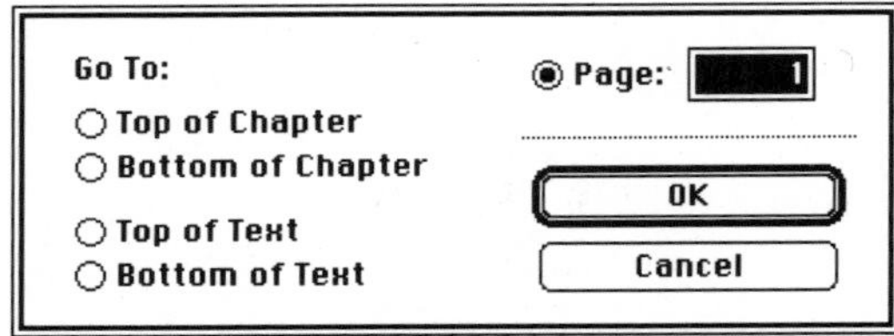

FIGURE 6-2. GO TO.
To display this FullWrite Professional dialog box, double-click on the page number in the lower left corner of the document window.

UNSIGHTLY TEMP FILE BUILDUP

Many applications open temporary files in the System Folder and elsewhere. Both Microsoft Word and Microsoft Write put your recent typing in a temporary file in the System Folder. If Word or Write runs low on memory when you save a document, it might open another temporary file in the System Folder. That file frees some memory by holding the contents of the Clipboard. In addition, Word might open temporary files in the folder that contains the Word application and in any folder that contains an open Word document; the same is true of Microsoft Write.

Applications are supposed to delete all their temporary files when you quit normally. If the power goes off, the application quits unexpectedly, or the Mac suddenly stops working, however, the application doesn't get a chance to delete its temporary files. If you're using Word, you might be able to reconstruct your work from the temporary files. Press Shift while choosing Open from the Word File menu to open them.

You can safely delete the Word and Write temporary files by dragging them to the Trash. If you're using Word or Write with MultiFinder, the Mac will not let you delete temporary files that are in use at the time. It complains, *That item is locked or in use and can't be removed.* When you click OK, the Mac puts the busy file back in the folder from which it came.

WINDOW TILES

Microsoft Word has several window-management features, including its Window menu and the Command-Option-W command, which rotates through the open windows in turn. In addition, this command tiles windows. Clicking the zoom box of each open full-size window (or double-clicking its title bar or size box) shrinks the windows and arranges them so that at least a portion of each window is visible.

There's an exception to Word's window tiling. If you resize or move a window after opening it and then, later, click its zoom box (or double-click its title bar or size box), Word zooms it to full size. Click again, and the window returns to the size and location you gave it earlier.

KEYBOARD CONTROL PAD

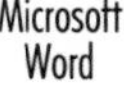

What's the fastest way to move around a Microsoft Word or Microsoft Write document and select text with the keyboard? The arrow keys work, of course, but if you have to look to find them, they're not very efficient. The numeric keypad has the same shortcoming. But pressing the Command and Option keys turns the right side of the keyboard into a directional control pad, which you can use without moving your hands from their standard typing position. Figure 6-3 on the following page shows how they work.

While you are holding the Command and Option keys down, pressing O moves the insertion point up one line, pressing L moves it right one character, pressing the comma key moves it down one line, and pressing K moves it left one character. Adjacent to those four keys are four more that move in the same direction as their neighbors but a greater distance: Command-Option-P moves the insertion point up one page, Command-Option-semicolon moves it right one word, Command-Option-period moves it down one page, and Command-Option-J moves it left one word. If you hold down the Shift key along with the Command and Option keys, Word or Write selects text as you move the insertion point. To intensify the action of the next control-pad key, press the apostrophe key while holding down the Command and Option keys. Release the Command and Option keys before you press the next control-pad key. For example, to move the insertion point to the left end of the line, press Command-Option-apostrophe and then press the K key by itself.

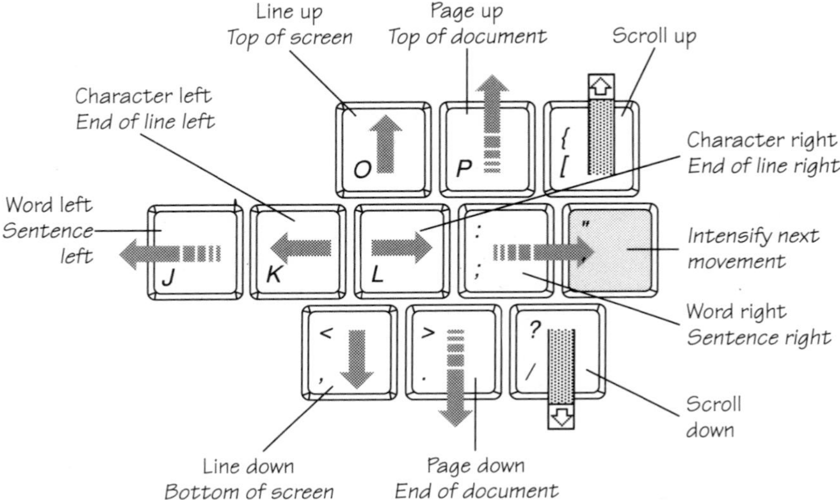

FIGURE 6-3. KEYBOARD MOUSE.

In Microsoft Word and Microsoft Write, holding down the Command and Option keys lets you move the insertion point and scroll from the keyboard without taking your hands from their normal typing position.

ENORMOUS WORD DOCUMENTS

Although theoretically there's no limit to the size of a Microsoft Word document, practical limits intrude when a document becomes very large. Obviously, the whole document must fit into the space available on a disk. Even if the disk has room for the document, you might want to break it down into chunks of 200 KB or less. Saving a mammoth document takes ages. Word lets you split a long document into manageable pieces and link them together. (For details, look up "Long Documents" in the Word reference manual.)

CONDENSING DOCUMENTS

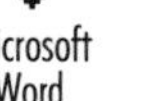

Microsoft Word Microsoft Write

After you do a lot of editing to a Microsoft Word or Microsoft Write document, it might take up significantly more space on disk (and in memory) than it needs. That's because Word and Write leave deleted and changed passages in the document—albeit in a form you can't see—when you save using the Save command. To clear out the deadwood, choose Save As from the File menu, turn off the Fast Save option, click the Save button, and click Yes when asked whether you want to replace the existing document.

CHANGING PRESET FORMATS

General Word Processing

How can you change your word processor's standard formatting ruler, font, font size, paper size, and other settings? In WriteNow 2.0, create an empty document with the settings you want. Save the document, naming it Stationery and placing it in the same folder as WriteNow. Every time you choose New from the File menu, WriteNow 2.0 opens an untitled copy of the Stationery document.

Similarly, in MacWrite II, create a document with the settings you want. Choose Save As from the File menu, select the MacWrite II Stationery format from the pop-up menu, name the document MacWrite II Options, and put the document in the System Folder. Every time you choose New from the File menu, MacWrite II uses the settings of the MacWrite II Options document.

If your word processor doesn't let you change its initial settings, you can work around the problem. Make a template document that sets up the conditions you want. Then, instead of using the New command each time you want to create a new document, open the template document and immediately use the Save As command to give the document its own name.

To create a template, choose New from the File menu. Then set up formatting rulers, headers, footers, paper size, orientation, and other paragraph and document formatting. Choose the font, size, and style with which you want to start the document. Enter any text and paste any pictures that will appear in every document. Choose Print, select the options you will normally use, and print a copy of the template by clicking OK. Finally, save the document, using a generic name such as Letter or Envelope.

SPELLING NONSENSE

The spelling checker dictionary in WriteNow contains strange "words" such as "allous" and "orgasmatronx." Although you might think you could remove such words by selecting them and clicking WriteNow's Forget button, don't do it. Removing these apparent nonsense words actually removes perfectly good words from the dictionary. You can't remove the nonsense words because they're not actually in the dictionary.

The nonsense words show up in lists of suggested alternatives to misspelled words. WriteNow constructs a list of alternatives by manipulating the currently selected word when you click the Guess button. It might create a thousand derivatives from one misspelled word, many of them synthetic words. To winnow the bogus derivatives from the list, Write Now checks the list against its dictionary. Because of the way WriteNow checks its dictionary, there's a statistical probability (1 in 50,000) that it won't catch a misspelled word. The nonsense words you see are spurious derivatives that WriteNow didn't catch.

WriteNow lets counterfeit words pass because it mistakes them for legitimate words in its dictionary. When WriteNow looks up a word in its dictionary, it actually looks up a numeric code it calculates from the word. If it finds the calculated code in the dictionary, it assumes the spelling is accurate. By chance, a nonsense word might generate the same code as a legitimate word. If so, the nonsense word seems genuine to WriteNow because its numeric code is in the dictionary.

Removing a nonsense word deletes the corresponding numeric code from the dictionary. This effectively removes the genuine word with the matching numeric code as well. Unfortunately, there's no way for a WriteNow user to tell which real word is deleted when a nonsense word is "removed."

CUSTOM MENUS

You can quickly add any Microsoft Word option that you normally select in a dialog box to a menu. Press Command-Option-plus and then go through the motions of selecting the option. While you are doing so, the pointer is the shape of a large plus sign. When you complete the action, the option is added to the appropriate menu. For example, when you select a font or font size with the Character command (on the Format menu) the font or size is added to the Font menu. Other options you select using the Character, Paragraph, and Section commands (on the Format menu) all appear on the Format menu. Styles you select with the Styles command (on the Format menu) and glossary entries you select with the Glossary command (on the Edit menu) appear on the Work menu. (If the Work menu doesn't exist, Word adds it to the right of the Window menu.)

You can remove a command from any Word menu by pressing Command-Option-hyphen and then choosing the command. While you go through the motions, the pointer is the shape of a large minus sign.

If you want to add or remove several items from menus one after another, press the Shift key while using the plus-shaped or minus-shaped pointer.

FILENAMES AS MENU COMMANDS

To add the name of an open Microsoft Word document to the Work menu, press Command-Option-plus and click the title bar of the document window. To add the name of a document that's not open, press Command-Option-plus and go through the motions of opening the document. While you are doing so, the pointer is the shape of a large plus sign.

To remove one or more documents from the Work menu, follow the steps mentioned in the previous tip, using Command-Option-hyphen.

WORD CREDITS

To see a hidden list of people who had a hand in developing Microsoft Word 4.0, choose About Microsoft Word from the Apple menu. Then press the Command key and click the Word icon.

SELECTING

SELECTING WORDS

How can you quickly select a whole word? Point to it and double-click the mouse button. If you hold down the mouse button on the second click, you can drag the pointer to select text in whole-word increments.

A few word processors, such as Microsoft Word, select the blank space after the word when you double-click. Most word processors—including MacWrite, FullWrite Professional, and WriteNow—select only the word.

General Word Processing

SELECTING LINES

What's the quickest way to select text a line at a time? Place the pointer in the left margin, hold down the mouse button, and then drag the pointer up or down in the margin. (Don't drag sideways across the line.) As you drag up or down, lines of text are highlighted. You can drag the pointer past the top or bottom edge of the window to scroll the document and select more lines as it scrolls.

In MacWrite II, click three times anywhere on the line you want to select. To select more than one line at a time, hold down the mouse button after triple-clicking, and drag up or down.

In Microsoft Word or Microsoft Write, place the pointer in the left margin—it changes to the shape of an arrow pointing to the right. Click once to select one line. To select more than one line at a time, hold down the mouse button and drag up or down in the margin.

General Word Processing

SELECTING SENTENCES AND PHRASES

To select a sentence or phrase quickly, double-click the first word of the sentence or phrase and, while holding the mouse button down, drag directly (diagonally, if appropriate) to the last word or punctuation mark of the sentence or phrase. Selecting word by word takes less precision, and therefore less work, than selecting letter by letter. Selecting phrases by dragging backward—right to left, and up—from the end of the phrase to its beginning might be easier than selecting by dragging from beginning to end. Your eye is already at the end of the phrase after reading from left to right, and it's easier to start there and drag backward than it is to look back and drag forward.

In Microsoft Word and Microsoft Write, you can select a sentence by holding down the Command key and clicking on any part of the sentence. To select several sentences, hold down the Command key, press the mouse button, and drag. After you start dragging, you can release the Command key. You can extend a selection made with the Command key to a distant sentence: Scroll to the sentence to which you want to extend the selection, press the Shift key, and click anywhere in that sentence.

SELECTING PARAGRAPHS

To select a paragraph quickly, place the pointer in the left margin next to the first line, hold down the mouse button, and then drag down the margin until the pointer is next to the line that follows the end of the paragraph. Dragging down that far ensures that the selection includes the invisible return character that marks the end of the paragraph. (You can also drag backward, from the start of the line after the end of the paragraph to the start of the paragraph.)

In MacWrite II, click four times anywhere in the paragraph you want to select. To select more than one paragraph at a time, hold down the mouse button after quadruple-clicking, and drag up or down.

In Microsoft Word or Microsoft Write, place the pointer in the left margin next to any line of the paragraph, and double-click the mouse button. If you hold down the mouse button on the second click, you can select adjacent paragraphs by dragging the pointer up or down.

SELECTING LARGE BLOCKS OF TEXT

To select a large block of text quickly, click at one end of the text block, use the scroll bar to bring the other end into view, and press the Shift key while clicking an insertion point there. This method is faster than forcing the word processor to scroll by dragging past the window boundaries.

SELECTING THE ENTIRE DOCUMENT

Word processors such as MacWrite II, Microsoft Works, WordPerfect, and WriteNow have a Select All command on the Edit menu. In MacWrite II, you can also click five times anywhere in the document to select the entire document. In Microsoft Word or Microsoft Write, either you press Command-Option-M or you place the pointer in the left margin next to any line, press Command, and click. In any other word processor, click at the beginning or the end of the document, scroll to the other end of the document, and hold down Shift while you click again.

Be careful what you do while an entire document is selected—anything you type replaces all selected type.

EDITING

CORRECTING TYPOS ON THE FLY

General Word Processing

The quickest way to correct a typo you just made is to use the Delete key. Mouse methods for text removal might be more powerful, but moving your hands away from the keyboard can interrupt your typing flow.

REPLACING TEXT DIRECTLY

General Word Processing

To replace one or two letters, click just after the last one, press Delete to erase as many as you want, and type the replacement. To replace a word or more, select the old text and then simply type the new. The selected text is deleted when you start typing. There's no need to press Delete first.

SUAVE MOVES

Microsoft Word

Microsoft Write

You can use a shortcut to move or copy text in Microsoft Word or Microsoft Write without using the Cut or Copy command. (With this technique, you bypass the Clipboard so that you retain what you last copied or cut for later pasting.) Here's what to do:

1. Select the text you want to move or copy.
2. Press Command-Option-X to move or Command-Option-C to copy. The message *Move to* or *Copy to* appears in the lower left corner of the document window.
3. Click an insertion point at the new location for the selected text. Alternatively, drag the pointer across anything you want the selected text to replace. (The text to be replaced is underlined with dots.)
4. Press Enter or Return to complete the move or copy. (To cancel, press any other key.)

INSERTING WHILE TYPING

Microsoft Word

Microsoft Write

While typing, you can move or copy text and graphics to the insertion point from anywhere else in the same Microsoft Word or Microsoft Write document.

1. Press Command-Option-X to move or Command-Option-C to copy. The message *Move from* or *Copy from* appears in the lower left corner of the document window.
2. Drag the pointer across whatever you want moved or copied to the insertion point. (The text to be moved or copied is underlined with a dotted line.)
3. Press Enter or Return to complete the move or copy, and then continue typing. (To cancel, press any other key.)

RECYCLING DELETED TEXT

General Word Processing

Today's trash might be tomorrow's treasure, so don't hastily condemn the sentences and paragraphs you delete to oblivion. Instead, cut and paste them into a recycling bin. Create a separate document to hold your semantic ore. If your word processor won't let you keep two documents open at once, you can put your remnants at the end of the document on which you're working. You can also store scraps in the Scrapbook, but you might find that method too slow if you don't have a hard disk. Don't delete the leftovers permanently until you have finished the final editing of the document.

EVALUATING PHRASING OPTIONS

General Word Processing

Trying to decide which of two phrasings works better in a certain passage? The following method lets you see first one passage, then the other, in context:

1. Type one option, select it, and type the other.
2. Ponder.
3. Choose Undo (on the Edit menu) or press Command-Z, the shortcut for the Undo command. The first option reappears.
4. Contemplate.
5. Choose Undo again. The second option reappears.
6. Repeat steps 2 through 5 until you either decide or fall asleep.

ALIGNING WITH TABS

Tabs are the only sensible tool to use for column alignment on the Mac. On a typewriter, where all letters are the same width, you can use spaces. It's hard to get precise alignment using spaces on a Mac because spaces in the Mac's proportional-width fonts are narrower than most letters and other characters. What's worse, subsequent changes in words, the font, or the font size will probably ruin the alignment if spaces are used.

REMOVING DOUBLE SPACES

After a lengthy editing session, your document might be sprinkled with double spaces between words. Although such blemishes won't stop the earth from rotating, they're ridiculously easy to eliminate with the Change command, so why put up with them? Get rid of them with your find-and-replace command. It might be called Change, Find/Change, Find/Replace, Replace, or something similar. Specify two spaces as the text to be found and one space as the replacement text. Then click the Change All button (or the equivalent). If your document might contain three, four, or more spaces between words, click Change All several times.

Don't worry about changing double spaces you might have used after periods to single spaces. Although using double spaces is standard procedure with typists, it is frowned upon by professional typesetters and word processors. A single space after a period is now the preferred style.

Caution: Replacing multiple spaces with a single space is safe if you use tabs and indention markers in formatting rulers for paragraph indentation, column alignment, and so forth. If you instead use multiple spaces for those purposes, don't use the procedure described in the previous paragraph. Or, instead of clicking Change All, use the procedure that lets you confirm each change before it is made.

TYPING SHORTHAND

Save time when typing by devising standard abbreviations for long or complicated words and phrases that you use often. Then substitute those abbreviations as you type a document. After you have finished, use the find-and-replace command to replace each abbreviation in turn with its proper expansion. (That command might be called Change, Find/Change, Find/Replace, Replace, or something similar.)

Try to choose unique abbreviations that won't appear in the middle of regular words. For example, *\ne* would be a poor abbreviation for *Nebuchadnezzar* because the *ne* in the word *prune* would then be expanded to *pruNebuchadnezzar*. You can guard against this type of unwanted expansion if the find-and-replace command lets you restrict it to finding whole words only.

HARD SPACES

How can you prevent a line from breaking at a particular blank space (when you are typing formulas and equations, for example)? Press Option-Spacebar to type a hard, nonbreaking space. You can use hard spaces anywhere you can use normal spaces, including dialog boxes. In Microsoft Word, you can also press Command-Spacebar to produce a nonbreaking space in regular documents, but this does not work in dialog boxes.

Caution: In a proportionally spaced font (Geneva, New York, Times, Helvetica, and so on), a hard space is twice the width of a normal space. In a fixed-width font (Monaco and Courier), a hard space is the same width as a normal space.

MANUAL HYPHENATION

If your word processor has automatic hyphenation, you can break lines manually by inserting strategically placed hyphens. Just before printing, go through your document looking for short lines. Put a hyphen in the first word following a short line. This solution is less than ideal because a hyphenated word might move to the middle of the line if you subsequently change the paragraph it's in. Ideally, you would like your hyphens to be invisible unless they occur at the end of a line. Some word processors offer this type of hyphen; see the next tip for details.

OPTIONAL HYPHENS

Most word processors let you type an optional hyphen by pressing Command-hyphen. An optional hyphen is invisible unless it falls at the end of a line. When a word that contains optional hyphens occurs at the end of a line, the word processor tries to divide the word at one of them and, if successful, shows a hyphen.

General Word Processing

DASHES

Unless you use the Courier font and strive for the typewritten look, you should not substitute double hyphens for dashes. An em dash (—) is the usual replacement for a double hyphen. You type it by pressing Shift-Option-hyphen. An en dash (–) is shorter than an em dash but longer than a hyphen. It's commonly used to separate numbers in a range. Type an en dash by pressing Option-hyphen.

Microsoft Word

Microsoft Write

COPYING FORMATS

If you want to copy the format of one character, paragraph, or section to another in a Microsoft Word or Microsoft Write document, don't overlook the shortcuts for format copying. Select the text from which you want to copy formats, and press Command-Option-V. Then select the text you want to apply the formats to, and press Return or Enter.

CHARACTERS AND WORDS

General Word Processing

TYPING RULES

To type a solid horizontal rule that is vertically centered in a line, use a series of em dashes (Option-Shift-hyphen). Underscore characters (Shift-hyphen) also create a solid rule, but below the line.

Microsoft Word

TYPING TABS

To type a tab character in a Microsoft Word 4.0 table (created with the Insert Table command), press Option-Tab. If you press Tab, you move to the next call in the table.

WriteNow

SPACEY, IRREGULAR TEXT

Text that seems spaced wrong or looks uneven might have been set to an uninstalled font size, such as 11 point or 13 point. That's not hard to do accidentally in WriteNow, where pressing Command-9 decreases the font size by 1 point and pressing Command-0 increases the size by 1 point. To fix bad-looking text, select it all and choose an installed size from WriteNow's FontSize menu. Installed sizes are always listed in the menu in outline style.

SIMPLE FRACTIONS

You can create acceptable fractions in almost any word processor by reducing the point size of the numerator and denominator and then superscripting the numerator. (See Figure 6-4.) This technique works in Word, WriteNow, FullWrite Professional, and MacWrite versions 5.0 and earlier. However, it does not work very well in MacWrite II or Microsoft Works.

Apple Pie

Prepare an unbaked crust in a 9-inch pie pan. In a bowl, mix together 1/4 cup **sugar**, 1 teaspoon **cinnamon**, 1/4 teaspoon **nutmeg**, 2 tablespoons **flour**, and 1/8 teaspoon **salt**. Sprinkle 1/3 of mixture over crust.

Peel, core, and slice 3 pounds **Pippin apples**. Pile apples high in crust, sprinkling remaining 2/3 of mixture over apples as you go.

Preheat oven to 450°F. With a pastry blender or two knives, mix 1/2 cup **sugar**, 3/4 cup **flour**, 3 tablespoons **brown sugar**, 1/4 teaspoon **salt**, and 1/3 cup **butter** until mixture is crumbly. Spread mixture over filling and pat down. Sprinkle with **cinnamon**.

Bake at 450° for 10 minutes, then reduce heat to 350° for 35 to 40 minutes more. When pie is done, fork should penetrate apples easily.

FIGURE 6-4. FRACTIONS IN TYPE.
To create fractions like these, reduce the numerator and denominator (but not the slash) by 1 to 3 points and superscript the numerator 1 or 2 points. The best amounts to use will depend on the font and size of the text surrounding the fraction.

TYPING TRUE QUOTES

To give your documents a more typeset, less typewritten look, use right and left quotation marks. For example, you can type *Hoagy Carmichael's "Stardust"* instead of *Hoagy Carmichael's "Stardust"*. Type Option-open bracket ([) for “, Option-Shift-open bracket for ”, Option-close bracket (]) for ‘, and Option-Shift-close bracket for ’.

Instead of typing those awkward combination keystrokes to get curved quotation marks, you can add the utility Curlers to your System Folder. It automatically replaces plain quotes with opening and closing quotes as you type. If you use Microsoft Word, click the "Smart" Quotes option of the Preferences command.

General Word Processing

REPLACING QUOTES

It's possible to replace plain quotation marks (") with opening and closing quotation marks (“ ”) using a word processor's find-and-replace command. The procedure is not foolproof, but it handles most cases. Substitute the opening quotation marks first. They're almost always preceded by blank spaces, and closing quotation marks aren't. Search for a blank space followed by a plain quotation mark ("), and replace that pair of characters with a blank space followed by an opening quotation mark (“). This won't replace opening quotation marks that begin a paragraph. If your word processor allows, you can replace all instances of a paragraph mark followed by a quotation mark with a paragraph mark followed by an opening quotation mark. In Microsoft Word, for example, search for ^p" and replace it with ^p“. Finally, replace all remaining plain quotation mark characters (") with closing quotation mark characters (”).

You can repeat the process to replace plain single quotation marks (') with opening and closing single quotation marks (‘’). This will also replace the apostrophes needed in contractions, possessives, and a few plurals with closing single quotation marks (’). If the document contains apostrophes but no opening single quotation marks, replacing all plain single quotation marks (') with closing single quotation marks (’) is sufficient.

HyperCard

SCRIPTED QUOTE REPLACEMENT

In addition to the quote-replacement method described in the previous tip, you can convert plain quotation marks (") to opening and closing quotation marks (“ ”) with HyperCard. The script shown in Figure 6-5 replaces pairs of plain quotes with pairs of opening and closing quotes.

```
on mouseUp
  global memory
  if the version of Hypercard < 2 then
    ask "Document to convert"
    if it is empty then exit to Hypercard
    put it into source
    ask "Save converted document as" with it & ".Q"
    if it is empty then exit to Hypercard
    put it into dest
  else
    answer file "Document to convert:" of type text
    if the result is "Cancel" then exit to Hypercard
    put it into source
    get lastThing(":",it) -- source filename from path
    ask file "Save converted document as: " with it & ".Q"
    if the result is "Cancel" then exit to Hypercard
    put it into dest
  end if
  set cursor to watch
  open file source
  open file dest
  put 0 into memory -- keeps track of whether quotes balance
  repeat
    read from file source for 16384 -- read 16 KB chunks
    if it is empty then exit repeat -- end of file?
    write convertQuotes(it) to file dest
  end repeat
  close file source
  close file dest
  set cursor to 0 -- normal
  if memory is 1
  then answer "Oops! Quotes didn't balance."
end mouseUp
```

(continued)

FIGURE 6-5. QUOTE CONVERTER.
This HyperCard script converts pairs of plain quotes (") in any text document to pairs of opening and closing quotes (“ ”).

FIGURE 6-5. *continued*

```
--Convert all "" in variable it to ""
--If the number of quotes is uneven, variable memory is 1
  function convertQuotes it
  global memory
  put 0 into qCount
  put offset(quote,it) into cNbr -- find the first plain quote
  repeat until cNbr is 0
    set cursor to busy
    add one to qCount -- count this conversion
    if qCount mod 2 is 1
    then put """ into char cNbr of it -- Odd nbr of quotes
    else put """ into char cNbr of it -- Even nbr of quotes
    put offset(quote,it) into cNbr -- find the next plain quote
  end repeat
  --keep track of whether quotes balance:
  put (qCount mod 2 + memory) mod 2 into memory
  return it
end convertQuotes
--Function lastThing extracts the part of string s
--that follows the last instance of character c
function lastThing c,s
  if c is in s
  then put lastThing(c,char offset(c,s)+1 to length(s) of s) into s
  return s
end lastThing
```

GETTING THE QUOTES RIGHT

A special utility, Macify, replaces plain quotation marks (") in a plain text document with opening and closing quotation marks (“ ”). The only requirement: You must save your document in text-only format. The utility also optionally changes pairs of apostrophes to opening and closing single quotes, double hyphens to em dashes, the *fi* and *fl* combinations to ligatures, and more. Macify is available from most user groups that have software libraries.

UNDERLINED BLANK SPACES

MacWrite

In MacWrite, the underline style apples only to text, not to blank spaces. You can underline a whole line, including any blank spaces, by creating a right-aligned tab with an underscore leader on the next line. (See Figure 6-6.) Choose the Tab command from the Format menu to set the fill character. To change the length of the rule, simply drag the tab marker in the formatting ruler. Choose the Paragraph command from the Format menu to adjust the amount of space between the rule and the line above it.

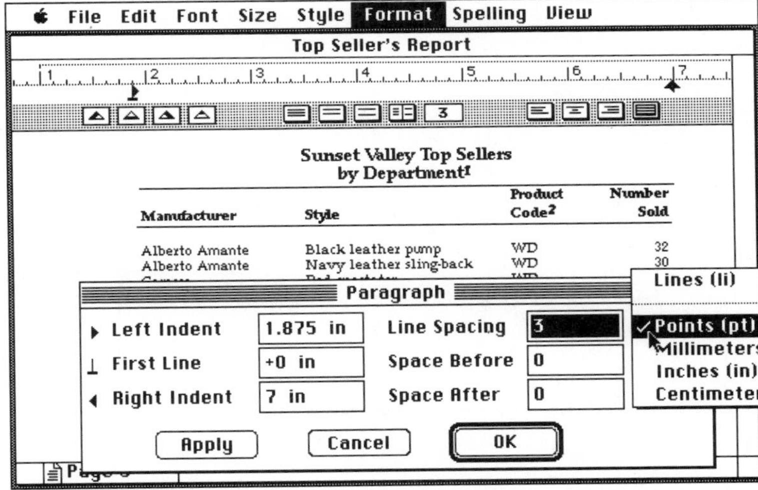

FIGURE 6-6. THE RULING PRINCIPLE.

In MacWrite, if the underline style doesn't underline blank spaces, draw a rule on the next line by using a right-aligned tab with an underscore as a fill character. Move the rule up or down by setting the line spacing of the rule and of the line above it in points.

ITALICS BEAT UNDERLINES

General Word Processing

Use boldface or italics in your documents instead of underlining. Underlined text is a fossil of the Early Pleistocene Typewriter period, when only typesetters had access to italics and boldface. You'll notice that typeset documents rarely contain underlined text (because it is generally considered hard to read). They use bold for headings and italics for emphasis, special terms, and book titles.

MATH WORKSHEETS

You can create math worksheets and complex formulas with a graphics program or with Microsoft Word's formulas feature. (Look it up in the Word reference manual.) But the simplest method is to use Expressionist, an editor for arithmetic and math expressions. (See Figure 6-7.) Be sure to get version 2.0 or later.

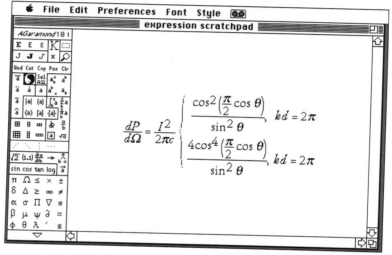

File Edit Preferences Font Style

expression scratchpad

$$\frac{dP}{d\Omega} = \frac{I^2}{2\pi c} \begin{cases} \dfrac{\cos^2\left(\frac{\pi}{2}\cos\theta\right)}{\sin^2\theta}, & kd = 2\pi \\ \dfrac{4\cos^4\left(\frac{\pi}{2}\cos\theta\right)}{\sin^2\theta}, & kd = 2\pi \end{cases}$$

FIGURE 6-7. EXPRESSION EDITOR.
Create math expressions with Expressionist, and then paste them into any other application.

CHOOSING FONTS

To choose a font in Microsoft Word without using a menu command, press Command-Shift-E, type the first few letters of the font name, and press Return. You must type enough letters to uniquely identify the font. The font name you type appears in the lower left corner of the document window.

FONT CONFUSION

The Font menu of Microsoft Word might not list the same fonts as the Character command. When you choose Character from the Format menu, you see all available fonts listed. The Font menu includes only the fonts that have been placed in it.

To add fonts to or remove fonts from the Font menu, use the Add To Menu command, as described in the tip "Custom Menus," earlier in this chapter.

REPEATED TEXT FORMAT CHANGES

For help in repeatedly changing text attributes such as fonts, sizes, and styles in blocks of text scattered throughout a Microsoft Word or Microsoft Write document, use the Find Formats and Find Again commands. First select some text that has the attributes you want to change. Don't change its attributes, however; instead, use the Find Formats command (or press Command-Option-R) to find and select the next instance of the same attributes. Now repeat the following steps as needed:

1. Change the attributes of the selected text, using menu commands or keyboard shortcuts. To change underlining to italics, for example, press Command-Shift-U to remove the underlining, and then press Command-Shift-I to apply italics.
2. Use the Find Again command (press Command-Option-A) to find the next instance of text with the same attributes as your original selection. (If you instead use the Find Formats command again, Word or Write will find the next instance of text having the new attributes of the current selection.)

Note: If your original selection uses any combination of boldface, italic, outline, shadow, strikethrough, small caps, all caps, and hidden text, the Find Formats command searches for those attributes and ignores any other formats the text might have, such as font, size, superscript, subscript, expanded characters, and condensed characters.

To further automate steps 1 and 2, use a macro utility such as AutoMac, MacroMaker, QuicKeys, or Tempo II. With MacroMaker, for example, you can record a macro that with one keystroke changes the attributes of the current text selection and "presses" Command-Option-A to find and select the next text to be changed.

TEXT FORMAT CHANGES IN BULK

You can change the text attributes (character formats) of a specific word or phrase throughout a Microsoft Word or Microsoft Write document with the Change command on the Search menu. First find an instance of the text you want changed and give it the attributes you want it to have. Select that text and choose Copy from the Edit menu to copy the text to the Clipboard. Click at the beginning of the document, and choose the Change command. In the Change dialog box, type the text you want found in the Find What box, and type *^c* (lowercase *c*) in the Change To box. This tells Word or Write to replace the text with the contents of the Clipboard.

Word or Write notes how the Clipboard text deviates from its normal character format and applies the same deviations to the normal character format of each instance of the search text. This method works best if all the text being changed has similar character formats. Applying a specific character style to text that already has that style results in text without the desired style. For example, applying the italic attribute to a word that is already italicized results in a nonitalic word.

Microsoft Word

Microsoft Write

FIND-AND-REPLACE TEXT FORMATS

Another way to change text attributes (font, size, and style) and make other formatting changes throughout a Microsoft Word or Microsoft Write document is to work with an RTF (Rich Text Format) version of the document. To convert a document to RTF, choose the Save As command, click its File Format button, select the Interchange Format (RTF) option, click OK, enter a new document name, and click the Save button. The document is saved as a plain text document with mnemonic codes for every format. For example, underline style is indicated by the three characters *\ul*. Other RTF codes are listed in the table in Figure 6-8. For complete RTF documentation, call Microsoft Customer Service at (206) 882-8088 or write to Microsoft Corporation, RTF/Applications, One Microsoft Way, Redmond WA 98052-6399.

After converting a document to RTF, you can replace one format with another by using the Change command. For example, replacing *\ul* with *\i* changes the format from underline to italic. When you finish changing formats, save the document and close it. Then open it again, clicking Yes when Word or Write asks whether it should interpret RTF codes. A little later, you'll see your formatted document with the changes you made.

Code	Format
\plain	Plain
\b	Bold*
\i	Italic*
\strike	Strikethrough*
\outl	Outline*
\shad	Shadow*
\scaps	Small caps*
\caps	All caps*
\v	Hidden*
\fx	Font number x**
\fsx	Font size: x half-points
\expndx	Expand or compress x quarter-points (negative x compresses)
\ul	Underline*
\ulw	Word underline*
\uld	Dotted underline*
\uldb	Double underline*
\ulnone	Cancel all underlining
\upx	Superscript x half-points
\dnx	Subscript x half-points

*These formats can be turned off by repeating the format code with a suffix of 0 (zero).

**A font table at the beginning of the document correlates fonts and font numbers. If you want to change to a font that's not listed in the font table, temporarily add some text in that font to the regular, non-RTF version of the document and then resave it as an RTF document.

FIGURE 6-8. RTF CODES.

To change the attributes of individual words throughout a Microsoft Word or Microsoft Write document, change their text attribute codes in the Rich Text Format (RTF) version of the document. Then convert the RTF version back to the Normal format.

WIDESPREAD TEXT STYLE CHANGES

WriteNow

WriteNow has a limited ability to change font, size, and style selectively throughout a document. If you press the Shift key while changing the text font, size, or style, WriteNow makes the changes only to currently selected text that has the same attribute as the first character of the current selection (before its change). For more control, you might be able to work with an RTF (Rich Text Format) version of the document.

To convert a WriteNow document to RTF, choose the Save As command, select its RTF (MS Interchange) option, enter a new document name, and click the Save button. Close the document. The document is saved as a plain text document with mnemonic codes for every format. For example, underlined text begins with the characters *ul* and ends with the characters *ulnone*. For other RTF codes, see the table in Figure 6-8. For complete RTF documentation, call Microsoft Product Support at (206) 454-2030 or write to Microsoft Corporation, RTF/Applications, One Microsoft Way, Redmond WA 98052-6399.

To make changes to an RTF document, open it as a plain text document: Choose Open from the File menu, select the Text document type, and double-click the document's name. In this plain text form, you can replace one text attribute with another using WriteNow's Change command. For example, replacing *ulnone* with *i0* (zero) and then replacing *ul* with *i* changes all underlined text to italics. When you finish changing attributes, save the document as a text document. Then open it as an RTF document. Soon you'll see your revised document with the text attributes changed.

Caution: WriteNow cannot always convert to and from RTF. Try converting your document to RTF and back and then checking over the document before using this tip.

MindWrite

PARAGRAPH LABEL FORMAT

A MindWrite heading label takes its font, size, and style characteristics from the last character in the paragraph it labels. If the period at the end of a paragraph is bold, for example, the label for that paragraph is bold also. To make the label plain text, add a space to the end of the paragraph, select the space, and change its style to plain text. This technique lets you make the style of your labels different from that of the paragraphs. Simply add a space at the end of a paragraph and change its font or style to the specifications you want.

Microsoft Word

Microsoft Write

QUICK SYMBOL

In Microsoft Word or Microsoft Write, press Command-Shift-Q to make the next character you type the Symbol font. This font change affects only a single character. As you continue typing, Word or Write reverts to the normal font. This feature is handy for formulas and technical documents.

OVERSTRIKE CHARACTERS

Microsoft Word

Microsoft Write

It's easy to create special symbols and characters by combining standard characters, using the commands for typesetting math formulas available in Microsoft Word and Microsoft Write. This lets you avoid the hassle of creating special fonts or having to use MacDraw or MacPaint to draw the special characters and then paste them into the Word or Write document. You create special characters by combining the overstrike command and the superscript/subscript command (not the *character formats* overstrike, superscript and subscript). For some examples of symbols often used in statistics and economics, see Figure 6-9.

Symbol	Formula	Characters Combined
$\bar{X}$	.\O(X,.\S.\UP11.\AI-11(_))	"X" and superscripted "_"
$\dot{P}_t$	.\O(P,.\S.\UP10.\AI-10(.).\S.\DO4(t)	"P", superscripted ".", and subscripted "t"
$\underset{\sim}{Y}$	.\O(Y,.\S.\DO7(~))	"Y" and subscripted "~"

FIGURE 6-9. COMBINING CHARACTERS.
Create special characters by using the math formula commands of Microsoft Word and Microsoft Write to combine standard characters.

To type formulas, you must make the Show ¶ option active. (Choose Show ¶ from the Edit menu or press Command-Y.) When you finish typing a formula, choose Hide ¶ from the Edit menu to see the results.

You begin every formula command and any command options with the formula character. To type it, press Command-Option-backslash. Word or Write displays this character as a backslash preceded by a dot (.\). (Do not type a period and a backslash.)

The overstrike command (.\O) superimposes two or more characters. Options let you align the superimposed characters at their center, left edge, or right edge. The displace command (.\D) is similar to the overstrike command. It lets you space forward or backward any number of points between two characters so that you can make them partially overlap. The superscript/subscript command (.\S) moves a character up or down the number of points you specify. Keep in mind that if you change fonts, styles, or font sizes, you might have to adjust the amount of displacement, superscript, or subscript. The Word and Write manuals and online help have

more information on formula commands, including a complete explanation of each formula command and its options. Look under "Formulas."

WORD COUNT

How can you count words in MacWrite II? Use MacWrite II's spelling checker. To count the number of words in a specific section of text, select the text and choose Check Selection from the Spelling menu. After a short time, you'll see the number of words in the lower right corner of the dialog box, as shown in Figure 6-10.

To count the total number of words in a document, you must count the number of words in the header, the footer, and the main body of text separately and add those totals together. To count the number of words in the main body of text, click in it and choose Check Main Body from the Spelling menu. To count the number of words in the header, click anywhere in it and choose Check Header. To count the number of words in the footer, click anywhere in it and choose Check Footer.

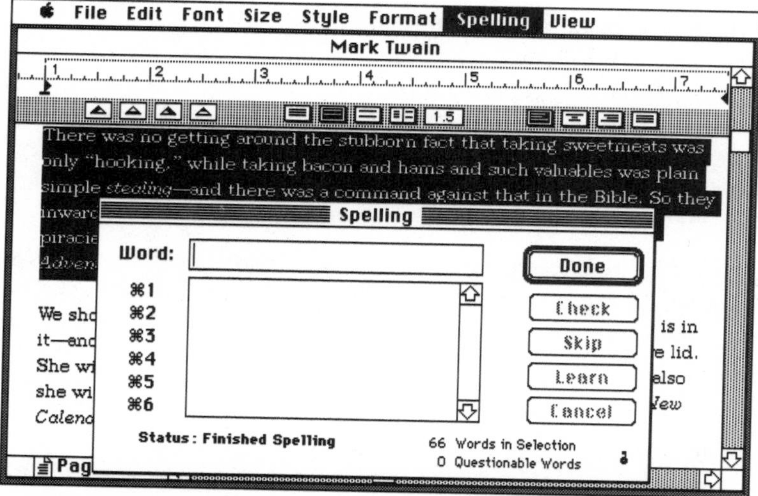

FIGURE 6-10. COUNT WORDS.

Use MacWrite II's spelling checker to count the words in the header, the footer, the main body of text, or any selected text.

LINES AND PARAGRAPHS

HAND-FIT SPACING

You can often squeeze an extra word onto a line without changing your margins, font, or font size. Simply reduce the font size of the spaces between the words. Furthermore, you can change the font of the blank space to one that takes less space. For example, Helvetica is smaller than the same point size of Geneva, and Times is smaller than New York. Of course, later editing might change the line breaks, necessitating additional fine-tuning.

The same trick also works with vertical spacing. When you need to fit one more line on a page, try reducing the font size and changing the font of any blank lines between paragraphs on that page.

To increase the height of a line in small increments, increase the font size of any blank space in the line. The larger the font size, the more space there is above the letters on the line. Giving the blank space the outline or shadow attribute increases the line height even more. Enlarging a blank space makes it not only taller, but wider as well. This side effect is invisible if you enlarge the blank space at the end of the line.

LINE SPACING

Many word processors give you precise control over the amount of space between lines of individual paragraphs or an entire document. You might also be able to specify whether the spacing is fixed or flexible. Flexible line spacing allows the word processor to increase the height of individual lines to accommodate superscripts, tall text, or graphics. Fixed line spacing freezes the line spacing of all selected paragraphs at the amount you specify. Letters that appear chopped off in fixed line spacing in fact print completely, although they may overstrike the line above or below. Figure 6-11 on the following page illustrates the differences.

To set the line spacing in WriteNow, use the linespacing controls at the right end of the formatting ruler. Click the closely spaced lines in the control to reduce line height by 1 point; click the widely spaced lines to increase line height by 1 point. The word *Flexible* or *Fixed* appears in the control to indicate which type of line spacing is set. Click the word to change the type of spacing.

To set the line spacing in Microsoft Word, choose the Paragraph command from the Format menu. For the Line option, enter a number and, optionally, the unit of measure: *pt* for points, *pi* for picas, *cm* for centimeters, or *in* for inches. If you don't enter a unit of measure, Word uses whatever unit of measure was set with the Preferences command. Word will set the line spacing according to the text size if you enter *Auto* instead of a number for the line spacing. Normally, Word uses flexible line spacing. To specify fixed line spacing, enter a negative number in the Line box.

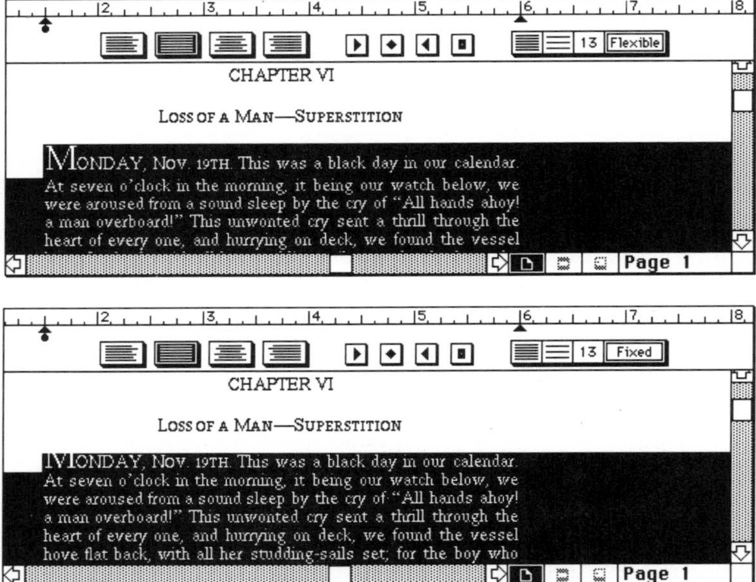

FIGURE 6-11. FIXED AND FLEXIBLE.
In WriteNow, you control the line spacing by indicating either "Fixed" or "Flexible" with the linespacing controls in the ruler.

CENTERING A LINE

When is a centered line not centered? When it has spaces at the beginning. Figure 6-12 illustrates the problem. (In WordPerfect and WriteNow, spaces at the end of a line also affect centering.) To remove all the extra blank spaces easily, click just before the first word of the line (or just after the last word), drag to the margin, and press Delete.

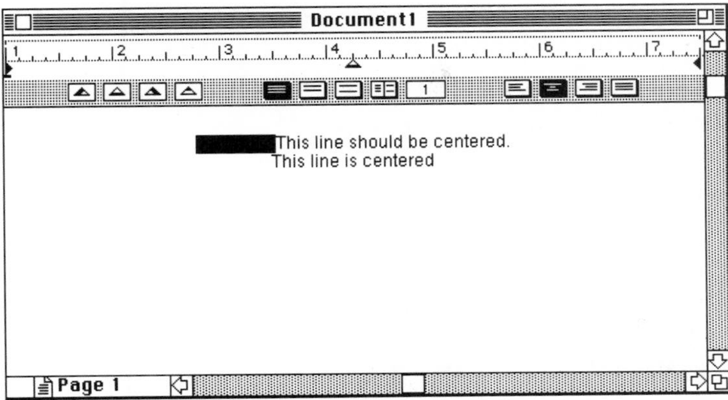

FIGURE 6-12. OFF-CENTERED.
Extra blank spaces at the beginning of a centered line throw the line off-center.

HANGING INDENT

To indent all lines of a paragraph below the first line (as opposed to indenting only the first line), place the left indent marker to the right of the first-line indent marker. Figure 6-13 on the following page shows how this looks in MacWrite II. In each paragraph, all the lines of text below the first line will be indented.

HANGING INDENT WITH TAB

In a paragraph with a hanging indent (the first-line indent is to the left of the left indent), most word processors treat the left indent marker as a tab stop. This feature makes it easy to type numbered lists and bulleted lists. (See Figure 6-14 on the following page.) You type the number or the bullet to start a paragraph and then press Tab to align the first word at the left indent marker.

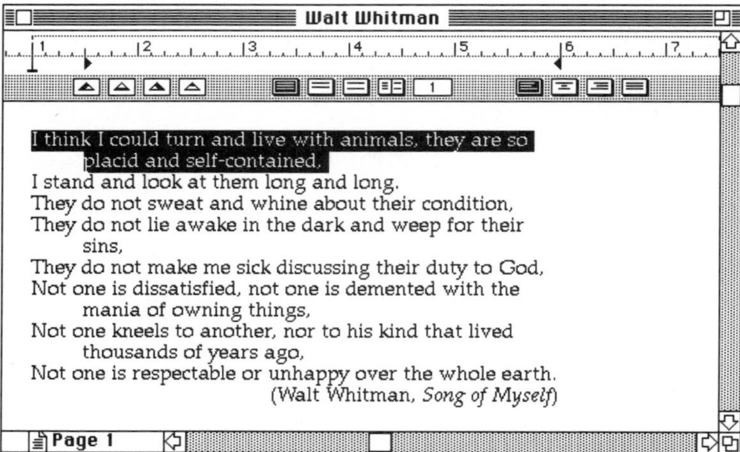

FIGURE 6-13. OUTDENT.

A left indent marker to the right of the first-line indent marker causes all but the first line of a paragraph to be indented.

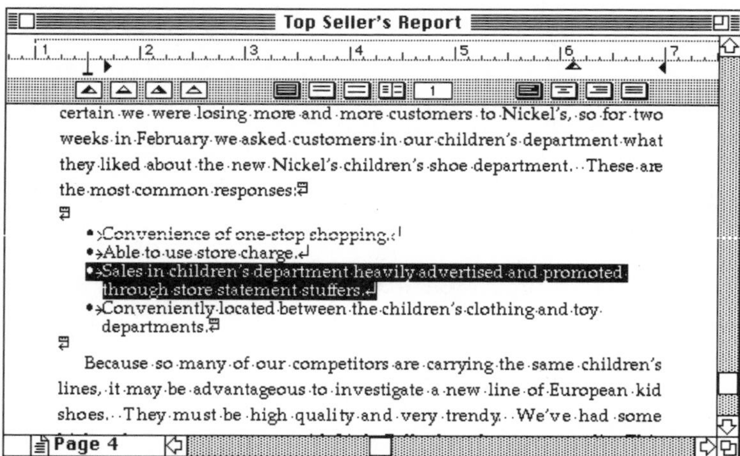

FIGURE 6-14. LIST CONSTRUCTION.

In this list, the first-line indent marker is to the left of the left indent marker. A tab aligns the text at the left indent marker.

FLUSH SUBHEADS

Here's one way to indent the first line of paragraphs but make subheads flush with the left margin with a minimum of formatting fuss. Set the first-line indent marker for indented paragraphs, and set an ordinary tab stop about two characters from the right margin. (See Figure 6-15.) When you come the end of a paragraph before a subhead, press Return and then Tab. (If you don't want a blank line before the subhead, press Tab without pressing Return.) When you begin typing, the line will wrap around so that the subhead is flush with the left margin. If you have other tabs set, you might need to press Tab more than once. And if the first word of the subhead is short, you might have to prefix it with a few blank spaces to make it wrap around to the left margin. You can also try moving the tab nearer the right margin. This method works with any word processor that allows automatic indents.

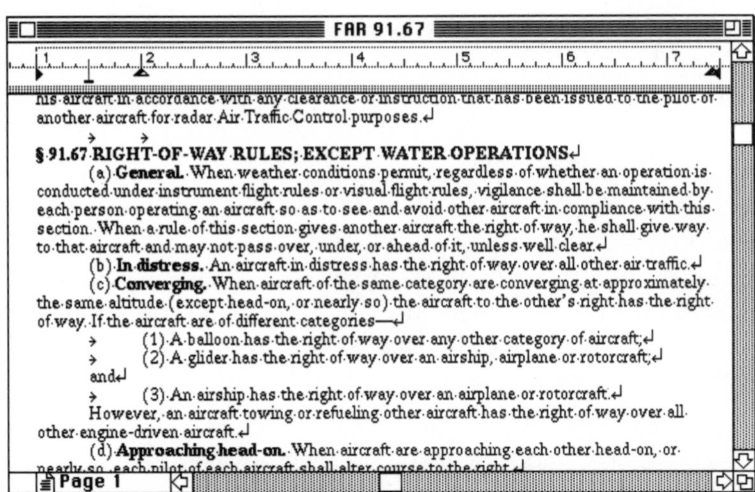

his aircraft in accordance with any clearance or instruction that has been issued to the pilot of another aircraft for radar Air Traffic Control purposes.

§ 91.67 RIGHT-OF-WAY RULES; EXCEPT WATER OPERATIONS

(a) **General.** When weather conditions permit, regardless of whether an operation is conducted under instrument flight rules or visual flight rules, vigilance shall be maintained by each person operating an aircraft so as to see and avoid other aircraft in compliance with this section. When a rule of this section gives another aircraft the right of way, he shall give way to that aircraft and may not pass over, under, or ahead of it, unless well clear.

(b) **In distress.** An aircraft in distress has the right of way over all other air traffic.

(c) **Converging.** When aircraft of the same category are converging at approximately the same altitude (except head-on, or nearly so) the aircraft to the other's right has the right of way. If the aircraft are of different categories—

(1) A balloon has the right of way over any other category of aircraft;

(2) A glider has the right of way over an airship, airplane or rotorcraft; and

(3) An airship has the right of way over an airplane or rotorcraft.

However, an aircraft towing or refueling other aircraft has the right of way over all other engine-driven aircraft.

(d) **Approaching head-on.** When aircraft are approaching each other head-on, or nearly so, each pilot of each aircraft shall alter course to the right.

FIGURE 6-15. FLUSH INDENTS.

This MacWrite II formatting ruler yields indented paragraphs when you press Return; it yields flush-left headings when you press Tab once or twice and enter a couple of blank spaces.

TAB STYLES

How can you set left, right, decimal, and center tabs in a Microsoft Works word processing document? Click in the blank area of the formatting ruler, below the ruler markings. Click once for a left tab, twice for a right tab, three times for a decimal tab, or four times for a center tab. If you accidentally click too many times, simply keep on clicking until Works cycles around to the tab style you want to set.

WriteNow

TAB LEADERS

Any character can be used as a tab fill in a WriteNow document. Simply type the desired fill character before releasing the Tab key. WriteNow displays the character at evenly spaced intervals up to the next tab stop. To adjust the spacing and appearance of the fill characters, change their font, size, and style.

WriteNow

WRITENOW STYLE SHEETS

WriteNow's lack of style sheets can be a problem if you frequently change paragraph formats within a document. To change formats quickly and ensure consistency throughout the document, set up a sample of all formats at the end of the document. Then use WriteNow's Copy Ruler and Paste Ruler commands to copy formats from the samples and paste them into the appropriate paragraphs in the text.

If you later need to change one of the formats—for example, from single spacing to double spacing—use WriteNow's Identical Settings feature. That is, select everything from the first paragraph that has the format you want changed to the end of the document, and then hold down the Shift key while making ruler changes. The changes you make affect only paragraphs having exactly the same format as the first one you selected.

The Copy Ruler and Paste Ruler commands do not copy character attributes such as font, size, and style. If you want to copy both character and paragraph formats, use the regular Copy and Paste commands with an appropriate sample paragraph from the end of your document. (Select the pasted sample text and type the actual text as a replacement.)

MacWrite II

Microsoft Works

MACWRITE STYLE SHEETS

Style sheets make changing paragraph styles a snap. MacWrite and Microsoft Works don't have style sheets, but you can fake them with a set of preformatted sample paragraphs at the end of your document. In MacWrite II, use the Copy Ruler and Paste Ruler commands from the Format menu to copy a format from the appropriate sample paragraph and apply it to the paragraph that needs formatting. In Microsoft Works, use the Copy Format and Paste Format commands from the Format menu.

This procedure copies only paragraph formats: justification, indention, tabs, and line spacing. If you want to copy character formats such as font, size, and style as well, use the regular Copy and Paste commands with an appropriate sample paragraph from the end of your document. (After pasting a copy of the sample paragraph, select the copy and type the actual paragraph as a replacement.)

KEEPING PARAGRAPHS TOGETHER

Microsoft Word

MacWrite

To keep paragraphs from breaking across page boundaries in a Microsoft Word document, scroll from the beginning of your document and look for undesirable page breaks. When you spot one, click an insertion point before it and insert a manual page break. This procedure also works in MacWrite versions 5.0 and earlier.

FOLLOWING STYLE

Microsoft Word

Microsoft Word resets the paragraph style each time you press Return at the end of a paragraph. The Next Style specification for the current paragraph style (set with the Define Styles command) determines the new paragraph style. For example, a heading style such as Heading 1 is usually followed by the Normal style.

You can retain the current paragraph format in subsequent paragraphs, bypassing the Next Style specification altogether. At the end of the current paragraph type a blank space, press the Left arrow key, and then press the Return key. Because the insertion point is not at the end of the paragraph when you press Return, Word ignores the Next Style specification. Instead, it uses the current paragraph style for the new paragraph. At the end of the new paragraph, simply press Return to continue the style.

When you want the next paragraph to use the Next Style, use the mouse, the Right arrow key, or any other method to move the insertion point to the end of the current paragraph (past your extra space character). Then press Return. Because the insertion point is at the end of the paragraph, Word uses the paragraph's Next Style specification for the following paragraph.

Microsoft Word

COPYING ALL STYLES

You can copy all styles of a Microsoft Word document into another Word document. With the destination document open, choose Define Styles from the Format menu. Then choose Open from the File menu, select the source document, and click Open. Incoming styles replace existing styles with the same name in the destination document.

Microsoft Word

COPYING A FEW STYLES

If you want to copy one or a few styles from one Microsoft Word document to another Word document without bringing in the entire style sheet, try the following:

First open the document that has the style or styles you want to copy. Select a paragraph that is formatted in the desired style and copy it to the Clipboard. To copy several styles at once, copy a series of paragraphs that contain all the desired styles. (Or, create paragraphs just for this purpose and use Cut instead of Copy.) Now open the document to which you want to copy the styles, and paste the paragraphs. The new styles will appear in the style sheet. You can then delete the text you pasted, and the styles will remain. Note that the incoming styles won't update or replace any styles already in the destination document, such as Normal. Existing styles take precedence over incoming styles with the same name.

Microsoft Word

Microsoft Write

NEW LINE, SAME PARAGRAPH

How can you start a new line without starting a new paragraph in a Microsoft Word or Microsoft Write document? Press Shift-Return to continue typing on the next line at the left margin. Text before and after the new line is all part of a single paragraph and is governed by one formatting ruler. Pressing Return alone starts a new paragraph, with its own formatting ruler.

Microsoft Word

Microsoft Write

FORMATTING-RULER CHICANERY

In Microsoft Word and Microsoft Write, every paragraph has its own formatting ruler. The ruler is associated with the return character (paragraph mark) at the end of the paragraph. If you move or remove a return character, you also move or remove a formatting ruler. For example, if you paste paragraph A into the middle of paragraph B, the format of the first part of

paragraph B changes to match the format of paragraph A. In other words, the first part of paragraph B becomes the first part of paragraph A. To copy the text from paragraph A but not the format, exclude the return character at the end of paragraph A when you select it.

Unintentional changes to a paragraph's format also occur if you accidentally remove the return character at the end of the paragraph. To avoid unintentionally including the return character in the selection, use caution when selecting text at the end of a paragraph.

Return characters are normally invisible, but you can see them by choosing Show ¶ from the Edit menu.

SCROLLING LEFT OF 0

To scroll to the left of 0 on the Microsoft Word ruler, press the Shift key and click the left scroll arrow at the bottom of the document window.

CONTROLLING FORMULAS

One of the Microsoft Word and Microsoft Write formula commands, .\I, can create the integral (∫), summation (Σ), and product (Π) operators. The size of the operator depends on the height of the operand, which is normally the third argument of the .\I command. As a result, you might end up with small, medium, and large operators on the same page of a document. To produce operators of uniform size, use a superscripted blank space as the third argument of the .\I command and put the actual operand after the .\I command. For example,

```
.\I(a,b,.\S.\UP5())f(x)dx
```

yields

$$\int_a^b f(x)\,dx$$

To adjust the size of the operator, change the value of the superscript. For example, UP20 makes a larger operator than UP5.

PAGES AND DOCUMENTS

CONTROLLING PAGINATION

Don't insert manual page breaks to control pagination in a Microsoft Word document. To keep all lines of a paragraph on the same page, select the paragraph and set the Keep Lines Together option, using the Paragraph command (in the Format menu). To keep two or more paragraphs on the same page, select all of them except the last one and set the Keep With Next ¶ option in the Paragraph dialog box.

EASY FOOTNOTES

If your word processor doesn't provide automatic footnoting, there's a fairly easy way to handle the deficiency. Enter the text of a footnote immediately after the line on which you place the reference to it, as shown in Figure 6-16. If your footnote style calls for a rule or a blank line separating footnotes from the main text, type one above each footnote.

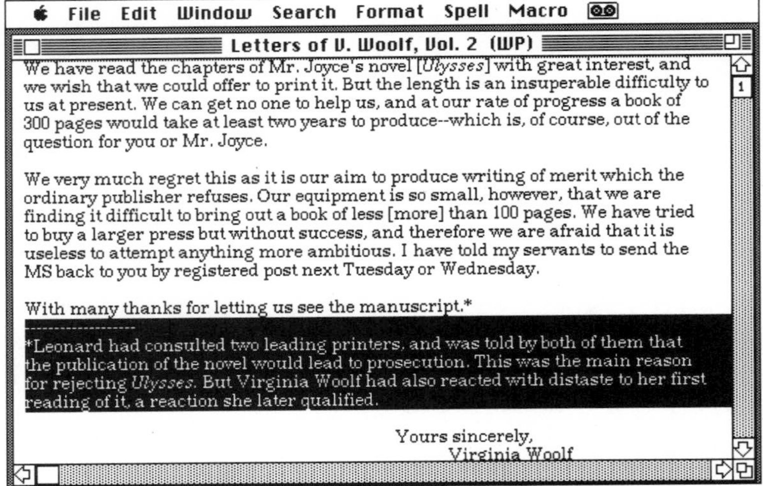

We have read the chapters of Mr. Joyce's novel [*Ulysses*] with great interest, and we wish that we could offer to print it. But the length is an insuperable difficulty to us at present. We can get no one to help us, and at our rate of progress a book of 300 pages would take at least two years to produce--which is, of course, out of the question for you or Mr. Joyce.

We very much regret this as it is our aim to produce writing of merit which the ordinary publisher refuses. Our equipment is so small, however, that we are finding it difficult to bring out a book of less [more] than 100 pages. We have tried to buy a larger press but without success, and therefore we are afraid that it is useless to attempt anything more ambitious. I have told my servants to send the MS back to you by registered post next Tuesday or Wednesday.

With many thanks for letting us see the manuscript.*

----

*Leonard had consulted two leading printers, and was told by both of them that the publication of the novel would lead to prosecution. This was the main reason for rejecting *Ulysses*. But Virginia Woolf had also reacted with distaste to her first reading of it, a reaction she later qualified.

Yours sincerely,
Virginia Woolf

FIGURE 6-16. NOTA BENE.

To simplify footnotes, type them just below the line to which they refer. Later, cut the footnotes and paste them at the bottom of the page.

Complete all your writing, editing, rewriting, and pagination. Then go back through the document one last time and cut and paste each footnote (with its separating rule or blank line) to the bottom of the page. Because you paste the same number of lines you cut, the page breaks are undisturbed. If you end up with too many rules at the bottom of a page, you can replace extra rules with blank lines.

ACCOMMODATING PRINTED LETTERHEADS

General Word Processing

When typing a letter that will be printed on letterhead stationery, you must plan for the space taken up by the letterhead. Change the top margin to the distance from the top of the page to the line on which you want to begin printing. For a multiple-page letter, enter blank lines at the beginning of the letter instead of changing the margin.

TOP-TO-BOTTOM CENTERING

General Word Processing

How can you vertically center text on a page if your word processor has no command for doing it? Add the correct number of blank lines above the text. Here's one approach:

1. Remove extra blank lines above and below the text to be centered.
2. Below the text, press Return repeatedly, counting the number of times you press Return, until a page break appears.
3. Press Delete half the number of times you pressed Return.
4. Select all the remaining blank lines below the text.
5. Cut the selected lines and paste them above the text.
6. If more text follows on another page, insert a page break below the centered text.

PASTING PICTURES PRECISELY

General Word Processing

Copying a picture from MacPaint, SuperPaint, PixelPaint, or another paint-style graphics application into a word processing document should be a simple task—a matter of cut or copy and paste. But sometimes the place where the picture ends up in the text document seems to be controlled by mysterious, supernatural forces. A picture that seems offset might have extra white space around it, as shown in Figure 6-17. Word processors treat the whole picture—surrounding white space included—as an indivisible unit. The extra white space results when you select too large an area with the selection rectangle. The graphics application might tighten the selection rectangle to eliminate extra white space if you press the Command key while dragging the selection rectangle. Alternatively, select with the lasso.

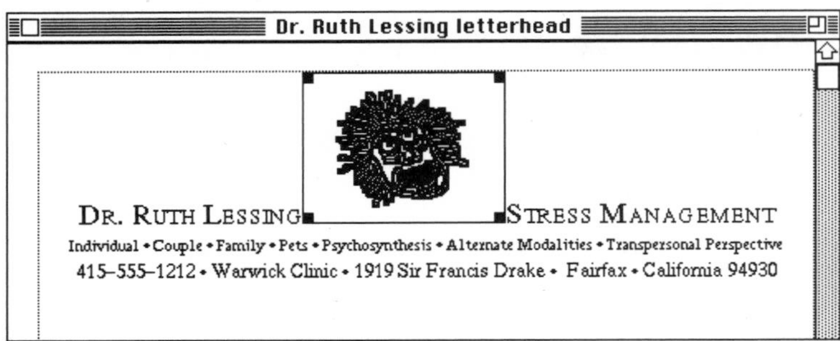

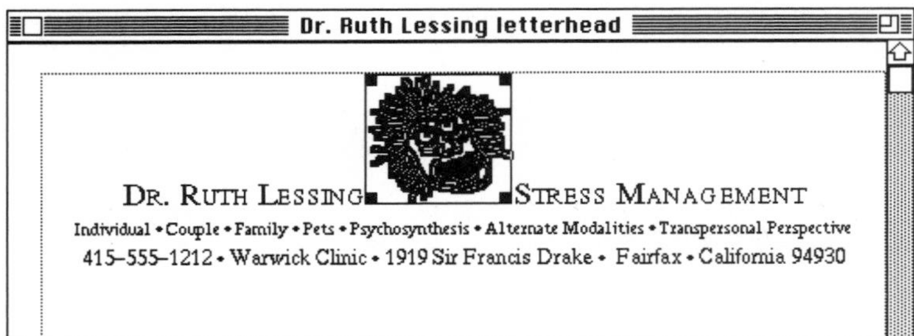

FIGURE 6-17. UNWANTED WHITE SPACE.
Bit-mapped graphics that you copy and paste from MacPaint or other paint-style graphics applications might have extra white space around the edges. You can avoid having the extra space by selecting very carefully before copying from the graphics application.

WriteNow

CHANGING DOCUMENT MARGINS

Normally, when you select some text and change the left margin in a WriteNow document, all paragraphs selected acquire that new left margin. However, if you press and hold the Command key while making the ruler change, the paragraphs will maintain their indentation relative to one another. With this technique, you can change the overall document margin and still maintain the relative indentation of individual paragraphs.

CHANGING ALL NORMAL PARAGRAPHS

Style sheets make it easy to change all normal paragraphs of a Microsoft Word document at once. Choose Define Styles from the Format menu; the dialog box shown in Figure 6-18 appears. Select the Normal style. Next use the commands in the Format menu and the Font menu to change the formatting. When the format is the way you want it, click the Define button and then close the Define Styles dialog box. If you click OK instead of the close box or the Cancel button, Word applies the selected style (Normal) to the paragraphs currently selected in your document. Note that clicking the Cancel button won't reverse any changes you make to the Normal style after you change it by clicking Define.

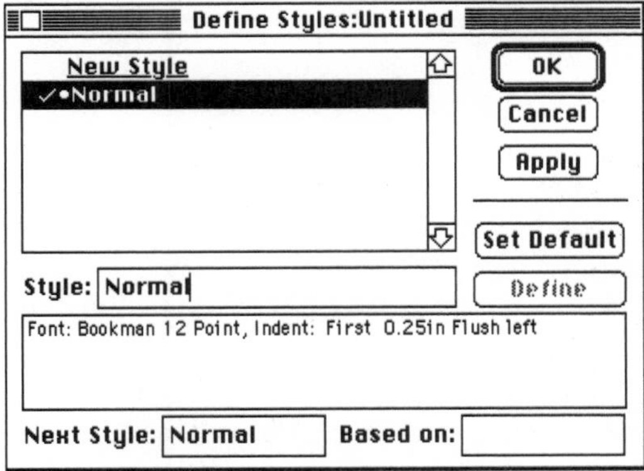

FIGURE 6-18. DEFINE STYLES DIALOG BOX.
This is the dialog box for Microsoft Word's Define Styles command, which you can use to change the character and paragraph format of all paragraphs having the same style throughout a document.

QUICK FORMATTING IN WORD

Store frequently used paragraph formats and section breaks in a Word glossary. Glossary entries are easily called up; you simply type a short mnemonic abbreviation or choose from a scrollable list. To insert a glossary entry at the insertion point, press Command-Delete, type the name of the entry, and press Return. Alternatively, choose Glossary from the Edit menu, select the name of the entry from the scrollable list that appears, and click the Insert button.

For fastest access to a few glossary entries, add them to the Work menu. To add an entry, press Command-Option-plus and go through the motions (described in the previous paragraph) of inserting the entry.

GLOSSARY USES

Word's glossary feature is more powerful than it might appear at first glance. It's not just for boilerplate text. You can store a template for an entire document—a letter, an invoice, or an envelope—as a single glossary entry. Simply create a sample of the document's character, paragraph, and division formats with dummy text. Then copy it all and paste it into the glossary. Similarly, you can use glossary entries for often-repeated parts of documents that you want formatted alike, such as tables, figure captions, chapter openings, and numbered lists.

MULTICOLUMN LASER LABELS

You can print a full page of multicolumn mailing labels on a LaserWriter by using Microsoft Word's Print Merge command. The directions in the Word manual for printing multicolumn labels on a LaserWriter might result in leaving the top and bottom row of labels blank. The trick is to use the Page Setup command (on the File menu) to set the US Legal option. Also, click the Option button and select the Larger Print Area option in the Page Setup dialog box. Then use the Document command (on the Format menu) to set the top margin to 0.194 inch (14 points), the bottom margin to 2.75 inches (198 points), and the left and right margins to 0.25 inch (18 points) each. Before clicking OK, be sure the Even/Odd Headers option is off. These settings enable you to print on all rows of labels.

The table feature of Word versions 4.0 and later makes it easy to prepare the main print-merge document, which specifies the format of the printed labels. Choose Insert Table from the Document menu and enter the number of columns you want to print. (Word calculates the proper column width.) In each column of the table, type a template for the labels in that column. Each template contains the field names in the order in which you want them to appear. (See Figure 6-19.) You can use *«if»* instructions to skip empty fields. More *«if»* instructions at the end of the first template compensate for skipped fields by inserting blank lines. (Only the first template needs to compensate because it determines the label height for all the labels.) All but the last template must end with a *«next»* instruction so that Word will read a new data record for the next template. Word automatically reads a new record at the end of the main print-merge document.

To get more than one row of labels per page, you must choose Section from the Format menu and select No Break for the Start option.

After choosing the Print Merge menu command, you must click the New Document button to create a new document of merged labels. Use the Print Preview command to double-check that an address will print on every label. If for some reason the last row of labels is blank, make the bottom margin smaller in the new document. Then use the Print command to print the new document onto label stock.

You can adjust the gap between rows of labels by selecting the last line of the first label in the template, choosing the Paragraph command, and changing the After option.

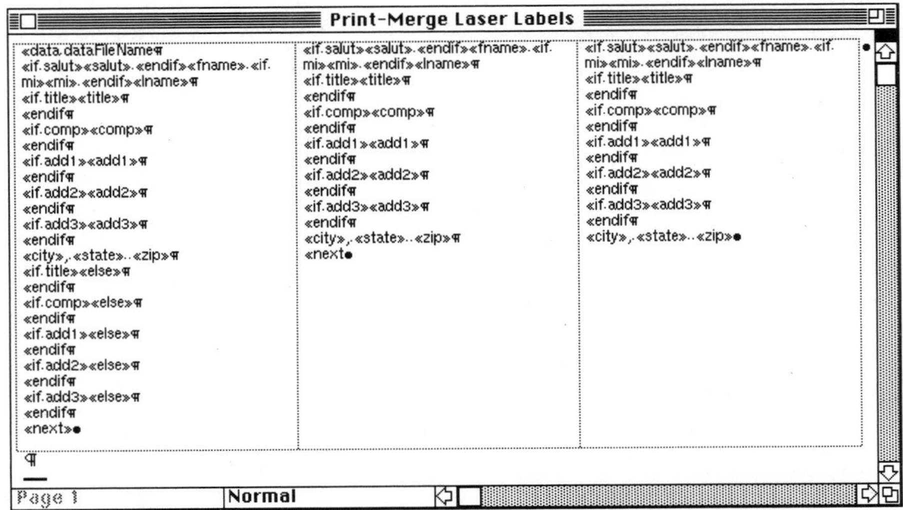

FIGURE 6-19. PRINT-MERGE LASER LABELS.

This Microsoft Word table specifies where information goes when you are printing three-column labels (twenty-four 1.375-inch labels per sheet) on a LaserWriter with the Print Merge command. Settings in the Page Setup and Document dialog boxes make it possible to print all labels on a page (no blank top or bottom row).

PRINT MERGE BY NUMBERS

Microsoft Word's Print Merge command lets you print a range of records from a data document. You specify the range by giving the beginning and ending record numbers. However, determining record numbers is tricky because you have to count them manually.

The solution to this problem is to number the records with the Renumber command on the Utilities menu. When you choose Renumber, specify a starting number of 0, which Word will assign to the first record—the header record—in the data document. Word places a tab character after every number, effectively adding another field at the beginning of every data record. The extra field does not interfere with the Print Merge command, nor does it appear in your form letters, mailing labels, or other merge-printed documents. Figure 6-20 shows a data document with numbers added using this method.

If your data document uses commas to separate fields, however, you must change the tab characters to commas. Click at the beginning of the document, choose Change from the Utilities menu, type *^t* in the Find What box and a comma in the Change To box, and click the Change All button.

Names

0.	name	street	city	state	zip
1.	Achilles de la Cruz	2349 Granger Lane	Abilene	TX	79624
2.	Babe Rothschild	944 Harrimore Road	Salina	KS	67410
3.	Fidel F. Flat	4309 Western Blvd.	Fort Collins	CO	80255
4.	Buck O. Racine	74202 Peach Blossom Hwy.	Marietta	GA	30063
5.	Venus Crooke	525 Shore Line Drive	Ely	NV	89601
6.	Plato Greenfield	72 Country Club Circle	Sheridan	WY	82801
7.	Cleopatra Kelly	828 Monument Ave.	Rapid City	SD	57305
8.	Zoltan Amadeus Power	175 Bolton Place	Cherry Hill	NJ	08004
9.	Bliss Hashimoto	6504 Bowsprit	Pawtucket	RI	02864
10.	Atlas Fang	4400 Glade Road, Apt. 500	Pampano Beach	FL	33066
11.	Biff Van Loo, Jr.	3850 Mt. Vernon Drive	Newport News	VA	23620
12.	Jezebel Lucretia Rodgers	888 Jack Tone Road	Wilkes-Barre	PA	18735
13.	Glory Vasquez	6003 Yavasupai Street	Las Cruces	NM	88008
14.	Zero McTush	2090 Avenue B	Paducah	KY	42001
15.	Aphrodite Elf	577 Warnock St.	Wausau	WI	54401

Page 1 Normal+...

FIGURE 6-20. NUMBERED MERGE RECORDS.

Use Microsoft Word's Renumber command to number each line of a document that contains data to be used with a Print Merge command. The line numbers make it easy to restrict printing to a range of records.

REPRINTING ONE FORM LETTER

After printing 150 form letters using a merge document and a database document in Microsoft Works, you discover that letter number 89 contains an error. To correct and reprint only letter 89, do the following:

1. Correct the information for letter 89 in the database.
2. Select (highlight) record 89 in the database.
3. Switch to the word processing letter, using the Window menu.
4. The revised letter 89 should appear in the form-letter window. If you see field names in the form letter instead of the information for field 89, choose Show Field Data from the Edit menu.
5. Choose Print—not Print Merge—from the File menu to print only letter 89.

SAVING COMPACTLY

To reduce the amount of disk space a WriteNow document occupies, press Option while choosing Save from the File menu. WriteNow normally keeps two copies of your document on disk. (This does not require twice the disk space because text that's common to both versions is shared between the two copies.) Pressing Option while saving deletes one copy.

To reduce the amount of disk space a Microsoft Word document occupies, use the Save As command instead of the Save command (in the File menu). Turn off the Fast Save option before clicking the Save button. Word normally reduces the time it takes to save a document by adding your recent changes to the end of the document on disk. With the Fast Save option off, Word saves the entire document. This takes longer but uses less disk space. Word turns the Fast Save option back on after it finishes saving.

To add Word's Fast Save option to the Edit menu, press Command-Option-plus and go through the motions of turning off the Fast Save option. As you do so, the pointer has the shape of a large plus sign. With the Fast Save option in the Edit menu, Word does not turn on the option after saving.

ILLUSTRATIONS AND SPECIAL EFFECTS

RESIZING AND MOVING GRAPHICS

MacWrite

To resize graphics pasted into MacWrite, grab a handle and drag in the direction you want the graphic to grow. To proportionally resize a graphic pasted into MacWrite II, click the graphic to select it and choose the Scale Picture command from the Format menu. When the Scale Picture dialog-box appears, enter the percentage by which you would like to alter the image. Enter the same number for horizontal and vertical scaling. Then click OK. If you are printing on a LaserWriter, some percentages work better than others. Specifically, multiples of 24 (24, 48, 72, 96, and so on) work best if the Page Setup command's Precision Bitmap Alignment option is off. If that option is on, multiples of 25 work best (25, 50, 75, 100, and so on).

To center or reposition the graphic on the page, select the graphic, grab one of the lines surrounding it (not a handle), and drag horizontally to the desired position on the page.

CROPPING GRAPHICS

MacWrite II

Sometimes a graphic you paste into a word processing document contains extra blank space, or you want only part of the graphic to show. To crop a graphic to fit in a MacWrite II document, press Option while dragging one of the handles at the corner of the selected graphic.

DECORATIVE BORDERS

General Word Processing

Character formats can transform a line of ordinary symbols into a decorative border. For example, an underlined underscore produces a double horizontal line. Figure 6-21 shows more examples.

Plain Border	Keystroke	Decorative Border	Style
************	Shift-8	************	Outline
----------------	Hyphen	----------------	Shadow
________________	Shift-hyphen	________________	Underline
000000000	0	00000000	Italic, outline
....	Period	....	Outline
::::::::::::::::::	Colon	::::::::::::::::	Italic, shadow
••••••••	Option-8	••••••••	Outline
÷÷÷÷÷÷÷÷	Option-/	÷÷÷÷÷÷÷÷	Bold, italic
◊◊◊◊◊◊◊◊◊◊	Option-Shift-V	◊◊◊◊◊◊◊◊◊	Bold, outline

FIGURE 6-21. BORDER LINE STYLE.
Combine characters and styles for decorative borders.

AUTOMATIC WRITING

FullWrite Professional can number figures, tables, equations, and other items for you and will renumber them and references to them as you move them within your document. The Classify command numbers an item, and the Insert Citation command puts a reference to the item in the text, such as *See Figure 2.* The FullWrite reference manual explains how to do that. But the manual doesn't tell you how to create a caption that Fullwrite will renumber if you move the item. For example, if you move your second figure to the beginning of your document, you want FullWrite to renumber its caption as well as all references in the text to the figure. You can achieve this by inserting a short citation, such as *Figure 2,* as a caption or part of a caption on a line adjacent to the figure. However, you have to remember to move that line whenever you move the figure.

A better solution is to create a new sidebar at the point where you want the figure or other item to appear, paste or otherwise place the item in the sidebar, and classify the item. Also in the sidebar, put a short citation as a caption or part of a caption. Now moving the sidebar moves the item with its caption and automatically changes all references to the item, including its caption. Figure 6-22 on the following page illustrates the process.

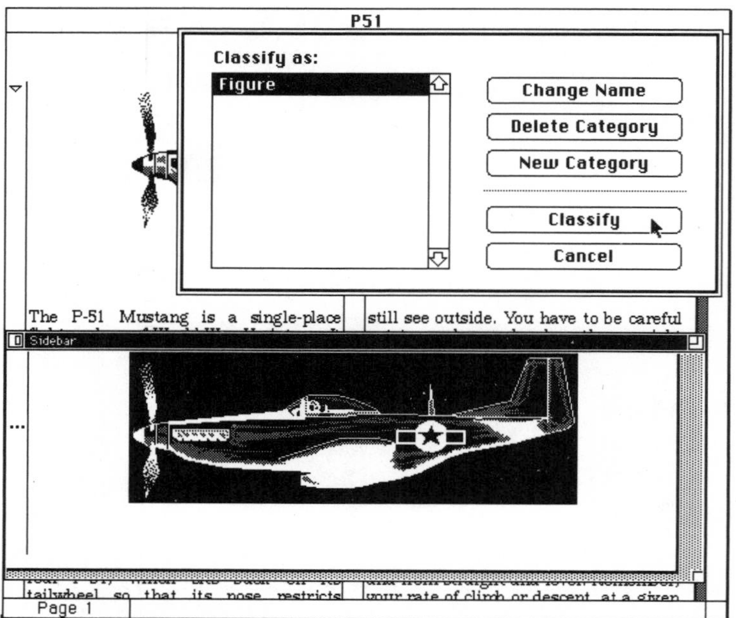

FIGURE 6-22. NUMBERED CAPTION.

To make a figure with a numbered caption in FullWrite Professional, first create a new sidebar, place the figure contents in the sidebar, and classify the contents (above). Next, insert a citation in the sidebar (top of next page). Then type any caption text and make any changes to the text font, style, and size (bottom of next page).

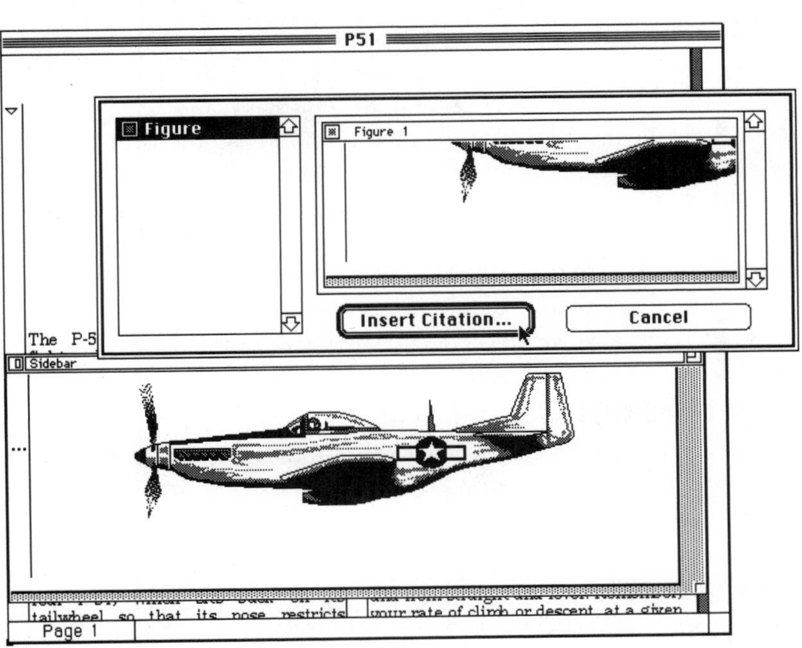
P51
Figure
Figure 1
Insert Citation...
Cancel
Sidebar
Page 1

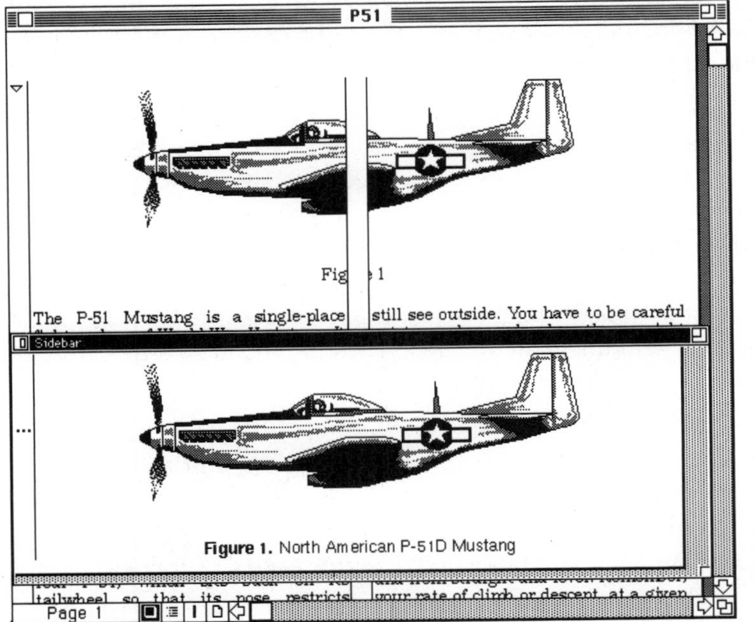
P51
The P-51 Mustang is a single-place
still see outside. You have to be careful
Sidebar
Figure 1. North American P-51D Mustang
Page 1

FullWrite Professional

OVERCLASSIFIED

It's easy to accidentally assign more than one number to an item in a FullWrite document—to call one figure both *Figure 3* and *Figure 4*, for example. To remove an extra classification number, use the Browse command to go to the line that contains the extra classification. Then look for a classification-mark icon next to that line in the icon bar. (If the icon bar contains only an ellipsis, double-click it to expand the icon bar and see the multiple icons attached to the line.) Double-click a classification-mark icon to have FullWrite identify it in a dialog box. Dismiss the dialog box, select the icon you want to remove, and choose Clear from the Edit menu.

Microsoft Word

POSTSCRIPT NO-SHOW

A PostScript program on a page by itself in your Microsoft Word document might not print. In such cases, put a blank line formatted in Normal style after the last PostScript line.

Microsoft Word

POSTSCRIPT IN WORD

To get special effects such as rotated text and gray type on a LaserWriter or other PostScript printer, you can include PostScript programs in your Microsoft Word documents. Word does not print PostScript programs. Instead, it sends them to the PostScript printer for interpretation.

Put a PostScript program between any two paragraphs on the page on which you want it to print. If you want a program to print on every page, include it in a header or footer. You can freely intersperse blank lines and blank spaces for better readability, but do not use tabs or the program won't work. After typing the program, you must format it in Word's standard PostScript style. Simply select the entire program, press Command-Shift-S, type the word *PostScript*, and press Return. Be sure you format the whole program, including blank lines. On screen, the PostScript program will be in the same font as the Normal style, but at a font size of 10 point and with the bold and hidden attributes.

A sample PostScript program appears in Figure 6-23, and its output appears in Figure 6-24 on the page after next. The first line of the program defines a macro named Inches, which converts inches to points. The next two lines set the initial text rotation to 90 degrees and the gray level to 0.9 (10 percent gray).

```
/inches {72 mul} def
/rotangle 90 def
/graylevel .9 def

/rotationloop {gsave
0 0 moveto
rotangle rotate
graylevel setgray
(Impact) show
/rotangle rotangle 2 sub def
/graylevel graylevel .02 sub def
grestore} def

/AvantGarde-DemiOblique findfont 28 scalefont setfont
.5 setlinewidth
gsave
36 wp$y 108 sub translate
45 {rotationloop} repeat
0 0 moveto 0 setgray (Impact Communications) show
0 0 moveto (Impact) true charpath gsave 1 setgray fill
grestore stroke
grestore
```

FIGURE 6-23. POSTSCRIPT SAMPLE.
This PostScript program sweeps the word "Impact" through a 90-degree arc, as shown in Figure 6-24 on the following page.

Next the program defines another macro, Rotationloop. The macro uses a Gsave operator to save the current graphics state. In the new graphics state, a Moveto operator places the pen at the lower left corner of the drawing area, Rotate and Setgray operators set the current rotation angle and gray level, and a Show operator draws the word "Impact." Then Sub operators decrease the rotation angle by 22.5 degrees and darken the gray level by 15 percent. The macro ends by restoring the graphics state to its previous condition with a Grestore operator.

With definitions and initializations done, the program sets the font to Avant Garde Demi Oblique, bold italic, 28 points. The Findfont, Scalefont, and Setfont operators do that. Then a Gsave operator saves the current graphics state. In the new graphics state, a Translate operator moves the lower left corner of the drawing area 2 inches to the right of and 3 inches above the absolute lower left corner of the page. Finally, a Repeat operator repeats the Rotationloop macro five times and a Grestore operator restores the graphics state to its previous condition.

FIGURE 6-24. SWEPT TEXT.
PostScript makes it easy to experiment with special effects such as text rotation. The text in this rotating sequence is 28-point Avant Garde bold italic. The gray level starts at 10 percent and darkens 2 percent with each line. The rotation angle ranges from 90 degrees to 0 degrees in 2-degree increments.

WATERMARK

Distinguish copies, drafts, and confidential documents created with Microsoft Word by watermarking them with ghosted outline text. Do this by adding a few PostScript lines to the document header. If you want to watermark only one page, put the PostScript lines at the beginning of it instead of in the header. After typing the PostScript commands into your document, select them all and apply the standard PostScript style. For more information on using PostScript in Microsoft Word, see the previous tip, "PostScript in Word."

The following PostScript lines print the word *Copy* in large outline type at a 45-degree angle across the page, as shown in Figure 6-25:

```
/NewCenturySchlbk-Bold findfont 140 scalefont setfont
/ShowOutline {true charpath stroke} def
200 250 moveto
45 rotate
.50 setgray
.1 setlinewidth
(Copy) ShowOutline
```

The text is printed in 50 percent gray outline. The font is 140-point New Century Schoolbook Bold. The following lines print the word *Confidential* in a slightly darker gray:

```
/NewCenturySchlbk-Bold findfont 110 scalefont setfont
/ShowOutline {true charpath stroke} def
150 70 moveto
60 rotate
.40 setgray
.1 setlinewidth
(Confidential) ShowOutline
```

The type is printed in 60 percent gray outline. The font is 110-point New Century Schoolbook Bold.

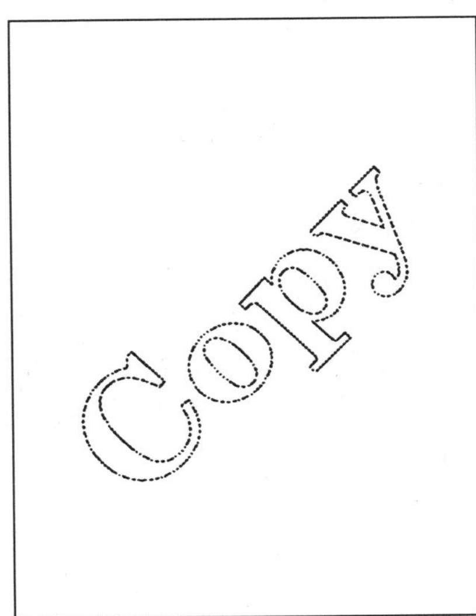

FIGURE 6-25. GHOST TEXT.
A few lines of PostScript code added to the beginning of a Microsoft Word document produce special effects such as the word Copy *shown here.*

Chapter 7

GRAPHICS

This chapter covers three types of programs that create graphics: drawing, painting, and combination. Each creates graphics in a different way. With a drawing program, you compose illustrations from graphic objects, such as lines, rectangles, ovals, arcs, and minimally formatted text. With a painting program, you create pictures as patterns of dots. With a combination program, you create composite illustrations using both graphics objects and dot patterns.

Drawing programs include MacDraw II, Cricket Draw, Drawing Table, Microsoft Works, Aldus Freehand, Adobe Illustrator 88, Swivel 3D, and Super 3D. Painting programs include MacPaint, FullPaint, PixelPaint, and Studio/8. Combination programs include SuperPaint and Canvas.

In this chapter, you will find tips on the following graphics topics:

- Tools and environment
- Selecting
- Lines and curves
- Patterns and fills
- Shapes
- Type (text)
- Erasing and removing
- Moving and copying
- Aligning
- Resizing and rotating

Some tips apply to drawing programs in general. Other tips apply to painting programs in general. Some tips apply to a specific drawing or painting program. The icons in the margin identify to which programs or types of programs the tips apply.

TOOLS AND ENVIRONMENT

CHANGING PRESETS

General Graphics

How can you change preset patterns, pen sizes, fonts, font sizes, and other standard settings so that new documents have the attributes you want? In MacDraw II, create a document that has the conditions you want. Choose Save As from the File menu, select the Stationery option, and save the document. When you open the stationery document, MacDraw opens a blank document having the conditions set in the stationery document.

In MacDraw II versions 1.1 and later, you can also change the presets used by the New command. First make a stationery document as described in the previous paragraph, and save it under the name MacDraw II Options. Put it in the System Folder or in the same folder as MacDraw II. (To override your settings and use MacDraw II's standard presets, press Option while choosing New or while opening MacDraw II.)

In Aldus Freehand, create a document with the conditions you want. Choose Save As from the File menu, select the Template option, and save the document. When you open the template, Freehand opens a blank document having the conditions set in the template. To change the presets used by the New command, make a template as just described and save it in the Freehand folder under the name Aldus Freehand Defaults.

If your drawing or painting program doesn't let you change its initial settings, you can work around it. Make a template document that sets up the conditions you want. Then, instead of using the New command each time you want to create a new document, open the template document and immediately use the Save As command to give the document its own name.

To create a template, choose New from the File menu. Then set up rulers, preferences, styles, paper size, orientation, and so forth. Enter any text and paste any pictures that will appear in every document. Choose Print, select the options you will normally use, and print a copy of the template by clicking OK. Finally, save the document, giving it a suitable name, such as Start MacPaint.

USING COPYRIGHTED MATERIAL

To use any copyrighted work, whether picture, film, writing, or music, you must request permission in writing from the copyright holder. You must include a line of text crediting the source. The only exception is the use of excerpts to illustrate or buttress your work, such as a quotation for purposes of criticism (the "fair use" doctrine). And it's probably all right to scan a picture and paste it into a letter to your mom. But distributing a document or a HyperCard stack that infringes a copyright is unethical whether you charge for it or not. Get permission or use public-domain material. (Anything published in the United States before 1906 can safely be assumed to be in the public domain. Copyrights for most European works, and U.S. works published after 1977, are in effect while the creator is alive and for 50 years after the creator's death.)

PICT AND PICT2 IMAGES

PICT and PICT2 are formats for graphic images that are defined by using the QuickDraw graphics imaging language built into the ROM (read-only memory) of every Macintosh. A PICT or PICT2 graphic consists of objects such as lines, rectangles, ovals, arcs, and minimally formatted text. You can edit individual objects any time after you draw them. For example, you can resize an object, fill an object with a pattern, change text, and so on. PICT2 graphics can be in full color or shades of gray. PICT images can contain only the eight standard QuickDraw colors: cyan, magenta, yellow, blue, green, red, black, and white.

Because PICT and PICT2 graphics are defined as sets of graphic objects, they're often called object-oriented graphics. They are created by drawing programs such as MacDraw, Canvas, Drawing Table, Cricket Draw, and the draw layer of SuperPaint. They're also created by the drawing tools in page-layout programs.

PICT and PICT2 are standard, general-purpose formats for Macintosh graphics. Many graphics, desktop publishing, and word processing programs can open and display with full fidelity documents saved in PICT and PICT2 formats. The Clipboard and the Scrapbook use the PICT and PICT2 formats for all graphic images.

BIT MAPS

A bit map is a graphics image defined by a pattern of dots. Bit-mapped graphics can't be edited as easily or as accurately as PICT graphics. In particular, you can't scale them to any size smoothly, and you can't edit text in them.

Bit maps are created at 72 dots per inch (the standard Macintosh screen resolution) by painting programs such as MacPaint, FullPaint, and the paint layer of SuperPaint. They're also created by HyperCard and SuperCard painting tools. Studio/8 and PixelPaint create color bit-mapped graphics. Screen snapshots made by pressing the Command-Shift-3 key combination are also bit-mapped graphics. Bit maps can be pasted into PICT graphics.

Scanners also create bit maps. Most scanners work at 72 dots per inch or at higher resolutions such as 300 dots per inch. The preferred format for high-resolution bit maps is called TIFF (Tag Image File Format).

SUPER SCROLL

To double the scrolling speed in MacPaint, press the Shift key while you use the scroll bars.

SCROLLING IN WORKS

You can scroll a Microsoft Works word processing document to see a draw object that extends past the end of text by adding blank space to the end of the document. To do that, be sure the draw layer is inactive. (If you can see the tool palette, choose Draw Off from the Edit menu.) Then click at the end of the word processing document and press Return enough times to allow for the height of the draw object.

PALETTE TRICKS

In Canvas 2.0 and later, you can tear off any of eight pop-up palettes by pressing the Spacebar and dragging the palette away. The eligible palettes are shown in Figure 7-1. The torn-off palettes do not float above the document window (as HyperCard's palettes do), however. You must position them so that the document window does not obscure them.

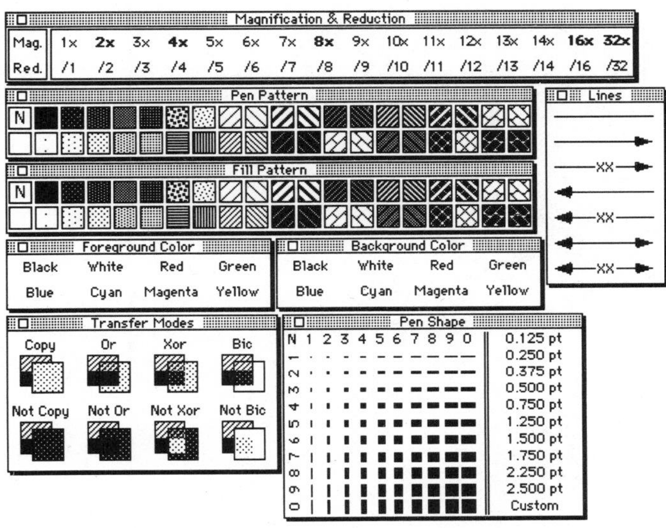

FIGURE 7-1. SHOW PALETTES.
These Canvas 2.0 palettes can be torn off.

INSTANT TOOLS AND PATTERNS

With any tool other than the text tool selected in MacPaint 2.0, pressing the T key places the tool palette's close box under the hot spot of the mouse pointer. If the tool palette is already open (torn off the menu bar), pressing the T key closes it. Similarly, pressing the P key alternately opens and closes the pattern palette. Thus, you can quickly get to MacPaint's tool palette or pattern palette from anywhere on the screen (even on a large screen) by pressing P or T once or twice.

TOOL INTENSIFIER

How can you make the eraser, selection rectangle, or lasso tool act on the entire screen? Double-click the tool in the tool palette. To make those tools act on the entire document, press the Shift key while double-clicking in the tool palette.

MacPaint

QUICK ZOOM

How can you quickly zoom in a MacPaint document to maximum magnification (8X)? Double-click the pencil tool in the tool palette. MacPaint zooms in on the area of most recent activity. To return to normal size, double-click the pencil tool again. To quickly zoom out to a reduced view, double-click the grabber (hand) tool.

MacPaint

PRECISION ZOOM

How can you zoom in on (magnify) a precise point in a MacPaint document? Select the pencil tool and then press the Command key while you click the area you want magnified. Each click adds 1X to the magnification up to a maximum magnification of 8X. To zoom out, hold down the Shift and Command keys while you click. Pressing Command or Command-Shift with the pencil tool changes the pointer to the shape of a magnifying glass to let you know what will happen.

General Painting

SWITCHING TO THE GRABBER

To scroll another part of your picture into view when using the pencil tool in most painting programs, you can switch temporarily to the grabber tool (the hand). Simply press the Option key. If the Option key doesn't work, try the Command key. This technique is particularly useful in magnified views.

MacPaint

WINDOW GRABBER

When the grabber tool is selected, holding down the Command key while dragging moves the whole MacPaint window, not only the drawing. (This doesn't work when you press the Option key to use the grabber tool temporarily while another tool is selected.)

MacDraw II

TOOL LOCK

After you draw with a tool, MacDraw II normally reverts to the selection tool (the arrow). To lock down a MacDraw II tool so that you can use it repeatedly without reselecting it each time, double-click the tool. The tool icon turns black (instead of the usual gray), and you can create as many objects with the tool as you want. To deselect the tool, click the selection tool. You can also deselect the line, rectangle, round rectangle, or oval tool by clicking in the document without dragging.

RESELECTING THE LAST TOOL

General Drawing

If your drawing program reverts automatically to the selection tool (the arrow) when you finish drawing, you can probably reselect the drawing tool you were using without schlepping to the tool palette (and back). In MacDraw II, simply press the Enter key or Command-Spacebar. You can also switch from a drawing tool to the selection tool by pressing Enter (but not Command-Spacebar).

In Cricket Draw and MacDraw 1.9, you can use the previous drawing tool by pressing the Command key and dragging.

ALTERNATING TOOLS

MacPaint

Most of the time, you can reselect the last tool you used in MacPaint by pressing Command-A. Use this technique to quickly alternate between two tools. Sometimes (often after you double-click in the tool palette), pressing Command-A won't reselect the last tool.

CONSTRAINED TOOLS

General Graphics

With most drawing and painting tools, pressing the Shift key before you start to draw restricts the tool's freedom of movement. For example, the Shift key restricts the line-drawing tool so that it will draw a line horizontally, vertically, or at a 45-degree angle. Figure 7-2 on the following page shows how most drawing and painting programs constrain tools when you press Shift. In some programs, you must press Shift before you start to use a tool, but you can release it after you begin drawing or painting. If you move in the wrong direction, choose Undo and try again.

COMMAND-KEY PAIRS

MacDraw II

Most Command-key shortcuts listed in MacDraw II menus have related effects if you also press the Shift key. The table in Figure 7-3 lists them.

Tool	Effect with Shift Key Pressed
	Selected object can be moved only horizontally or vertically
	Selected object can be moved only horizontally or vertically
	Scrolls only horizontally or vertically
A	No effect
	No effect
	Sprays only horizontally or vertically
	Brushes only horizontally or vertically
	Draws a line only horizontally or vertically
	Draws a line only horizontally, vertically, or at a 45° angle
	Erases only horizontally or vertically
	Draws only a square
	Draws only a rounded-corner square
	Draws only a circle
	Draws a polygon with only horizontal, vertical, and 45° angle sides

FIGURE 7-2. SHIFT EFFECTS.
The Shift key restricts freedom of movement for drawing and painting tools in many programs.

Key	Command-Key	Command-Shift-Key
E	Smooth	Unsmooth
F	Move Forward	Move To Front
G	Group	Ungroup
H	Lock	Unlock
J	Move Backward	Move To Back
K	Align	Alignment
M	Fit To Window	Full Size

FIGURE 7-3. SHIFTED COUNTERPARTS. *(continued)*
These MacDraw II keyboard shortcuts come in pairs. You get one effect by not using the Shift key and a related effect by using the Shift key.

FIGURE 7-3. SHIFTED COUNTERPARTS. *(continued)*

Key	Command-Key	Command-Shift-Key
O	Open Document	Open Library
W	Close Window	Move Window To Back
Y	Turn Autogrid On	Turn Autogrid Off

OPEN, NOT NEW

MacPaint

To get the Open dialog box instead of a blank document when starting MacPaint 2.0, hold down the Option key.

SCRAPBOX

General Drawing

When using a drawing program, you can keep a "scrapbox" of commonly used objects right on your drawing. First place all the objects in an unused area of the drawing and draw a white, borderless box over them. Then type a name on the invisible box so that you don't lose it. When you need an object, drag the white cover away, copy the object, and drag the cover back. Just before printing, cut the typed name from the box. After printing, paste the name back. This technique saves trips to the Scrapbook.

SLOW ON THE DRAW

Adobe Illustrator

Don't waste time waiting for Adobe Illustrator 88 to redraw a complex graphic each time you zoom in or out one power of magnification. Instead, move the image out of view by dragging the scroll box to the bottom of the scroll bar, and then zoom. Finally, drag the scroll box back to its former position. This technique is especially helpful when you are working in the Preview Illustration view.

Having the artwork out of view also helps immensely when you are using Illustrator with other applications. Whenever you move, resize, open, or close any window that covers an Illustrator window, the program redraws the window contents.

You can also accelerate Illustrator's redrawing by choosing Template Only or Artwork Only from the View menu before zooming, scrolling, or switching to a different program.

FINDING A LOST OBJECT

Have you ever lost an object in a drawing program? Here are three ways to find a small object that is hidden behind a larger object:

- Select the object you can see and choose the None pattern from the Fill menu.
- Select the object you can see and choose Send To Back from the Arrange menu.
- Drag the object you can see off to the side.

SELECTING

HANDLING SMALL OBJECTS

The mouse pointer gets in the way when you try to select, move, or resize small objects in drawing and painting programs. To get around this problem, work with small objects in a magnified view. In Adobe Illustrator 88, for example, select the magnifier tool and click an area that you want to magnify.

SELECTION RECTANGLE OR LASSO?

As shown in Figure 7-4, the selection rectangle and the lasso tool in painting programs do not handle white space in the same way. The selection rectangle, sometimes called the marquee, selects every dot (black or white) within a rectangular region. Typically, this means that an object is selected along with some surrounding white space.

The lasso selects the black dots it encircles. If some of the selected black dots completely enclose a region, any white dots inside the region are also selected. The result is that the lasso selects objects without selecting surrounding white space.

SELECTING ADJACENT OBJECTS

What's a quick way to select (or deselect) several adjacent objects in a drawing program such as MacDraw? Drag a selection rectangle around them, as shown in Figure 7-5. First imagine a rectangle around the group of objects. Place the pointer at one corner of the imaginary rectangle and hold down the mouse button. Then drag to the diagonally opposite corner

of the imaginary rectangle and release the mouse button. As you drag, you see a dotted-line rectangle. When you release the mouse button, that rectangle goes away and the objects it enclosed are all selected. If any of the enclosed objects were already selected, those objects become deselected.

If you miss an object, try again with a larger selection rectangle. Or add objects to the group selection by holding down the Shift key while you click

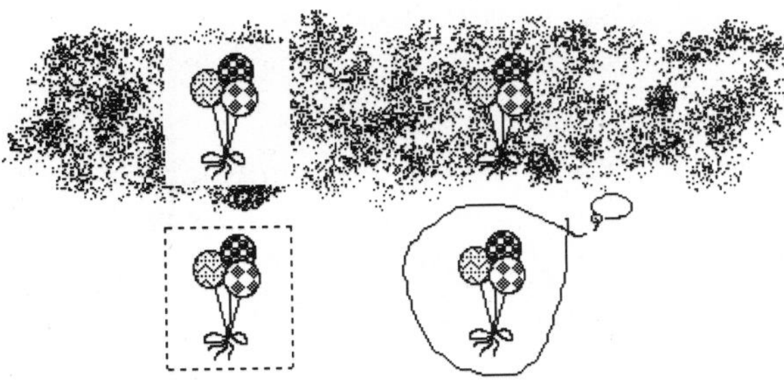

FIGURE 7-4. WHITE SPACE.
The selection rectangle includes extra white space around an object (left), but the lasso does not (right). Notice, however, that the white space enclosed by the black strings of the balloons is selected by both tools.

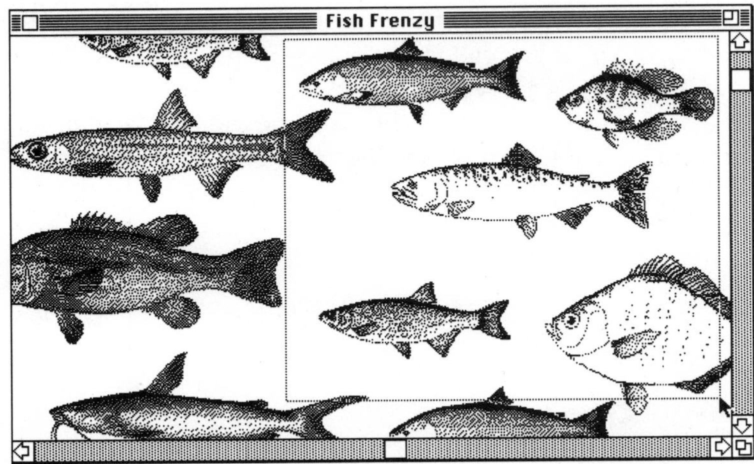

FIGURE 7-5. NET SELECT.
Drag a selection rectangle around adjacent objects you want to select.

them one by one. (You can also use the Shift key to deselect objects without deselecting the whole group.)

General Drawing

SELECTING MULTIPLE OBJECTS

How can you select (or deselect) multiple, possibly nonadjacent, objects in a drawing program? Hold down the Shift key as you click them one by one. Shift-clicking an unselected object selects it without deselecting any other objects already selected. Similarly, Shift-clicking a selected object deselects it.

If you need to select more than half the objects in a document, it's faster to select all the objects and then exclude the ones you don't want selected. Most drawing programs have a Select All command on the Edit menu.

General Drawing

SELECTING OVERLAPPING ITEMS

Trying to select a graphic or text object that's beneath another object in a drawing program can be frustrating. Too often you select the wrong object. When this happens, use the Send To Back command to get the undesired object out of the way. Then you can easily select the desired object.

General Painting

TIGHTENING THE NOOSE

Don't bother to completely encircle objects as you select them with the lasso in a painting program. Instead, drag the "rope" three-quarters of the way around whatever you want selected and release the mouse button, as shown in Figure 7-6. The painting program takes the rope straight back to your starting point and tightens it around the black dots it encircles.

General Painting

SHRINKING TO FIT

To make a selection rectangle shrink to fit the image it surrounds in a painting program such as MacPaint, press the Command key while you select the image.

MacDraw II

SELECTING BY TOUCH

When you drag a selection rectangle in MacDraw II, it normally selects only objects that are completely surrounded. To select all objects that a selection rectangle touches in MacDraw II, as shown in Figure 7-7, press the Command key while dragging.

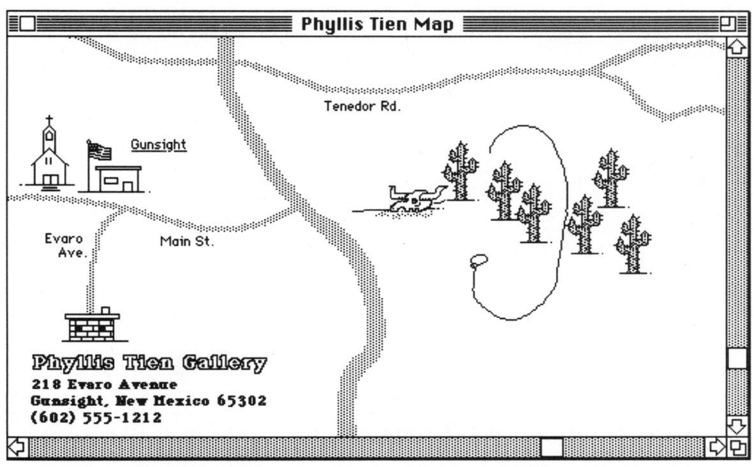

FIGURE 7-6. LAZY LASSO.

Plan your lassoing so that the painting program does the hard part. When you release the mouse button, the program will take the lasso on a straight line back to the starting point, no matter how tight the passage.

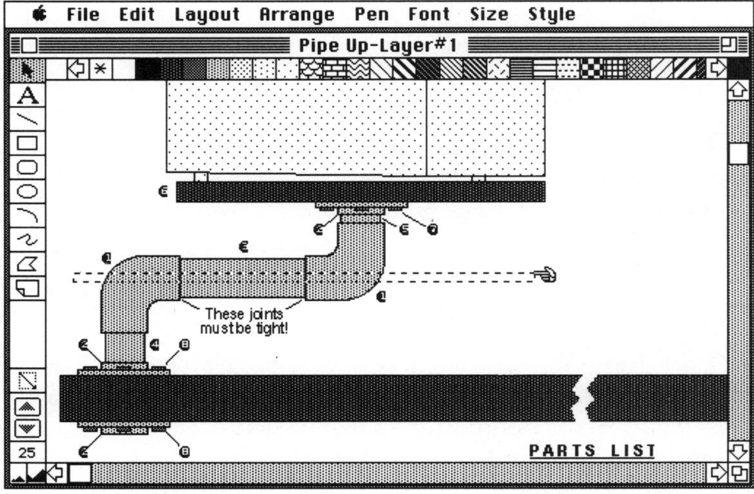

FIGURE 7-7. TOUCHED.

Pressing the Command key causes a MacDraw II selection rectangle to select all the objects it touches, not merely those it surrounds.

Canvas

MacDraw II

SELECTING ALL OF A KIND

You can quickly select all objects in a Canvas document that have a common attribute. First press the Option key while choosing the Select All command. Then select an attribute from one of the following pop-up palettes: fill pattern, pen pattern, foreground color, background color, pen shape, arrow type, ink type (transfer mode), or zoom (magnification/reduction). (Torn-off palettes don't work with the Select All command.) All objects with the specified attribute then become selected. After selecting a set of similar objects, you can choose any attributes you want them all to have. In effect, this gives you a graphic search-and-replace capability.

You can also select all instances of a particular type of object in a MacDraw II document (all the rectangles, for example). First select the tool you'd use to draw that type of object. Then choose the Select All command from the Edit menu.

PixelPaint

SELECTING TEXT

To select several text characters in PixelPaint, select the lasso and press the Command key while you click on each letter. Pressing Command while clicking with the lasso selects all points that are both connected to the point clicked and in the same color.

Aldus Freehand

DESELECTING WITH CERTAINTY

In an enlarged view, it's hard to be sure which objects are selected and which are not. To deselect all objects in an Aldus Freehand document, eliminating the risk of deleting or moving the wrong objects, press the Tab key.

Microsoft Works

PREVENTING SELECTION

You can freeze objects in the Microsoft Works draw layer so that they can't be selected and inadvertently moved or changed. First select the objects you want to freeze. Then press the F key while you click any one of the selected objects. To unfreeze an object, press F and click the frozen object again.

GRAY HANDLES

Some MacDraw II objects you select have gray handles instead of black, as shown in Figure 7-8. Why?

Gray handles mean an object is locked. Use the Unlock command (on the Arrange menu) to unlock it.

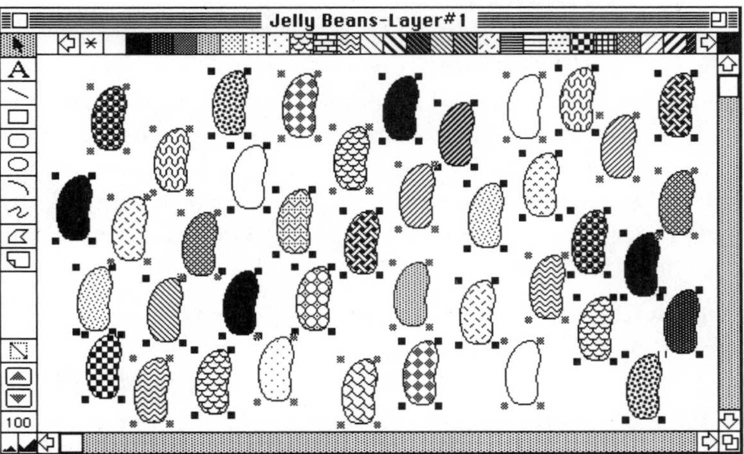

FIGURE 7-8. GRAY AND BLACK.
MacDraw II objects with gray handles can't be moved or changed.

LINES AND CURVES

PARALLEL LINES

When you need to place parallel lines close together, it's hard to keep them from overlapping. Even if they look like they aren't overlapping on the screen, they might print as one thick line. Instead of using two lines of identical thickness, superimpose a thin white line over a thicker black line. For example, draw a thick black line, copy it, paste it exactly over the original, and change the copy to a narrow white line. To create parallel dashed lines, overlay a thick patterned line with a thin white line.

THICK LINES

To create extra-thick lines in any painting or drawing program, draw a rectangle or parallelogram instead of a line. Fill it with the color or pattern you want for the line.

DIMENSION LINES WITH FRACTIONS

When MacDraw II creates lines that display their dimensions when drawn (called autosize lines), the dimensions might be decimal fractions, rational fractions, feet and inches, or picas and points. Figure 7-9 illustrates the many forms of measurements. The form that fractional measurements take depends on the setting of the Autogrid command (in the Layout menu). Some settings of the Rulers command (in the Layout menu)—specifically Drawing Ruler Units, Actual Size Units, and Divisions—also affect the form of fractional measurements.

To have MacDraw II show decimal fractions in autosize lines, turn off Autogrid before drawing the lines. MacDraw II also shows decimal fractions regardless of the Autogrid setting if the Actual Size Units setting is Miles or any metric unit of measure.

To show rational fractions in autosize lines, several settings must be in effect before you draw the lines. Autogrid must be on. In addition, Drawing Ruler Units must be Inch, and Actual Size Units must be either Inch or Feet. If Actual Size Units is Inch, then Divisions/Inch must be 2, 4, 6, 8, 16, 32, or 64. If Actual Size Units is Feet, then Divisions/Feet must be 12, 24, 48, 96, or 192.

To show picas and points in autosize lines, Autogrid must be on. Also, Drawing Ruler Units and Actual Size Units must both be Pica. If Units/Pica is 12, 24, 48, 96, or 192, then MacDraw II shows fractional points as rational fractions (3p3 ½). With other Units/Pica, fractional points are shown as decimal fractions (3.9p).

SUPERPAINT LINE LENGTH

If you need to shorten or lengthen several lines in SuperPaint's draw layer, select them all and choose Scale Selection from the Edit menu. Select or enter the amount of scaling needed. For example, scaling by 200 percent doubles the line lengths. Click OK to have the scaling take effect.

1.875"

1 7/8"

2'-5 1/2"

14p10

FIGURE 7-9. FRACTIONAL DIMENSIONS.
Fractions in MacDraw II's autosize (dimension) lines can take several forms, depending on the Autogrid setting and on ruler settings.

PATTERNED LINES AND BORDERS

Although most drawing and painting programs normally draw solid black lines and borders, the majority let you draw patterned lines as well. Most patterns make thin lines and borders look dashed or dotted. The spacing of the dots and dashes and the length of the dashes that make up the line or border depend on the pattern you choose, the angle of the line, and the location of the line or border in the document. These factors determine which part of the pattern definition is used to draw the line or border, as shown in Figure 7-10 on the following page.

To draw a patterned line or border in MacPaint and many other painting programs, select a pattern and press the Option key as you begin drawing. You can release Option after you start to draw.

To draw a patterned line or border in most drawing programs, select the line pattern (also called the pen pattern) and draw. Alternatively, you can select an existing object and then select a line pattern for it. To quickly select a pen pattern in MacDraw II, press the Option key while you click in the pattern palette. MacDraw II displays the pen pattern at the right end of its pattern palette.

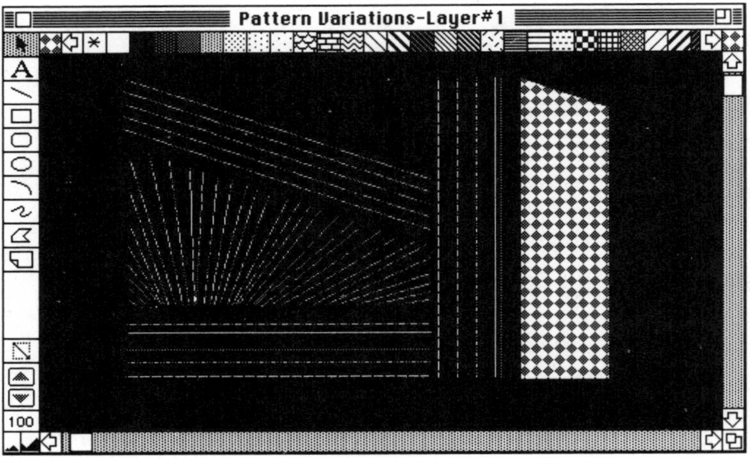

FIGURE 7-10. PATTERN VARIATIONS.

These dotted and dashed lines were all drawn over a black background using the line pattern shown. Their different angles and locations account for the variations in appearance.

Microsoft Works

ARC LENGTH

How can you change the length of an arc in the draw layer of Microsoft Works? If the arc has been grouped (if you see eight selection handles around it when you select it), use the Ungroup Picture command (in the Format menu) to ungroup it. Then select the arc and drag either endpoint.

Microsoft Works

THICK ARC

You can make an arc in the Microsoft Works draw layer that looks as though it were drawn with an extra-thick line. (See Figure 7-11.) Follow these steps:

1. Draw the arc, copy it, and paste it.
2. Drag the copy on top of the original, and choose Group Picture from the Format menu.
3. Choose Grid On from the Format menu and then reduce the copy until the space between it and the original is the thickness of the line you want.

4. Fill the large arc with the color or pattern you want for the thick line. Fill the small arc with the color or pattern of the draw layer's background.
5. Select the two arcs and choose Group Picture from the Format menu.

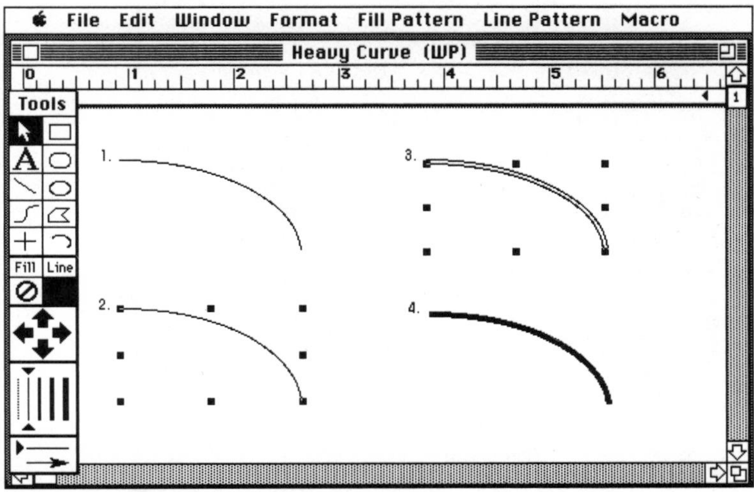

FIGURE 7-11. HEAVY CURVE.
Use two arcs to construct a thick-line curve. Fill the outside arc with the pen color and the inside arc with the background color.

SMOOTH CURVES

For a smooth curve in MacPaint and other painting programs, lasso part of a circle or oval and drag it into position.

PATTERNS AND FILLS

PICKING UP MACPAINT PATTERNS

As shown in Figure 7-12 on the following page, you can quickly transfer a custom pattern from a MacPaint drawing window to the pattern palette. Here are step-by-step instructions:

1. Scroll the drawing so that the pattern you want to put in the palette appears in the bottom third of the drawing window.

2. Tear off the pattern palette, and double-click the pattern swatch you want to replace. A pattern-editing window appears.

3. Point to the pattern you want to copy from the drawing window, and click the mouse button. The center of the arrow, not the tip, determines which pattern is picked up. If the pattern looks wrong, move the pointer slightly and click again. When the pattern looks right, click OK to install the pattern in the palette.

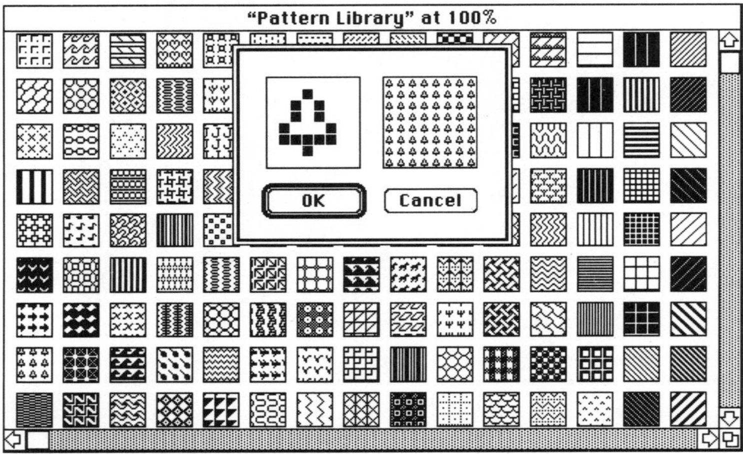

FIGURE 7-12. PATTERN PICKUP.
Copy a pattern from the drawing window to the pattern-editing window by pointing to it and clicking.

COPYING MACPAINT PATTERNS

Using the pattern-pickup technique described in the previous tip, you can copy a custom pattern from the pattern palette of one MacPaint document to the pattern palette of another document. Follow these steps:

1. Open the document that contains the pattern you want to copy, and find or create a swatch of the pattern in the drawing window.

2. Select part of the swatch and choose the Copy command from the Edit menu to copy the selection to the Clipboard.

3. Open the destination document, locate an empty spot in it, and choose the Paste command (on the Edit menu) to put the pattern swatch there. For best results, scroll the pasted pattern so that it's near the bottom of the drawing window.
4. Tear off the pattern palette, and double-click the pattern you want to replace. Then pick up the imported pattern by clicking on it in the drawing window. If the pattern looks wrong, move the pointer slightly and click again. When the pattern looks right, click OK to install the pattern in the palette.

If you want to copy several patterns from the same document, collect samples of them in one area and copy them all to the Clipboard in step 2. (Don't worry about clobbering the source document; remember, you can always choose not to save these changes when you close it.) When you paste into the destination document, the whole group of patterns appears in the drawing window. Repeat step 4 for each pattern you want to pick up.

COPYING MACDRAW PATTERNS

MacDraw & MacDraw II

You can easily copy and paste a custom pattern from one MacDraw document to another. In the source document, fill an object with the pattern and copy the object. Go to the destination document and paste the object. MacDraw II adds the custom pattern to the right end of the pattern palette, so you might need to scroll to see it.

CREATING A PATTERN LIBRARY

MacPaint

Copying a pattern from one MacPaint document to another is easy, but finding a particular pattern can be difficult unless you know where to look. To keep track of your MacPaint patterns, create a pattern library in a MacPaint document that you've created for that purpose. Each time you create a custom pattern, copy a small swatch of it to the Scrapbook or to your pattern-library document. If the library document fills up, start another. When you want to copy a pattern, you need to search only through your library, not through every document you've created.

MASKED PAINT OBJECTS

As the SuperPaint 2.0 manual mentions, bit-mapped (paint) objects have a transparent fill when pasted into the draw layer. The manual describes a rather tedious and painstaking method for creating an opaque mask with the freehand Bezier tool. Creating a mask is far easier with the AutoTrace command (in the Paint menu). Figure 7-13 illustrates the effect.

To create a mask that makes bit-mapped artwork opaque in SuperPaint's draw layer, follow these steps:

1. Select the bit-mapped artwork in the paint layer, and use the AutoTrace command to send an outline of the selection to the draw layer.
2. Go to the draw layer and choose Group from the Draw menu; this allows you to treat the outline as one object. In the pattern palette, select solid white for both the line and the fill of the mask.
3. Go back to the paint layer, select the bit-mapped artwork again, and choose Copy To Drawing or Cut To Drawing from the Edit menu.
4. Return to the draw layer, select the bit-mapped artwork and its mask, and choose the Group command to make them one.

This method makes an incomplete mask if the artwork lacks a solid perimeter. Also, the AutoTrace command sometimes creates a very complex drawing—with lots of objects in the mask—that slows SuperPaint

 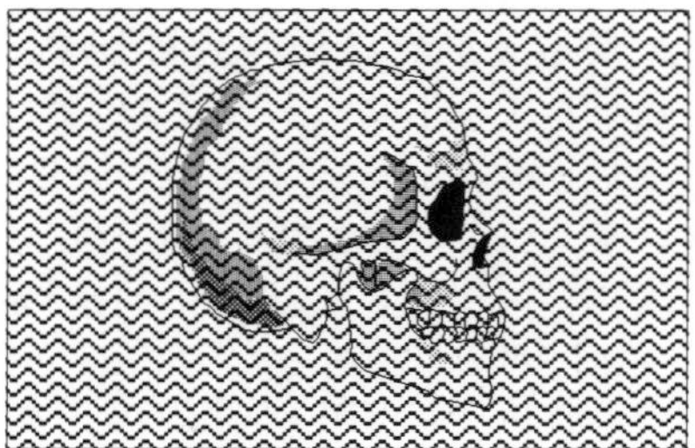

FIGURE 7-13. MASK.
Bit-mapped artwork such as this picture of a skull is normally transparent when pasted into SuperPaint's draw layer (right). A white or solid-color mask created with the AutoTrace command and placed behind the artwork makes the artwork opaque (left).

appreciably. With some bit-mapped artwork, you can minimize this side effect by choosing the AutoTrace Settings command from the Paint menu and setting the Outline Only option. If an autotraced mask is a bit too big, try making its line pattern identical to the fill pattern of the object behind it in the draw layer.

CREATING CROSSHATCH PATTERNS

Cricket Draw

To easily create crosshatch patterns in a Cricket Draw version 1.1 document, as shown in Figure 7-14, follow these steps:

1. Use the Grids & Guides command (in the Layout menu) to set the Show Guide Lines and Snap To Guide Lines options. Then drag out four guide lines to define the area where you want the pattern.
2. Use the grate tool to draw a grate inside the guide lines. With the grate still selected, use the Rotate & Tilt command (on the Arrange menu) to rotate the grate 45 degrees. If you want, you can modify the grate by using the Attributes command (on the Edit menu). Then choose Edit Grate from the Edit menu and drag each of the grate's four corners to the nearest intersection of guide lines.
3. Repeat step 2, but rotate the second grate –45 degrees.

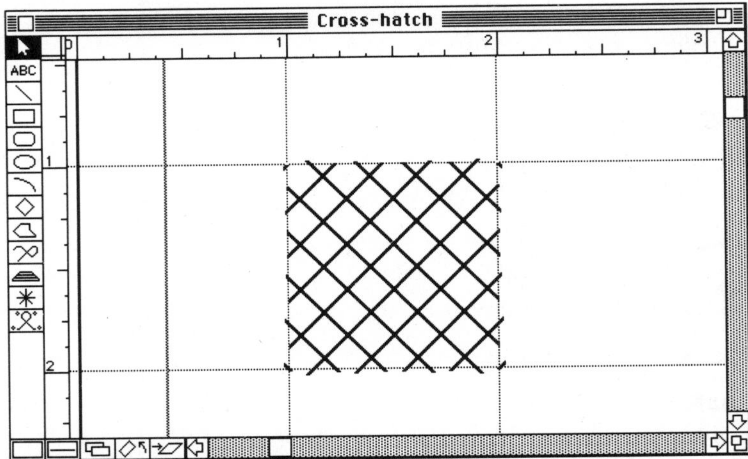

FIGURE 7-14. CROSSHATCH.
In Cricket Draw version 1.1, create crosshatch patterns like this one by rotating and reshaping two grates.

CRISSCROSS INTERSECTION

To create the effect of a crosshatch pattern where two objects overlap in MacDraw II, create a polygon to cover the overlap region. Fill each of the two overlapping objects with one of the two diagonal-line patterns. Fill the polygon with the crisscross-lines pattern, as Figure 7-15 illustrates.

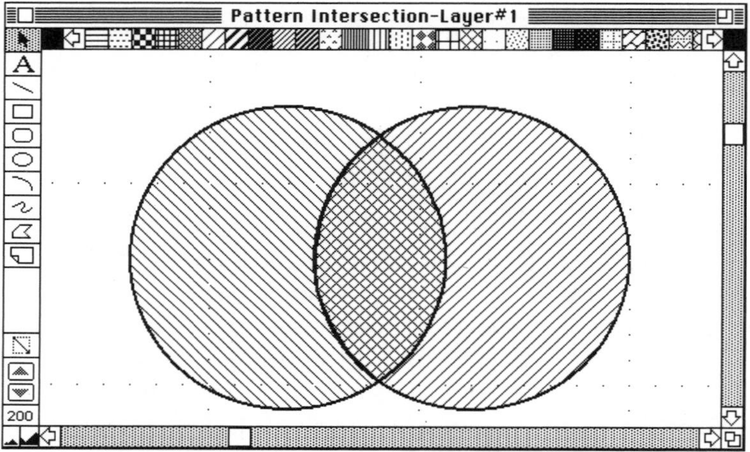

FIGURE 7-15. PATTERN INTERSECTION.
Although an object won't show through another object that covers it in MacDraw II, you can create the illusion that it does.

NEON EFFECT

To create a neon look along any path in Adobe Illustrator 88, similar to the one shown in Figure 7-16, use the blend tool as follows:

1. Select the object you want to give a neon look, and set its stroke to a dark color (black) and a thick weight (15 points), using the Paint command (in the Style menu). Set the Fill option to None.
2. Copy the object and paste the copy on top of the original.
3. Change the stroke of the copy to a light color (white) and a thin weight (1 point).
4. Zoom in and offset the copy by 2 or 3 points. (Use the Preferences command and the arrow keys as suggested in the tip "Temporary Move," later in this chapter.)

5. Select all points of both the original object and the copy. If they're grouped, choose the Ungroup command from the Arrange menu to ungroup them. Save your work at this point.
6. Select the blend tool. Click an end point on the original object and the corresponding point on the copy. When the Blend dialog box appears, enter *20* as the number of steps, and click OK. Preview your work. If you're not satisfied, close the document without saving your changes. Then reopen the document and repeat this step, specifying a different number of steps in the Blend dialog box.

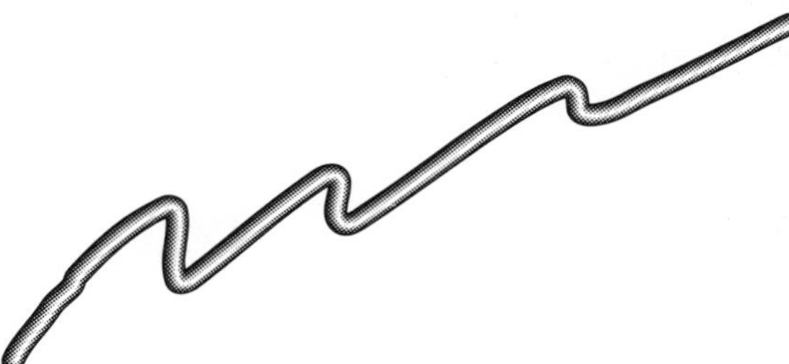

FIGURE 7-16. GLOW.
Adobe Illustrator 88's blend tool was used to create this neon look.

TILE STYLE

Aldus Freehand

Aldus Freehand lets you fill an object with square tiles that you design, but it always places the tiles adjacent to one another. To get the effect of space around each tile, place your tile image on a background square of the desired color. Then copy the background along with the image as your paste-in tile art. (See Figure 7-17 on the following page.)

EDITING FILL, LINE, AND COLOR STYLES

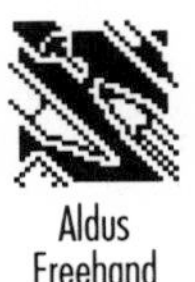
Aldus Freehand

What's the quickest way to edit the styles listed at the bottom of Aldus Freehand's Fill, Line, and Color menus? Press the Option key and choose the style you want to change from the bottom of one of those menus. After a style has been edited, Freehand applies the changes to all objects in the document that have that style.

This method lets you change the name and color of a style. For a line style, you'll also be able to change the pattern, weight, cap, join, and miter limit. For a color style, you'll be able to change the tint. However, you can't

change the type of fill (basic, graduated, patterned, PostScript, radial, or tiled), line (basic, patterned, or PostScript), or color (tint, spot, process, or PANTONE). To do that, use the Edit Fill, Edit Line, or Edit Color command.

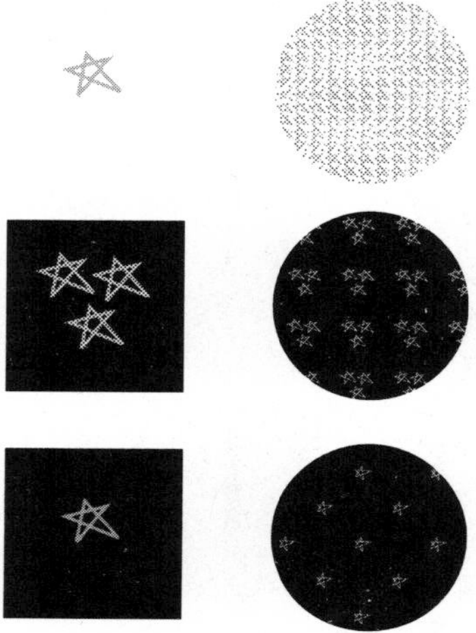

FIGURE 7-17. LAYING TILE.
Aldus Freehand has filled each circle with the tile pattern to its left. All the tiles are scaled 30 percent, and in the bottom circle, they are laid at a 45-degree angle. Increasing the amount of background in the tile results in a sparser-looking fill.

MacPaint

SCREENING WITH PATTERNS

It's impossible to produce a true gray color in MacPaint, but you can simulate shades of gray with a technique used in the publishing industry. Black-and-white books and newspapers often contain photographs and other illustrations that seem to have been printed in shades of gray. To get the apparent gray tones, the print shop photographs the original illustration through a mesh screen, breaking the continuous gray color into a pattern of closely spaced black dots on a white background. Where the dots are large, the image looks dark gray, and where the dots are small, the image looks light gray. The result is called a halftone. Dot spacing in a normal halftone screen is regular, but other screens can be used for special effects. Figure 7-18 shows a few of the possibilities.

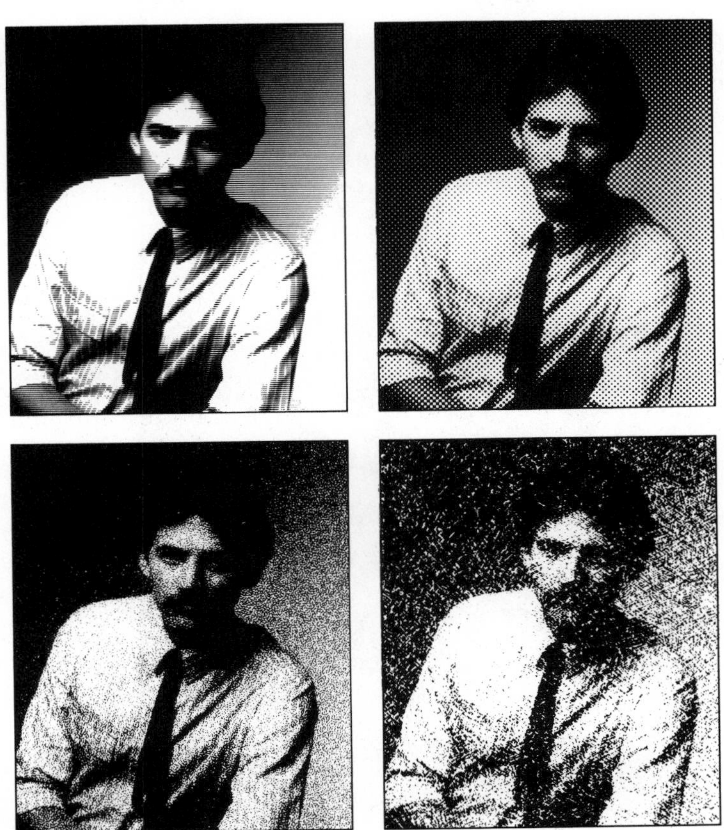

FIGURE 7-18. TRUE HALFTONE SCREENS.
These four halftone variations were rendered by the following special-effect screens (clockwise from top left): horizontal line, normal halftone, random line, and mezzotint.

If you are willing to give up detail for startling results, you can get the effect of halftone screens with MacPaint patterns, as shown in Figure 7-19 on page 283. Here's how:

1. Choose Preferences from the Goodies menu, and set the Pattern Effect option to Transparent.
2. Select the image to be screened and choose Invert from the Edit menu.

3. Select the pattern you want to use as a screen.
4. With the inverted image still selected, hold down the Command and Option keys while choosing Fill from the Edit menu. (Press the keys before pulling down the menu.) This forces MacPaint to fill with transparent paint.
5. With the inverted, screened object still selected, again choose Invert from the Edit menu.

MacPaint

SHADING WITH TRACE EDGES

Ordinarily, MacPaint's Trace Edges command (in the Edit menu) outlines everything you select with the selection rectangle. If you press the Shift key as you choose Trace Edges or if you press Command-Shift-E, the resulting outline will have a shadow on the right and bottom edges. The result of using Trace Edges with Shift and using it without is similar to the difference between the outline and shadow text styles.

MacPaint

MacDraw & MacDraw II

FILLING AROUND AN OBJECT

Would you like to fill the area around an object or image, using any available pattern or color? Here's one method for doing so:

1. If you're using a painting program, select the image with the lasso and copy it to the Clipboard. (This step is unnecessary in a drawing program.)
2. Draw a filled rectangle, oval, polygon, or other shape to serve as the background. The filled object covers the original object.
3. If you're using a painting program, paste the original image on top of the background you just drew. In a drawing program, use the Send To Back command to put the background behind the original object.

Cricket Draw

COMPLICATED FILL

In Cricket Draw version 1.1, the Fill control of the Attributes command (in the Edit menu) doesn't work with straight lines, arcs, or Bezier curves, even when the lines connect to form a closed object. To fill an arc or a more complicated curved object in Cricket Draw, trace a closed polygon over it and fill the polygon. Tracing is easier if you magnify the drawing. If necessary, fine-tune the polygon by using the Edit Polygon command (in the

1

2

3

4

FIGURE 7-19. ERSATZ HALFTONE.

For special-effect screens in MacPaint, invert an image, fill it with transparent paint, and invert it again.

Edit menu). Then either delete the original object or else make its fill None, make the line intensity of the new polygon None, and group the objects.

General Drawing

FILLING ODD SHAPES

Drawing programs do not always completely fill a shape constructed from a grouped collection of arcs and lines. You could trace the entire shape with the polygon tool to create a similar shape that can be filled. But in most cases, drawing patches with the freehand and rectangle tools is faster and easier. (See Figure 7-20.)

To fill a void in a complex graphic object, draw a patch that covers the object, make its fill pattern the same as that of the shape around it, and make its border pattern transparent. For a concave shape, use a pattern for the patch fill, but use white for the fill of the arcs and bring them to the front.

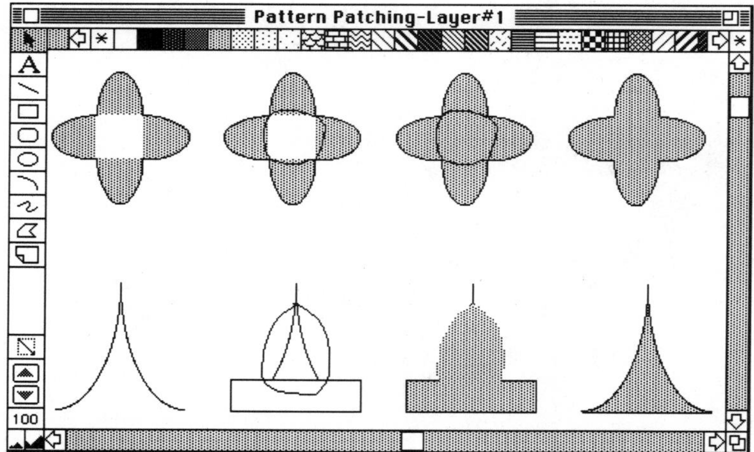

FIGURE 7-20. PATTERN PATCHING.
If your drawing program leaves a void in the fill of a complex object, cover the void with a filled patch.

General Graphics

DROP SHADOWS

You can easily add a drop shadow to any image in a painting program that has a Fill command, as shown in Figure 7-21. Here's how:

1. Lasso the image and choose Copy from the Edit menu to put a copy of the image on the Clipboard.

2. With the image still lassoed, select a dark pattern for the shadow from the pattern palette, and choose the Fill command.
3. Choose Paste from the Edit menu to get a copy of the original image from the Clipboard.
4. Drag the copy of the original image over the filled image, leaving only a shadow showing on two adjacent sides.

Follow these steps in a drawing program:

1. Select the object and choose Duplicate from the Edit menu. If your drawing program has no Duplicate command, choose Copy and then Paste from the Edit menu.
2. Select the rearmost of the twin objects and fill it with a dark pattern for the shadow.
3. If necessary, fill the original object with a nontransparent pattern or color. Move it over the dark object, leaving only a shadow showing on two adjacent sides.

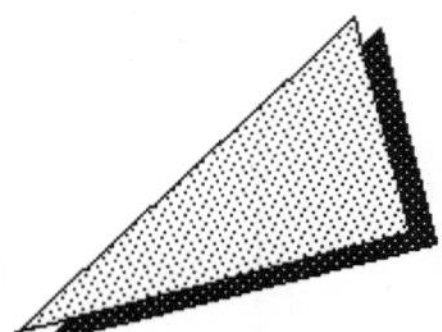

FIGURE 7-21. SHADOW.
Add shadows in a drawing or painting program.

CASTING SHADOWS

To create a shadow in Adobe Illustrator 88, as shown in Figure 7-22 on the following page, use the shear and scale tools as follows:

1. Select the object that you want to have cast a shadow.
2. Select the shear tool, and click the selected object at the bottom corner nearest the light source.
3. With the pointer in the middle of the object, hold down the Shift and Option keys and drag horizontally until the shadow is at the angle you want.

4. Select the scale tool and click the same point that you clicked in step 2.
5. With the pointer near the top of the object, press Shift and drag vertically until the shadow is the length you want.
6. Choose Send To Back from the Edit menu to place the shadow behind the object. Make the shadow an appropriate color by using the Paint command (in the Style menu). If necessary, adjust the shadow corners to match the base of the shadowed object. Preview your work.

FIGURE 7-22. SHEAR SHADOW.
To create this shadow, a copy of the object was transformed by using Adobe Illustrator's shear and scale tools, constrained by the Shift and Option keys.

SHAPES

BRUSH-MIRROR SYMMETRY

MacPaint

MacPaint's brush mirrors make it easy to draw symmetrically. But it's hard to end symmetrical drawing neatly at the center of the image unless you start on the selected brush-mirror axis (the axis of symmetry). If you select more than one brush-mirror axis, you should start drawing at the center of the drawing window. Figure 7-23 shows a symmetrical drawing that converges at the center of the image.

Finding the best starting point can be vexing, but not if you take advantage of the Undo feature, as follows:

1. Choose Brush Mirrors from the Goodies menu, and select the brush-mirror axes you want to use. Click OK.

2. Estimate the location of the axis of symmetry in the drawing window, and click there with the brush tool. If, for example, you have selected two or more axes, you must estimate the location of the center of the drawing window and click there. One or more pairs of dots appear, bracketing the preferred starting point.
3. Center the pointer by eye between all the dots. Do not click.
4. Without moving the mouse, undo the dots by pressing Command-Z or the tilde (~) key.
5. Press the mouse button and draw the symmetrical image.

FIGURE 7-23. FLORAL.
Use MacPaint's Brush Mirrors feature to draw symmetrically. Start drawing at the center of the drawing window to be sure your drawing closes perfectly, as shown here.

SYMMETRY

You can draw symmetrically in almost any painting or drawing program. You don't need a Brush Mirrors command or reflection tool. Use the following procedure, the result of which is illustrated in Figure 7-24 on the following page.

1. Draw half of the object—left or right for horizontal symmetry, or top or bottom for vertical symmetry.
2. Duplicate the half.
3. Flip the duplicate horizontally or vertically, as appropriate, to create the opposite half.

4. Put the two halves together and group them.

When you need symmetry on both horizontal and vertical axes, apply this method to one-fourth of the object to create a symmetrical half. Then apply the same method to the symmetrical half to create a completely symmetrical whole.

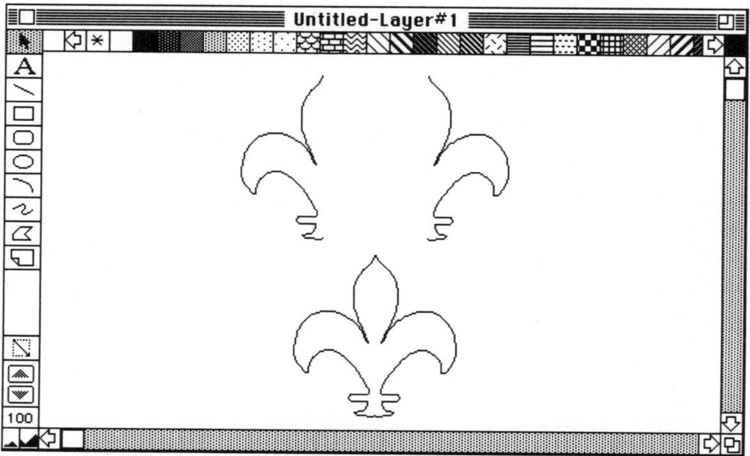

FIGURE 7-24. REFLECTIONS.
Create symmetrical objects by drawing half the object, duplicating it, flipping the duplicate, and dragging the duplicate into place.

MacDraw II

MacPaint

AVOIDING POLYGON CLOSURE

When you draw a polygon in MacDraw II or MacPaint, clicking the starting point normally closes the polygon. In MacPaint, a line of a polygon drawn anywhere near the start of the polygon tends to snap toward the starting point. To keep a polygon from closing when you click on or near the starting point, press the Option key. You'll be able to continue drawing the polygon.

Adobe Illustrator

DRAWING POLYGONS

To create a polygon having any number of equal sides in Adobe Illustrator 88, as shown in Figure 7-25, follow these steps:

1. Select the pen tool and click where you want one corner of the polygon.

2. Press the Option key and click the selection tool (arrow) in the tool palette to display the Move dialog box. Enter the length of one side of the polygon, and click the Copy button.
3. Select the rotate tool, place the pointer over the first point you drew, press Option, and click to display the Rotate dialog box. Enter the rotation angle, which equals 360 divided by the number of sides, and click the Copy button.
4. Repeatedly choose Transform Again from the Arrange menu until all corners have been placed.
5. Select any two adjacent points and choose Join from the Arrange menu. Repeat this step until the entire polygon is drawn.

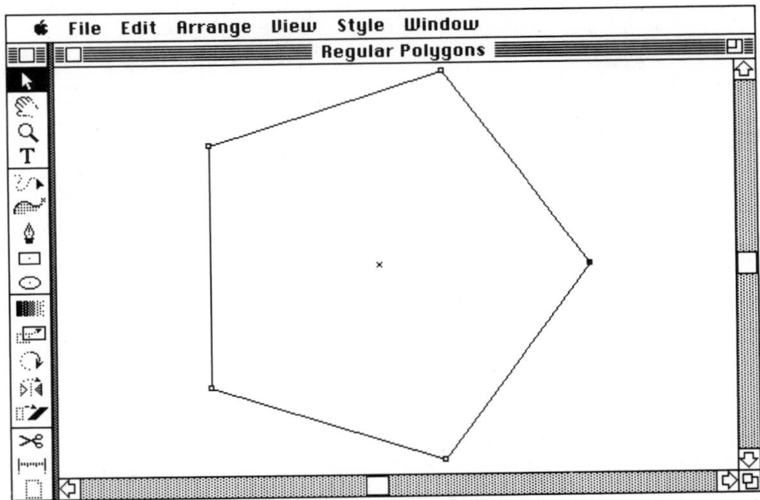

FIGURE 7-25. REGULAR POLYGONS.
Adobe Illustrator 88's Rotate and Transform Again commands make drawing regular polygons easy.

DRAWING SMOOTH CURVES

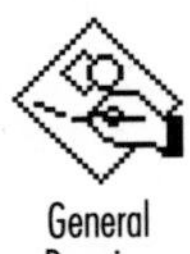

Take advantage of the Smooth and Reshape commands when you need to draw curved objects in MacDraw II and other drawing programs.

1. Draw an approximation of the curved object by using either the freehand tool or the polygon tool. If you use the polygon tool, you'll find that lots of short sides and wide-angled corners produce the best approximations. (Remember the connect-the-dots drawings from childhood?)
2. Use the Smooth command to smooth your rough picture. (Smoothing a freehand shape converts it to a smoothed polygon.)
3. Use the Reshape command to see and manipulate the handle (a black square) at each vertex of the smoothed shape.
4. Drag the handles to change the object's shape. If you miss the handles and drag the edge of the shape, the object moves. Watch out for this problem, because you might want to undo the move.

As you begin reshaping, some programs redraw the object with no fill so that you can see through it (even if it had a fill pattern to begin with). This takes a few seconds, so be patient with your first adjustment. When you finish reshaping and click elsewhere, the original fill pattern (if any) is restored.

Cricket Draw

DRAWING SMOOTH POLYGONS

Cricket Draw has a hidden feature that allows you to draw smooth polygons directly instead of smoothing a polygon after drawing it. Select the polygon tool, and press the Shift key while you click the first point. After placing the first point, release Shift and click the remaining points. The polygon will become smooth as you go.

Also, you can easily edit a smooth polygon by selecting it and choosing Edit Polygon from the Edit menu. You can then move individual vertices and see the effect as you go along.

MacDraw II

UNSMOOTHABLE CUSPS

You can create an object that has some smooth curves and some angular corners in MacDraw II, as shown in Figure 7-26.

While drawing with the polygon tool, designate a sharp corner, called a cusp, by holding down the Option key and double-clicking. Corners so designated will not be smoothed when you later choose Smooth from the

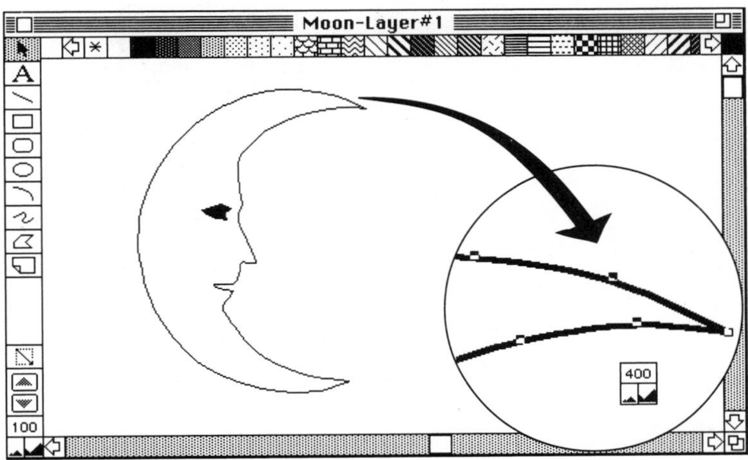

FIGURE 7-26. ANGLES AND CURVES.
MacDraw II's polygon tool, in conjunction with the Smooth command, can create shapes that have both smooth curves and pointed corners.

Edit menu on the object. Any corner at which you click once, with or without the Option key pressed, is not a cusp and will be smoothed. Double-clicking without holding down Option closes the polygon.

Reshaping a smoothed polygon that has cusps can be difficult. Each cusp appears to have one handle but actually has two handles stacked one on top of the other. If you drag the cusp, the handles separate, turning the cusp into two smoothed "corners." You can also drag two handles together to form a cusp, but you lose one corner in the process.

PULL-APART CUSPS

You can add a sharp corner, or cusp, to a Bezier curve in a Canvas document by clicking twice at the point at which you want a corner. Sharp corners in a polygon or free-form shape consist of two superimposed points. You can pull apart a cusp by selecting the curve, choosing Edit Bezier Curve from the Object menu, and pressing the Tab key while dragging the cusp.

MacDraw II

EASY TRACING

To easily trace over bit maps or scanned images in MacDraw II, use the layers feature. Paste the bit-mapped image into a new document. Then use the Layers command (in the Layout menu) to add a new layer. As you add the new layer, click alongside its name to make it the current (active) layer. You can now use the freehand tool or the polygon tool to trace the image without accidentally selecting it.

To trace accurately and quickly, enlarge the view to 200 or 400 percent and use the polygon tool. You could use the freehand tool, but it doesn't autoscroll when you draw past the edge of the window as the polygon tool does. You'll likely have to draw past the edge of the window when the document is enlarged.

After tracing, reduce the view to 100 percent and check your work. If you used the polygon tool, try smoothing jagged edges by choosing Smooth from the Edit menu. Choose Reshape from the Edit menu in an enlarged view to fine-tune your tracing as needed.

Aldus Freehand

STOPPING A TRACE

To stop Aldus Freehand from tracing an image, press Command-period and wait a few seconds. To clear the partial tracing, choose Undo Trace from the Edit menu.

General Graphics

CONCENTRIC SHAPES

You can draw equally spaced concentric circles, squares, ovals, or rectangles—without measuring—in a painting or drawing program. Figure 7-27 on the page after next illustrates the procedure. Here are the steps for a painting program:

1. Draw a diagonal line long enough to span the largest shape. For circles or squares, make it a 45-degree diagonal by holding down the Shift key as you start to draw.
2. At the top of the diagonal line, draw two short horizontal lines to mark off the distance you want between two concentric shapes.
3. Lasso the segment of the diagonal line that contains the two marks and include the marks in the selection.

4. Hold down the Option key, drag away a copy of the selected segment, and place the copy on the diagonal line so that the upper mark on the copy coincides with the lower mark on the original. Repeat this step until the entire diagonal line has been marked off.
5. Lasso the diagonal line with its marks, and choose Copy from the Edit menu to place a copy of the diagonal line on the Clipboard. You will use the copy to erase the original after drawing the circles.
6. Draw the shapes, starting and ending them only where a mark crosses the diagonal line. If you draw circles or ovals, they will not cross the diagonal line at the marks, but the imaginary squares that bound the circles or ovals will.
7. Erase the diagonal line and the horizontal marks. To erase with the copy of the diagonal line from the Clipboard, choose Paste from the Edit menu and drag the copy that appears exactly over the original diagonal line. While the copy is still selected, choose Invert from the Edit menu. Then click the mouse button anywhere, and the line disappears.

A similar method works in drawing programs:

1. Draw a diagonal line that's long enough to span the largest shape. For circles or squares, make it a 45-degree diagonal by holding down the Shift key as you start to draw.
2. Draw a horizontal line across the top of the diagonal line.
3. Duplicate the horizontal line and drag the copy down the diagonal line to mark the distance you want between shapes.
4. Select the two lines and group them. Then duplicate the lines and drag them until the top line of the copy is positioned over the bottom line of the original set.
5. Duplicate again and again, until the entire diagonal line is marked off. If some of the duplicates don't cross the diagonal line, drag them left or right (but not up or down) until they do.
6. Select all the lines, including the diagonal. (Hold down the Shift key as you click each line in turn.) Then group the selected lines so that they will be treated as a single object.

7. Draw the shapes. Start and end them only where a mark crosses the diagonal line. If you draw circles or ovals, they will not cross the diagonal line at the marks, but the imaginary squares that bound the circles or ovals will.
8. Select the group of lines and delete them.

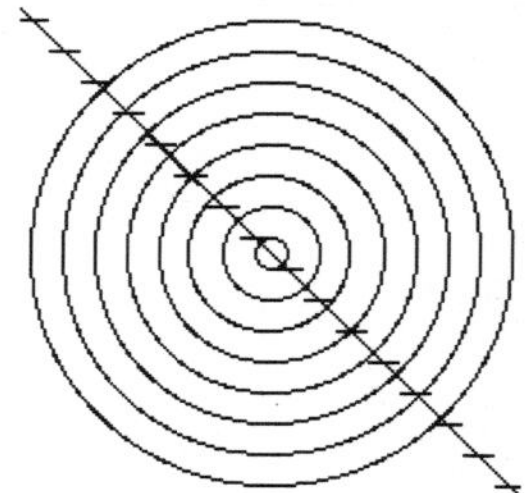

FIGURE 7-27. NEST.
Using a diagonal line as a guide, you can draw equally spaced concentric circles, squares, ovals, and rectangles.

EQUILATERAL TRIANGLES

Using three equal circles, you can construct an equilateral triangle in a painting application. Figure 7-28 illustrates the procedure, which is described in the following steps:

1. Draw a small circle and put a dot at its center. For best results, draw the circle with the grid feature activated, and make the circle an even number of grid units in diameter.
2. Lasso the circle, hold down the Option and Shift keys, and drag a copy of the circle to one side so that it barely touches the original circle.
3. With the duplicate circle still lassoed, hold down Option (but not Shift) and drag a second copy of the circle until it barely touches the other two circles.
4. Erase the circles, leaving the center dots. Connect the dots, using the polygon tool. The resulting triangle is equilateral.

If the triangle you construct is too large, simply draw a horizontal line above the existing base and erase the part below the line. If the triangle is too small, extend the sides, add another base below the existing one, and then erase the existing base. You could use the selection rectangle and, holding down the Command and Shift keys, drag the triangle to another size, but doing that distorts the lines that make up the sides of the triangle.

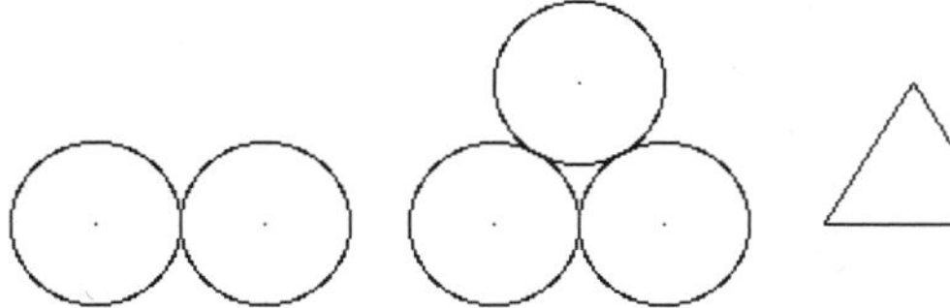

FIGURE 7-28. TRIANGULATE.
You can construct an equilateral triangle in a painting program by connecting the centers of three equal circles, each of which barely touches the other two.

3-D BOXES

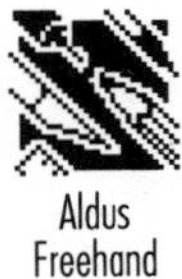
Aldus Freehand

To construct a three-dimensional box in Aldus Freehand, follow these steps, the result of which is illustrated in Figure 7-29 on the following page.

1. Draw a rectangle and fill it. Select the skew tool, press the Shift key, and slant the rectangle. This is the front of the box.
2. Duplicate the rectangle and fill it with a different shade of the color used for the original rectangle. Select the reflection tool, press Shift, and click anywhere on the duplicate to reflect it 90 degrees. Then drag the duplicate to align its right edge with the left edge of the original rectangle. (Zoom in to match the two edges precisely.)
3. Duplicate the original rectangle again, and fill it with a third shade. Position this duplicate so that its lower left corner touches the upper left corner of the reflected side.
4. With the third side still selected, choose Ungroup from the Element menu. Then move the top two corners of the third side to meet the top two corners of the first side.

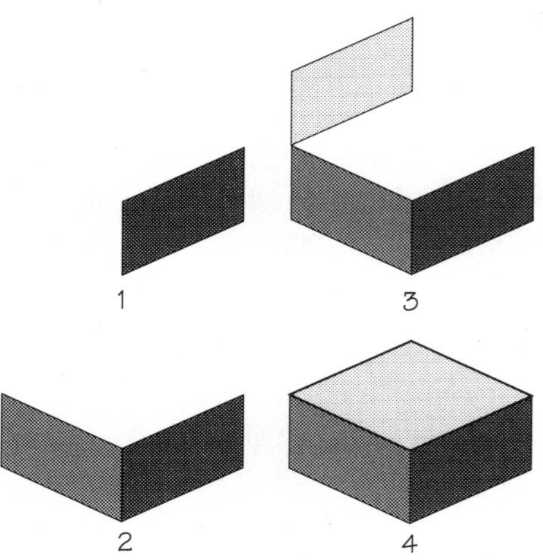

FIGURE 7-29. CUBIC.
You can construct a three-dimensional box by transforming and duplicating a rectangle.

OVALS AT PRECISE ANGLES

You can construct an oval of any desired angle in Adobe Illustrator 88 by using the method illustrated in Figure 7-30. The same basic method works in any drawing program that lets you rotate a line to the angle at which you want to draw the ellipse. Here are the steps:

1. Draw a circle with the diameter equal to the desired major axis of the ellipse. (To force a circle, hold down the Shift key while dragging.)
2. Using the pen tool, draw a radius while holding down Shift. (Be sure the Preferences command's Snap To Point option is checked.)
3. With both ends of the radius selected, select the rotate tool. Hold down the Option key, and click the center point of the circle. In the Rotate dialog box that appears, type the number that is equal to 90 minus the desired ellipse angle. (To create a 30-degree oval, as shown in Figure 7-30, type *60* in the Rotate dialog box.) Then click the Copy button.

4. Using the pen tool, draw a horizontal line (holding down Shift) from the end of the rotated radius past the opposite edge of the circle.
5. Select the circle and move it to the front (press Command-equal sign). With the scale tool selected, click the center point of the circle. Holding down Shift, select and drag down the top handle of the circle until it meets the horizontal line.

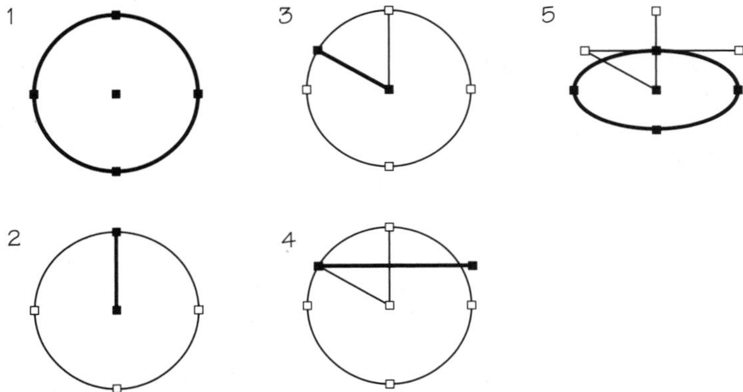

FIGURE 7-30. OVAL ANGLE.
Make a circle into an oval of any particular angle by performing five steps.

LINEAR PERSPECTIVE

Aldus Freehand

For assistance in placing and sizing objects in a perspective drawing in Aldus Freehand, you can create guidelines that converge on the vanishing point. Carry out the following steps, the result of which is illustrated in Figure 7-31 on the following page:

1. Decide on the vanishing point of your illustration. Reset the ruler origin to the vanishing point. To show the horizon, drag a guideline from the horizontal ruler to the zero point on the vertical ruler.
2. On layer 0, draw a line with one end on the vanishing point. To easily place one end of the line on the vanishing point, move that end of the line until the information bar (below the menu bar) shows the end point is at 0,0.

3. From the first guideline, clone any other perspective guidelines you might need. Move only the outer end of a new guideline so that the beginning stays at the vanishing point.

The guidelines in layer 0 appear under your illustration. If you want to see guidelines on top of your illustration, put them in layer 200. Before printing, either delete the guidelines from layer 200 or send them to layer 0. Objects in layer 200 print, but objects in layer 0 don't.

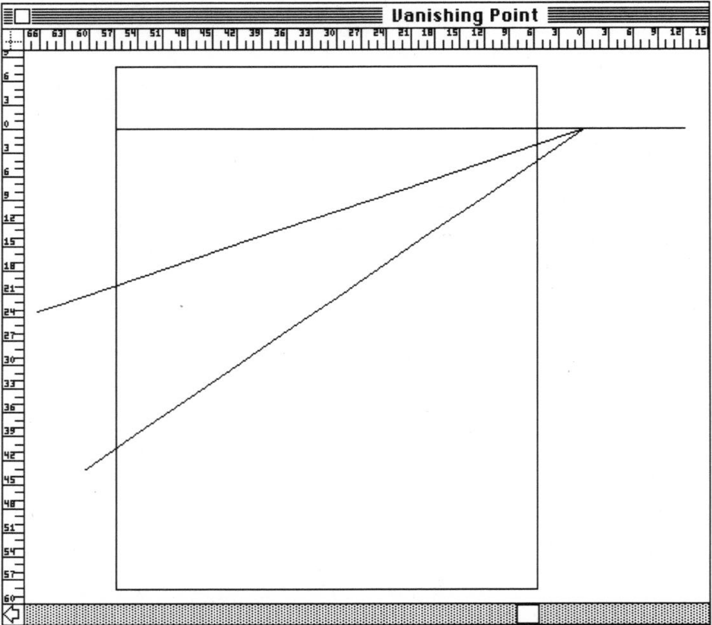

FIGURE 7-31. VANISHING POINT.
Drawing in linear perspective is easier if you move the origin to the vanishing point and create nonprinting guidelines that converge on it.

TYPE

Print Shop

A BLANK LINE'S POINT SIZE

You can't change the point size of a blank line when creating a sign with Broderbund's Print Shop. To work around this limitation, put a single blank space on each blank line. Then you can adjust the line spacing by changing

the size of the blank space. Similarly, you can adjust the height of a line that's not blank by changing the size of a blank space on it.

CONDENSED SHADOW AND OUTLINE TEXT

To get condensed outline-style text in MacPaint, use the Trace Edges command (in the Edit menu). For a condensed shadow style, press the Shift key while choosing Trace Edges. Figure 7-32 compares the Trace Edges method with MacPaint's Outline and Shadow commands (in the Style menu).

Standard Outline Style
Standard Shadow Style

Condensed Outline Style
Condensed Shadow Style

FIGURE 7-32. ALTERNATE OUTLINE AND SHADOW.
Compared to the standard outline and shadow styles (top), MacPaint's Trace Edges command yields more compact text (bottom).

ILLUSTRATOR TYPE STYLES

If you use Adobe Illustrator, don't overlook its ability to create typographic variations and alterations quickly and inexpensively. To create unique type treatments, copy some type, paste once or twice, and adjust the fill and stroke of the original type and the copies.

Figure 7-33 on the following page shows eight type variations you can create in about 10 minutes. The first line in Figure 7-33 shows the word *Bookman* set in 60-point Bookman Demi. Illustrator's standard for type fill and stroke are 100 percent black fill and no stroke.

Bookman

Bookman

Bookman

Bookman

Bookman

Bookman

Bookman

FIGURE 7-33. AFFECTED TYPE.
With Adobe Illustrator, you can create an endless variety of typographic effects. All these variations were made using the Copy, Paste In Front, Paste In Back, Paint, and Type commands.

The second line shows the same type as the first, still filled with 100 percent black, but with a 100 percent black stroke of 1.5 points. To get the three-dimensional effect, copy the type, paste it in back of the original, and change the paint specifications to white fill with a 100 percent black stroke of 0.2 point. Pressing Command-C, Command-B, and Command-I with the type selected will quickly copy the type, paste the copy behind the original, and open the Paint dialog box. After setting the paint attributes, move the back copy 4 points to the right.

The third line has the same type as the second, this time filled with white with a 1-point, 100 percent black stroke. Set the fill and stroke of the back copy to 20 percent black to create the gray shadow.

For the fourth line, keep the original 100 percent black fill, but give the type a 6-point, 100 percent black stroke. Next, copy it, paste it to the front, and change the top layer to white fill with a 4-point white stroke. Then paste to the front again and give the top layer 100 percent black fill and no stroke to create the bold inline effect.

The fifth line is a copy of the fourth line, with all three layers grouped and then scaled 130 percent horizontally.

The sixth line shows that a white stroke with a black fill can make characters thinner. Kern a copy of the original type a half-point by choosing the Type command and setting the Spacing option to –0.5 point. Then set the Paint options to 100 percent black fill and 0.5-point white stroke.

Line seven uses three layers of type to get the shaded inline effect. The bottom layer has black fill and an 8-point black stroke. The middle layer has white fill and a 7-point white stroke. The top layer is filled 20 percent black with no stroke.

The last line is simple. The top layer is filled with 20 percent black and given a 1-point stroke in 100 percent black. The back layer is moved 4 points to the right and given a 100 percent black fill and stroke.

In Illustrator, you set the fill and stroke for type as you do for any other object. First select the type and choose Paint from the Style menu (or press Command-I). In the Paint dialog box, select a fill color, a stroke color, and a stroke weight. If you set a stroke color other than None for some type, set the miter limit to 3 or lower to prevent strange spikes from appearing on some characters.

PASTED-TEXT ATTRIBUTES

MacPaint

Text pasted into MacPaint takes on that program's currently selected font, style, size, and alignment. Immediately after pasting text into MacPaint, you can easily change the text's font, style, size, alignment, and margins. Simply choose the attributes you want from the MacPaint menus. To change the margins, adjust the size and shape of the selection rectangle that surrounds the pasted text.

When you change the font attributes or reshape the selection rectangle, MacPaint re-forms the lines of text to fit within the selection rectangle. Excess text is chopped off at the bottom of the selection rectangle. To retrieve it, choose a smaller font size or stretch the selection rectangle.

QUICK FONT AND SIZE CHANGES.

MacPaint

MacPaint, like most programs, provides no shortcuts for choosing a specific font name or font size. However, you can use the keyboard to step

consecutively up or down through the list of fonts or the list of sizes. Only text that has just been pasted and is still selected—or text that you are currently typing—is affected.

- Press Command-Shift-period to advance to the next font.
- Press Command-Shift-comma to back up to the previous font.
- Press Command-period to advance to the next larger font size.
- Press Command-comma to back up to the next smaller font size.

Notice that the symbols < and >, which are the uppercase symbols on the comma and period keys, suggest direction.

MIXING MACPAINT TEXT ATTRIBUTES

MacPaint

How can you mix text attributes while typing in MacPaint?

Press the Enter key (not the Return key) before choosing a different font, size, or style. The attributes of previously typed text will be unchanged, but any new text you type will have the new attributes and will be perfectly aligned with the text you were typing when you pressed Enter. Figure 7-34 illustrates this condition.

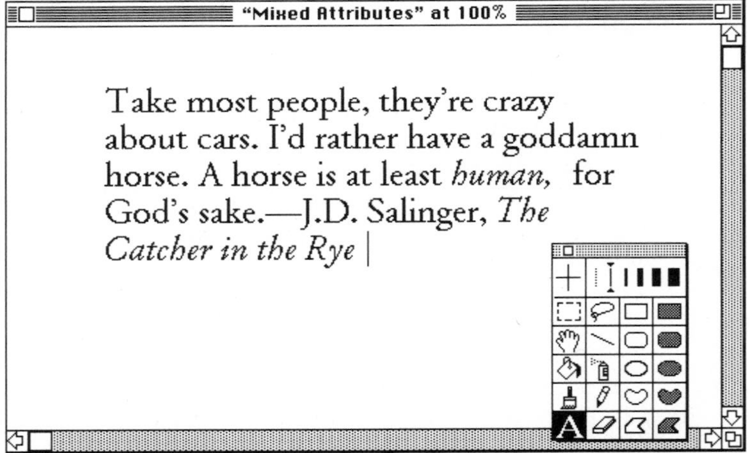

FIGURE 7-34. MIXED ATTRIBUTES.
Press Enter when you want to change text attributes in MacPaint without clicking a new insertion point and losing text alignment.

You can press Enter as many times as you want while typing a text passage. However, you can backspace only as far as the last place you pressed Enter.

If you make changes to the font, size, or style without first pressing Enter, the changes affect all the text in the block you're typing.

MORE STYLE

General Painting

You can use the Mac's screen snapshot feature to import elaborately formatted text into a painting program. You must copy the text one screenful at a time, and you cannot change it in the painting program. Here's the procedure:

1. Create the formatted text you want to copy, or open the document that contains the text. With the formatted text in view, press Command-Shift-3 to take a snapshot of the screen. The snapshot is saved as a MacPaint document named Screen 0.
2. Open the screen snapshot document, select what you need and copy the selection by using the Copy command (in the Edit menu).
3. Open the destination document from the painting program, and insert the copied text image by choosing Paste from the Edit menu.

If you take additional snapshots, the Mac increments the number in the filename by 1 each time. A beep when you press Command-Shift-3 means either that you have reached the maximum number of files (10) or that the disk is too full to record another snapshot. To take more than 10 snapshots, rename the existing snapshot files or move them into a folder.

PAINT-TEXT EDITING

General Painting

In MacPaint and other painting programs, you cannot simply select text you typed previously and change its content, font, size, or style. To change text in a painting program, follow these steps:

1. Type a replacement for the text in an empty area of the document. Be sure to begin or end it with a couple of letters that you aren't changing. These extra letters will help you align the replacement text with the existing text.
2. Erase the existing text that you're replacing.

3. Select the replacement text with the lasso and drag it into place, as shown in Figure 7-35.

"She Got the Gold Mint, I Got the Shaft"
a song by Jerry Reed
Mine

"She Got the Gold Mine, I Got the Shaft"
a song by Jerry Reed

"She Got the Gold Mine, I Got the Shaft"
a song by Jerry Reed

FIGURE 7-35. TEXT REPAIR.
To edit text in a painting program, you must type a "patch" in an unused area of the document and then drag it into place.

PATTERNED TEXT

Would you liked to create gaudy titles in a painting program? Change ordinary black text into patterned text. Simply lasso the text, click the pattern you want in the pattern palette, and choose Fill from the Edit menu (or use the paint bucket tool).

WHITE TEXT

You can create white text against a dark background in a painting program. Type normal black text on a white background. Then select it with the lasso and invert it. Finally, drag (or cut and paste) the inverted text over the dark background. If the background is a dark pattern (not straight black), you might want to fill the holes in letters like O and P with the pattern. Figure 7-36 illustrates the results.

COLORED TEXT

You can create colored text in MacDraw II. Select the text, using either the pointer tool (the arrow) or the text tool (the I-beam), and press the Option key while clicking the solid color you want.

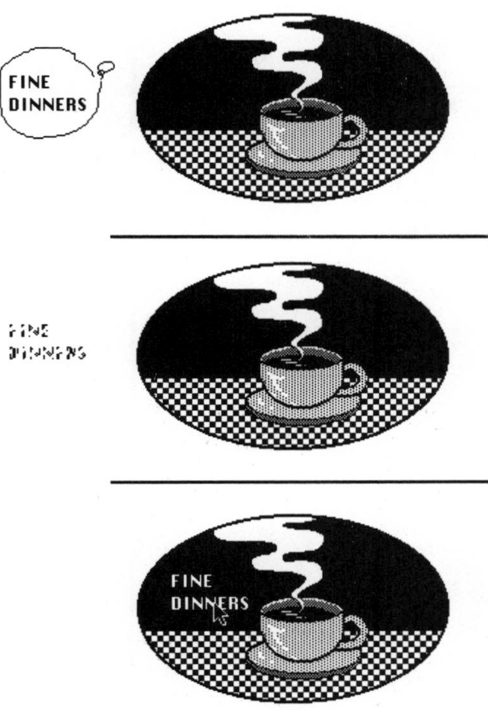

FIGURE 7-36. WHITE ON BLACK.
Inverted black text appears white when dragged over a dark background.

ULTRABOLD

Many commercial typefaces come in an "ultrabold" or "heavy bold" weight that is even larger than the regular bold available on the Mac. Figure 7-37 shows two bold weights. You can create ultrabold lettering in a painting program as follows:

1. Type the text in the outline and, optionally, boldface styles.
2. After typing, use the paint can to fill the hollow letters with black or a dark pattern. For small sizes and italics, you might have to fill the letters in a magnified view.
3. Use the pencil tool in a magnified view to clean up the notches in letters such as a, e, h, i, n, r, s, and T.

Phyllis Tien Gallery

Phyllis Tien Gallery
Phyllis Tien Gallery
Phyllis Tien Gallery

FIGURE 7-37. EXTRA BOLD FACE.
You can simulate an ultrabold style by filling outline-style letters with the paint can tool and touching up with the pencil tool.

CURVED TEXT

To center text at the top of a circle or oval in Aldus Freehand 2.0, choose center alignment for the text, join it to the circle, and rotate the joined text and circular path 90 degrees. Centering text at the top of an oval requires that you first draw the oval on its side. You can then join center-aligned text to the sideways oval and rotate them 90 degrees.

To center the text at the bottom of a circle or oval, rotate it –90 degrees instead of 90 degrees, and then reflect it 90 degrees to make it read correctly. Figure 7-38 shows several examples of text joined to circles and ovals.

Freehand normally joins the baseline of the text to the circle (or other path). Alternatively, you can position the joined text above or below the path by using the Element Info command (in the Element menu).

BINDING TEXT TO AN ARC

You can always tell where text will bind to an arc in a Cricket Draw document by selecting the arc and choosing Edit Arc from the Edit menu. Text

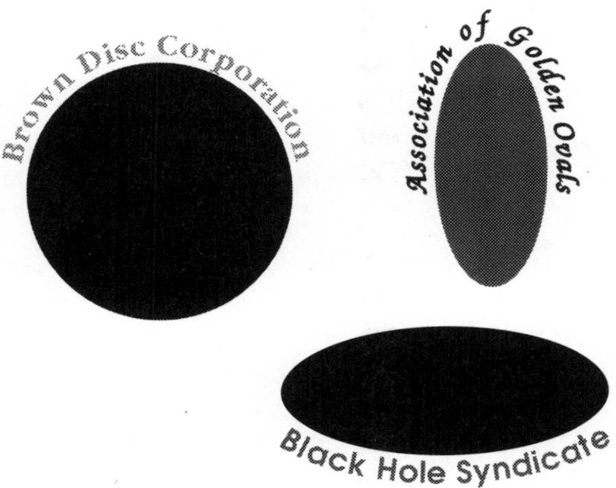

FIGURE 7-38. ABOVE AND BELOW.
In Aldus Freehand, you can easily center text above and below circles and ovals by rotating the text after joining it to the curved shape.

binds to the arc starting at the endpoint marked with a little circle. (The other endpoint is marked with a little square.) Also, Cricket Draw always binds the baseline (not the tops of the ascenders or the bottoms of the descenders) to the top of the arc (the edge nearest the top of the page).

BINDING TEXT TO A CIRCLE

To bind text to the top and bottom of a circle so that none of the text is upside down in Cricket Draw, split the text into two blocks and bind each to a semicircle. Figure 7-39 on the following page shows the result. Follow these steps:

1. Draw a circle to act as a guide.
2. Draw an arc from 12 o'clock to 3 o'clock on the circle. Use the Edit Arc command (on the Edit menu) to make the arc large enough for all the text you want at the top of the circle. Simply guess at the arc's size for now—you can modify it later. As you move the endpoints of the arc, watch the vertical ruler and make each endpoint the same distance from the top of the circle.

3. Draw a second arc from 6 o'clock to 3 o'clock on the circle. Use the Edit Arc command (in the Edit menu) to make the endpoints of the second arc almost touch the endpoints of the first arc.
4. Type the two blocks of text you want bound (or split it into two text blocks if it's already typed).
5. Select the upper arc and the upper text block and use the Bind Text command (in the Special menu) to bind the text to the arc. With the bound text still selected, select the Center option of the Attributes command (in the Edit menu) to center the bound text. If the text is longer than the path (indicated by a pattern of plus signs after binding), unbind the text and edit the arc sizes.
6. Repeat step 5 with the lower arc and the lower text block. Because the lower text is inside the circle and the upper text is outside the circle, you'll want to drag the lower text below the circle. Then drag the handles of the bound text to make its curvature match the circle.
7. Delete the circle you drew as a guide.

When ideas fail, words come in very handy.

FIGURE 7-39. BOUND TEXT.

Although this appears to be one block of text bound to a circle, it is actually two text blocks bound to separate arcs.

SPREADING TEXT AROUND AN OVAL

As shown in Figure 7-40, you can spread text around an arc in the Microsoft Works Draw layer. Copy the text to the Clipboard. Draw an arc. (Press the Shift key to make it a quarter-circle.) Drag the endpoints of the arc to lengthen it. Select this arc. Choose Spread Text from the Format menu.

In text spread in this manner, every character is a separate object that you can move, delete, or edit.

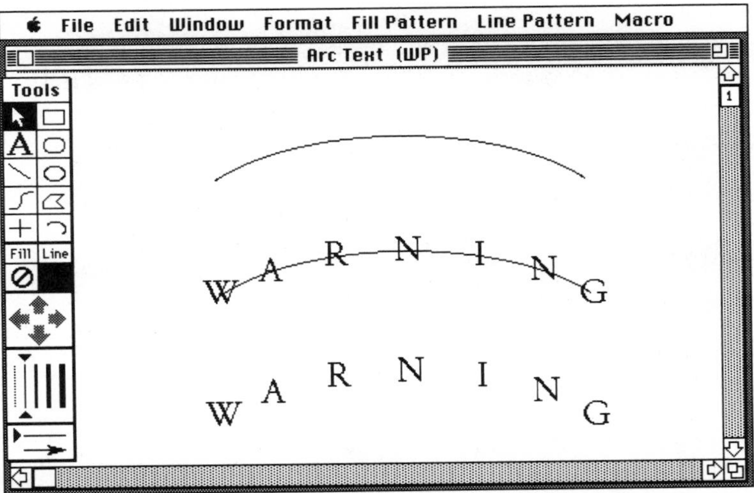

FIGURE 7-40 ARC TEXT.
Text can be spread across an arc in the Microsoft Works Draw layer.

EMBOSSED TEXT

You can create an embossed look in Aldus Freehand, Adobe Illustrator, Canvas, or any other program that lets you color text in shades of gray. Basically, you add two drop shadows behind the text you want embossed, as shown in Figure 7-41 on the following page. One drop shadow is a shade darker than the text, and the other drop shadow is the same amount lighter. Follow these steps:

1. Select the text to be embossed and make it a medium shade of gray (40 percent).

2. Duplicate the text. (Use the Copy and Paste, the Duplicate, or the Clone command.) Make the duplicate a dark gray (60 percent). Send it to the back. Move the duplicate slightly to the left of and down from the original text. For example, move 1 point for 24-point text.
3. Duplicate the original text again. Make this second duplicate light gray (20 percent). Send it to the back. Move this duplicate slightly to the right of and up from the original text. For example, move 1 point for 24-point text.
4. Draw a rectangle (or other shape) as a background for the text. Make it the same shade of gray as the original text (40 percent). Send it to the back.

ars est celare artem

de gustibus non disputandum

FIGURE 7-41. BOLD RELIEF.
This embossed look is created from three copies of the same text, each a different shade of gray. The frontmost copy is the same shade of gray as the background "paper."

Canvas

EDITING SPECIAL-EFFECTS TEXT

How can you edit text in Canvas to which special effects (rotation, flipping, skewing, distortion, and perspective) have been applied? Select the text by using the pointer tool (the arrow), and choose Restore Original from the Effects menu. Then edit the text. When you finish editing, reapply the special effects.

Aldus Freehand

TEXT SPACING

You can change the letterspacing, word spacing, or leading (line spacing) in Aldus Freehand by selecting a text block and dragging its different handles. To change the letterspacing, drag the middle handle on the left or right side of the text block. To change the word spacing, press the Option key and drag the middle handle on the left or right side of the text block. To

change the leading, drag the middle handle on the top or bottom of the text block. As you drag, watch the information bar (normally located just below the menu bar) for precise spacing measurements.

ELASTIC TEXT

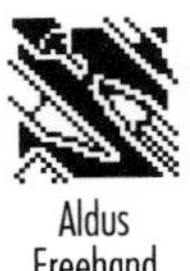

To stretch or shrink text in Aldus Freehand, press the Option key while you drag any corner of a selected text block. To stretch or shrink proportionally, press Option-Shift while dragging a corner. Figure 7-42 shows an example of the effects you can create.

St. Louis

Cape Girardeau

Memphis

Greenville

Vicksburg

Natchez

Baton Rouge

New Orleans

FIGURE 7-42. FLEX TEXT.

When you drag it by the corners while pressing the Option key, text in Aldus Freehand acts as though it was printed on rubber. All of this text was stretched from 24-point Palatino.

TEXT BOUNDS

To enter text on (or in) a graphic object in MacDraw II versions 1.1 and later, simply draw the object and enter the type while the object is still selected. If the object is already drawn, select it and start typing. Either way, text remains within an imaginary rectangle bounding the object.

UNWANTED TEXT CROP

You can prevent text in a MacDraw II document from becoming cropped when the contents of the document are imported by another program. Try turning off the Fractional Character Widths option of the Preferences command (in the Layout menu). Or, if the importing program supports fractional character widths, be sure that feature is on in that program. Also see the tip "Export Alignment," later in this chapter.

ERASING AND REMOVING

DETAILED ERASING

The paintbrush tool makes a good eraser in most painting programs. Simply choose a pattern to match the background, and paint over unwanted parts of a picture. For detail work, use a small brush shape.

ERASING LINES BY FILLING

You can erase black lines by filling them with white paint from the paint can tool in a painting program. But be ready to undo: If the lines you're erasing touch another part of the picture, it will be erased too.

ERASING WITH RECTANGLES

Use a borderless white rectangle to erase large swaths across a painting program's drawing window. As you draw the rectangle, you can adjust its size and shape without permanently erasing what it covers. When its size and shape are just right, release the mouse button to finalize the erasure.

HIDING BEHIND MASKS

You can't erase part of an object in a drawing program, but you can hide part of one object with another. The object that does the hiding is called a mask. A mask can be any simple object—a rectangle, oval, free-form shape, polygon, and so on—or it can be a composite of several simple objects. After a mask is in place, group it together with the object it covers so that both objects will be treated as one.

MOVING AND COPYING

PRECISION POINTER

When you need precise control over pointer movement, use Apple's Easy Access utility software to move the pointer by pressing keys on the numeric keypad. For information on using Easy Access, see "Keyboard Mouse," in Chapter 1, "General Macintosh Operations."

OUTLINE DRAG

If you want to see outlines of the MacDraw II objects you are dragging instead of the usual generic rectangle, hold down the Command key as you drag. Figure 7-43 illustrates this effect. (In MacDraw I, use the Option key instead of the Command key.) All types of objects, including text, freehand shapes, and polygons, are then represented by their true outlines.

Holding down the Command key continuously greatly slows the speed at which objects move on the screen, especially when you're dragging a complex object such as a smoothed polygon. To speed things up, press Command only when you want to take a reading on the exact location of the object or objects you are dragging rather than continuously.

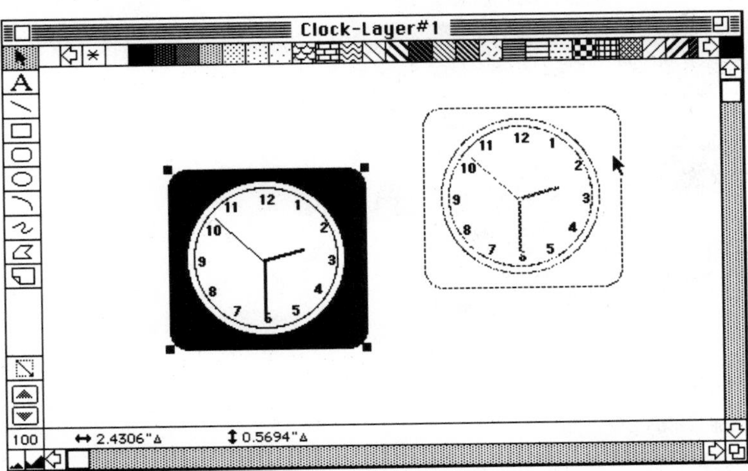

FIGURE 7-43. NO BLIND DRAG.
When dragging an object in MacDraw II, press the Command key to see the outline of the object.

MacPaint

PERIMETER DRAG

To see the dashed lines of the selection rectangle when you drag a selection in MacPaint, press the Spacebar. Normally, MacPaint hides the selection rectangle lines when you drag.

MacPaint

INTERACTIVE DRAG

In MacPaint, you can choose among four ways for a selection to interact with the part of the picture it is being dragged over. The selection can block out the picture beneath it (opaque interaction). The picture can show through the selection above it (transparent interaction). The black parts of the selection can become white where they cover black parts of the picture (reversed interaction). Finally, the selection can act like a patterned eraser on the picture (erased interaction). In addition, you can have MacPaint invert the selection before it applies the interaction. Figure 7-44 illustrates the various types of interaction.

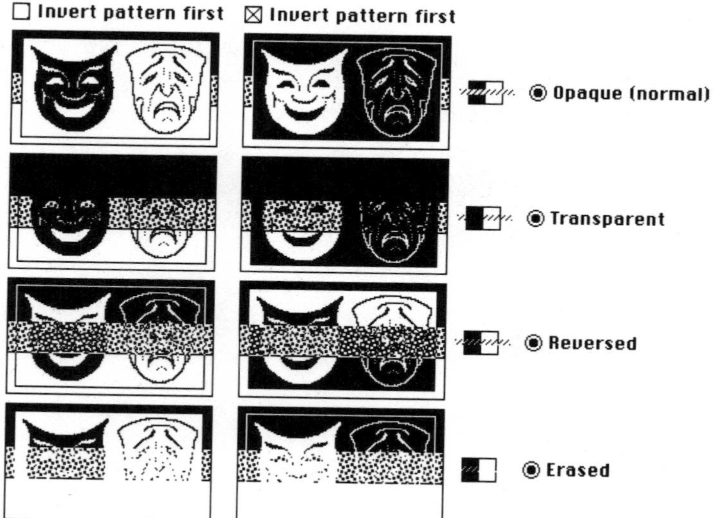

FIGURE 7-44. PATTERN EFFECTS.

The Pattern Effect setting of MacPaint's Preferences command determines what happens when you drag a selection over another part of the picture while pressing the Tab key. Here, the two masks on a white rectangle are dragged over solid black, a pattern, and solid white.

You set the type of interaction with the Preferences command (in the Goodies menu). You make the interaction happen by pressing the Tab key as you start to drag the selection.

DRAGGING TINY OBJECTS

General Drawing

Moving a small object in a drawing program can be difficult. Instead of moving the object, you might inadvertently drag one of its handles, resizing the object instead of moving it.

In MacDraw, the trick is to be sure the object you want to move is not selected. To deselect it, click in an empty area of the document. Then select the object and drag it all in one motion, without releasing the mouse button.

In any drawing program, you can work around this difficulty by selecting a large object with the small one. (For example, press the Shift key while clicking the additional object.) Drag the large object, and the small one will follow. (See Figure 7-45.)

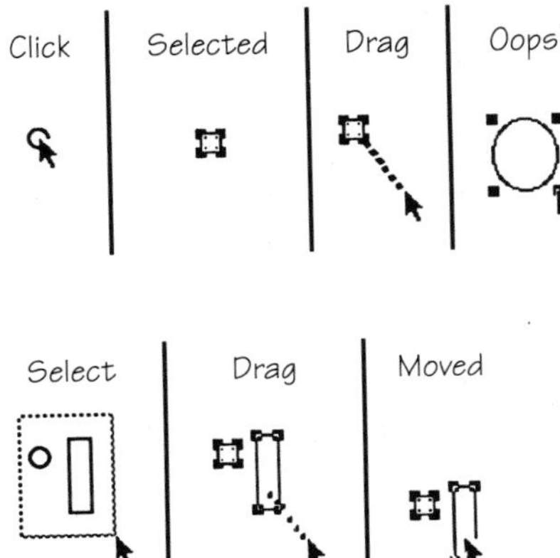

FIGURE 7-45. DRAG TOGETHER.
When trying to drag a small object, you often end up enlarging it (top). To avoid this, use a large object as a tow bar (bottom).

MacDraw II

GAUGING GROUP MOVEMENT

MacDraw II shows two dotted outlines when you drag several objects at once. A dotted-line rectangle shows the group's overall size and location. Inside that rectangle is an outline of the object at which you pointed when you started to drag.

If you start by pointing at a piece of text, a freehand shape, or a polygon, MacDraw uses a rectangle that represents its overall size and position within the group selection. All other objects are represented by their true outlines.

You can use the two outlines to gauge how far and in which direction to move. For best results, start by pointing to the object of the group that will best enable you to tell whether the group is correctly positioned in its new location.

Canvas

GUIDED MOVE

To move all objects aligned to a guideline in a Canvas document, press the Option key and drag the guideline. Objects that touch the guideline but that are not aligned to it do not move.

Adobe Illustrator

TEMPORARY MOVE

To move an object aside in an Adobe Illustrator 88 document, use an arrow key (also called a cursor key in Illustrator). Set the distance by which you want to move the object by using the Cursor Key Distance option of the Preferences command (in the Edit menu). Then select the object you want to move and press an arrow key. When you are ready to move the object back to its former location, select it again and press the opposite of the arrow key you used to move the object aside.

MacDraw II

SAVING MEMORY WITH DUPLICATE

To save memory when using many copies of a scanned image or other bit-mapped image in MacDraw II (such as a logo in a presentation), use the Duplicate command instead of copying and pasting. When you duplicate a bit-mapped object and don't change it, MacDraw II saves memory by keeping only a single copy and displaying it multiple times.

EQUALLY SPACED DUPLICATES

MacDraw II's Duplicate command makes it easy to create a series of equally spaced identical objects. The first time you duplicate an object, MacDraw II records what you do next. If you move the copy of the object, MacDraw II remembers where you moved it in relation to the original object. If you use the Duplicate command again, MacDraw II places the third object in the same position relative to the second object as the second is to the first.

To take advantage of this feature, you must create the entire series of objects before doing anything else. If you draw a new object or select an existing one between uses of the Duplicate command, MacDraw II forgets the relative position of the duplicated objects.

DUPLICATES

General Painting

You can make multiple separate and complete copies of a selected image in MacPaint and most other painting programs. Hold down the Option key and drag away a copy. After you have started dragging, you can release the Option key. When you release the mouse button, the copy of the image is selected instead of the original. You can make another copy by again holding down the Option key and dragging the selection.

MULTIPLES

General Painting

You can create continuous multiple copies of a selected image in MacPaint and most other painting programs, as illustrated in Figure 7-46. Drag the selected image while holding down both the Command and Option keys.

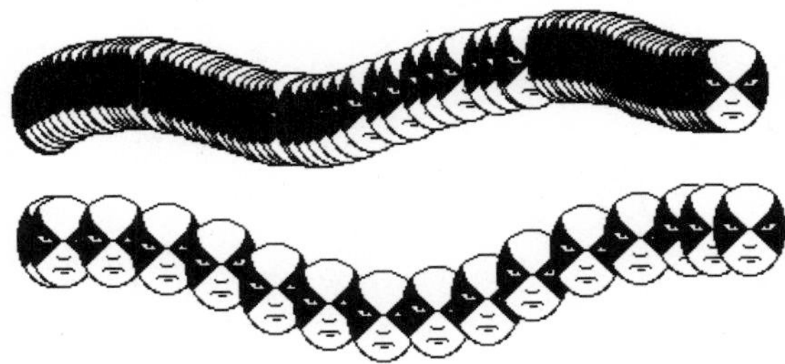

FIGURE 7-46. TRAIL OF COPIES.
Dragging a selected image while pressing Command-Option leaves a trail of multiple copies of the image.

The speed at which you drag affects the spacing between copies. If you drag the selected object slowly, each new copy overlaps most of the previous copy. If you drag quickly, the copies overlap less. If you drag erratically, you will get sporadic, out-of-sequence, chaotic fragments of the selection instead of multiple copies. The currently selected line thickness also affects the spacing of copies.

MAKING QUICK DUPLICATES

Adobe Illustrator

To quickly duplicate an object at regular intervals in an Adobe Illustrator 88 document, use the arrow keys (also called cursor keys in Illustrator). First set the distance you want between each duplicate by using the Cursor Key Distance option of the Preferences command (in the Edit menu). Then select the object you want to duplicate and press the Option key while you repeatedly press and release one of the arrow keys.

COPYING FROM ILLUSTRATOR

Adobe Illustrator

You can't use ordinary copy-and-paste methods to transfer artwork from Adobe Illustrator to another program. Illustrator, like most programs, maintains a private clipboard, but unlike other programs, it does not automatically convert artwork on the private clipboard to the standard PICT format when you switch programs.

To copy Illustrator artwork by means of the Clipboard to another program, select the artwork in Illustrator (choose Select All from the Edit menu to select the whole document), press the Option key while choosing Copy from the Edit menu, switch programs, and choose Paste from the Edit menu. Pressing Option while choosing Copy converts the selected artwork to PICT format with Encapsulated PostScript (EPS). In this form, the artwork is compatible with any program that accepts graphics from MacDraw. (However, text rotation and a few other special effects print correctly only from a program that supports EPS.)

ALIGNING

ADJUSTING GRID SPACING

MacDraw II

If invisible grid lines are too widely spaced, you might not be able to size and place objects accurately. You can change MacDraw II's grid spacing by using the Rulers command (in the Layout menu) to change the ruler. The

number of divisions per inch in the ruler determines the grid spacing. The more divisions, the shorter the distance between the invisible grid lines.

Note that the rulers might not show all the divisions you select. For example, if you set 32 divisions per inch, the ruler shows divisions only every 1/16 inch. The finer grid lines are there, but they're not marked on the rulers.

ALIGNMENT RULES

MacDraw II

MacDraw II provides a visual display of the different alignment options when you choose Alignment from the Arrange menu. To see where on the drawing the Alignment command will line up objects you have selected, refer to the table in Figure 7-47.

Aligns	Where
Top edges	Top edge of topmost object
Centers (vertical)	Halfway between topmost and bottommost objects
Bottom edges	Bottom edge of bottommost object
Left edges	Left edge of leftmost object
Centers (horizontal)	Halfway between leftmost and rightmost objects
Right edges	Right edge of rightmost object

FIGURE 7-47. LINE UP.
MacDraw II follows these rules when aligning selected objects.

LINKED ALIGNMENT

Swivel 3D

To facilitate the alignment of objects in a Swivel 3D document, link them first. After a child is linked to a parent, the child's position is dependent on the parent's. It's easier to specify the child's position relative to the parent's than it is to situate both objects by giving absolute coordinates.

CENTERING PICTURES IN MACPAINT

MacPaint

How can you center a picture on a MacPaint page? Use the Zoom Out command (in the Goodies menu) to view your document reduced by 50 percent. (The window title includes the percentage of reduction or enlargement.) At 50 percent, you can see an entire page on a Mac with a large screen, and you can edit the whole drawing without scrolling. To center the drawing, first select all of it—excluding extra white space around the edges—by tearing off the Tool menu and pressing Command-Shift while double-clicking the selection tool. Then drag the drawing until it looks centered on the page.

Centering a drawing on a smaller screen is not so easy, however. On a small screen you can see the whole width of the page but not the whole height. In that case you can center the drawing horizontally by eye and vertically by using the mouse-position inset window. First select the whole drawing, as described in the previous paragraph. Drag left or right until it looks centered horizontally. Then press the Shift key to constrain movement to one direction, and drag the drawing to the top of the page. Next choose Show Mouse Position from the Goodies menu to display the mouse-position inset. Measure the distance from the bottom of the drawing to the bottom of the page by watching the middle of the mouse-position inset while dragging a selection rectangle between those two locations. Select the whole drawing again, press Shift, and drag the drawing down the page half the distance you just measured.

TEXT THAT WON'T ALIGN

When your drawing program won't properly align a single line of text with other objects, there might be blank spaces at the beginning of the text, or the text boundary box might be wider than the line of text. To see the true size of a line text, select it by clicking on it with the selection tool (the arrow). Figure 7-48 shows both these situations.

Remove extra blank spaces by selecting them with the text tool and then either choosing Clear from the Edit menu or pressing the Delete key. Make the text boundary narrower by selecting the text with the selection tool and then dragging one of the boundary's corners.

These two lines should be centered in the box,

but this line has extra blanks at the beginning.

FIGURE 7-48. TOO-WIDE TEXT.

Text with extra blank spaces at the beginning or with a wide boundary box might not align correctly in a drawing program.

DISABLED GRID

To disable the alignment grid in Canvas temporarily, press the Tab key while dragging. Drawing, resizing, and moving of objects will not be restricted to grid intervals. You turn the alignment grid on and off with the Snap To Grid command (in the Layout menu).

EXPORT ALIGNMENT

MacDraw II graphics sometimes drift out of alignment when pasted or imported into page-layout and word processing documents. This problem occurs because QuickDraw (the Mac's built-in graphics system) and PostScript (the graphics system used by the LaserWriter IINT and other printers) use different coordinates to locate objects. To forestall misalignment of an exported MacDraw II graphic, choose Rulers from the Layout menu and set the Divisions/Inch to 72.

RESIZING AND ROTATING

PRECISE ROTATION

To rotate objects in MacDraw II more precisely, magnify the view. Use the Preferences command (in the Layout menu) to set the Custom Mouse Constraint option to the exact rotation angle. Then choose Rotate from the Arrange menu and hold down the Shift key while rotating. The object will rotate to the precise angle specified.

ROTATION POINT

MacDraw II can rotate an object around either of two points: the center of the object, or the corner of the object diagonally opposite the corner you drag when doing the rotation. The corner/center control determines the rotation method. The control is located near the lower left corner of the drawing window.

To rotate an object around its center in MacDraw II, set the corner/center control for a center origin. To rotate an object around one of its corners, set the corner/center control for a corner origin. Figure 7-49 on the following page shows the two settings of the control.

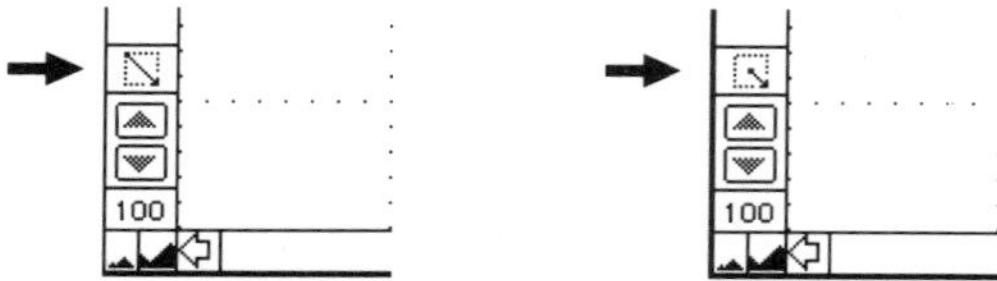

FIGURE 7-49. CENTER/CORNER ROTATION.
When the center/corner control is set for a corner origin, MacDraw II rotates an object around its corner (left). When the control is set for a center origin, the program rotates an object around its center (right).

MacDraw II

RESIZING OR MOVING?

In MacDraw II, how can you tell whether you're changing an object's size or moving it? Choose Show Size from the Layout menu and then watch the statistics at the bottom of the drawing window as you drag. You're moving, not resizing, if little triangle-shaped symbols appear alongside the size statistics when you drag. Figure 7-50 shows what the symbols look like.

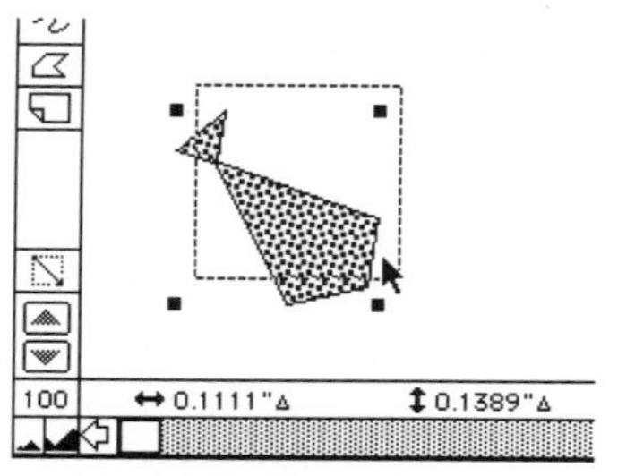

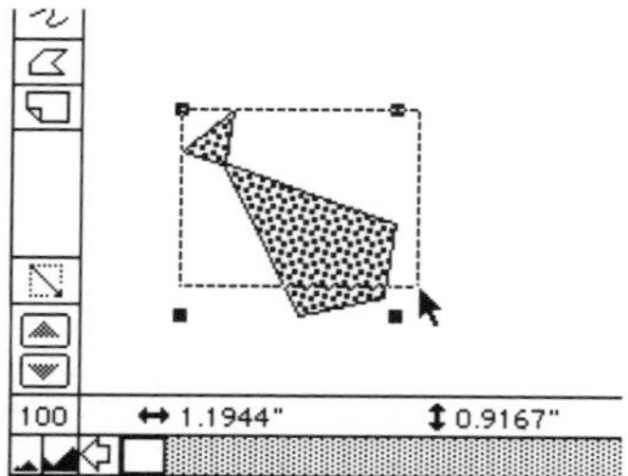

FIGURE 7-50. DELTA MOVE.
The Greek letter delta (Δ) appears next to MacDraw II's size statistics when you move an object but not when you resize an object.

General Painting

NEW SIZE AND SHAPE

How can you change the size or shape of an image in a painting program? Select the image, using the selection rectangle, and press the Command key while dragging on or inside the flashing edge of the rectangle. To resize horizontally, drag from a side edge. To resize vertically, drag from the top or bottom edge. To resize both horizontally and vertically, drag from a corner. Resizing an image in a painting program distorts the lines and patterns, so be ready to undo should you dislike the results.

NEW SIZE, SAME SHAPE

General Painting

How can you keep the ratio of height to width constant while you resize an image in a painting program? Simply hold down the Command and Shift keys as you start to drag a corner of the selection rectangle.

ALIGNED RESIZING

Canvas

When resizing multiple objects as a group in Canvas, the Scale command (in the Object menu) normally maintains the positions of the objects in the drawing. To maintain the relative distances and alignment of multiple objects that you're resizing, press the Option key while clicking OK in the Scale dialog box. Pressing Option when doubling the size of two objects also doubles the distance between them.

RESIZING WHILE PASTING

MacPaint

You can preset the size, shape, and location of an object you plan to paste into a MacPaint picture. Before using the Paste command, draw a selection rectangle where you want the object to be. Make the selection rectangle the size and shape you want the imported object to have. When you paste, MacPaint resizes the contents of the Clipboard to fit within the selection rectangle.

KEEPING SIZE IN PERSPECTIVE

Aldus Freehand

To scale an object along lines of perspective in Aldus Freehand, as shown in Figure 7-51 on the next page, follow these steps:

1. If you haven't already done so, move the ruler origins to the vanishing point and drag vertical and horizontal guides to the origin. (See the tip "Linear Perspective," earlier in this chapter.)
2. Select the object you want to scale.
3. Select the scale tool and place the pointer at the vanishing point. Watch the information bar for precise placement.
4. With the pointer at the vanishing point, press the Shift key and drag. Drag away from the selected object to reduce it or toward the selected object to enlarge it.

PRECISE ENLARGEMENT AND REDUCTION

You can enlarge or reduce an object by a precise percentage or ratio by using a 1-inch square as a gauge. Your drawing or painting program must provide some means of measuring objects—rulers, grids, or a size readout. In MacDraw, for example, use the Show Size command (in the Layout menu) to turn on the display of sizes. In SuperPaint 2.0, use the Grids & Rulers command (in the Options menu). In Microsoft Works's draw layer, use the Grid On command (in the Format menu).

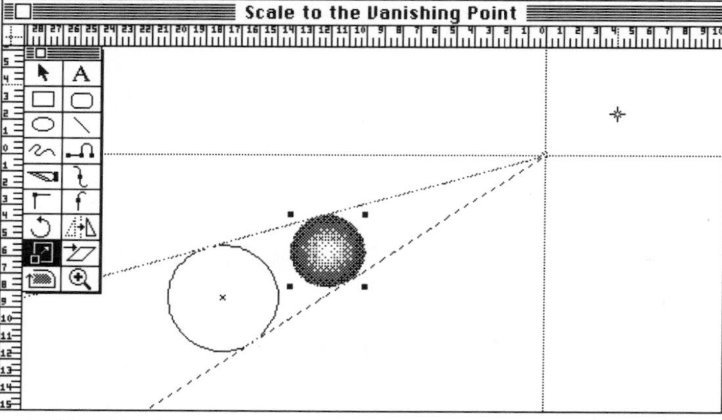

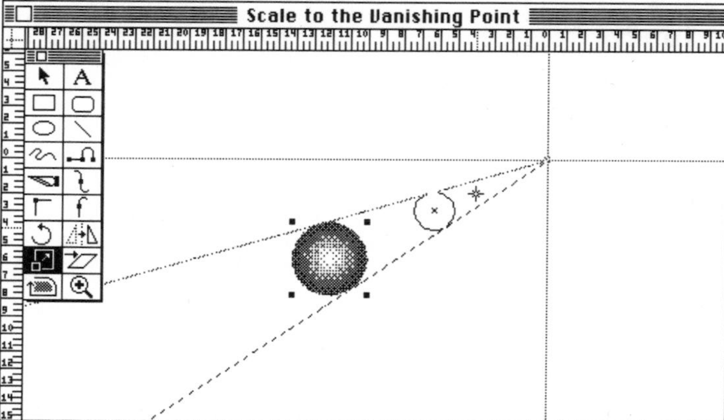

FIGURE 7-51. SCALE TO THE VANISHING POINT.

In Aldus Freehand, keep an object's size in perspective by placing the scale tool at the origin and pressing Shift while dragging away from the object (top) or toward the object (bottom).

Draw the 1-inch square near the object to be scaled. Select both the square and the object to be scaled. Then scale the square and the other object along with it by dragging one of the square's corners. Scale the square to the percentage or ratio of its original size that you want applied to the other object. For example, scale the square to ½ inch if you want a ½, or 50 percent, reduction. Finally, erase the square.

THE THREE-FINGER STRETCH

You can stretch only the middle of an object in a painting program. The two opposite ends of the image are unchanged and parallel lines connect them, as illustrated in Figure 7-52. For example, a circle can be widened into a shape that has semicircular sides and straight top and bottom edges.

Drag a selection rectangle to select one end of an image. Select the left end if you want to stretch horizontally to the left, the top end if you want to stretch vertically upward, and so on. Then hold down the Command, Option, and Shift keys and slowly drag the selection rectangle in the direction of the stretch. As you drag, parallel lines appear in the wake of the selection rectangle.

If you drag too quickly, the parallel lines can be jagged. In that case, drag slowly back in the other direction, far enough to clean up the jaggedness, and then drag ahead again. This method has been dubbed the "three-finger stretch" by MacPaint's author, Bill Atkinson.

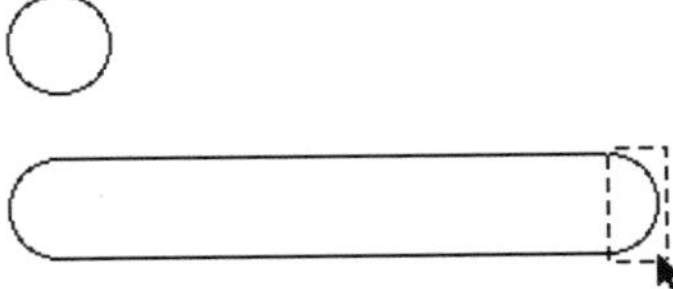

FIGURE 7-52. DRAG OUT.
Widen or heighten an image in a painting program by selecting one side and dragging while holding down Command-Option-Shift.

THE THREE-FINGER STRETCH AND THE GRID

The results of the three-finger stretch described in the previous tip are unsatisfactory with patterned images because the pattern is disrupted. To maintain the pattern during a three-finger stretch, be sure the painting program's grid option is set. Figure 7-53 shows the results with and without the grid active.

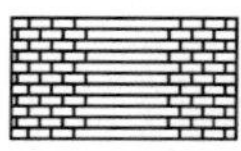

FIGURE 7-53. GRIDDED DRAG.
For patterned images, the three-finger stretch works better if the grid option is on.

ENHANCING ENLARGEMENTS

The enlargements you produce in a painting program by dragging the corner of a selection rectangle while pressing the Command key are relatively crude. You can touch them up with the paintbrush and other tools, but there is a more mechanical method for improving the appearance of proportional enlargements that are some exact multiple—two, three, four, and so on—of the original image. First you make the crude enlargement, and then you thin its blocky texture, as shown in Figure 7-54. Carry out these steps:

1. Select the image and make it two, three, or any other whole number of times larger. If your painting program has a Scale command, use it.

   To enlarge without a Scale command, create a gauge for enlargement by arranging copies of the original side by side. For example, to triple the size of the object, arrange three copies of the original next to and touching one another. Then select the topmost original with the selection rectangle and proportionally enlarge it by pressing the Command and Shift keys as you start to drag the lower right corner. Continue to drag until the enlargement covers the bottommost copy of the original. The large, blocky dots in the enlargement should all be the same size.

2. To thin the enlarged image, start by inverting the crude enlargement. This yields a negative image of the crude enlargement. Fill the inverted image with a dark gray transparent pattern. Invert again to get a light positive image. Save your work now so that you can revert to this point later.

In MacPaint, for example, select the image and choose Invert from the Edit menu. Then select the pattern in the top right corner of the standard pattern palette, and press the Command and Option keys while choosing Fill from the Edit menu. Choose Invert again from the Edit menu.

3. Now darken the light positive image by lassoing it, holding down the Option key, and dragging a copy one or two dots away. Release the mouse button without moving the mouse.
4. The light positive image is still selected. Darken it still more by holding down the Option key again and dragging another copy of the image a dot or two in another direction. Release the mouse button without moving the mouse.

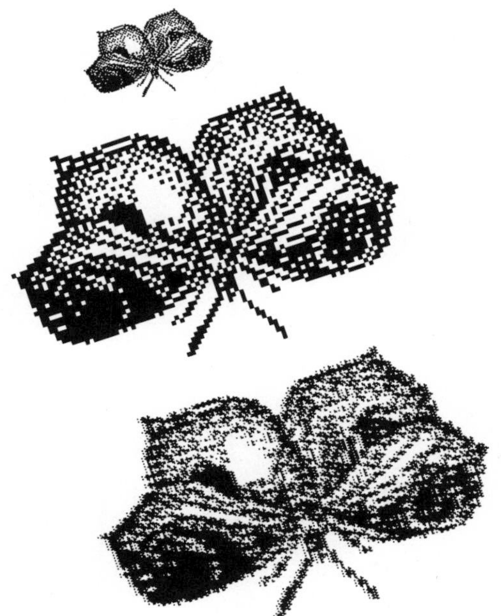

FIGURE 7-54. THIN AND BLUR.
Coarse enlargements in a painting program can be enhanced without a lot of freehand touch-up work, providing a smoother transition from black to white.

Repeat this step until you get the look you want. You'll have to experiment. If you clobber the enlargement, revert to the single light positive image you saved in step 2, and begin darkening anew.

Chapter 8

PUBLISHING AND PRESENTATIONS

Desktop publishing and desktop presentations let you systematically lay out text and graphics on pages or slides. This chapter covers publishing and presentations in general as well as several specific page-layout and slide-layout programs. You'll find tips on the following topics:

- Desktop environment
- Typography
- Artwork and photos
- Layout
- Hard-copy output

Both publishing and presentations combine text and graphics and sometimes spreadsheets. Those topics are covered separately in Chapters 6, 7, and 9. Printing on a LaserWriter or ImageWriter is covered in Chapter 4.

DESKTOP ENVIRONMENT

PICAS, POINTS, OR INCHES?

General Publishing

If you're new to publishing, you need to become accustomed to working in picas and points instead of inches. If you live outside the United States, you might want to use ciceros and cicero points instead of millimeters. By working in picas (or ciceros) and points, you avoid dealing with fractions.

1 inch = 6 picas = 72 points
1 pica = 12 points

PageMaker

SEE THE WORLD

To view the entire PageMaker pasteboard, press the Shift key while choosing Fit In Window from the Page menu. You can use this whole-world view for spreading out items on the pasteboard while you decide where to place them. (See Figure 8-1.)

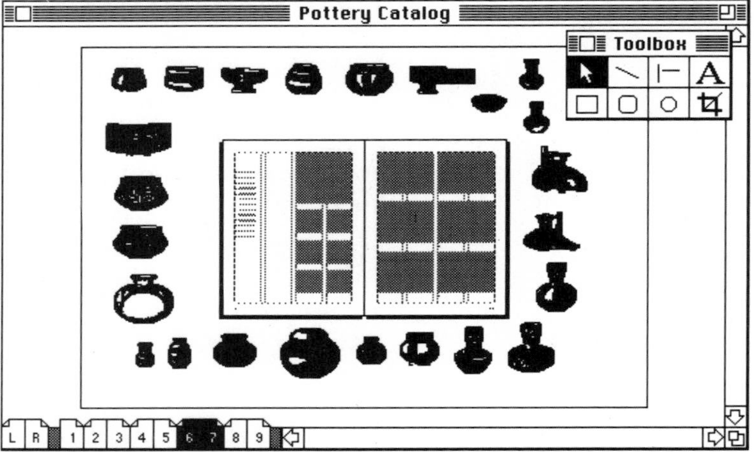

FIGURE 8-1. WORLD VIEW.
Use the Shift key with PageMaker's Fit In Window command (in the Page menu) to see the whole pasteboard.

QuarkXPress

THUMBNAIL VIEW

You can quite easily view thumbnails of a QuarkXPress document on the screen. First shrink the document window by dragging its size box (located at the lower right corner of the window) toward the upper left corner of the screen. The window height at this point determines the size of the thumbnails. Next reduce the page view by choosing Fit In Window from the View menu. Finally restore the document window to its original size by clicking the zoom box at the right end of the window's title bar or by dragging the window's size box. QuarkXPress displays multiple thumbnails in the window, as shown in Figure 8-2. If you want to see facing pages side by side, be sure the Facing Pages command (in the Pages menu) has a check mark beside it.

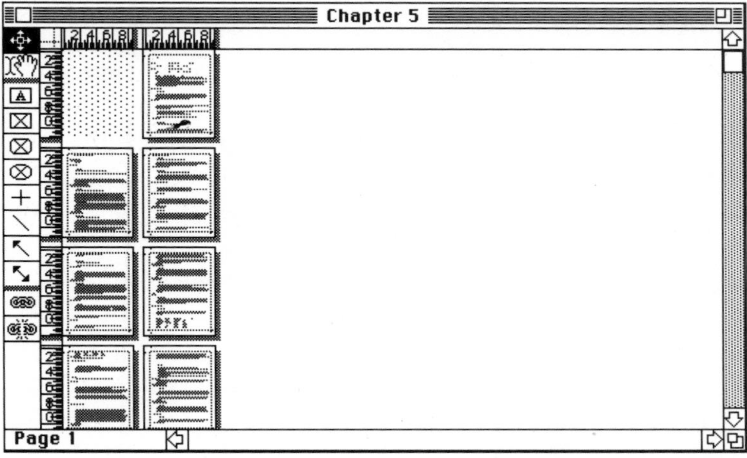

FIGURE 8-2. FIT MORE IN WINDOW.

QuarkXPress displays several pages immediately after you shrink the document window, apply the Fit In Window command (in the View menu), and then make the window taller again.

OPTIONAL VIEWS

When you are working on a QuarkXPress document, sometimes the Actual Size view is too small and the 200% view is just too much. To magnify the view to 150%, press the Option key before pulling down the View menu, and hold it down while choosing 75%. Likewise, you can magnify the view to 400% by pressing Option while choosing 200%. (This Option-key technique doubles the other view sizes too, but only 75% and 200% yield sizes not on the View menu.)

GETTING CLOSER

PageMaker versions 3.0, 3.01, and 3.02 have an undocumented page view of 400 percent. To use it, press the Shift key while choosing 200% from the Page menu. There doesn't seem to be a keyboard shortcut for the 400 percent view.

QUICKER PAGE CHANGE

You can shorten the amount of time it takes to display the next page in PageMaker, especially if you are using Adobe Type Manager (ATM) and are viewing your document at less than full size. As you click the page icon at the bottom of the window, press the Shift key. Doing this makes the upcoming page appear in the Fit In Window view regardless of which view was last used for the page. In that view, most of the type is displayed faster because it is greeked (illegible), relieving ATM from rebuilding the screen fonts.

From the Fit In Window view, you can go quickly and precisely to any part of a page. To do so, press Command-Option (for actual size) or Command-Shift-Option (for 200 percent enlargement) while clicking on the area you want to see. By comparison, scrolling at actual size or at a magnified view is much slower and less precise.

SLIDE ADVANCE

How can you go to the next slide or the previous slide in Aldus Persuasion without using the menus? Go to the next slide by pressing Command-Down arrow once. Press Command-Up arrow to view the previous slide. You can skip several slides by keeping the keys pressed down. The slide numbers advance quickly in the slide-number indicator at the lower left corner of the window, without pausing to display each slide. When you release the keys, Persuasion displays the current slide.

TOOL SWITCH

To change from any PageMaker tool to the pointer tool without huffing and puffing to the toolbox, press Command-Spacebar. To switch back to the tool you were using, press Command-Spacebar again.

NO-HANDS PAGE TURNING

You can cycle automatically and continuously through all the pages of a PageMaker publication. To do so, press the Shift key while choosing Go To Page from the Page menu. Each page appears in the same view in which it was last displayed. To stop the slide show, click once anywhere.

SELECTING A BURIED OBJECT

PageMaker

You can easily select an object buried beneath other objects in a PageMaker publication without moving the overlapping objects aside. With the pointer tool selected, press the Command key and click twice or more where the buried object resides. Each successive Command-click selects the object buried one level lower. You can generally tell which object is currently selected by the configuration of selection handles. You can change most attributes of a selected object without affecting its level, but moving it brings it to the top level.

GROUP MOVE

QuarkXPress

To move several items from different boxes in QuarkXPress as a group, you must put them all in one box. Draw a new box of any type—text or picture. Then cut each item from its current parent box and paste it into the new box. The new box becomes the parent of the items you paste in it, and moving it moves all items it contains.

UNIQUE COLORS

QuarkXPress

You can create and save your own colors in QuarkXPress. Choose Colors from the Edit menu and click the New button to get the Edit Color dialog box. Select the Pantone option to see color swatches from the Pantone color matching system. Click a color close to what you have in mind. Next select the RGB option to see the standard Macintosh color wheel and convert the selected color to RGB color space. You can now change the percentage of the red, green, and blue values while viewing the color change on the screen. When the screen displays the color you want, name it and click OK, thereby dismissing the Edit Color dialog box. Save your new color for future use by clicking the Save button in the Default Colors dialog box. If you create a color when no document is open, QuarkXPress adds it to the standard color palette so that it will be available in all documents.

NEW STANDARDS

PageMaker

PageMaker applies standard type specifications, paragraph formatting, and scores of other settings and options to every document you create. You can change the options and settings that PageMaker initially applies to a new publication by making menu choices and dialog box settings when no publication is open.

After you create a new publication, PageMaker remembers that publication's standard options and settings separately. You can change the standard settings and options that apply only to the currently open publication. First select the pointer tool and click once in an empty area of the publication window to be sure no text or graphic is selected. Then make the menu choices and dialog box settings that you want PageMaker to apply to objects you subsequently add to the publication.

PageMaker

DISMISSING EXTRA GUIDES

You can quite easily clear away a clutter of ruler guides you no longer need on a particular page of a PageMaker publication. Be sure the Lock Guides command (on the Options menu) is not checked, and choose Copy Master Guides from the Page menu. PageMaker will clear the page of all ruler guides. Any master guides you have set up will remain in place.

PageMaker

DIMENSION OVERRIDE

Regardless of the measurement system you set by using PageMaker's Preferences command (in the Edit menu), you can include any unit of measurement that makes sense along with a value you enter in a dialog box. When specifying column spacing with the Column Guides command (in the Options menu), for example, you can enter a number of inches or a number of picas and points. Add the letter *i* for inches or *m* for millimeters, like this: *0.75i* or *190.05m*. For picas and points, suffix the letter *p* followed by the number of points (if any), for example: *4.5p*, *4p6*, or *0p54*. Do not enter a space between the number and the abbreviated unit of measurement that follows.

Aldus Persuasion

TRANSITION TROUBLE

Transition effects in Aldus Persuasion version 2.0 stop working between slides in on-screen presentation if you press the Caps Lock key or if Persuasion doesn't have enough memory available to create the upcoming slide off-screen. If you suspect that Persuasion has run out of memory and MultiFinder is active, try quitting Persuasion, selecting the Persuasion icon in the Finder, and using the Finder's Get Info command (in the File menu) to increase the Application Memory Size setting. Alternatively, try restarting

with MultiFinder inactive. If MultiFinder is inactive and transition effects still don't work, you must either add memory to your computer or simplify your presentation.

The amount of additional memory required depends on the size of the screen and the number of colors displayed. On a Mac Plus or SE, transition effects require 25 KB extra. On a Mac II with a 13-inch screen, transition effects require 40 KB for black and white, 155 KB for 16 colors, 310 KB for 256 colors, and 1.2 MB for millions of colors.

TYPOGRAPHY

PASTEBOARD GLOSSARY

If you will be repeatedly using symbols, dingbats, and other special text in your PageMaker publication, keep one copy of each item on the pasteboard. As you work, use the text tool to select what you need on the pasteboard, copy it, and then paste it into place on the page.

LEADING WITH INITIAL CAPITAL LETTERS

A large initial capital letter throws off automatic leading, leaving a big gap after the line that contains the capital letter. (Leading is the typographic term for the space between lines.) To keep leading consistent when you use a large initial capital letter, select the capital letter and set the leading equal to the leading of the regular text. In Ready,Set,Go! and DesignStudio, you must set the leading of the entire paragraph. (In Ready,Set,Go!, leading is called line spacing.) After you change the leading, the initial capital letter might appear beheaded on screen, but it will print correctly.

You can compute the amount of leading to use for the initial capital letter when regular text has automatic leading. In PageMaker and QuarkXPress, automatic leading is usually 20 percent larger than the text size. In Ready,Set,Go! and DesignStudio, automatic leading is usually exactly the same as the text size. To check the automatic leading factor in PageMaker 4.0, click the Spacing button of the Paragraph command (in the Type menu). In PageMaker 3.0x, use the Spacing command (in the Type menu). While you're checking the automatic leading factor in PageMaker, be sure the leading method is set to Proportional. To check the automatic leading

factor in QuarkXPress, use the Preferences command (in the Edit menu). In DesignStudio, use the Preferences command (in the Document menu). In Ready,Set,Go!, use the Preferences command (in the Special menu).

PageMaker

DROP-IN CAPITAL LETTERS

To customize a large drop capital letter (a capital letter that is larger than and "drops" below the rest of a line) in PageMaker, create it in a PostScript drawing program such as Aldus FreeHand or Adobe Illustrator and save it as an EPS graphic. Bring that graphic into PageMaker as an independent graphic by using the Place command (in the File menu). From the Element menu, choose the appropriate Text Wrap option for the placed graphic. (In PageMaker 3.0x, Text Wrap is located in the Options menu.) You can manipulate the text-wrap border by selecting it and dragging the handles so that the text wraps to the irregular outline of the drop capital letter, as shown in Figure 8-3. To postpone changes in the text flow while you're adjusting text-wrap handles, hold down the Spacebar.

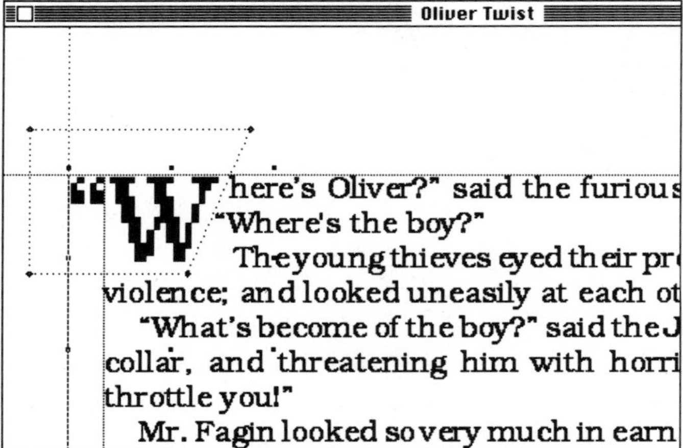

FIGURE 8-3. DROP DOWN.
This drop cap is really an EPS graphic imported into PageMaker. Adjust the text-wrap handles to fit the text around the shape of the letter.

OBJECT TYPE

To make an ad headline look good in PageMaker, you must custom-fit it to the ad space, adjusting its height and width precisely. You can set headline copy with any drawing program and then import the graphic headline into PageMaker by cutting and pasting or by using PageMaker's Place command. After the headline is in PageMaker, you can stretch this graphic object into the headline space as if it were rubber type. This strategy is fine for simple headlines, but a drawing program's kerning and line-spacing control are too primitive for multiline copy.

With Super Glue from Solutions International, you can get much more effective results without quitting PageMaker. Set your type in PageMaker with the kerning and leading you want. Then print the document, using Super Glue to transform the PageMaker text into a graphic object. Use Super Glue's ViewerDA desk accessory to cut and paste the object type back to PageMaker. Then make the type any shape you please.

This technique works equally well on both individual headlines and a whole ad. See Figure 8-4 for examples.

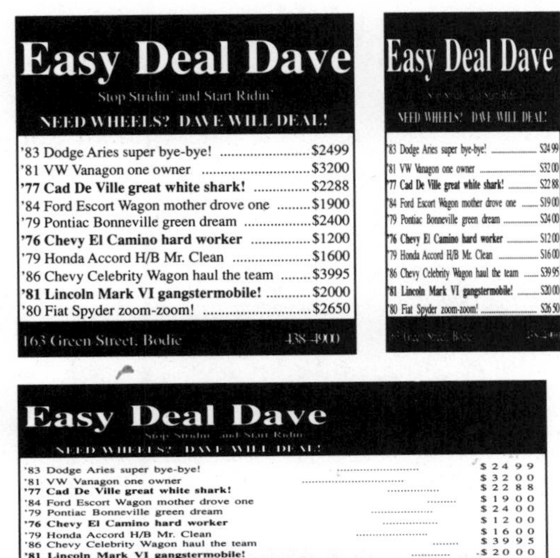

FIGURE 8-4. RUBBER TEXT.
Use Super Glue to transform PageMaker text so that you can stretch it to fit any shape.

PageMaker

FORCE-FITTING A HEADLINE

PageMaker offers three ways to fit a headline into a space that's slightly too narrow. First try selecting the headline and choosing Justify from the Alignment submenu of the Type menu. Justified text uses the minimum allowable letterspacing, whereas left-justified text uses the desired letterspacing.

If that technique doesn't work, left-align the headline and be sure it's in a separate text block. (Cut it and paste it into a blank spot if it's not.) Then select it and change the desired letterspacing to a negative number, such as –10%. To do that in PageMaker 4.0, choose Paragraph from the Type menu and click the Spacing button. In PageMaker 3.0x, choose Spacing from the Type menu.

If neither of these methods works, select the headline text and reduce the point size by 1 or 2 points.

DesignStudio

Ready, Set,Go!

HYPHENATION EXCEPTIONS

How can you prevent DesignStudio or Ready,Set,Go! 4.5 from hyphenating specific words, such as proper names? Leave hyphenation turned on (in the Text menu), and type a soft hyphen by pressing Command–hyphen in front of the word you want to keep unbroken. The halves of the currently hyphenated words immediately reunite and drop to the next line. If the word isn't currently hyphenated, this will prevent it from being broken in the future.

General Publishing

EQUATIONS FROM WORD

You can import equations created in Microsoft Word intact into any page-layout document. In Word, select the equation and copy it as a graphic by pressing Command-Option-D. Then switch to the page-layout program and paste the graphic form of the equation into your document. Because the equation is a graphic, you cannot edit it, but you can move it, resize it, and crop it.

General Publishing

LEVEL FRACTIONS

To create a fraction that sits level on the baseline and looks attractive, type the whole number and the fraction with no space between them. Type a fraction bar (Option-Shift-1) instead of a slash. Make the numerator a

superscript, and set the size of the denominator to about half the size of normal text. If necessary, kern the fraction.

For best results in PageMaker, use the Position option of the Type Specs command (on the Type menu) to make the numerator a superscript and the denominator a subscript. Then select the fraction, click the Options button of the Type Specs command, and set the Subscript Position option to 0. With some fonts and point sizes, you might also need to adjust the Super/Subscript Size option and the Superscript Position option to make the fraction the same height as a capital letter.

NON-BREAKING SLASH

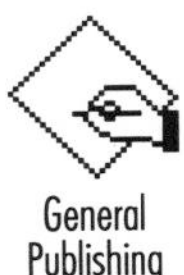
General Publishing

A word or acronym that includes a slash, such as OS/2 or A/UX, might break at the slash when it falls at the end of a line. Replacing the slash with a fraction bar (Option-Shift-1) keeps it "glued" together. The bar slants at a different angle than the slash and might change the kerning of the word or acronym, but in most fonts the differences are slight enough to let you mix the slash and the fraction bar in the same text block.

INSIDE-OUT TEXT FLOW

PageMaker

PageMaker normally flows text around the outside of a graphic object, but it can flow text inside an object instead. The key to flowing text inside an object is the text-repelling graphic boundary that PageMaker creates around the object, and the trick is to turn the boundary inside out. Figure 8-5 on the following page illustrates the procedure. Here are the steps:

1. Select the object and choose Text Wrap from PageMaker's Options menu (the Element menu in PageMaker 4.0). In the dialog box that appears, select the middle Wrap option and click OK. PageMaker draws a rectangular graphic boundary with diamond-shaped handles at each corner.
2. Select the pointer tool from the toolbox, and drag the upper right handle to the left, near the upper left handle. Then drag the upper left corner to the right. Repeat with the lower handles. The graphic boundary is now inside out.
3. Adjust the handles to get the amount of standoff you want inside the graphic object. For a nonrectangular graphic boundary, add diamond-shaped handles by clicking anywhere along the graphic boundary.

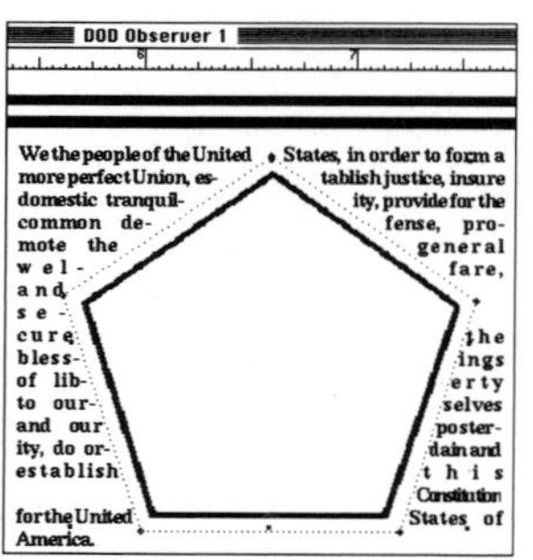

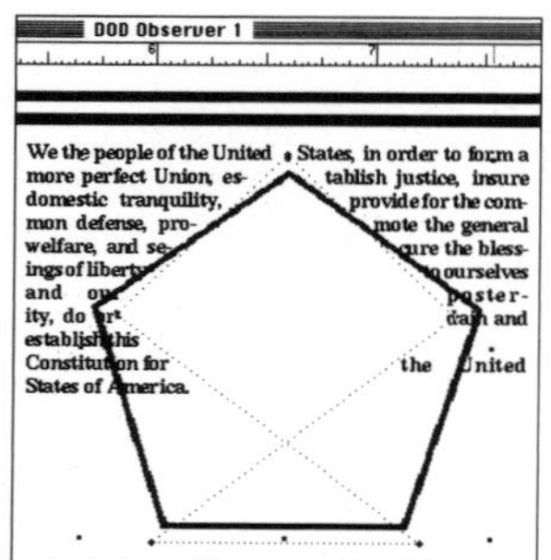

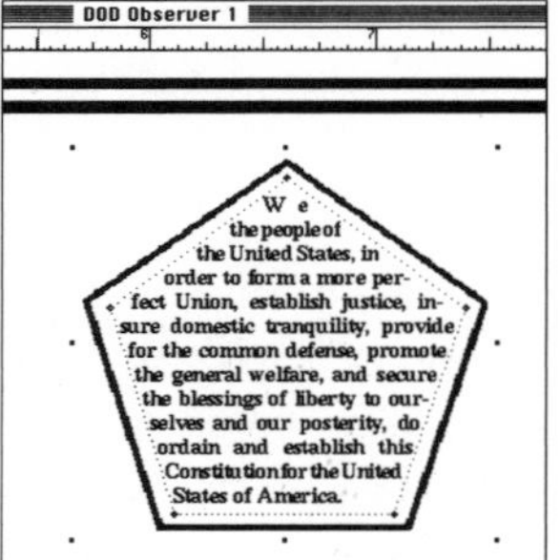

FIGURE 8-5. FLOW WITHIN.

PageMaker wraps text around graphics by constructing a graphic boundary that repels text (left). By dragging the handles on the right side of the graphic boundary to the left side and dragging the handles on the left side to the right side (center), you turn the graphic boundary inside out. As a result, PageMaker wraps text inside the graphic boundary (right).

One last important note: You might have to experiment with the text handles to make the inside wrap work. For example, the text will not wrap to the inside of an inside-out graphic boundary if the text is narrower than the widest part of the graphic boundary.

TEXT WRAPS TEXT

Normally you can't wrap text around other text in Ready,Set,Go! One way to get around this is to use MacDraw or some other drawing program to create the text to be surrounded and then import it into Ready,Set,Go! as a graphic. Text can be wrapped around a graphic.

There's an easier way to convert text to a graphic, however. First create the text, using a standard Text Block. Make all the adjustments you need to the text, such as adding style options or changing the point size. Then, when the text looks exactly the way you want it, select the text block (not the text itself) and copy it to the Scrapbook. This converts the text block to a graphic block. With the Scrapbook still open, copy again. Finally, close the Scrapbook, prepare a graphic block, and paste. The Scrapbook does all the work you might have used a drawing program for.

RULER REGISTRATION

Dragging the zero point of the screen ruler from the upper left corner of the document window to the left edge of the active text block puts the screen ruler and the tab ruler in registration—that is, the measurements on the two rulers match.

SLANTED MARGINS

You can easily create slanted margins in most page-layout programs, even though most programs don't let you set them directly. The first step is the same in PageMaker, Ready,Set,Go!, and QuarkXPress: Use the line-drawing tool to draw a line at the angle at which you want the margin to slant. From here on, the process is different for the various programs.

In QuarkXPress versions 2.0 and later, the margin-defining line should intersect a text box so that you can later flow type along the line. While the line is selected (showing endpoints), press Command-M to modify it. Set the shade to 0 percent Black or to White, and be sure it is not transparent. Now text flowed into the adjoining text box slants along the invisible line. (See Figure 8-6.) This method works for left and right margins if you use the appropriate paragraph format option (Left or Right).

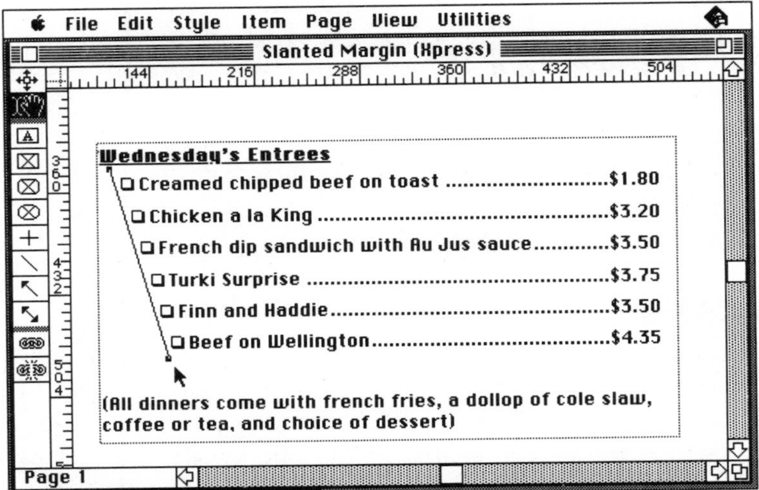

FIGURE 8-6. MARGINAL ANGLE.

QuarkXPress 2.0 and other page-layout programs can align text along a diagonal line, creating the effect of a slanted margin.

In PageMaker, use the Text Wrap command (in the Options menu in 3.0x; in the Element menu in 4.0) to set the middle Wrap option. With the line selected, drag the diamond-shaped handles of its graphic boundary to make a rhomboid boundary around the line. Choose None from the Lines menu to make the line invisible. Place or type text at the top of the slanted line.

In Ready,Set,Go!, draw the margin-defining line on top of the text box. With the line still selected, use the Specifications command (in the Edit menu) to set the Runaround option. Then choose None from the Pen menu to make the line invisible.

General Publishing

ALIGNING LISTS

To ensure uniform alignment of text in a bulleted or numbered list, type a tab instead of a space after each bullet or number. Set the leftmost tab stop to fix the amount of space between the bullet or number and the text that follows it. If items on the list run longer than one line, set the left indent even with that first tab stop. This left-aligns all text evenly at the point established by the leftmost tab stop.

PageMaker

NO BOLD LEADERS

PageMaker doesn't let you directly set the type specs of the leader characters that fill the space before a tab stop. It formats tab leaders using the type specs of the letter or symbol that precedes them. If you need the leaders to be in a different style from the preceding text, insert a hard space (press Option-Spacebar) immediately ahead of each tab character and set the style of the hard space to the style you want for the tab leader. (See Figure 8-7.) You can make the hard space unobtrusive by reducing its font size, but that has the side effect of reducing the subsequent tab leader.

General Publishing

FOREIGN CAPITALS

How can you figure out which keys to press to produce accented letters, both lowercase and uppercase? The Key Caps desk accessory shows the letter or other character each key generates when you press it alone or in combination with one or more modifier keys (Option, Shift, and Control). But it does not show many letters with accents or other diacritical marks because typing them is a two-step process.

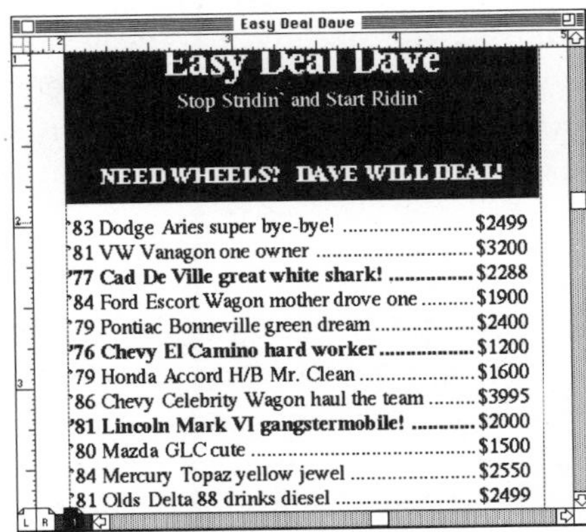

FIGURE 8-7. LEADER STYLE.
The type specs for leaders in PageMaker are normally the same as those of the letter or symbol that precedes them (left). To make them different from the preceding symbol, insert a hard space before the tab and give it the specs you want (right).

First you simultaneously press the Option key plus one other key to indicate which diacritical mark you want. To find out which key to press to set up a particular diacritical mark, look at Key Caps while pressing the Option key. (See Figure 8-8.) Then type the letter over which you want the diacritic placed. For example, pressing Option-U and then typing *u* or *U* creates

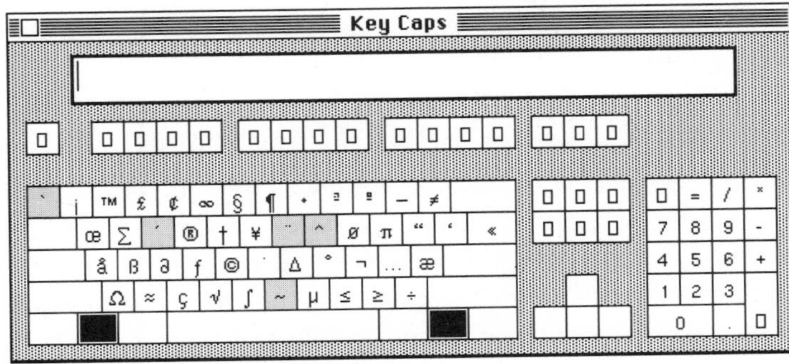

FIGURE 8-8. DIACRITICS REVEALED.
Pressing the Option key along with one of these highlighted keys tells the Mac which diacritical mark you want to put above the next letter you type.

ü or Ü. This method works equally well for lowercase and uppercase letters. However, some letters cannot have diacritical marks above them. You'll know you've found such a letter when your screen displays a diacritical mark followed by the letter—for example, ′C.

General Publishing

NOT QUITE CENTERED

A centered headline ending in a comma, a period, or an apostrophe might not seem truly centered to the eye. Compensate by inserting a duplicate punctuation mark at the beginning of the headline. Then make the duplicate white type. The character will become invisible but will push the headline slightly to the right, visually compensating for the ending punctuation.

To get white type in PageMaker, use the Reverse command (on the Type Style submenu of the Type menu). In QuarkXPress, choose 0% from the Shade submenu of the Style menu.

PageMaker

BAD STYLE

Avoid problems with Microsoft Word style sheets you plan to place in PageMaker by being sure that the Word style names do not include colons, semicolons, backslashes, hyphens, or parentheses.

General Publishing

MAKING CHANGES TO REDUCED TYPE

Some people print camera-ready copy at 200 percent on a laser printer and then have a print shop photostatically reduce the printing plate by 50 percent, improving the final resolution. If you do this and need to make a last-minute change by pasting in some type, be sure to print your change at 200 percent and have it photostatically reduced before pasting it in. If you print your last-minute corrections directly in the final type size, the insert might not match the rest of the type. (See Figure 8-9.) Adobe fonts and some other PostScript fonts include special instructions, called hints, that improve the look of a typeface in small sizes. Usually, the hints make very thin lines slightly thicker and add more space to counters (open spaces). The hints are not used for the larger sizes you typically get when printing at 200 percent.

does does

FIGURE 8-9. MYSTERIOUS MISMATCH.

These two samples of 11-point Palatino type do not exactly match. The left sample was printed at 200 percent—effectively making it 22 points—on a LaserWriter IINT and then photostatically reduced by 50 percent. Because it was printed at 22 points, it does not use Adobe's built-in hints that enhance the quality of type printed at small sizes. The right sample does use the hints because it was printed at 100 percent on a LaserWriter IINT. Both examples have been enlarged to make the differences more apparent.

TWO SHADOWS

The PageMaker manual does not document all the differences between Apple's LaserWriter printer driver and Aldus's printer driver. As shown in Figure 8-10, text formatted in the Shadow style prints differently depending

"Over the Mountains
Of the Moon,
Down the Valley of the Shadow,
Ride, boldly ride,"
The shade replied—
"If you seek for Eldorado!"
—Edgar Allen Poe, Eldorado

"Over the Mountains
Of the Moon,
Down the Valley of the Shadow,
Ride, boldly ride,"
The shade replied—
"If you seek for Eldorado!"
—Edgar Allen Poe, Eldorado

FIGURE 8-10. DARK SHADOWS.

PageMaker can print two outline styles on a LaserWriter, depending on whether you choose the Aldus (top) or the Apple (bottom) printer driver.

on which printer driver you use. The Aldus driver prints black text with a gray drop shadow, whereas the Apple driver prints outline text with a black drop shadow.

SPLIT-LINE TREE CHARTS

Here's a tip for anyone who uses More II and creates a lot of tree charts. When you create headlines, use the vertical line (type Shift-backslash) to separate parts of a headline that you want on individual lines in the More tree chart. (See Figure 8-11.)

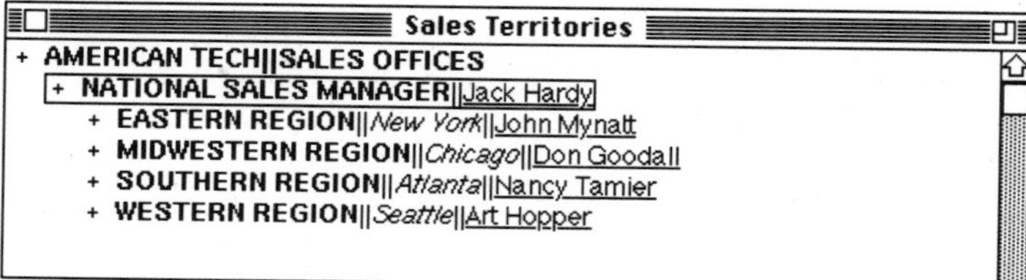

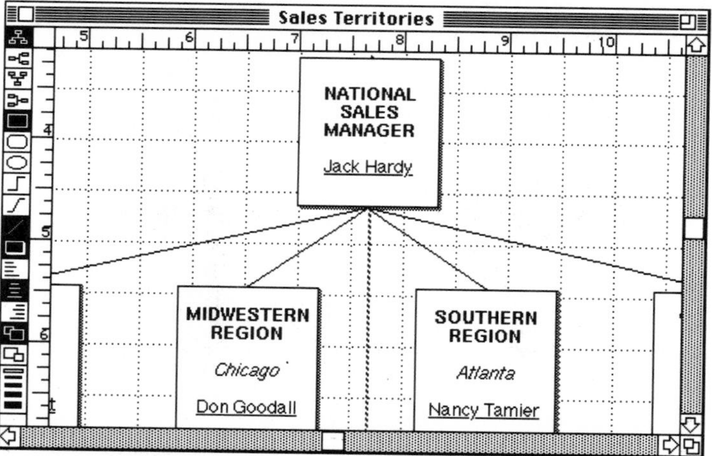

FIGURE 8-11. DIVIDING LINE.

In More II, vertical lines (type Shift-backslash) in headline text divide the text into multiple lines on a tree chart.

ARTWORK AND PHOTOS

LABELS OVER PHOTOS

Ready, Set,Go!

PageMaker

White text with a black drop shadow shows up well over a photograph where either black or white alone would be hard to read. (See Figure 8-12.) To get this effect in Ready,Set,Go! version 4.5, follow these steps:

1. Create a text block, and with it selected, use the Specifications command (in the Edit menu) to set the Ignore Runarounds option. Type the label in the text box and set its font, size, and other type specs.
2. Duplicate the text block and offset the second block slightly. You can use the Duplicate command (in the Edit menu), specifying vertical and horizontal offsets of −0.03.
3. Select the top text, and use the Color command (in the Text menu) to make the color of the top text white.

Although Ready,Set,Go! doesn't display white text on the screen unless the text has a nonwhite fill, the white text does print properly.

FIGURE 8-12. SHADOW LABEL.
For labels that stand out from a photograph or drawing, use white text with a black drop shadow.

You can get the same effect in PageMaker and in most paint and draw applications. Use the Copy and Paste commands to duplicate the text, and offset the duplicate by dragging.

PageMaker

DASHING LINES

You can create dashed lines that have weights, densities, and rhythms not available on PageMaker's Line submenu (in the Element menu) by overlaying reversed text on a horizontal rule. (In PageMaker 3.0x, line selections are located in the Lines menu.) First draw a horizontal rule of the weight and the length you need. Next create a text block the same length. Pick suitable Zapf Dingbats characters such as ❚ (lowercase y) or ❘ (lowercase x), and type them into your text block continuously or with whatever pattern, spacing, and frequency you want.

For additional variations, experiment with different text styles and sizes. After the text block is set, position it over the rule, select the text, and choose Reverse from the Type Style submenu of the Type menu. When the type turns white, the underlying rule appears dashed.

General Publishing

BLEMISH COVER-UP

You can remove a small dot or line from an imported graphic in a page-layout document without going back to the source program and changing the graphic. Use the drawing tools in the page-layout program to draw a square, circle, or other shape. Then set the shape's fill and line color to white. You can drag this patch anywhere on the page and resize it as needed to cover mistakes in an imported graphic.

PageMaker

CENTERING OBJECTS

In PageMaker, you align text blocks, graphics, or both along their left or right edge by dragging them to a guideline. You can use a similar technique to center objects without measuring, as shown in Figure 8-13. Start by drawing a rectangle that exactly spans the width of the page or column in which you want to center objects. Next drag a vertical guideline to the rectangle's center handle. (Zoom in for precise alignment.) Select the rectangle and press the Delete or Backspace key to eliminate it.

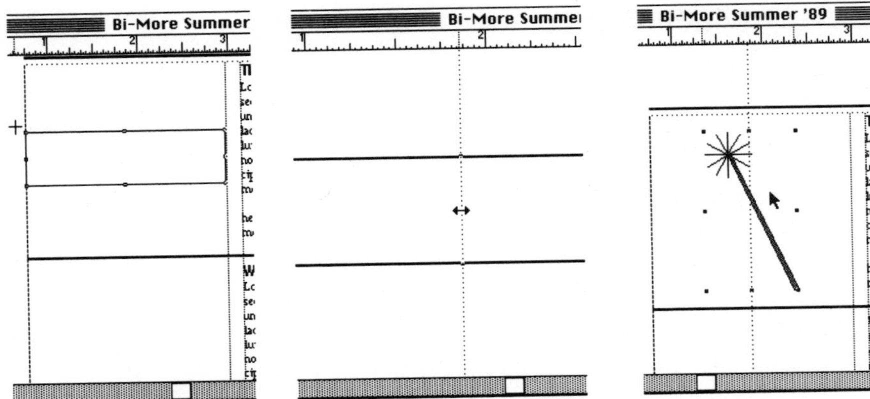

FIGURE 8-13. NO-MEASURE CENTERING.

Establish the center of a PageMaker column or other space by drawing a rectangle across it (left). Then zoom in and drag a guideline to the rectangle's center handle (center). Delete the rectangle and use the guideline to center other objects (right).

Now you can center any object that has center handles, including a text block, by moving it so that its center handles straddle the guideline. For precise positioning, use Easy Access so that you can move the pointer by pressing keys on the numeric keypad. (See the tip "Keyboard Mouse," in Chapter 1.) Be sure to remove excess white space around an imported graphic by cropping before you try to center it. Some asymmetrical images might need to be positioned off-center to appear centered.

You can also use the same vertical center guideline to set up an automatic centering ruler. Simply drag the zero point of the horizontal ruler to the guideline. Now, to center an object, move it until the dashed lines that indicate its left and right edges in the ruler are both on the same number. For example, the edges of a 24-pica object will be at 12 and 12 on opposite sides of the horizontal zero point.

DRAGGING EMPTY SHAPES

When moving an unfilled shape made using a PageMaker drawing tool, drag from the outline only. Dragging one of the handles resizes the object, and dragging within an unfilled shape deselects it.

KEEPING GRAPHICS TRIM

Crop away unneeded white space from around a graphic to reduce problems in selecting objects adjacent to the graphic. The boundaries of a graphic in PageMaker are the handles you see when you select the graphic, not the image itself. Cropping close to the image also allows you to effectively use the Print command's Proof Print option, which substitutes placeholders for graphics. Without cropping, a placeholder might block out surrounding objects.

PROPORTIONAL RESIZING

To preserve a graphic's proportions while resizing it, imagine (or actually draw) a rectangle around the graphic and draw a diagonal line from one corner to the opposite corner of the rectangle. If you're going to enlarge the graphic, extend the diagonal line beyond the point to which you plan to enlarge the graphic. Place the diagonal line behind the graphic. Now you can proportionally resize the graphic by dragging its corner along the diagonal line, as shown in Figure 8-14. Delete the diagonal line (and the bounding rectangle, if you drew one) when you finish resizing. Many programs also let you resize proportionally by holding down the Shift key while you drag a corner handle.

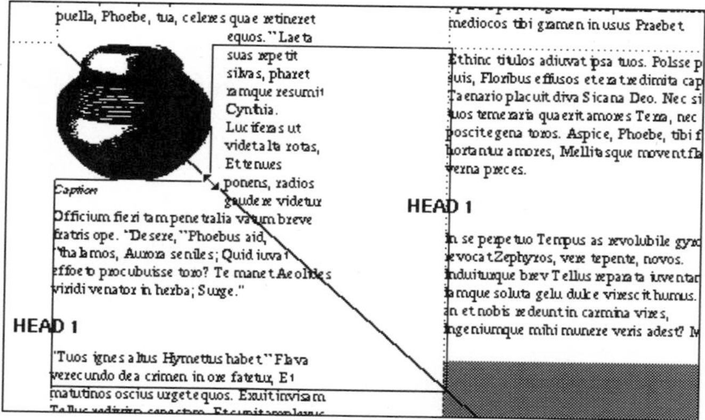

FIGURE 8-14. DIAGONAL DRAG.

A temporary diagonal line shows the path along which you must drag the corner of a graphic that you want to resize proportionally.

MAGIC SIZES

When you reduce a bit-mapped image (72 dots per inch) in PageMaker by dragging the corner of the image, PageMaker does not tell you the percentage of reduction. Unless you luckily reduce to exactly the right size, moiré patterns and jagged edges appear in the printed work. But if you use the Place command (not the Paste command) you can proportionally reduce a graphic image to a magic percentage—96, 72, 48, or 24—when you put it in your PageMaker publication. Because these percentages match the image's 72-dpi resolution to the LaserWriter's 300-dpi resolution, you get no moiré patterns or jagged edges. Reducing a 72-dpi image to 24 percent results in an apparent 300 dpi when it is printed on a 300-dpi printer.

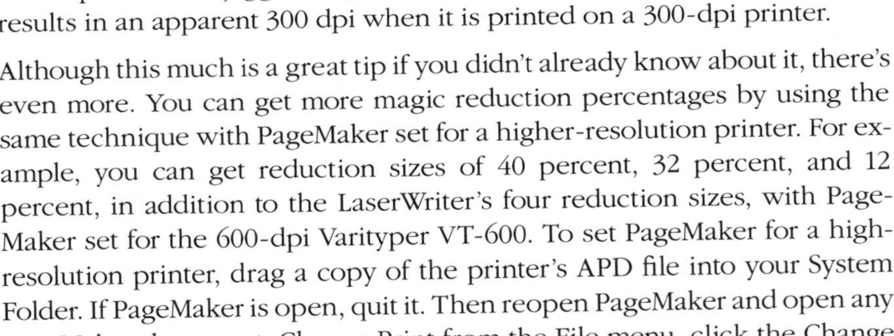
Although this much is a great tip if you didn't already know about it, there's even more. You can get more magic reduction percentages by using the same technique with PageMaker set for a higher-resolution printer. For example, you can get reduction sizes of 40 percent, 32 percent, and 12 percent, in addition to the LaserWriter's four reduction sizes, with PageMaker set for the 600-dpi Varityper VT-600. To set PageMaker for a high-resolution printer, drag a copy of the printer's APD file into your System Folder. If PageMaker is open, quit it. Then reopen PageMaker and open any PageMaker document. Choose Print from the File menu, click the Change button, select the new type of printer, click OK to confirm the printer change, and press Cancel to dismiss the Print dialog box.

SECRET DESIGNSTUDIO SHORTCUTS

DesignStudio has several undocumented arrow-key features. Kerning with Command-Left arrow and Command-Right arrow is documented (0.05 ems per tap), but adjusting baselines with Command-Up arrow and Command-Down arrow (0.1 point up or down per tap) is not.

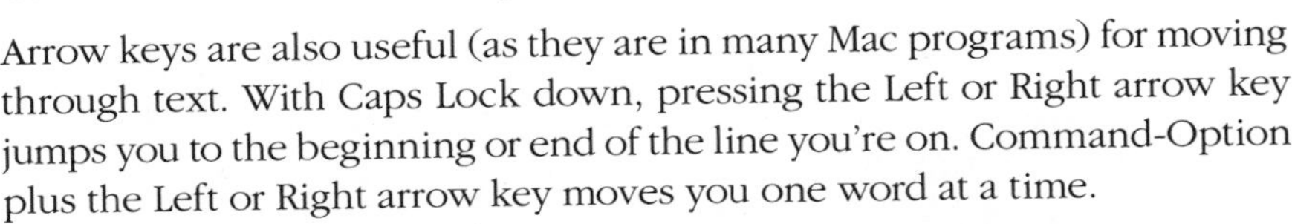
Arrow keys are also useful (as they are in many Mac programs) for moving through text. With Caps Lock down, pressing the Left or Right arrow key jumps you to the beginning or end of the line you're on. Command-Option plus the Left or Right arrow key moves you one word at a time.

When you're not editing text, the arrow keys are handy for precise adjustment of objects' positions. A selected object (or group) moves 1 point for each tap on an arrow key. If Caps Lock is down, the selected object jumps 10 points.

General Publishing

BAGGING THE BIG ONES

Have you ever scanned an image at a service bureau only to discover that it wouldn't fit on a floppy disk? You have room for it on your hard disk but no way to get it there. Next time take along a file-compression program such as StuffIt or a backup program such as HD Backup in addition to several blank floppy disks. The file-compression program reduces file size by 40 to 50 percent and can segment a large file across several disks. A backup program can also segment a single large file across multiple disks. When you return to your Mac, the file-compression program or backup program can reverse the process you performed at the service bureau.

Aldus Persuasion

PERSUASION EPS FONTS

Aldus Persuasion 2.0 does not intelligently scan imported EPS graphics for downloadable fonts. This limitation means you must manually download the fonts (using, for example, Adobe's Font Downloader utility) to your printer before printing. You might not care to download fonts manually, or you might be unable to download because you're imaging slides on a non-PostScript device, using Freedom of Press utility software. If so, you can get Persuasion to download the fonts in imported EPS graphics for you automatically. Simply type some hidden text on the master slide, including at least one character for each font used in the imported EPS graphics.

PageMaker

Adobe Illustrator

REVISING AN EPS GRAPHIC

You can revise an EPS graphic that was originally created in Adobe Illustrator 88 and later placed in PageMaker, even if you don't have the original graphic. It doesn't matter if the graphic has been cropped or resized in PageMaker. In most cases you can edit text in the graphic even if your system doesn't have the proper font.

Basically, you export the graphic with PageMaker's Print command, revise the exported graphic in Adobe Illustrator 88, and place the revised graphic back in PageMaker. Follow these steps:

1. Open the PageMaker document and copy the EPS graphic you want to change.

2. Close the PageMaker document and paste the EPS graphic into a new, empty PageMaker document. You don't need to save this document.
3. Choose Print from the File menu. If the Print dialog box contains a PostScript button, click it. If it doesn't have a PostScript button but does have an Options button, click that. Otherwise, press the Option key while clicking the OK button. A PostScript Print Options dialog box appears. (See Figure 8-15 on the following page.)
4. Select the Print PostScript To Disk and EPS options. Click the File Name button and, in the directory dialog box that appears, decide where you want to save the exported EPS graphic and what you want to name it.
5. If the PostScript Print Options dialog box has a Print button, click it. Otherwise, click its OK button and then click the OK button in the Print dialog box. PageMaker saves a PostScript file to disk, giving it the name you specified.
6. Switch to Adobe Illustrator (no need to save that PageMaker document). Use Illustrator's Open command (in the File menu) to open the PostScript file just saved by PageMaker's Print command. The exported graphic appears, ungrouped and ready for revising. Any stretching or cropping that was done in PageMaker is not present in this pristine graphic.
7. After you revise the graphic, use the Save As command to save it in a new file. Be sure to select the Macintosh Preview option when you save the graphic.
8. Back in PageMaker, open the PageMaker document that contains the old graphic, select that graphic, and use the Place command to replace it with the revised graphic. If you select the Place command's Replace Entire Graphic option, PageMaker scales and crops the revised graphic to match the old one. (If you resized the graphic using Adobe Illustrator, PageMaker resizes it so that at least one side of it fits the space of the old graphic.)

FIGURE 8-15. EPS EXPORTER.
Use PageMaker's PostScript Print Options dialog box to export an EPS graphic for revision in Adobe Illustrator 88.

LAYOUT

PAGE-LAYOUT GUIDES

To get accurate spacing between objects in a page-layout document, use boxes as guides. They're perfect for matching the space throughout a publication between a headline and body text, between body text and a graphic, and so on. Unlike rulers, guide boxes are completely visual and involve no arithmetic. You drag the guide to the edge of one object and then drag the other object to the other side of the guide. Figure 8-16 shows some guides in use.

SNAPPING TO THE BASELINE

You can accurately and easily align the baselines of text blocks in different columns in a PageMaker document by synchronizing the vertical ruler with the text leading. This same procedure helps you position horizontal rules below lines of text, which can be useful in designing forms.

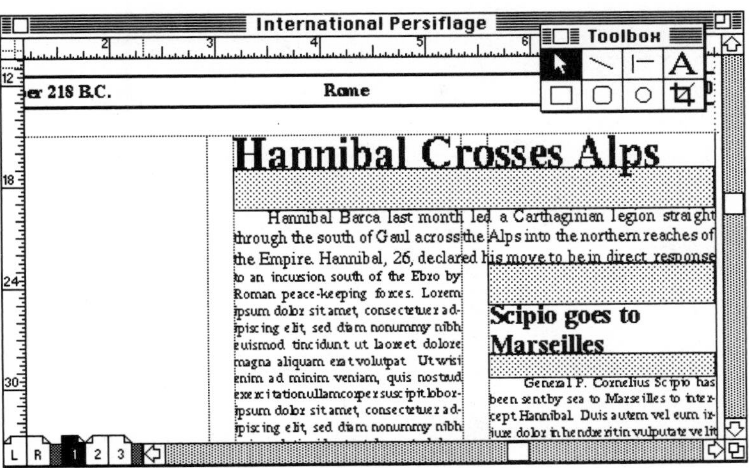

FIGURE 8-16. GUIDE BOX.

Draw a box (shaded or not) to use as a spacing guide when laying out the pages of a publication. The shaded boxes here, which facilitate standard spacing between headlines and body text, will be removed before printing.

First set a specific amount of leading for all text you want aligned, overriding the standard setting of Auto. Next use the Preferences command (in the Edit menu) to specify the same amount for custom vertical ruler spacing, as shown in Figure 8-17 on the following page. Be sure the Snap To Rulers command in the Options menu is selected. If you want to match the ruler grid to an existing baseline, drag the vertical ruler's zero point down from the upper left corner of the window to that baseline. Now, when you drag a text block or other object, PageMaker snaps it to the nearest baseline.

TABLE TAB GUIDES

To quickly set up tabs for a new table in a PageMaker publication, use the vertical ruler guides as visual aids. At the Fit In Window view, drag ruler guides onto the page to mark off your intended columns. Then go to the Actual Size view, choose Rulers from the Options menu, and align the zero mark on the Indents/Tabs ruler with the left edge of the table. That's usually either the left margin guide or a column guide. Now you can use the vertical ruler guides to determine the placement of tabs along the Indents/Tabs ruler. (See Figure 8-18 on the following page.)

Preferences
OK
Cancel
Layout view:
Measurement system: Inches
Vertical ruler: Custom 12 points
Greek text below: 6 pixels
Guides: Front Back
Detailed graphics: Gray out Normal High resolution
Show layout problems: Loose/tight lines "Keeps" violations
Story view:
Size: 12 points Font: Geneva

FIGURE 8-17. CUSTOM RULER GRID.

PageMaker's Preferences dialog box lets you specify a custom interval for the vertical ruler—12 points here. Matching this interval to the text leading in the document and checking the Snap To Rulers command (in the Options menu) makes it simpler to align the baselines of text blocks in adjacent columns.

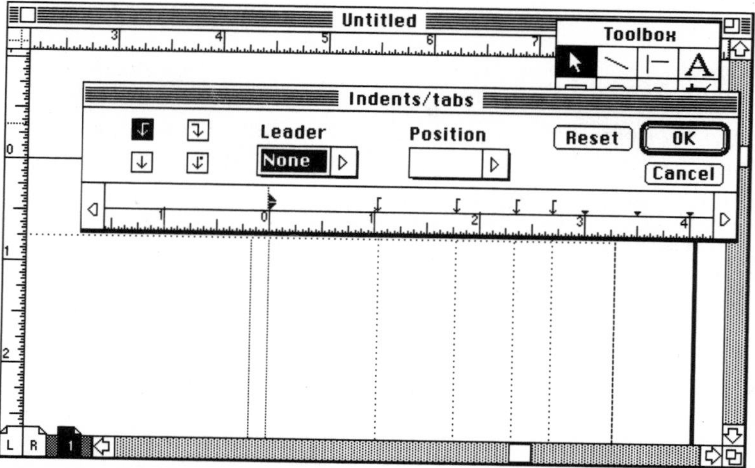

FIGURE 8-18. TABLE LAYOUT.

PageMaker's vertical ruler guides facilitate table layout. After you align the zero point of the Indents/Tabs ruler with the left edge of the table, the ruler guides show where to put tab stops.

FORMATTED TABLES FROM WORD

You can export all or part of a table from Microsoft Word into any page-layout program with all formatting intact by copying the table as a graphic. Start in Word by turning off the Show Hidden Text and Show Table Grid-lines options, using Word's Preferences command (in the Edit menu). Next select the part of the table that you want to export and press Command-Option-D. This copies the table as a graphic. Then switch to the page-layout program and paste the graphic form of the table into your document. Because the table is a graphic, you cannot edit it, but you can move, resize, and crop it.

TABLE SPACING

To include extra space between categories in an Aldus Persuasion chart that has multiple data series, insert an extra row or column, as though you were inserting another data series. Instead of entering numbers for the values of the new series, however, type a blank space in each cell. Persuasion plots a blank row or column—a space the width of one column—between the non-blank columns.

If the chart includes a legend, Persuasion will add a key for the new blank series. To remove the key from the legend, you must ungroup the chart, remove the extra key, adjust the position of the remaining legend parts, and regroup the chart. Do this only as a final step—if you later must replot the chart, you'll have to remove the extra key again.

TABLE SETUP

Before you copy and paste a table from a spreadsheet program to PowerPoint, you must set tab stops on the PowerPoint text ruler for the text block where the table is going. Otherwise, the spreadsheet's columnar formatting will be lost. To see the ruler for the currently selected text block, use PowerPoint's Show Text Ruler command (in the Text menu). Set one tab stop for each column you're copying. Remember that you are limited to 10 tabs per text block.

FORMATTED TEXT FROM WORD

If you copy and paste text from a word processing program to a presentation program, you lose text formatting. You can import formatted text from

Microsoft Word to a presentation program one slide at a time by copying the text as a graphic.

In Word, turn off the Show Hidden Text and Show Table Gridlines options, using Word's Preferences command (on the Edit menu). Then select the formatted text you want to put on one slide and press Command-Option-D. Switch to the presentation program and paste the graphic form of the text into a slide. You can move, resize, and crop the graphic, but you can't change the text in it.

PageMaker

PRINTING OUTSIDE OF CROP MARKS

It is possible to print a job ID or other text outside the crop marks of a PageMaker document. You can't simply put a block of text on the master page below the page boundary, however, because PageMaker sees this text as being on the pasteboard, not on the page, and so the text will not print on the regular pages. One solution is to create the job ID as a graphic, using any drawing program. Alternatively, you can type the job ID in PageMaker, copy it, paste it into the Scrapbook, and use PageMaker's Place command (in the File menu) to convert the text into a graphic.

If you're putting the graphic at the bottom of the page, be sure to include blank space at the top of the graphic. If you're putting the graphic at the top of the page, include blank space at the bottom of the graphic. Place the graphic on the master pages, with the blank space on the page and the job information hanging off the page, as shown in Figure 8-19. The graphic is printed on all pages where master items are showing.

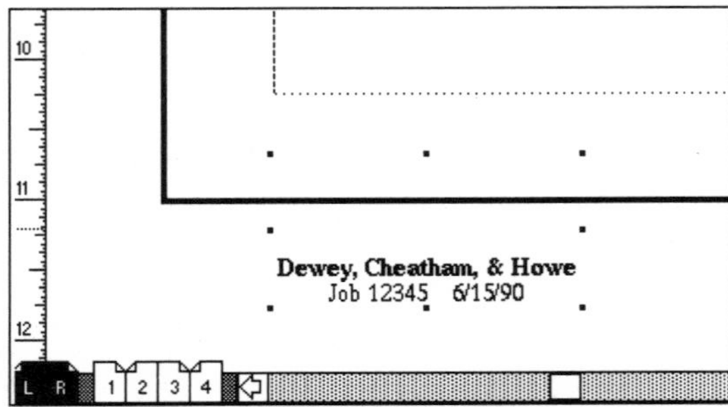

FIGURE 8-19. JOB INFO.

To print text outside the crop marks of your PageMaker publication, create a graphic that contains the text, and position it as shown here.

UNNUMBERED TITLE PAGE

PageMaker always starts its automatic page numbering with the first page of a document. You might want the title page, table of contents, and other front matter to be unnumbered. To achieve this, put those pages at the end of the document. Hide the page numbers on those pages by deselecting Display Master Items on the Page menu.

You can also hide a page number by covering it with a small, borderless, opaque rectangle. (Choose None from the Lines menu and Paper from the Shades menu.)

COMBINATION BACKGROUND

By combining two slides having different background shading or graphic elements, you can create a PowerPoint background with unique special effects. From the slide sorter view, select one of the slides you want to combine, and choose Copy from the Edit menu to copy it. Then go to the other slide and choose Paste As Picture from the Edit menu. You can resize the top slide at this point. Choose Send To Back from the Edit menu to see the graphics merged.

SPOTLIGHT EFFECT

Create a spotlight effect on a PowerPoint slide such as the one shown in Figure 8-20 on the following page by following these steps. (You need a Mac II with 256 colors.)

1. Draw a small circle the size you want the highlighted spot to be. Use the oval tool to do this, pressing the Shift key as you draw to force a perfect circle.
2. With the circle still selected, choose Set As Title from the Edit menu.
3. Make the circle invisible by turning off the Filled command and the Framed command in the Draw menu.
4. Shade the background by choosing Color Schemes from the Color menu, clicking the Shade Background button, selecting the From Title option, clicking the OK button, and then clicking the Apply button.

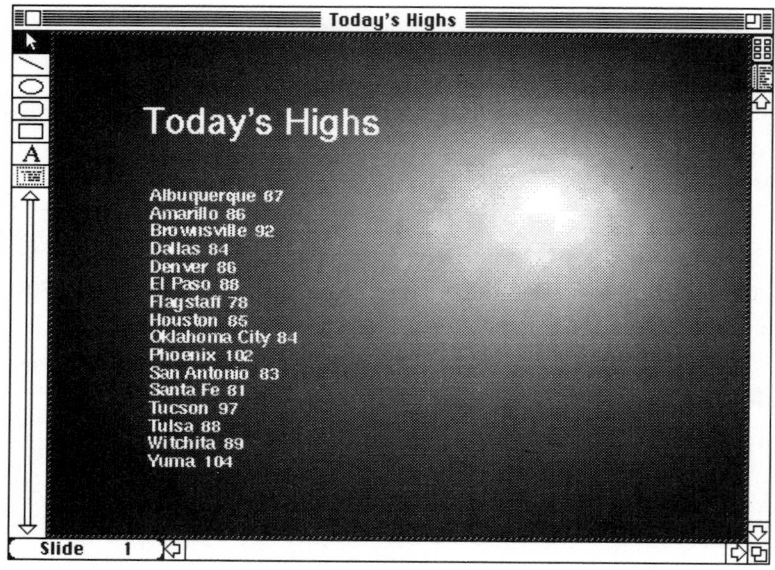

FIGURE 8-20. SHADE SPOT.
Spotlight shading adds impact to a slide and is easy to achieve in PowerPoint.

PowerPoint

REUSING A COLOR SCHEME

You can easily transfer a color scheme from one PowerPoint presentation to another. With both presentations open, activate the presentation whose color scheme you want to copy (by choosing that presentation from the Window menu or clicking its window). Next choose Color Scheme from the Color menu to open the Color Scheme window. In it you should see the color scheme you want to transfer. Now activate the presentation you want to have the color scheme. Choose Color Scheme from the Window menu (not the Color menu), and in it set the Apply To All Slides option and click the Apply button. Then close the Color Scheme window.

General Presentations

IMAGE-SAFE AREA

Don't let a film recorder or slide mount unexpectedly cut off the edges of your presentation. Measure the safe area on a sample mounted overhead transparency or slide, and draw a round-cornered rectangle that size on the master slide. Make another sample to double-check your rectangle, and

adjust it as needed. As you make new slides, keep their contents inside the rectangle. Don't forget to delete the rectangle before you output your slides.

COMP TEXT

PageMaker

When you need dummy text for a preliminary layout that shows what a publication will look like, use the Lorem Ipsum text file that comes with PageMaker. You can change the font, size, and style to match the type specifications you want in the final publication.

DUMMY SCAN

General Publishing

If you are planning a layout that includes an irregular graphic and you don't have a scanned image to work with at that stage, photocopy the graphic onto a sheet of transparency film. Set the page view to Actual Size and place the photocopied dummy over the monitor where the graphic should appear. Adjust the text wrap or other layout elements around the overlaid dummy. You might need to trace an outline of the graphic for use as a placeholder in the document. Finally, paste the final art into the document, or have it stripped in using traditional methods.

SPOT COLOR FPO

PageMaker

You can scan photos or artwork and use them in PageMaker for position only (FPO) when printing proofs. For final printing, though, you might want to drop out the scanned pictures and have the printer strip in conventional halftones. A problem occurs, however, if you have run text around an irregular picture and you then remove the picture. The text re-wraps to fill the void where the scanned picture was. You can solve this by assigning the scanned picture a color you're not using from the color palette. Then you print, specifying the Spot Color Overlays option. The space for the image retains the correct shape, and you throw away the color overlay.

ARRANGING PAMPHLET PAGES

General Publishing

Arranging pages of pamphlets, catalogs, and other small publications in the correct sequence can be tricky if you're printing two pages per sheet of paper. Each page fills half the sheet so that when the paper is folded and stapled you have a little booklet. The following technique works in any

page-layout or word processing program that can automatically adjust page margins for double-sided printing:

1. Use the Page Setup command (in the File menu) to set wide orientation.
2. Set up the document for double-sided printing. In PageMaker, use the Page Setup command (in the File menu) to turn on the Double Sided option and to turn off the Facing Pages option. In QuarkXPress, use the Page Guides command (in the View menu) to set the Double Sided option and to specify paper dimensions (such as 11 by 8.5 inches). In Ready,Set,Go!, choose Design Grids from the Special menu, select the Grid Setup option, click OK, and then set the Double Sided option. In MacWrite II, set the Left/Right Pages option of the Pages command (in the Format menu). In Microsoft Word, use the Document command (in the Format menu) to turn on the Mirror Even/Odd Margins option.
3. Enter the top, bottom, and outside margins you want. Then add the width of one booklet page (5.5 inches for US Letter-size paper) to the size of the inside margin. Use the Page Setup command in PageMaker, the Page Guides command in QuarkXPress, the Grid Setup option of the Design Grids command in Ready,Set,Go!, the Pages command in MacWrite II, and the Document command in Word.
4. When you're ready to print the pamphlet, determine the smallest multiple of 4 that is greater than or equal to the number of pages. Print a number of pages equal to half the multiple of 4 you just computed. Arrange the pages face up in reverse order (page 1 on the bottom) and return them face up to the paper tray. (A LaserWriter Plus automatically puts pages in reverse order; a LaserWriter II does so if you open its face-up exit door.) Then print the rest of the pages. If your pamphlet has 17 pages, for example, the smallest multiple of 4 containing 17 is 20. You would print the first 10 (20 divided by 2) pages, rearrange them, return them to the paper tray, and print the last 7 pages.

You now have a set of single-sided originals, each bearing two pamphlet pages. After appropriate double-sided copying, the copies of your pamphlet are ready for folding and stapling.

ORGANIZATIONAL CHART ALIGNMENT

PageMaker can help you make a neat organizational chart with boxes that are all the same size aligned in even rows and equally spaced columns. You can achieve uniform box width and equally spaced columns more easily with column guides than with ruler guides. The number of columns and the column spacing that you specify with the Column Guides command (on the Options menu) determine the number of boxes across the page and the spacing between boxes. For horizontal alignment at one level of the chart, drag a guide down from the horizontal ruler. Draw one box between the guides, using the rectangle tool. Make additional boxes the same size by copying and pasting the first box.

HARD COPY

LASER CARDS

Laser printers aren't designed to print on card stock heavier than 36-pound, but you can create an interesting equivalent by fusing transparency film to label stock. The resulting "cards" are not quite as rigid as regular card stock, but they are extremely durable and cannot be readily creased. In addition, the toner is protected from cracking by being sandwiched between the label stock and the transparency sheet. The price per hundred is around $5. The technique is useful for printing cards for special promotions, address changes, and other short runs.

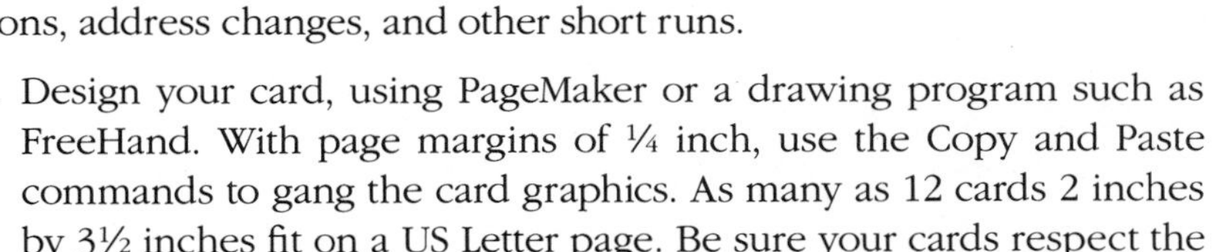

1. Design your card, using PageMaker or a drawing program such as FreeHand. With page margins of ¼ inch, use the Copy and Paste commands to gang the card graphics. As many as 12 cards 2 inches by 3½ inches fit on a US Letter page. Be sure your cards respect the ¼-inch margin limit, or the LaserWriter will crop them.
2. Print a mirror image of the page of cards on a sheet of transparency film. To do that, choose the Page Setup command (on the File menu), click the Options button, and then set the Flip Horizontal and Larger Print Area options. To get a mirror image in PageMaker version 4.0 using the Aldus LaserWriter driver, choose the Print command from the File menu, click the Options button, and set the Spot Color Overlays option and the Mirror option. In PageMaker version 3.02 Color Extension, set the Spot Color Overlays option before clicking

the Change button and setting the Mirror option. In versions 3.02 and earlier, click the Changes button and set the Mirror option.

3. Peel the backing from a sheet of solid label stock (Avery number 5353 or the equivalent). Carefully press the toner side of your transparency sheet onto the sticky side of the label stock, as illustrated in Figure 8-21.
4. Use a paper cutter, scissors, or an X-acto knife to slice off the ¼-inch margin on all sides and to cut the individual cards.

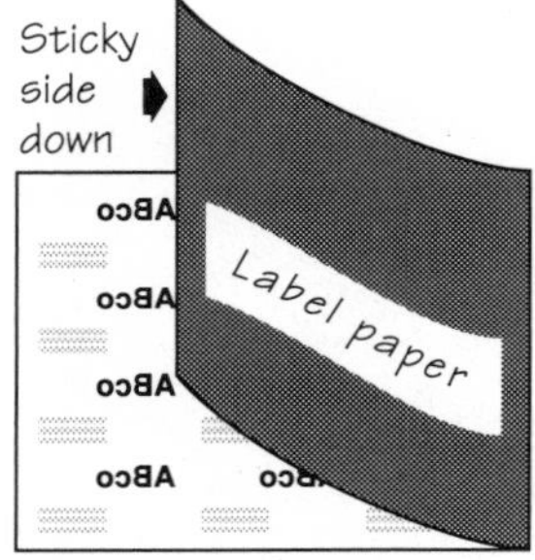

FIGURE 8-21. MOCK CARDS.
A laser printer can't print on card stock, but you can get a similar effect by printing a mirror image on transparent film and affixing that to uncut label stock. For two-sided cards, print the label stock before fusing.

PowerPoint

PRESENTATION IN GRAY

You can print color PowerPoint presentations in shades of gray on a LaserWriter for proofing or for use as handouts and note pages. Although PowerPoint itself can convert colors to shades of gray for printing, you'll get better results if you let the latest version of Apple's LaserWriter software do the conversion for you. (See Figure 8-22.) Be sure you have version 6.0 or later of the LaserWriter and Laser Prep files in your System Folder. When you use the Print command, set its Print option to Color/Grayscale and its Slide Color option to Normal.

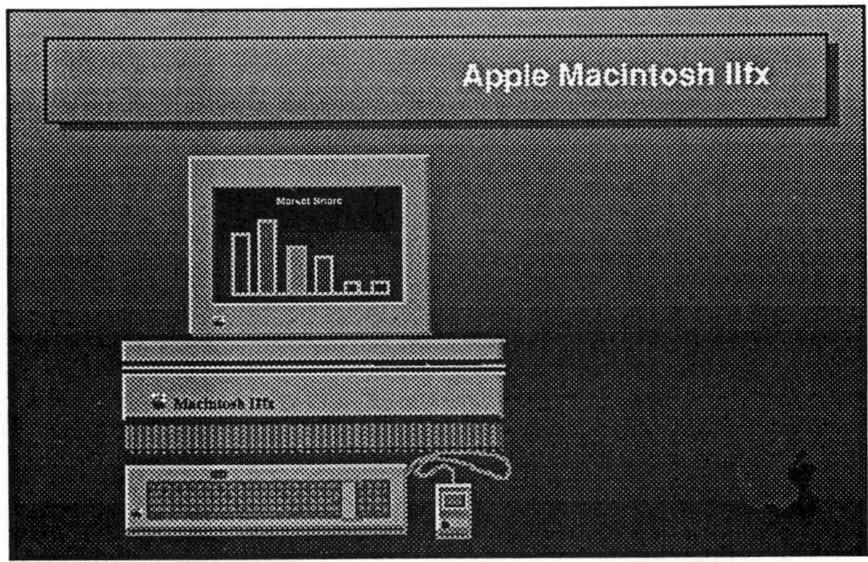

FIGURE 8-22. GRAY DIFFERENCE.

When printing a color PowerPoint presentation on a LaserWriter, the LaserWriter software does a better job of converting colors to grays (top) than does the PowerPoint program (bottom).

You can get acceptable results if you must use an earlier version of the LaserWriter software, such as version 5.2. In that case, set the Print command's Slide Color option to Gray Scale or to Inverse Gray Scale. With this version, the Print command has no Print option.

POSTSCRIPT OUTPUT (GENERAL)

Fonts in a desktop publishing document might get mixed up when you send the document to a service bureau for typesetting. Sending your service bureau a PostScript derivative of your document avoids mixed-up fonts. The service bureau might ask you to send a copy of your System file, which it uses to start its Mac before printing your document. But sending a Postscript derivative of the document is faster and cheaper. To make a PostScript file from most programs, follow these steps. (See the next tip if you use PageMaker.)

1. Use the Chooser to choose a LaserWriter and to turn off background printing (if it's on).
2. If you're using a third-party print spooler such as SuperLaserSpool, deactivate it for now.
3. Choose Print from the application's File menu.
4. Click the OK button in the Print dialog box and immediately press Command-F. (To make a PostScript file that includes the Laser Prep file, press Command-K.) Keep holding down the keys until you see the message *Creating PostScript® File.* If the document prints instead of the message appearing, you weren't fast enough at pressing Command-F.

This procedure creates a file with a name such as PostScript0. If you can't find the file, use the Find File desk accessory.

POSTSCRIPT OUTPUT (PAGEMAKER)

The procedure described in the previous tip doesn't normally work with PageMaker because PageMaker has a nonstandard Print command. The following steps tell you how to create a PostScript file from PageMaker, using an Aldus printer driver (APD):

1. Be sure your System Folder contains the APD file for the particular PostScript device that will ultimately print your publication.

2. Open the publication in PageMaker.
3. Choose Print and verify that the printer type, page size, and so on are set correctly for the printer the service will use for output.
4. If you have PageMaker 4.0, click the Print command's PostScript button. If you have PageMaker 3.02, click the Options button. If you have any other version, press the Option key while clicking OK. The Post-script print options shown in Figure 8-23 appear.
5. Select the Print PostScript To Disk and Normal options. Click the File Name button and, in the directory dialog box that appears, decide where you want to save the exported EPS graphic and what you want to name it. Set the other options according to advice from your service bureau.
6. If the PostScript Print Options dialog box has a Print button, click it. Otherwise, click its OK button and then click the OK button in the Print dialog box. PageMaker saves a PostScript file to disk, giving it the name you specified.

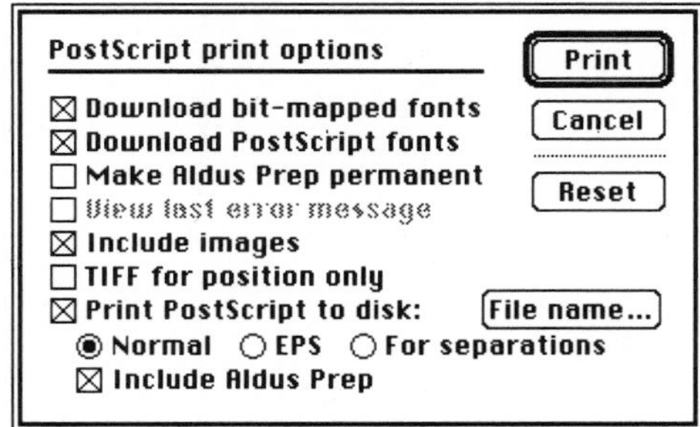

FIGURE 8-23. POSTSCRIPT PRINT OPTIONS.
PageMaker provides these options when you "print" a PostScript derivative of your publication.

RECEDING HAIRLINE

Don't use hairline rules or fill with a 10 percent shade when printing to a high-resolution device such as a Linotronic. At high resolution, hairline rules and the dots of a 10 percent fill are so fine that they're nearly invisible. Use a half-point rule and a 20 percent fill instead.

SAVING TIME AND SPACE

If you use outside printing services to produce your desktop publishing output, you should shrink your PageMaker files for minimum transmission time or disk space. All you do is use the Save As command when you finish the publication. This command produces a file that is about 40 percent smaller than the same file saved with the Save command, which retains the previous version as well as the latest version, in case you want to revert while you are editing.

SLOW COLLATING

The Collate option of PageMaker's Print command slows down printing. Because each collated copy prints in correct page-number sequence, the printer must prepare each page image anew for every copy of the document. Preparing a page with lots of graphics can take a long time. With the Collate option off, the printer prepares each page image one time and quickly prints the requested number of copies at once.

Chapter 9

SPREADSHEETS AND CHARTS

If you use spreadsheets (some people call them worksheets) to deal with formulas, numbers, and bits of text arranged in orderly rows and columns, try the hints in this chapter.

Spreadsheets and charts go hand in hand, so this chapter also includes tips on charting. The tips are organized into the following sections:

- Windows and cells
- Selecting and manipulating
- Formulas and formats
- Charts
- Performance
- Macros and scripts
- Importing and exporting

WINDOWS AND CELLS

SAVING WINDOW POSITION

Would you like to save a window's position when you close a Microsoft Excel 2.2 document so that you don't have to click the zoom box every time you open the document? Use the Save Workspace command (in the File menu) to save a document that contains a list of all open windows and their sizes and positions. Later you can open that workspace document and Microsoft Excel reopens the same windows—or repositions them if they're already open—at their previous positions.

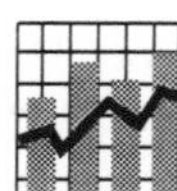

GOING QUICKLY TO A1

How can you scroll quickly to cell A1 in a MacCalc spreadsheet or a Microsoft Excel spreadsheet? Click the upper left corner of the spreadsheet window, above row 1 and to the left of column A. (See Figure 9-1.) This selects all cells. Then press the Enter key in MacCalc or Command-Enter in Microsoft Excel.

Alternatively, in MacCalc you can enter *A1* at the left end of the entry bar and either click the adjacent Go To icon or press Enter or Return.

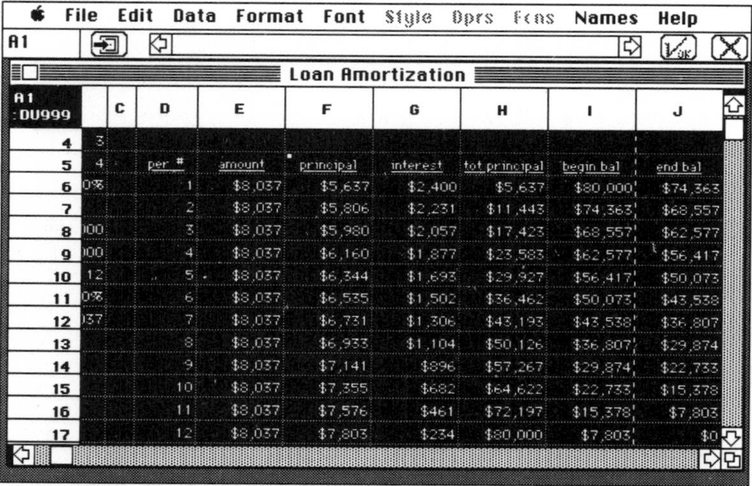

FIGURE 9-1. SCROLL HOME.
After you click the upper left corner of a MacCalc spreadsheet window to select all cells, press the Enter key to scroll quickly to cell A1.

MULTIPLE DATA SETS

When you use a single spreadsheet for more than one set of data, put each set in a separate work area. Arrange the work areas along an imaginary diagonal line running from the upper left corner of the spreadsheet to the lower right corner. (See Figure 9-2.) That way, if you later need to insert or delete rows and columns in one set of data, the action won't affect the other sets. If you lay out your sets of data side by side, changes to one set might unintentionally affect other sets.

	A	B	C	D	E	F	G	H
1	123456789	123456789	123456789	123456789				
2	123456789	123456789	123456789	123456789				
3	123456789	123456789	123456789	123456789				
4	123456789	123456789	123456789	123456789				
5	123456789	123456789	123456789	123456789				
6	123456789	123456789	123456789	123456789				
7	123456789	123456789	123456789	123456789				
8	123456789	123456789	123456789	123456789				
9	123456789	123456789	123456789	123456789				
10	123456789	123456789	123456789	123456789				
11	123456789	123456789	123456789	123456789				
12	123456789	123456789	123456789	123456789				
13					123456789	123456789	123456789	123456789
14					123456789	123456789	123456789	123456789
15					123456789	123456789	123456789	123456789
16					123456789	123456789	123456789	123456789
17					123456789	123456789	123456789	123456789
18					123456789	123456789	123456789	123456789
19					123456789	123456789	123456789	123456789
20					123456789	123456789	123456789	123456789
21					123456789	123456789	123456789	123456789
22					123456789	123456789	123456789	123456789
23					123456789	123456789	123456789	123456789
24					123456789	123456789	123456789	123456789

FIGURE 9-2. DIAGONAL CONSTRUCTION.
By organizing different parts of a spreadsheet along an imaginary diagonal, you keep changes in one part from inadvertently affecting other parts.

RESTORING THE PRINT AREA

If you want to print an entire Microsoft Excel spreadsheet after having printed part of it, simply do the following: Select the whole spreadsheet (click in the upper left corner of the spreadsheet window, above row 1 and to the left of column A), and choose Set Print Area again. Alternatively, choose Define Name from the Formula menu, select Print_Area in the scrollable list of names, and click the Delete button. Be careful, however; you can't undo name deletion.

MYSTIC GRID LINES

Sometimes grid lines are displayed on the screen but they aren't printed. Other times they are printed but they aren't displayed on the screen. How can you control the printing and display of grid lines in Microsoft Excel? Use the Display command (in the Options menu) to control grid lines on the screen. Use the Page Setup command (in the File menu) to control grid lines on the printed page.

Trapeze

TINY GRID MEANS TROUBLE

To avoid difficulty in aligning blocks in Trapeze, don't set the horizontal or vertical grid size to below 5. If you need more precision, you can use the Shift key to move or resize a block 1 point at a time. Press Option-Shift to move a block or Command-Option-Shift to resize a block.

Microsoft Excel

EASY ROW, COLUMN INSERTION

You can quickly insert single or multiple rows, columns, or cells in a Microsoft Excel spreadsheet or macro. To do so, press the Option key and click or drag a row label, a column label, or a cell.

Full Impact

CELLS AS A GRAPHIC IMAGE

You can create a range of cells in a Full Impact spreadsheet that you can treat as if it were a graphic, a chart, or a paragraph. You do so by copying and pasting a picture of the cells rather than the cell contents. To create a picture of a cell range, select the cells and press the Option key while choosing Copy from the Edit menu. Then choose Paste from the Edit menu to place a copy of the picture on the spreadsheet. You can move the picture, resize it, group it with other objects, and put a border around it as you would any Full Impact object.

Microsoft Works

CELL NOTE AND ATTRIBUTES SHORTCUTS

To open a cell note in a Microsoft Works spreadsheet, press the Command key and double-click the cell.

To open the Set Cell Attributes dialog box, simply double-click the cell.

Microsoft Excel

Microsoft Works

DIALOG BOX SHORTCUTS

Microsoft Excel has a number of keyboard shortcuts that work in dialog boxes. You can usually operate the buttons you see by pressing the Command key as you type the first letter of the button name. For example, in an Open dialog box, you can eject a disk by pressing Command-E. Pressing Command-period cancels the dialog box, as if you had clicked Cancel.

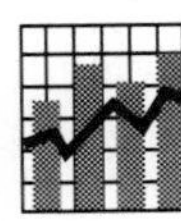

The same keyboard technique works for other options listed in dialog boxes. In a dialog box where there is no place to enter text, you can simply type the first letter of the button name, without pressing the Command key. You can also select a dialog box option and click the OK button by pressing the Command key and typing the first letter of the option twice. In some cases, you can use the mouse to effectively select an option and click the OK button simply by double-clicking the option.

SELECTING AND MANIPULATING

SELECTING LARGE AREAS

General Spreadsheets

Here's a quick way to select a large block of cells. Click the cell at one corner of the block, scroll to the opposite corner, press the Shift key, and click the cell at that corner. This method is faster than dragging from one corner of the block to the opposite corner.

SELECTING NONADJACENT CELLS

General Spreadsheets

You can select nonadjacent cells in Full Impact, Microsoft Excel, Multiplan, or Wingz by pressing the Command key as you click the cells or drag across the blocks of cells you want selected. You can change the shape of the most recently selected block by pressing the Shift key instead of the Command key and clicking or dragging.

SELECTING PAST WINDOW EDGES

General Spreadsheets

As you're selecting a block of cells in a spreadsheet, how can you extend the cell selection into an area out of view? Drag the pointer into the column headings, the row headings, or one of the scroll bars. The spreadsheet scrolls as long as you hold down the mouse button and keep the pointer just outside the cell area.

SELECTING CELLS BY NAME

General Spreadsheets

Most spreadsheet programs offer an easy way to select a large or complex group of cells more than once. While a group of cells is still selected, you can name it and subsequently select it again by that name. Use the commands listed in the table in Figure 9-3 on the following page.

Program	To Name Selected Cells	To Select Cells by Name
Full Impact	Named Ranges command (Display menu)	Go To command (Display menu), and then Named Ranges command (Misc menu), and then Return or Enter
MacCalc	Names command (Name menu)	Name menu
Microsoft Excel	Define Name command (Formula menu)	Goto command (Formula menu)
Multiplan	Define Name command (Select menu)	Goto command (Select menu)
Trapeze	Name command (Block menu)	Goto command (Sheet menu)
Wingz	Define Name command (Go menu)	Name command (Go menu)

FIGURE 9-3. CELL NAMES.
Use these commands to name a selected group of cells so that you can subsequently reselect the same block quickly.

Microsoft Works

MOVING CELLS

How can you move information from one cell to another in a Microsoft Works spreadsheet without using the menus? Select the cell whose contents you want to move, and then press the Command and Option keys while clicking the cell to which you want to move the information.

FORMULAS AND FORMATS

General Spreadsheets

BYPASSING FORMULA ERRORS

Most spreadsheet programs won't let you put an erroneous formula in your spreadsheet. When nothing you do seems to rid a formula of an elusive error and you'd like to set the formula aside for awhile, remove the equal sign at the beginning of the formula. (See Figure 9-4.) Without the equal sign, the formula is treated as text. Later, you can return for another try at resolving the error. (In MacCalc, turn a formula into text temporarily by prefixing it with a single quotation mark.)

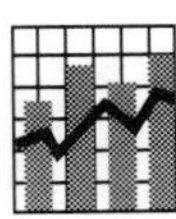

FIGURE 9-4. TEMPORARY IGNORANCE.
Sometimes a spreadsheet program insists that you fix an error in a formula before moving to another cell (top). Removing the equal sign (bottom) lets you ignore the error temporarily.

CHANGING CALCULATED VALUES TO CONSTANTS

If you need to convert formulas to constants in Wingz, use the Cut, Copy, and Paste commands with the Scrapbook, as follows:

1. Select the cells and choose Copy from the Edit menu. This places a copy of the cell contents, including any formulas, on the Clipboard.
2. Choose Scrapbook from the Apple menu, and then choose Paste from the Edit menu. The Paste command evaluates any formulas on the Clipboard and places the resulting values in the Scrapbook.
3. Choose Cut from the Edit menu to replace the formulas on the Clipboard with the calculated values. If you want to, you can now close the Scrapbook.
4. The cells you selected in step 1 should still be selected. Choose Paste to return the calculated values to their respective cells.

INSTANT EVALUATION

It's easy to convert one formula or part of one formula to a constant in a Microsoft Excel spreadsheet. Here are the steps:

1. Select the cell containing the formula.
2. Select the part of the formula you want evaluated, or click anywhere if you want the whole formula evaluated.
3. Choose Calculate Now from the Options menu.

SUBTRACTING DATES

Calculating the number of days between two dates is easy in Microsoft Excel: Simply subtract the earlier date from the later date. To express the difference between two days in years, months, and days, use this formula:

```
=TEXT(YEAR(DATE2-DATE1)-1904,"#0")&" Years,
"&TEXT(MONTH(DATE2-DATE1)-1,"#0")&" Months,
"&TEXT(DAY(DATE2-DATE1),"#0")&" Days"
```

In this formula, DATE1 names the cell containing the earlier date, and DATE2 names the cell containing the later date.

CROSS-TABS

Suppose you want to cross-tabulate two types of data in order to tally the number of times each combination of input values occurs. For example, let's say you've gathered hundreds of complaints in each of 10 categories for dozens of field offices. You want to know how many complaints of each category there were from each office. You can use Microsoft Excel to perform this cross-tabulation. Figure 9-5 shows a spreadsheet that cross-tabulates customer complaints by complaint category and site.

To prepare a cross-tabulation spreadsheet, enter each item of raw data on a separate line in a two-column list (A7:B19 in Figure 9-5). Put column headings at the top of the list. Select the list, along with the headings, and choose the Set Database command from the Data menu. This defines the selection as a Microsoft Excel database named Database.

To count occurrences in the database you just defined, put the formula *=DCOUNT(Database,,Criteria)* in an unused cell (C3 in Figure 9-5). Use the Define Name command (in the Formula menu) to name that cell Count.

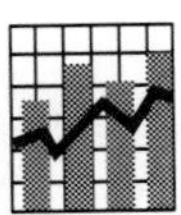

Reserve space for the criteria needed by the DCOUNT function by selecting cells on two lines above the database (A2:B3 in Figure 9-5) and choosing Set Criteria from the Data menu. Copy the headings from the database to the first line of the criteria space.

At this point, your simple database could count the occurrences of any single pair of inputs. However, you would have to specify each possible combination of inputs separately and manually record the count for each.

To complete the cross-tab system, add a table to an unused area of the spreadsheet. In the leftmost column of this table, enter as row headings all the possible values for one input. In the topmost row, enter as column headings all the possible values for the other input. In the upper left corner (cell D6 in Figure 9-5), put the formula *=IF(Count=0,"",Count).* Select the block of cells containing the row and column headings, plus an extra row at the bottom and an extra column on the right for totals (D6:I12 in Figure 9-5). Make this selection a two-input table by choosing Table from the

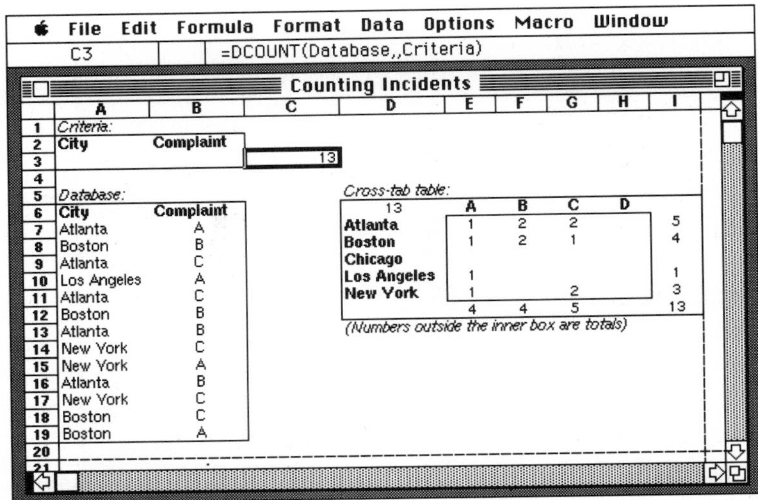

FIGURE 9-5. COUNTING INCIDENTS.

This Microsoft Excel spreadsheet combines a database and a table to cross-tabulate the values of two inputs. Range A6:B19 is defined as Database, and range A2:B3 is defined as Criteria. Cell C3 is named Count and contains the formula =DCOUNT(Database,,Criteria). *Cell D6 contains the formula* =IF(count=0,"",count). *Range D6:I12 is a table, with row input taken from cell A3 and column input from cell B3.*

Data menu; in the dialog box that appears, set the Row Input Cell to the second criterion used by the DCOUNT function and set the Column Input Cell to the first criterion (B3 and A3 in Figure 9-5).

Microsoft Excel fills in the table by calculating the formula in the corner of the table, using all combinations of the two inputs. When the calculation is complete, the table contains the cross-tabulation of the data in the database. With a large database, calculation could take a while.

Microsoft Excel

MONTHLY HEADINGS

In a Microsoft Excel spreadsheet that lists information by month, the Series command (in the Data menu) can help you quickly create the January through December row or column headings. For example, the following steps create three-letter abbreviations Jan through Dec in cells A1 to A12:

1. Enter *1/1* in cell A1.
2. Select cells A1 through A12.
3. Choose Number from the Format menu. In the dialog box that appears, type *mmm* as the format. Click OK to dismiss the dialog box.
4. Choose Series from the Data menu. In the Series dialog box, select the Columns, Date, and Month options. Be sure the Step Value is 1 and the Stop Value is blank. Figure 9-6 shows how the dialog box should look.

General Spreadsheets

SPREADSHEET INDENTS AND TABS

Tabs and indents are essential to effective, organized spreadsheets, but spreadsheet programs generally don't allow for tabs. Aligning by indenting with typed blank spaces is tedious and hard to change later. However, you can insert extra columns to provide uniform horizontal spacing.

To set up an indent at the left edge of the spreadsheet, make the width of the first column the size of the indent, and make the second column wide enough for the widest of the indented and nonindented entries. Put indented entries in the second column and nonindented entries in the first column. (The nonindented entries in the narrow first column automatically extend into the second column.) Figure 9-7 demonstrates the technique.

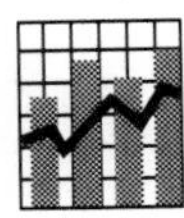

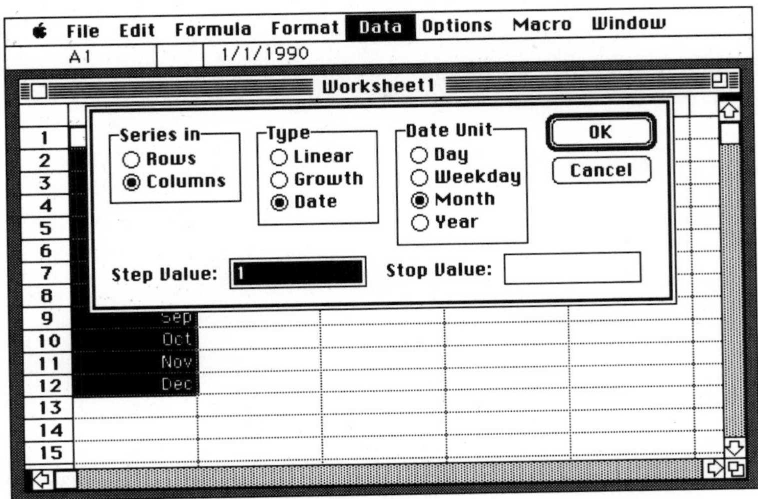

FIGURE 9-6. MONTHLY PROGRESSION.
Create a monthly progression in a column of cells with these settings for Microsoft Excel's Series command.

1040:1

	A	C–O	R
35	35	Subtract line 34 from line 32. Enter the result here.	35
36	36	Multiply $1,950 by the total number of exemptions claimed on line 6e.	36
37	37	**Taxable Income.** Subtract line 36 from line 35. Enter the result (if less than zero, enter zero)	37
38		**Caution:** If under age 14 and you have more than $1,000 of investment income, check here	
39		and see page 17 to see if you have to use Form 8615 to figure your tax.	
41	38	Enter tax. Check if from: Tax Table, Tax Rate Schedules, or Form 8615	38

1040:2

	A	C–O	R
35	35	Subtract line 34 from line 32. Enter the result here.	35
36	36	Multiply $1,950 by the total number of exemptions claimed on line 6e.	36
37	37	**Taxable Income.** Subtract line 36 from line 35. Enter the result (if less than zero, enter zero)	37
38		**Caution:** If under age 14 and you have more than $1,000 of investment income, check here	
39		and see page 17 to see if you have to use Form 8615 to figure your tax.	
41	38	Enter tax. Check if from: Tax Table, Tax Rate Schedules, or Form 8615	38

FIGURE 9-7. VIRTUAL TABS.
As a rule, spreadsheet programs don't support indentation and tabs, but you can simulate them by using narrow columns for spacing. The upper window here shows the effects of this technique. Grid lines in the lower window show where the extra columns are.

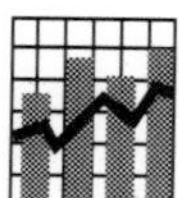

For x levels of indentation, set the widths of the leftmost x columns to the size of an indentation space, and make the next column to the right wide enough for the widest indented entry.

OUTLINING CELL BLOCKS

How can you put a border around every cell of a selected block of cells in a Microsoft Works spreadsheet, as shown in Figure 9-8? After selecting the range, use the Outline, Right, and Bottom commands (in the Border submenu of the Format menu), in that order. The Outline command by itself puts a border only around the perimeter of the selection. The Right and Bottom commands add the other border lines. After you apply this method, the Border submenu imprecisely indicates that the selection has Outline-style borders.

File Edit Window Select Format Options Chart Macro

Sales Projections (SS)

	A	B	C	D	E	F	G
1							
2		**Region**	**June**	**July**	**August**	**Summer Total**	**Percent**
3							
4		Africa	$80	$87	$95	$262	10.6%
5		Asia/Pacific	$100	$109	$119	$328	13.3%
6		Northern Europe	$99	$108	$118	$325	13.2%
7		Central Europe	$200	$219	$240	$659	26.8%
8		Southern Europe	$70	$76	$83	$229	9.3%
9		North America	$95	$104	$114	$313	12.7%
10		South America	$105	$115	$126	$346	14.1%
11							
12		**Total**	**$749**	**$818**	**$895**	**$2462**	**100.0%**
13							

FIGURE 9-8. CELL BLOCK BORDERS.

Which Microsoft Works commands would you use to put borders around each cell of a block in a spreadsheet?

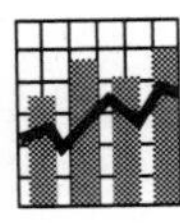

HIDING COLUMNS

Spreadsheets often contain tables, auxiliary and intermediate calculations, proprietary formulas, or other information that you'd rather keep out of the public eye. In most spreadsheet programs, you can hide private cells by putting them in columns outside the public part of your spreadsheet and then setting the widths of those columns to 0.

Incidentally, if you set all the column widths to 0 and turn off the display of row and column headings, you can make the spreadsheet appear to have vanished.

HIDING NUMBERS

Would you like to hide numeric values on a Microsoft Excel spreadsheet without affecting the cell values or formulas? Don't bother with the Cell Protection and Protect Document commands; they hide formulas but not values. Simply select the cells you want to hide, choose Number from the Format menu, press Backspace or Delete, type one or two semicolons, and press Return. This gives the selected cells a blank number format. The blank format will then appear as a choice in the Format Number dialog box, where you can use it on other cells having numeric values. (See Figure 9-9.)

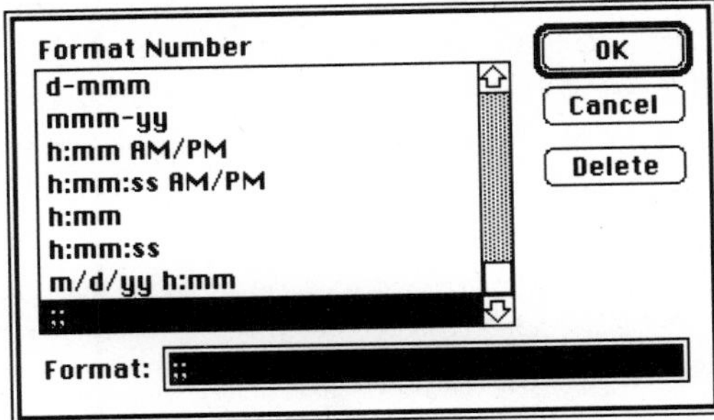

FIGURE 9-9. CELL BLANK.
Use this number format to hide cell values in a Microsoft Excel spreadsheet.

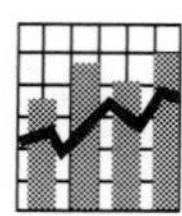

HIDING CELLS

To hide text in a Microsoft Excel spreadsheet, select the text cells you want to hide, choose Number from the Format menu, type *[White]*—that is, the word "White" enclosed in square brackets—and press the Return key. That format uses white "ink" to hide any value, text or numeric. It overrides the font color you set with the Font command (in the Format menu). The only values it won't hide are error values, such as the #NAME? and #DIV/0! error values.

LINING UP DECIMAL POINTS

When dealing with dollars and cents, an accountant typically prefixes the first and last numbers in a column with dollar signs and omits the dollar signs in the middle of the column. You could use two of Microsoft Excel's standard number formats, $#,##0.00 ;($#,##0.00) and #,##0.00, to accomplish this. However, the space ahead of the semicolon in the first format means that the decimal points don't quite line up. (The space appears in positive numbers to balance the parentheses used in negative numbers.)

To be sure numbers line up exactly when you are using both dollar formats and regular formats in the same column, make your own format for numbers without dollar signs. Choose Number from the Format menu and select the $#,##0.00 ;($#,##0.00) format. Remove the dollar signs and click OK. You'll end up with the format #,##0.00 ;(#,##0.00). (See Figure 9-10.) Use the new format for every cell except the first and last in the column.

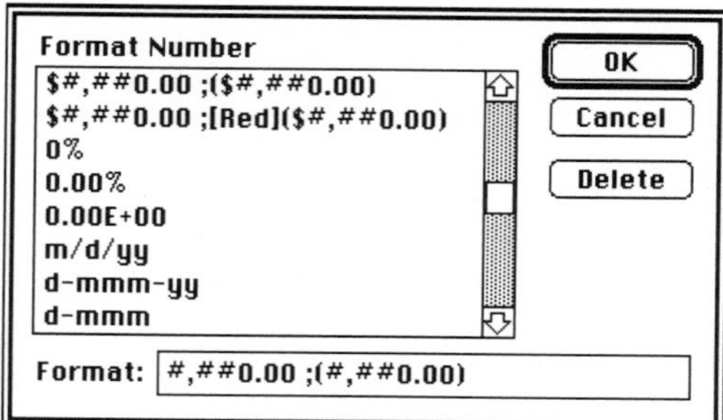

FIGURE 9-10. DECIMALS AND DOLLAR SIGNS.
Amounts having the standard format at the top of the list will align correctly with amounts given the new format shown in the editing area.

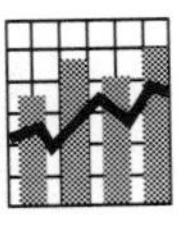

TABLE LOOKUPS

MacCalc

You can use MacCalc's CHOOSE and INDEX functions together to do table lookups. The INDEX function will look for a match in a table of keys and will return the offset of the match from the beginning of the table. The CHOOSE function will use this offset to pick out an entry from a corresponding table. For example, suppose the range F2:F5 is named ITEMS and contains the text values "Nuts," "Bolts," "Screws," and "Nails." The corresponding range G2:G5, named PRICES, contains the numeric values 0.10, 0.15, 0.25, and 0.05. If B2 contains "Nails" and C2 contains the formula *=CHOOSE(INDEX(B2,ITEMS),PRICES),* then the value of C2 is 0.05. The INDEX function in this formula returns 4 because it finds a match for B2 in the fourth cell of ITEMS. The CHOOSE function therefore returns the value of the fourth cell of PRICES, which is 0.05. (See Figure 9-11.)

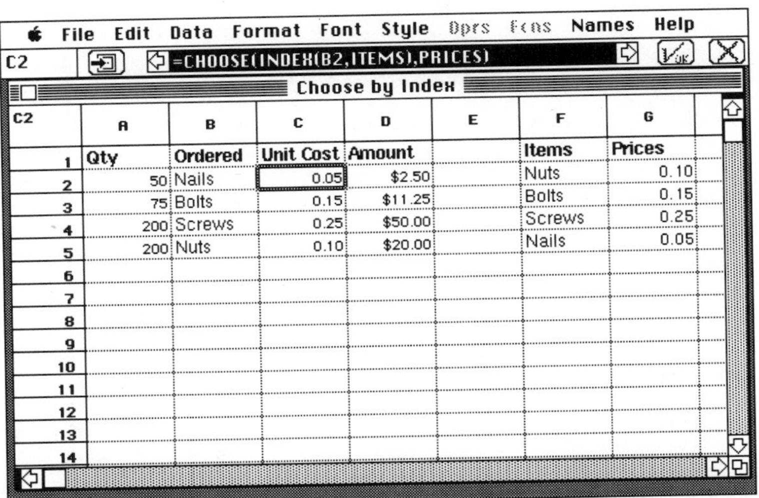

FIGURE 9-11. CHOOSE BY INDEX.

The formula in cell C2 looks up an amount associated with the contents of cell B2 in the table in cells F2:G5.

FLEXIBLE EXTERNALS

Microsoft Excel

External references in a Microsoft Excel spreadsheet don't have to be locked to a specific cell or range of cells in a supporting spreadsheet. You can create an external reference that adjusts automatically when the cells to which it refers change location in the supporting spreadsheet. First you name the cell or range of cells in the supporting spreadsheet. Then in the dependent spreadsheet, use an external reference to that name. The dependent formula will always have the correct information even if the named cell or range moves in the supporting spreadsheet. For example, you could link a cell in an Annual_Expenses spreadsheet to a total for January from a January_Expenses spreadsheet by following these steps:

1. On the January_Expenses spreadsheet, select the cell that contains the total for January. Use the Define Name command (in the Formula menu) to name that cell Jan_Total.
2. Activate the Annual_Expenses spreadsheet, and select the cell that will have the external reference.
3. Enter this formula in the cell: *=January_Expenses!Jan_Total.*

SUM EASY FORMULA

Microsoft Excel's SUM function is very powerful but is tedious to enter. The following two-line macro relieves the tedium:

```
=FORMULA("=SUM(R[-"&(ROWS(SELECTION())-1)&"]C:R[-1]C)")
=RETURN()
```

This macro builds a SUM formula that adds all cells but the last one in a one-column range, and enters the formula in that last cell. After entering the macro on a macro sheet, name it and give it a keystroke shortcut, using the Define Name command.

To use the macro, select the cell where you want the formula to be placed, and then extend the selection up to the first cell of the range to be summed. The macro works only if the active cell is the last one in the selection. After selecting the range to be summed, press the keystroke shortcut that you defined for the macro.

You can use the same type of macro to automate entry of other Microsoft Excel functions that operate on a range of cells, such as AVERAGE, MAX, COUNT, MIN, VAR, and STDEV.

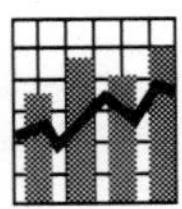

DAMAGE CONTROL

You can sometimes recover values from a damaged Microsoft Excel spreadsheet by constructing external links from a new spreadsheet. First open a new spreadsheet and select a range of cells that is the same size as or larger than a range that you want to recover. Type a formula that consists of an external reference to the range of cells on the damaged spreadsheet, and press Command-Enter to enter the formula. For example, the formula *='Bad Spreadsheet'!$A$1:$F$30* is an external reference to cells A1 through F30 of the spreadsheet named Bad Spreadsheet. If the program asks you to locate the spreadsheet, locate it and open it. Microsoft Excel then imports any values available from the cell range you specified.

CHARTS

PAIR PLOTTING

A scatter graph is normally used to analyze the relationship between two variables, usually called the *x* variable and the *y* variable. If you can establish a high degree of correlation in observed values of the two variables, you can predict with some certainty the value of one variable given a hypothetical value of the other. There's a trick to plotting data pairs on scatter graphs in Microsoft Excel that not everyone knows. If you simply select the columns of data and create a new chart, Microsoft Excel treats the horizontal-axis values as another set of vertical-axis values. Collect your observed data and proceed as follows:

1. Arrange the data so that the first column contains the values for the horizontal axis (the *x* values) and subsequent columns each contain a set of corresponding values for the vertical axis (the *y* values).
2. Select all the data and copy it to the Clipboard by choosing Copy from the Edit menu.
3. Create a new chart by choosing New from the File menu.
4. Choose Paste Special (not Paste) from the Edit menu. Select the Categories In First Column option and click OK. (In Microsoft Excel parlance, categories are the horizontal-axis values.) If you had chosen Paste, the program would assume that you did not want category-axis labels on your chart and would plot both the *x* and *y* values along the

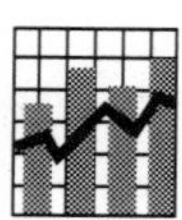

value axis (the *y*-axis) as two data series, instead of plotting one point for each pair of *x* and *y* values.

5. Choose Scatter from the Gallery menu, and select one of the scatter graph formats to replace the standard column-chart choice.
6. Label the axes and the data points with the Attach Text command from the Chart menu. Unfortunately, you cannot link labels from the spreadsheet to the axes or data points in the chart; you have to re-type them.

In step 1, you can arrange the *x* and *y* values in rows instead of columns. In that case, the *x* values go in the first row and the option in the Paste Special dialog box becomes Categories In First Row.

You can also use a short macro to do most of the work of steps 2 through 5. After setting up the two-column table of *x* and *y* values, select it and then run this macro:

```
ScatterGraph
=COPY()
=NEW(2)
=PASTE.SPECIAL(2,FALSE,TRUE)
=GALLERY.SCATTER(1)
=RETURN()
```

Note that if you use the row-wise arrangement mentioned earlier, you must change the third line of the macro to *=PASTE.SPECIAL(1,FALSE,TRUE)*.

A resulting graph might look like the one in Figure 9-12.

SCATTER-PLOT ORIGIN

If you need to have the origin of a Microsoft Excel scatter plot in the upper right or upper left corner, rather than the lower left corner, you can easily change the origin of both axes independently. Click the axis to select it, choose Scale from the Format menu, and select the option Values (or Categories) In Reverse Order.

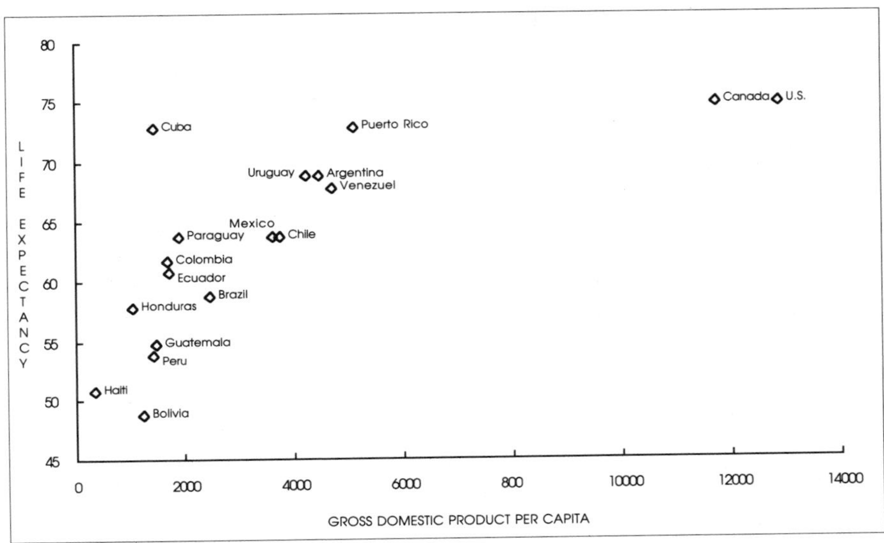

Source: United Nations 1982 Statistical Yearbook

FIGURE 9-12. SCATTER GRAPH.
Creating a proper scatter graph in Microsoft Excel requires the use of the Paste Special command (in the Edit menu).

DOUBLE-Y SCATTER

Cricket Graph can create a scatter plot of two vertical *y*-axis variables, as shown in Figure 9-13 on the following page. First choose DoubleY from the Graph menu. In the dialog box that appears, select a variable from the left list for the horizontal axis and two variables from the right list for the vertical axis. Then press the Option key while clicking the New Plot button.

REVERSING AXES

To reverse an axis in Cricket Graph, you must change the signs of the data column you plan to plot on it. Use the Simple Math command (in the Data menu) to multiply all selected data columns by –1 and place the results in new data columns. Doing this leaves your original data untouched. After plotting the negative values, you can mask the minus signs in the axis labels with blank text. Do this with the text tool, which you can select after choosing Show Tools from the Goodies menu. (See Figure 9-14 on the page after next.)

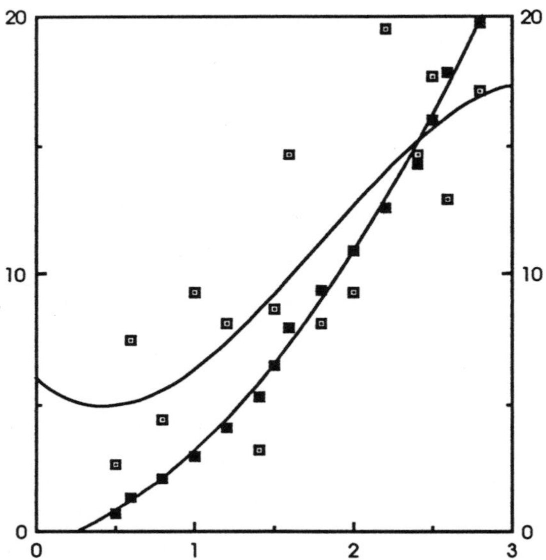

FIGURE 9-13. DOUBLE-Y SCATTER PLOT.
Pressing the Option key while plotting a double-Y graph in Cricket Graph produces a scatter plot of the two vertical-axis variables. Curves have been added with the Polynomial command (in the Curve Fit menu).

CHART SHADOW

You can make a Trapeze chart look more interesting by putting a shadow behind it, as shown in Figure 9-15. After creating the chart, select it and choose Duplicate from the Edit menu. Click the duplicate chart block to bring up the chart format dialog box. In that dialog box, set the Show Data Only option, and change the fill pattern for every data series in use on the chart to a solid color. To change a fill pattern for a data series, click the pattern in the chart format dialog box. Another dialog box opens in which you can use pop-up menus to set the fill pattern and color.

After changing the formats of the duplicate chart, move it slightly to one side and down or up. (Press Option-Shift to move the block 1 point at a time.) Next use the Color command (in the Style menu) to change the pen color to match the paper color. Finally, use the Send To Back command (in the Block menu) to put the duplicate behind the original chart.

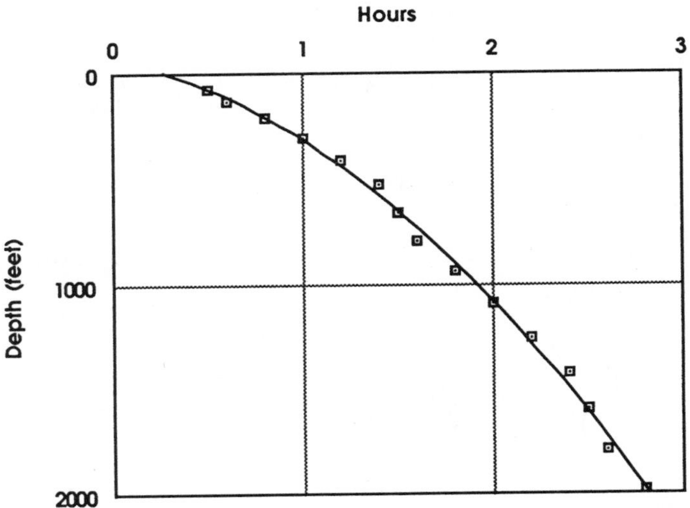

FIGURE 9-14. PLOT ORIGIN.
Changing the origin of a Cricket Graph plot involves changing the signs of the data before plotting and covering the resulting minus signs with blank spaces after plotting.

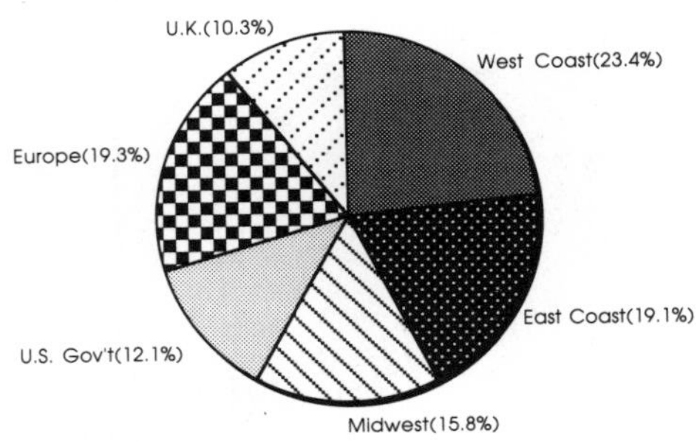

FIGURE 9-15. DROP SHADOW.
Create a drop shadow behind a Trapeze chart from a duplicate that you fill with a solid color, offset slightly, and put behind the original.

3-D SHADOW

To make a chart or graphic object stand out on a Full Impact spreadsheet, put a drop shadow behind it. Figure 9-16 illustrates the effect. Follow these steps to create a drop shadow:

1. Using the Rectangle command (in the Draw menu), draw a rectangle the same size as the whole chart or other object you're shadowing. Drag the rectangle sideways and down or up to offset it slightly from whatever it's shadowing.
2. With the rectangle selected, choose Black or another solid color from the Fill submenu of the Draw command. Then use the Send To Back command (in the Draw menu) to put the rectangle behind whatever it's shadowing.
3. Combine the drop shadow and the object it's shadowing by selecting both (press Shift while clicking each in turn) and choosing Group from the Draw menu.

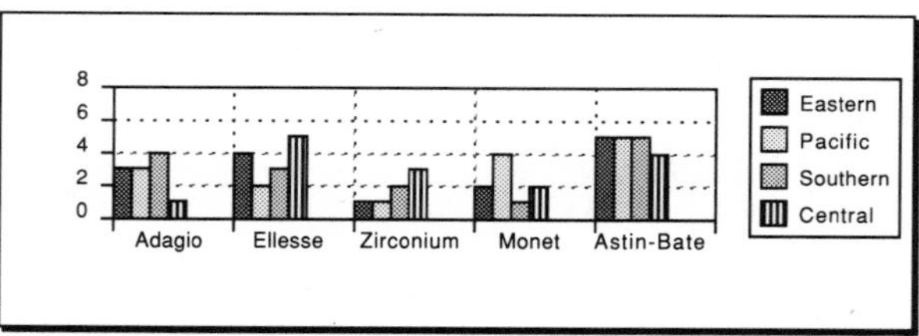

FIGURE 9-16. STAND OUT.
A drop shadow makes a chart stand out on a Full Impact spreadsheet.

COMPOSITE CATEGORY LABELS

You can't always find a chart format in Microsoft Excel's Gallery menu to show all the information you want to present. For instance, no standard pie chart shows both category names and percentages like the one in Figure 9-17.

This problem is easily overcome in the spreadsheet on which the chart is based. There you can use the Text function to convert numbers to text, and you can use the concatenation operator to combine text from various sources. The following formula combines category labels from column A

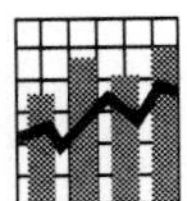

with percentages from column D and puts the result in column B, which can then be used for chart labels:

```
=A2&" "&TEXT(D2,"0.00%")
```

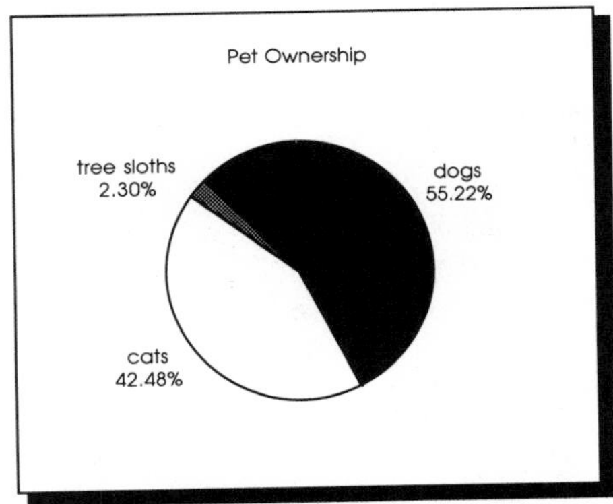

Name and Number table

	A	B	C	D
1	Pet Type	Chart Category	Number	Percentage
2	dogs	=A2&" "&TEXT(D2,"0.00%")	312	=C2/TOTAL
3	cats	=A3&" "&TEXT(D3,"0.00%")	240	=C3/TOTAL
4	tree sloths	=A4&" "&TEXT(D4,"0.00%")	13	=C4/TOTAL
5				=C5/TOTAL
6	TOTAL		=SUM(C1:C5)	=C6/TOTAL

FIGURE 9-17. NAME AND NUMBER.
To combine values for use as a data point label in a Microsoft Excel chart, use the concatenation operator (&) and the Text function in the linked spreadsheet. Here, the formulas in column B combine the text in column A with the percentage in column D. The chart graphs cells in the range B2:C4.

CREATING A LEGEND

Legends that Microsoft Excel draws for charts change the chart size, are immobile, and can't be resized. You can create your own legend without these limitations by using unattached text, as shown in Figure 9-18 on the following page.

First make a background and, optionally, a border for the legend. To do that, create some blank, unattached text by first pressing the Spacebar and

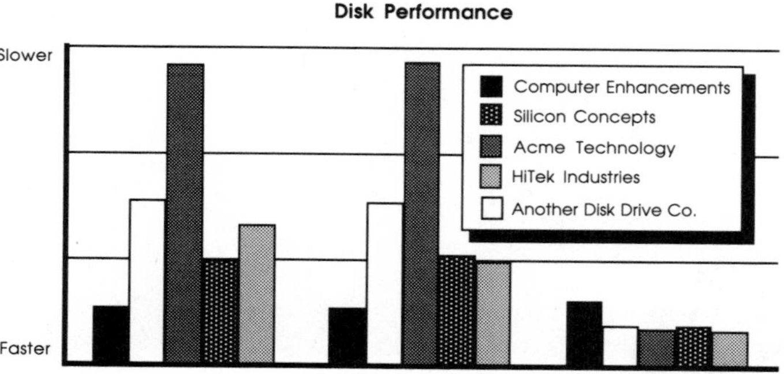

FIGURE 9-18. CUSTOM CHART LEGEND.
When Microsoft Excel's standard legends won't do, create your own, using unattached text.

then the Return key. Select this blank text and use the Patterns command (in the Format menu) to set the background pattern and the border attributes. You can resize the background/border by dragging a handle at one of its corners or sides. Move the background/border by dragging its center.

Next make and label keys for the markers in the chart. To make a key, type some blank, unattached text and use the Patterns command (in the Format menu) to set border and area patterns that match the marker. With the Font command (in the Format menu), set the text background option to Transparent. Move a key by dragging it, and resize it by dragging its handles. Label the key with additional unattached text.

Custom legends created from unattached text have a couple of limitations. For one, you might have difficulty finding space for a custom legend in the chart window because Microsoft Excel always draws the chart to fit the window. Also, moving an entire custom legend is tedious because you have to move the unattached text elements individually and then realign them all at the legend's new location.

Full Impact

TWO CHARTS IN ONE BORDER

You can easily produce the effect of two or more charts inside one chart border on a Full Impact spreadsheet, as shown in Figure 9-19. Here's how:

1. Select one of the charts and choose Get Chart Info from the File menu and set the Freeze Current Graph Size option. Then enlarge the border of the selected chart by dragging one of the selection handles.
2. Select another chart and drag it inside the enlarged border of the first chart. If the first chart overlays the second chart, choose Bring To Front from the Draw menu. Eliminate the second chart's border by choosing None from the Line Pattern submenu of the Draw menu.
3. Select all the charts (by pressing Shift while clicking each in turn) and choose Group from the Draw menu to make Full Impact treat them as one object.

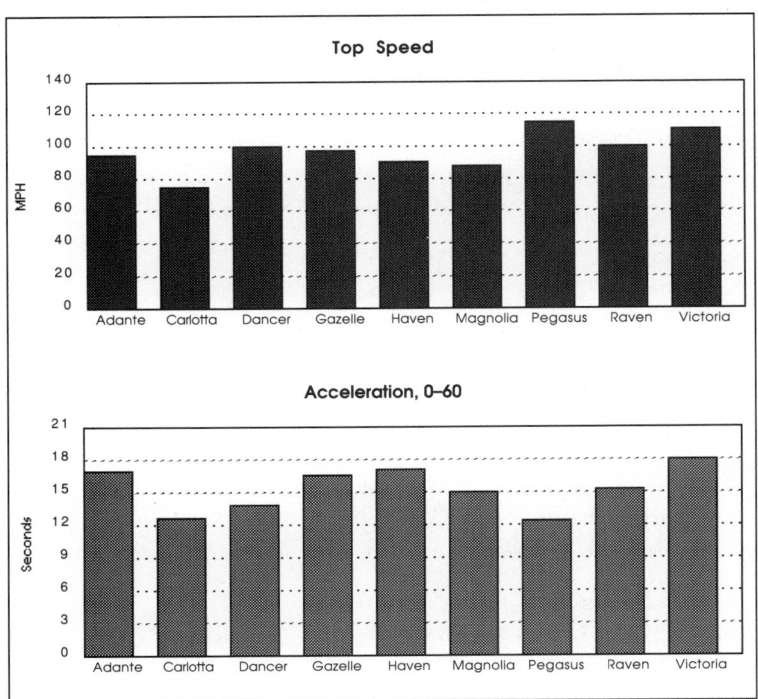

FIGURE 9-19. COMBINED CHARTS.

You can enlarge the border of a chart in Full Impact to make room for more than one graph. To prevent the graph from being enlarged along with the border, set the Freeze Current Graph Size option of the Get Chart Info command.

VERSATILE CHARTS

One chart in Microsoft Excel can graph amounts for any one task that is taken from a database of multiple tasks. The chart simply graphs data from a dedicated area of the spreadsheet that contains a copy of the amounts for one task. To switch the chart to a different task, you put a copy of that task's data into the spreadsheet area that the chart uses. You do this by using the Copy and Paste commands (in the Edit menu) or the Extract command (in the Data menu). You make no changes to the chart. In Figure 9-20, for example, cells AB2:AD14 contain a copy of the budgeted and actual expenses for one task extracted from the database of task expenses in cells A2:G15. By extracting each task in turn and printing the resulting chart, you can easily graph every task in the database.

You can also make a Microsoft Excel chart show only past data—not future data—by using named cell references defined with the Index and Match functions. The data must be arranged in chronological order from oldest to newest. The chart in Figure 9-20, for example, graphs budgeted and actual expenses, using the following two series formulas:

```
=SERIES(Expenses!$AC$2,Expenses!DATES,Expenses!ACTUALS,2)
=SERIES(Expenses!$AD$2,Expenses!DATES,Expenses!BUDGETS,1)
```

In these formulas, the first item is an explicit cell reference that supplies the legend text. The name DATES specifies the chart's category (horizontal) axis. DATES refers to cells AB3:AB14 in the Expenses spreadsheet, which contain the names of all 12 months. (The month names are actually dates, such as 1/1/88, formatted by using a number format of MMM.)

In the first formula, the name ACTUALS specifies the actual expense values for past months. It is defined on the Expenses spreadsheet with the following formula:

```
=$AC$2:INDEX($AC$2:$AC$13,MATCH(CURRENT_DATE,DATES,1))
```

This formula defines ACTUALS as the range of cells from the first date to the current date. The name CURRENT_DATE is defined as the cell that contains the current date. The Index and Match functions reset the range of cells to be plotted. A similar formula, using column AD instead of AC, defines the name BUDGETS.

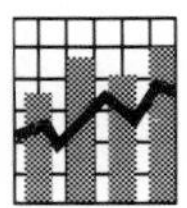

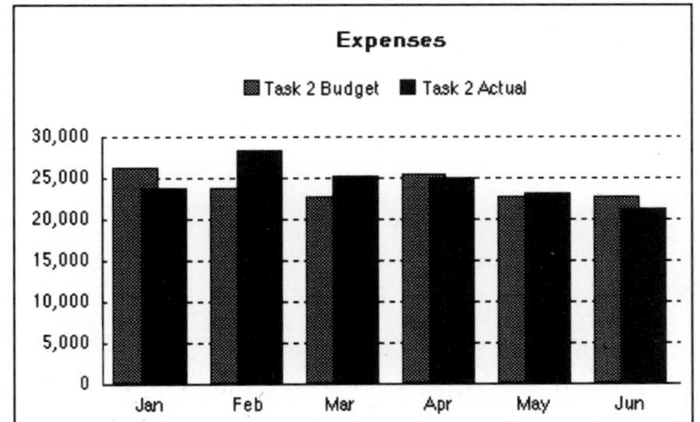

Expenses:1

	AB	AC	AD
1	*One task extracted from the Database*		
2	Date	Task 2 Actual	Task 2 Budget
3	Jan	23,715	26,065
4	Feb	28,246	23,751
5	Mar	25,101	22,696
6	Apr	24,861	25,437
7	May	23,017	22,696
8	Jun	21,179	22,696
9	Jul		22,696
10	Aug		22,696
11	Sep		22,696
12	Oct		22,696
13	Nov		22,696
14	Dec		27,752

Expenses:2

	A	B	C	D	E	F	G
1				*The Database*			
2	Date	Task 2 Actual	Task 3 Actual	Task 4 Actual	Task 2 Budget	Task 3 Budget	Task 4 Budget
3	Jan	23,715	28,072	3,317	26,065	30,478	6,741
4	Feb	28,246	29,684	3,754	23,751	30,478	6,741
5	Mar	25,101	29,382	4,803	22,696	30,478	6,741
6	Apr	24,861	33,628	5,232	25,437	30,478	6,741
7	May	23,017	30,057	5,902	22,696	28,545	6,741
8	Jun	21,179	28,810	6,512	22,696	29,601	6,741
9	Jul				22,696	28,545	6,741
10	Aug				22,696	28,545	6,741
11	Sep				22,696	28,545	6,741
12	Oct				22,696	28,545	6,741
13	Nov				22,696	28,545	6,741
14	Dec				27,752	30,230	6,741
15	Cumulative	146,119	179,633	29,520	284,573	353,013	80,892
16							
17							
18							
19				*The Criteria for the Extract menu command*			
20		Task 2 Actual	Task 3 Actual	Task 4 Actual	Task 2 Budget	Task 3 Budget	Task 4 Budget
21							

FIGURE 9-20. ONE FOR ALL.

This Microsoft Excel chart works for any one task from the database in cells A2:G15 because it graphs the data for whichever task has been copied to cells AB2:AD14. Only past months are graphed; future months are excluded. The chart's series formulas determine which months to show by using names defined in the spreadsheet (not explicit cell references).

Wingz

SURFACE AND CONTOUR SHADING

In a surface or contour plot, you typically want a smooth gradation of color bands or gray shades across the z (height) axis. As Figure 9-21 shows, however, Wingz uses a seemingly random standard set of colors that makes contour graphs and surface graphs not only ugly but more confusing than if they had no color bands.

The Wingz script in Figure 9-22 solves the problem. It sets the z-axis for 16 shades of gray. Doing so produces good results when printed on a 300-dpi LaserWriter using LaserWriter driver 6.0 or later. (For more gray levels, you can change the script to set the zones variable to a number greater than 16.) To use the script, simply select the contour or surface graph to be converted and run the script.

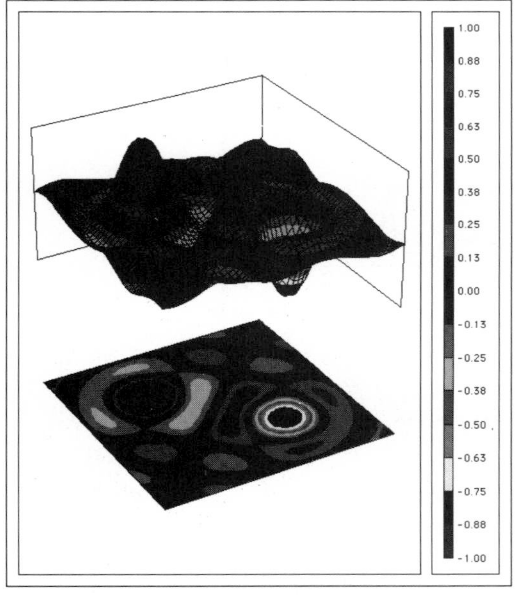

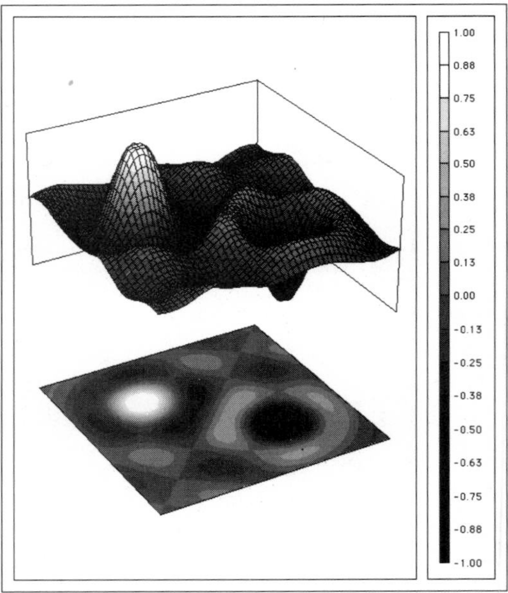

FIGURE 9-21. SHADED SURFACE.

Standard Wingz colors in surface and contour charts don't provide useful shading information (left). Applying the script in Figure 9-22 to those graphs achieves smooth, intuitive shading (right).

```
{Define the variables needed for the script}

{"chartnum" refers to the selected chart}
DEFINE chartnum

{"min" and "max" are the}
{minimum and maximum}
{values on the z-axis}
DEFINE min, max

{"Z" and "Z1" are}
{the current z-axis}
{division and subdivision}
DEFINE Z, Z1

{"colorvalue" is the RGB number of the color or gray shade }
{for one z-axis division}
DEFINE colorvalue

{"zones" is the number of shading zones (i.e. z-axis divisions}
DEFINE zones

{set the number of gray shades}
zones = 16

{prevent redrawing the graph after each command}
REPAINT OFF

{get the number of the selected chart}
chartnum = NUMBER()

{select the z-axis}
SELECT CHART chartnum AXIS 3
```

FIGURE 9-22. SMOOTH VARIATIONS. *(continued)*

This Wingz script smoothly shades a surface or contour graph. The script remaps the Z-axis to have 16 divisions and makes each division a lighter shade of gray than the division below it.

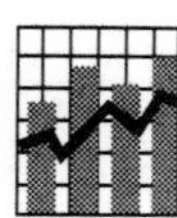

FIGURE 9-22. SMOOTH VARIATIONS. *(continued)*

```
{get the minimum and maximum z-axis values}
min = SCALEMINIMUM()
max = SCALEMAXIMUM()

{set z-axis scaling and number of major divisions}
MANUAL SCALING FROM min TO max WITH zones MAJOR AND
 1 MINOR DIVISIONS

{loop through each z-axis division, }
{assigning the next gray shade to it}
FOR Z = 1 TO zones

       {calculate the RGB number for gray shade}
       colorvalue = Z * 255 / zones

       {select z-axis division}
       SELECT CHART chartnum SERIES Z

       {set gray shade}
       FILL FG RGB(colorvalue,colorvalue,colorvalue)

END FOR
{end loop}

{now redraw the graph}
REPAINT OBJECTS
```

Cricket Graph

THICKENING A PLOT

In Cricket Graph, the Overlay Plot button (visible in the Graph dialog box of compatible plots) lets you add points from a new data set to an existing scatter or line plot. However, it won't let you overlay a data set with only one data point or a data set containing data that fall on a perfect vertical or horizontal line. If you try, a message pops up, telling you that you can't use zero-range data. Even when the data points fall easily within the bounds of the established axes on the current plot, adding zero-range data is impossible. This issue arises in many situations with real scientific data.

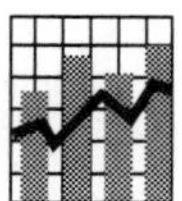

You can trick Cricket Graph into overlaying a single data point on an existing scatter or line plot. First copy the point from the data table and paste it to the next row in the data table. Then change the values in one of the two rows by some minuscule amount. Finally, overlay both data points on the existing graph. Cricket Graph will plot the two nearly identical points one on top of the other, as if there were only one point. For instance, suppose you wanted to add the data point x=3.5, y=2.6 from case 11 to a scatter plot already overlaid with cases 1 through 10. You would create a second data row in the case 11 data table with x=3.50001 and y=2.60001. If you overlaid the two points, they would appear as one.

A similar trick applies when adding or creating plots of data that fall on a vertical or horizontal line. To plot a horizontal line, for instance, simply change one of the y values (on the vertical axis) by a trivial amount to make the y range nonzero. After the data is plotted, you can change the range of the axes at will.

PERFORMANCE

CLEARING THE CLIPBOARD

General Spreadsheets

After cutting or copying and then pasting a particularly large range of spreadsheet cells, you should clear the cells from the Clipboard. The contents of the Clipboard occupy valuable space in the Macintosh's memory and therefore reduce the amount of space available for your spreadsheet.

To clear the Clipboard completely, select a single cell and choose Copy from the Edit menu twice. The first Copy command clears the Clipboard but holds its contents in another area of memory so that you can, if necessary, undo the copy operation. The second Copy command clears the large cell selection from the "undo" area of memory.

SPREADSHEET BLOAT

Microsoft Works

How can you be sure a Microsoft Works spreadsheet isn't taking more RAM or disk space than it needs? Use the Last Cell command (in the Select menu) to find the last cell that contains a value. If the last cell is to the right of or below the cells you're actually using, you can probably reduce the amount of RAM and disk space used by the spreadsheet.

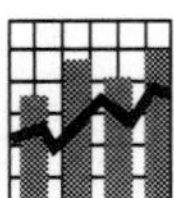

1. Select all columns from the column that contains the last cell up to but not including the last cell you're actually using. Choose Clear from the Edit menu.
2. Select all rows from the row that contains the last cell up to but not including the last cell you're actually using. Choose Clear from the Edit menu.
3. Save, close, and then reopen the spreadsheet.

COPYING QUICKLY TO MANY CELLS

Here's a quick way to copy the contents of one cell to any group of cells in a Microsoft Excel spreadsheet:

1. Select the group of cells to which you want to copy. Use the Shift key for large selections and the Command key for nonadjacent selections.
2. Press the Command key and then click on the cell whose contents you want to copy.
3. Click in the formula-editing area. Edit the cell contents or enter the new contents if necessary.
4. Press Option-Enter, or press Option and click the enter box in the formula-editing area.

Using the Option key to propagate cell contents adjusts relative cell references in a formula in the same way that using the Copy and Paste commands does. Relative cell references in each copy of a formula refer to different cells from those referred to in the original formula.

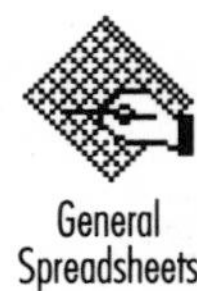

INCREASING ACCURACY

Spreadsheet calculations might appear to be incorrect if they involve cells whose precise values have more decimal places than the cell formats show on the screen. For example, the result of adding 62.118 to 37.876 is 99.994. If the cells containing those three values are formatted to show only two decimal places, the result looks wrong: 62.12 + 37.88 = 99.99.

To be sure calculation results are shown correctly, you can incorporate the ROUND function into spreadsheet formulas so that cell values are stored at the same precision as they are displayed. You can get the same effect in

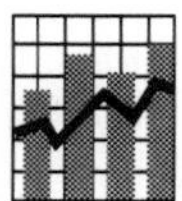

Microsoft Excel without using the ROUND function by setting the Precision As Displayed option of the Calculation command (in the Options menu). The trade-off for using this command is slower spreadsheet calculation, because Microsoft Excel rounds every cell value to its formatted precision. Also, any constant values you entered by using extra decimal places are permanently rounded; you can't restore the extra precision later by turning off the Precision As Displayed option.

ORDER OF ENTRY

Microsoft Excel

Multiplan

It's possible to preselect a group of cells in a Microsoft Excel or Multiplan spreadsheet for which you will later enter values, and to designate in advance the order in which the selected cells' values must be entered. To do this, open the spreadsheet and proceed as follows:

1. Select the group of cells for which values must be entered, using the Command key and possibly the Shift key, as described in the tip "Selecting Nonadjacent Cells," earlier in this chapter. Select the cells in the order in which you want their values entered.
2. After selecting the last cell in the group, press the Enter key once. This makes the first cell of the group the active cell.
3. Give the group of selected cells a name, something like Entry, using the Define Name command, as described in the tip "Selecting Cells by Name," earlier in this chapter.
4. Save the spreadsheet.

When it's time to enter values, open the spreadsheet and use the Goto command to select the named group of cells. Enter the value for the active cell, which has a heavy white border. Then press the Enter key, not the Return key, to end the entry and advance to the next selected cell. If you need to back up to a previous cell, press Shift-Enter.

SAVING TIME WITH MANUAL CALCULATION

General Spreadsheets

Save time when working on a large spreadsheet by using the manual calculation option. In Microsoft Excel, set the Manual option of the Calculation command (in the Options menu). In Full Impact, set the Manually Recalculate option of the Recalc Options command (in the Display menu). In MacCalc, choose Manual Recalc from the Data menu. In Trapeze, choose

Manual Recalculation from the Environment menu. In Multiplan, choose Manual Calculation from the Calculate menu. In Wingz, choose Manual Recalc from the Recalc Info submenu of the Go menu. In Microsoft Works, choose Manual Calculation from the Options menu. You can force any of these spreadsheet programs to calculate at any time by pressing Command-equal sign.

MACROS AND SCRIPTS

Microsoft Excel

PERSONAL SHORTCUTS

It's easy to create Microsoft Excel macros that not only choose commands from a menu, but that also select specific options in the dialog boxes that accompany the menu choices. And you can execute each command macro with a keyboard shortcut that you designate. For example, you could record a macro to left-align the values of selected cells as follows:

1. Choose Record from the Macro menu. In the dialog box that appears, enter *AlignLeft* as the macro name and *L* as the keyboard shortcut. Click OK to dismiss the dialog box.
2. Choose Alignment from the Format menu. In the dialog box that appears, set the Left option. Click OK to dismiss the dialog box.
3. Choose Stop Recorder from the Macro menu.

To use this macro, select the cell that you want left-aligned and press Command-Option-L. When you quit the program, it asks you whether you want to save the macro sheet. Name it and click OK. The next time you open Microsoft Excel, you must open that macro sheet in order to use the LeftAlign macro.

Full Impact

Microsoft Excel

A MACRO FOR MULTIPLE FORMATS

One handy use of macros—even for beginners—is to apply multiple formats all at once to cells you have selected. To record such a macro in Full Impact, follow these steps:

1. Select one (or more) cells.
2. Choose New Macro from the Macros menu. In the dialog box that appears, type a name for the macro, select the Global Macro option, and click the Record button.

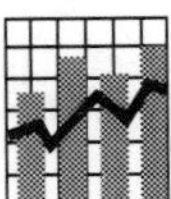

3. One at a time, choose the formats you want the macro to apply: the font, the size, the style, the alignment, and so on.
4. Choose Stop Recording from the Macros menu.

To use the macro, select the cells you want formatted and choose the macro from the Run Macro submenu of the Macro menu.

To record a similar macro in Microsoft Excel, follow these steps:

1. Select one (or more) cells.
2. Choose Record from the Macro menu. In the dialog box that appears, type a name for the macro and a key you'll use as a shortcut in running the macro. Then click OK.
3. One at a time, choose the formats you want the macro to apply: the number format, the font attributes, the border style, and so on.
4. Choose Stop Recorder from the Macro menu.

To use the macro, select the cells you want formatted and either press the keyboard shortcut you assigned in step 2 or use the Run command (in the Macro menu) to select and run the macro.

A MACRO FOR COPYING FORMATS

Why write separate macros for specific formatting options in Microsoft Excel? There's nearly always a cell right on the spreadsheet that has the format you want. Simply copy the source cell, select the target cell or cells, and execute the following two-line macro:

```
paste_format;=opt/command/f
=PASTE.SPECIAL(4)
=RETURN()
```

MULTIFACETED MACROS

By combining multiple Microsoft Excel command macros, you can run them in rotation with the same keyboard shortcuts. As a simple example, one macro can cyclically change the alignment of the current spreadsheet selection. (See the script in Figure 9-23 on the following page.) Each time you run the macro, it changes to the next alignment in its cycle: Left, Center, Right, and repeat.

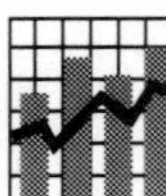

	A
1	**ALIGNMENT**
2	**left**
3	=IF(cycle=0,ALIGNMENT(2),GOTO(center))
4	=SET.VALUE(cycle,cycle+1)
5	=RETURN()
6	**center**
7	=IF(cycle=1,ALIGNMENT(3),GOTO(right))
8	=SET.VALUE(cycle,cycle+1)
9	=RETURN()
10	**right**
11	=ALIGNMENT(4)
12	=SET.VALUE(cycle,0)
13	=RETURN()
14	**cycle**
15	0

FIGURE 9-23. ROTATING MACRO.
Each time you run this macro, for example, by entering its keyboard shortcut, the spreadsheet selection changes to the next alignment in this cycle: Left, Center, Right, and repeat. Cell A15 in the macro keeps track of the cycle. Cell A3 must be named "center," A7 must be named "left," and A11 must be named "right."

OFF-SCREEN SPREADSHEET

Use the following macro in Microsoft Excel to move the frontmost spreadsheet window off the screen:

```
HideTopWindow
=MOVE(-GET.WINDOW(5),0)
=RETURN
```

To move the window back, use this macro:

```
ShowTopWindow
=MOVE(0,0)
=RETURN
```

CUSTOM WINDOW SIZE

To change a Microsoft Excel window to a size you've preset, create a macro that positions the window by using the Full, Size, and Move functions. You can use the macro recorder to have the program create the macro for you, as follows:

1. Choose Record from the Macro menu. In the dialog box that appears, type a name for the macro and a key you'll use as a shortcut in running the macro. Then click OK.

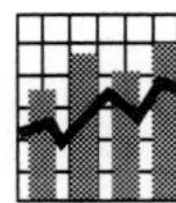

2. Resize and reposition the window as you want the macro to do. The program records your actions as a macro on a new macro sheet.
3. Choose Stop Recorder from the Macro menu.

To use the macro, either press the keyboard shortcut you assigned or use the Run command (in the Macro menu) to select and run the macro.

SAVING ALL

Saving all open Microsoft Excel documents can be quite bothersome. The Close All command helps, but it prompts with dialog box after dialog box asking if you want to save each document. You can use a macro to save every open Microsoft Excel document except the macro itself, without any prompting. To create the macro, use the following procedure:

1. Choose New from the File menu to create a new macro sheet.
2. Transcribe the macro shown in Figure 9-24 into the new macro sheet.
3. Select the whole macro, and choose Define Name from the Formula menu. In the dialog box that appears, name the macro CloseAnd-SaveAll and optionally type a key you'll use as a shortcut in running the macro. Then click OK.
4. Use the Save command (in the File menu) to save the macro sheet under the name CloseAndSaveAll. If you want to save it under a different name (for example, to incorporate this macro into an existing macro sheet), you must also substitute the new name for the name CloseAndSaveAll in the three places where it appears in the macro.

	A	B
1	**CloseAndSaveAll**	by Scott Silverman
2	=MESSAGE(TRUE,"Saving and closing all Excel documents")	Display advisory below menu bar.
3	=ECHO(FALSE)	
4	=IF(NOT(WINDOWS()=""),GOTO(A5),GOTO(A11))	If no windows left, then end macro.
5	=IF(INDEX(WINDOWS(),1)="CloseAndSaveAll",GOTO(A6),GOTO(A8))	If top window is this macro,
6	=ACTIVATE.NEXT()	activate the next window.
7	=IF(INDEX(WINDOWS(),1)="CloseAndSaveAll",GOTO(A11),GOTO(A8))	If top window is this macro, skip it;
8	=SAVE()	otherwise, save it
9	=CLOSE()	and close it.
10	=GOTO(A4)	Go check the next window.
11	=ECHO(TRUE)	
12	=MESSAGE(FALSE)	Erase advisory message.
13	=RETURN()	End of macro.

FIGURE 9-24. CLOSEANDSAVEALL.

This macro closes and saves all open Microsoft Excel documents except the macro itself, without asking whether you want to save each one.

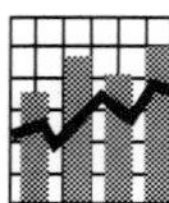

To use the macro, either press the keyboard shortcut you assigned in step 3 or use the Run command (in the Macro menu) to select and run the macro.

EXCEL DIALOG BOX DEFAULTS

In Microsoft Excel, you can create custom dialog boxes by using the DIALOG.BOX macro functions with dialog box definition tables located on the macro sheet. A dialog box definition table specifies each item in a dialog box: static text, edit boxes, buttons, and so on. (See Figure 9-25.) The last column of a definition table specifies the initial, or default, value of each item that can have a user entry or selection. The program replaces those initial values with the entries and selections made when someone actually uses the dialog box and clicks its OK button.

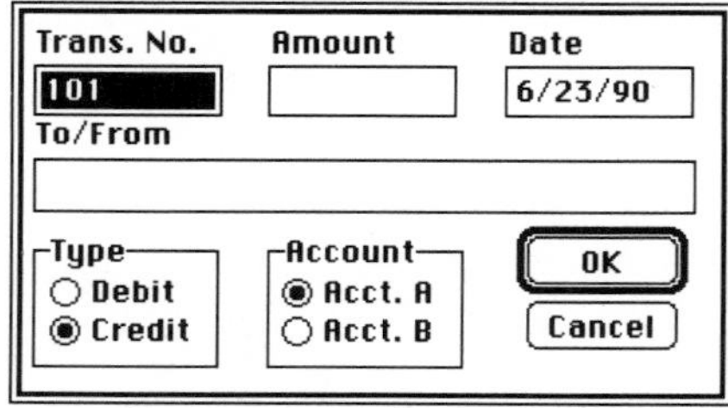

	C	D	E	F	G	H	I	J
1	Description	Item	Horizontal	Vertical	Width	Height	Text	Initial/Result
2								
3	Trans. No. field name	5	1	1			Trans. No.	
4	Trans. No. entry field	7	1	20	80			101
5	Amount field name	5	100	1			Amount	
6	Amount entry field	8	100	20	80			
7	Date field name	5	200	1			Date	
8	Date entry field	8	200	20	80			31585
9	To/From field name	5	1	45			To/From	
10	To/From entry field	6	1	65	280			
11	Type group	11	1	100			Type	2
12	Debit button	12					Debit	
13	Credit button	12					Credit	
14	Account group	11	100	100			Account	1
15	Acct. A button	12					Acct. A	
16	Acct. B button	12					Acct. B	
17	OK	1	210	100			OK	
18	Cancel	2	210	130			Cancel	

FIGURE 9-25. CUSTOM DIALOG AND DEFINITION TABLE.

This custom dialog box (top) serves as an entry form for a database in a Microsoft Excel spreadsheet named Checks. A table (bottom) in the macro sheet that creates the dialog box contains the dialog box specifications, including the default (initial) values shown here.

The macro that displays a dialog box can reset a dialog box to its initial values in one of two ways. It can copy the values from another part of the spreadsheet and paste them into the last column of the dialog box definition table; or it can use the SET.VALUE macro function, as illustrated in Figure 9-26.

	A	B
1	**Initialize and Display Checks Dialog Box**	**Option-Command-d**
2	=ECHO(FALSE)	
3	=SET.VALUE(J4,INDEX(Checks!Database,ROWS(Checks!Database),1)+1)	Set Trans. No. field default
4	=SET.VALUE(J6,"")	
5	=SET.VALUE(J8,TEXT(NOW(),"m/d/yy"))	Set Date field default
6	=SET.VALUE(J10,"")	
7	=SET.VALUE(J11,2)	Set Type field default
8	=SET.VALUE(J14,1)	Set Acct. field default
9	=DIALOG.BOX(D2:J18)	Display dialog box
10	=RETURN()	End of macro

FIGURE 9-26. RESETTING CUSTOM DIALOG BOX DEFAULTS.
This Microsoft Excel macro resets the default (initial) values in the custom dialog box shown in Figure 9-25. The macro function in cell A9 displays the dialog box according to the specifications in the definition table in cells D2:J8.

For general information about custom dialog boxes, see the *Functions and Macros* manual provided with Microsoft Excel.

SELECTING THE WIDEST CELL

To set the width of a column to accommodate the column's widest value, you could take a "brute force" approach. You would scroll up and down looking for a too-wide value, adjust the column width so that the value fits, and repeat until all values fit. In Microsoft Excel, you can instead use the macro shown in Figure 9-27 on the following page to find and select the cell with the longest value in a column of text values.

The key to this macro is in cell A9. The LEN function normally works with one cell, but here it is used on a column of cells—that is, an array. Basically, the MATCH function compares the longest value against each cell in the column using the formula MAX(LEN(SELECTION 0)). It reports the row number of the first cell whose length matches the length of the longest cell. The formula in cell A9 subtracts 1 from that row number to get an offset from the first row. Using that offset, the formula in cell A10 then selects the desired cell.

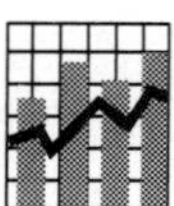

	A	B
1	**SelectWidestCell**	**Option-Command-w**
2	=ECHO(FALSE)	Turn off screen update
3	=COLUMN(SELECTION())	Determine which column
4	=SELECT("R1C")	Select first row from that column
5	=DEFINE.NAME("col")	Call that cell "col"
6	=SELECT.LAST.CELL()	Select last cell on worksheet
7	=ROW(SELECTION())	Determine its row number
8	=SELECT(!col:OFFSET(!col,(A7-1),0))	Select all cells in column
9	=MATCH(MAX(LEN(SELECTION())),LEN(SELECTION()),0)-1	<==COMMAND-ENTER this cell—
10	=RETURN()	uses array processing to find widest cell
11	=SELECT(OFFSET(!col,A9,0))	Select the widest cell
12	=DELETE.NAME("col")	Delete cell name
13	=ECHO(TRUE)	Turn on screen update
14	=RETURN()	End of macro

FIGURE 9-27. FAT FINDER.

You select a cell in your spreadsheet, and this Microsoft Excel macro selects the cell with the most characters from the same column. You can then adjust the column width to fit that longest cell value.

You must hold down the Command key when you either press the Enter key or click the Enter box to enter the formula in cell A9. This tells the program to make the formula an array formula. The macro won't work otherwise.

This macro has some limitations. For one, the longest cell isn't always the widest—because of the variable characters widths of most Macintosh fonts—although it usually is. Also, the macro doesn't work well with columns containing dates or numbers. The LEN function reports the length of dates and numbers in their internal format, which is usually different from their displayed format. For example, dates always have a length of 5 characters, and all numbers except whole numbers have a length of 15 characters.

IMPORTING AND EXPORTING

Microsoft Excel

TAKING PICTURES

You can copy Microsoft Excel spreadsheets and charts as pictures, with the font, style, formatting, and display or printing options intact. Pressing the Shift key as you pull down the Edit menu changes the Copy command to a Copy Picture command. (See Figure 9-28.) The Copy Picture command places on the clipboard a picture of the selected part of the spreadsheet or a picture of the chart in the active window. The program gives you a choice of copying the picture exactly as it appears on the screen or as it would appear if printed. After pasting, you can resize the picture with good results.

Edit
Can't Undo ⌘Z
Repeat Close ⌘Y
Cut ⌘X
Copy Picture...
Paste ⌘V
Clear... ⌘B
Paste Special...
Paste Link
Delete... ⌘K
Insert... ⌘I
Fill Left
Fill Up

FIGURE 9-28. COPY PICTURE COMMAND.
Press the Shift key to change Microsoft Excel's Copy command to a Copy Picture command, which puts selected cells on the Clipboard as a picture.

All of the commands on the Format menu affect both the displayed and the printed appearance of the picture. The Display command (in the Options menu) also affects the displayed and printed appearance of a spreadsheet. However, the Page Setup command (in the File menu), not the Display command, controls whether grid lines and row and column numbers are printed. You can check the results without leaving Microsoft Excel by choosing Show Clipboard from the Window menu.

CREATING A TABLE

To base a table in a word processing program on values of cells in a spreadsheet, follow these steps:

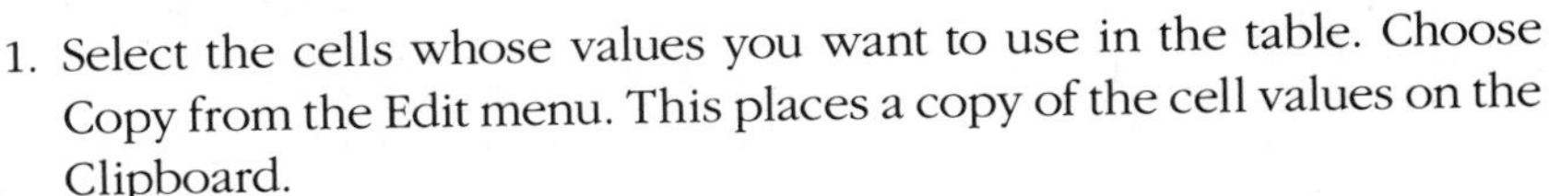

1. Select the cells whose values you want to use in the table. Choose Copy from the Edit menu. This places a copy of the cell values on the Clipboard.
2. Switch to the word processing program, open the document in which you want the table to appear (or create a new document), and choose Paste from the Edit menu. This inserts a copy of the cell values from the spreadsheet into the document as text. The values are not aligned in columns, but they are separated by invisible tab characters.

3. Align the columns of the table by setting tabs at appropriate places. (Check your word processor's manual for instructions on setting tabs.) Generally, you will use a left-alignment tab to align text and a decimal-alignment tab to align numbers. You can also change the font, size, and style of any part of the text.

Trapeze

LOCKING DOWN AN IMPORTED BACKGROUND

You can avoid trouble when manipulating blocks located on top of an imported background in Trapeze by locking down the background. This makes it unselectable and unmovable. Follow these steps:

1. Select the block that contains the background. If it's not already behind the other blocks, use the Send To Back command (in the Block menu) to put it there.
2. Set the Locked option by using the Attributes command (in the Format menu).
3. Activate all locks on the spreadsheet by setting the Locked option of the Setup command (in the Sheet menu).

Cricket Graph

IMPORTING DATA TO CRICKET GRAPH

How can you read data into Cricket Graph from a spreadsheet? In the Finder, put the spreadsheet document and the Cricket Graph program in the same folder or on the desktop. Select both (by pressing the Shift key while clicking each, for example) and choose Open from the Finder's File menu. Cricket Graph opens and reads the spreadsheet data. The imported spreadsheet data is formatted as alphanumeric text. Before you can plot it, you must select the column you want plotted as the *y*-axis and use the Column Format command (in the Data menu) to give it one of the numeric formats.

Cricket Graph can import data that has been saved in plain text format or in SYLK format by a spreadsheet program.

Chapter 10

INFORMATION MANAGEMENT

The Macintosh, like all other computers, is great at storing and retrieving organized information. Managing the information is up to you, with the help of three types of programs: HyperCard, flat-file managers such as FileMaker, and relational databases such as 4th Dimension. In this chapter, you'll find tips on the following information-management topics:

- Environment
- Manipulating information
- Searching and sorting
- Design
- Scripting and programming

The HyperCard tips in this chapter apply to versions 2.0 and later. Many also work with earlier versions with little or no modification.

ENVIRONMENT

MESSAGE WINDOW READY

HyperCard

When you want to paste into the HyperCard message window or type something into it without clicking a text insertion point first, press the Delete key (the Backspace key on a Mac Plus). This places the insertion point in the window and deletes any message residing there.

HIDING THE POINTER

HyperCard

If you want to hide the pointer while using HyperCard's browse tool, press the slash (/), asterisk (*), plus (+), or hyphen (-) key on the numeric keypad. All regular keys have the same effect if the Blind Typing option is set on the User Preferences card of the Home stack. But for the four keys mentioned, HyperCard always acts as if Blind Typing were set.

HyperCard

SWITCHING PROGRAMS

When using HyperCard with MultiFinder, you can switch to another open application program by using the doMenu command from the message window or within a script. For example, *doMenu MacDraw* switches to MacDraw, assuming MacDraw is already open. (If not, HyperCard displays an alert saying it can't find the menu item.) This procedure works because the doMenu command has the effect of choosing a menu item, and the names of open programs appear in the Apple menu. (This tip might not work with System 7.)

Panorama

AUTO-SCROLL SUBSTITUTE

Panorama doesn't scroll automatically if you try to drag or resize an object past the boundary of a forms window in graphics mode. You can lessen the likelihood of bumping into the window boundaries by working in a reduced view. To reduce the view, select the magnifying glass tool, press the Spacebar, and click. All the tools work in reduced views. It's also possible to resize or to place an object beyond the window boundaries by using the Dimensions command (in the Edit menu).

To return the view to actual size, select the magnifying glass tool, press the Command key, and click.

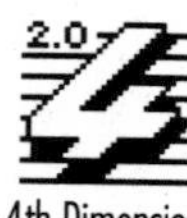

4th Dimension

CHOOSING FILES OR LAYOUTS

In the User environment in 4th Dimension, pressing Command-Spacebar alternately shows and hides the List Of Files window. Figure 10-1 shows a sample List Of Files window. From this window you can choose which file you want to view. You can also specify which layout is the Input layout and which is the Output layout for any file.

Employees: 60 of 60

First Name	Last Name	Start Date	Sal	
Tom	Johnson	1/2/80		
Alice	Bentley	3/6/87		
Biff	Davis	1/2/80		
Shirley	Ransome	1/11/80		
Dennis	Hanson	1/14/80		
Lydia	Vernon	1/15/80		
Andy	Venable	1/15/80		
Jim	Borrell	1/22/80		
Bryan	Pfaff	1/22/80		
Nancy	Heizer	1/23/80		
Kathy	Forbes	1/28/80		
Garth	Hammons	2/6/80		
Mary	Smith	2/7/80	26500	Engineer
Frederic	Bell	2/14/80	25200	Director
John	Martin	4/25/83	56144	Supervisor
Shirley	Nalevanko	2/21/80	41050	Designer
Marlys	Wilson	2/27/80	36500	Supervisor
George	Lyle	2/28/80	47900	Salesperson

List of files

I O Employees

I O Departments

FIGURE 10-1. FILE LIST.

The small List Of Files window is always open in 4th Dimension, but it is usually hidden behind the current document window. To bring it to the front, press Command-Spacebar.

INITIAL ENVIRONMENT

4th Dimension opens a database in the Design environment unless you designate otherwise. You can easily change the initial environment by using the Preferences command (in the File menu) while in the Design environment. This setting is stored separately for each database, so it can be different for each database that you create.

FAST CLEANUP

To quickly close all the open windows in the 4th Dimension Design environment, press the Option key and then click the close box of the front window.

MEMORY SHORTAGE

If you get the message "Not enough memory to use the painting tools" when you try to paint on a card or you get the message "Can't open script editor" when you try to edit a script, you need to make more memory available to HyperCard.

One or more of the following courses of action might help:

- Quit HyperCard, select the HyperCard program icon, and choose Get Info from the Finder's File menu. In the information window, you can allocate more memory to HyperCard by increasing the Application Memory Size setting. Try increasing in 50-KB increments until you are able to use the paint tools and edit scripts. This is relevant only if MultiFinder is active.
- Remove startup documents (INITs) from your System Folder. Also remove any control panels (CDEVs) whose icons appear on the screen during startup. Then restart your Mac.
- Restart with MultiFinder inactive. You can deactivate MultiFinder by using the Finder's Set Startup command (in the Special menu). (With System 7, you can't deactivate MultiFinder.)
- Turn off the RAM Cache option in the General Control Panel. HyperCard doesn't use it. (You can't turn off the RAM Cache option in System 7.)
- Install more RAM in your Macintosh.

HyperCard

CHILDPROOFING

Altering one line in the stack script of your Home stack can protect your HyperCard stacks from accidental changes by others (for example, your 9-year-old son). Find the line that begins as follows:

```
set the userLevel to cd fld "User Level" of cd user
Preferences" -- hidden field
```

Replace the entire line with this:

```
ask "Password?" with "-----"
if it is "myPassword"
then set the userLevel to cd fld "User Level" ¬
of cd "User Preferences" -- hidden field
else set userLevel to 1
```

After you have done this, the script asks for a password at startup. Entering the correct password selects the user level on the User Preferences card; entering the wrong password selects the browse level. This keeps newcomers out of trouble, but lets experienced users change the user level.

MANIPULATING INFORMATION

KEYBOARD BROWSING

How can you move forward and backward one record at a time in a FileMaker database without using the mouse? Press Command-Tab to move forward and Command-Shift-Tab to go backward.

SHOWING CARDS FOREVER

The HyperTalk command Show All Cards shows each card in the stack one time. However, the Show Cards command continues to show the cards in the stack forever—or until the mouse button is clicked. To see this work, try typing both commands, one at a time, in the message window.

EDITING CALCULATED TEXT

In FileMaker, you can edit a text field whose value has been calculated by a formula. Choose Define from the Select menu, and change the field type for the field from Calculation to Text. The field retains its calculated value as it becomes a text field, and you can now edit the value. The formula previously used to calculate the value is lost.

CALCULATED QUESTION MARK

When browsing through records in FileMaker, you might find that some records have a question mark in numeric fields, as shown in Figure 10-2 on the following page. This happens when a field is not large enough to display a formatted number. A question mark signifies a number that has overrun the field. Be sure that you've entered the number correctly. If you did, use the Layout command (in the Select menu) to edit the layout. Widen the field by selecting the pointer tool (the arrow) and dragging the black square handle at the lower right corner of the field until the number fits.

COPYING SELECTED INFORMATION

You can omit field names when copying information from a Microsoft Works database document to a Works word processing document. Use the Copy command (in the Edit menu) as you normally would, but press the Option key while choosing Paste from the Edit menu in the word processing document.

Orders/Invoices

The Spokesman — ORDER FORM

12 Bearing Street Wheeling, W. VA 26055 817/245-7854

Order # 0-101 **Customer #** 235PETJ **PO #** 99887 **Date** 3/17/91

SOLD TO:
John W. Petersen
4455 W. Hammerslag Road
Worchester WV 26345
Phone # 817/359-4909 x899

SHIP TO:
John Petersen, Jr.
890 Beachtree Ct. #55
Redding MA 02155
Ship Via UPS

Bank Code VISA **Card #** 344-578-22346 **Card Expiration** 5/31/89

Qty	Item No.	Description	Unit Cost	% Tax	Tax	Amount
1	LSV21	Leather Seat	?	6.5	?	?
2	AWW27	27" Alloy Wheel	42.00	6.5	5.46	89.46
1	HTM11b	Handlebar Tape, black	3.75	6.5	0.24	3.99
2	AFM27	Alloy Forks—27" wheel	35.95	6.5	4.67	76.57

Subtotal ? **Total Tax** ? **Total Shipping** 12.50 **Total Amt** $1065166.55

Browse

FIGURE 10-2. QUESTIONABLE NUMBERS.
A question mark in a FileMaker field means the field isn't large enough to display a formatted number.

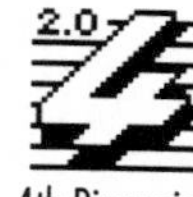

WIDESPREAD CHANGES

When you're working in the User environment in 4th Dimension, you can apply a change to all currently selected records by using the Apply Formula command (in the Enter menu). Choosing that command brings up the formula editor. Create a formula that will effect the change you want. For example, the following formula converts the contents of the State field to uppercase letters:

```
State:= Uppercase (State)
```

If you think you might want to reuse your formula or one like it, click the Save button to save it on disk. To retrieve a saved formula, click the Load button. Edit the formula as necessary, and then click the OK button to apply the formula to the selected records.

GLOBAL CHANGE

In FileMaker, you can quickly change the contents of a field to contain a single new value in every record, or you can make the change only in selected records. First find the records to be affected. Choose Find All from the Select menu if you want to change all records, or choose Find from the Select menu to extract some of the records. Then go to the first record and enter the new value in the field to be changed. While the flashing text insertion point is still in that field (or while the field is selected), choose Replace from the Edit menu to propagate the new value through all currently found records.

FRACTIONAL INPUT AND OUTPUT

Sometimes you'll want to allow input of fractions, such as ½ or 1¼, and to produce them as output. For instance, a cutting order for a carpenter who uses a tape measure would be most convenient if the cutting sizes were expressed in fractions.

To accomplish this in FileMaker, you need three fields: PP is a text field used for input of fractions and mixed numbers. RR is a calculation field that converts PP to a decimal value for use in any calculations involving other fields. SS is another calculation field that converts RR to a mixed fraction. Define field RR as follows:

```
if(position(PP,"/",1)=0,TextToNum(PP),if(position(PP," ",1)=0,0,
TextToNum(left(PP,position(PP," ",1)-1)))+TextToNum(middle(PP,
position(PP," ",1)+1,position(PP,"/",1)-position(PP," ",1)-1))
/TextToNum(right(PP,length(PP)-position(PP,"/",1))))
```

The following definition of SS converts the decimal value in field RR to the nearest sixteenth:

```
if(RR=int(RR),RR,if(int(RR)=0,"",NumToText(int(RR))&" ")
&if(2*RR=int(2*RR),NumToText(2*(RR-int(RR)))&"/2",
if(4*RR=int(4*RR),NumToText( 4*(RR-int(RR)))&"/4",
if(8*RR=int(8*RR),NumToText(8*(RR-int(RR)))&"/8",
NumToText(int(16*(RR-int(RR)))&"/16")))))
```

When entering the formula for field SS, select the Text option for the result of the calculation. Also, do not type any extra blank spaces in these long formulas. FileMaker allows only 256 characters per formula, and spaces count toward that limit.

You could make these formulas simpler by breaking them into subcalculations. For instance, you could define a field AA = position(PP,"/",1) and use AA in the formula for RR. However, keeping track of intermediate calculations is more confusing than dealing with the two messy calculations defined here. By the way, you can reduce the character count in these formulas by using single-letter field names instead of PP, RR, and SS.

HyperCard

NUMBER, PLEASE

The address stack and the phone dialer stack provided with HyperCard send Touch Tone dial tones through the Mac's speaker. On most phones, you can have the Mac dial the number simply by holding the mouthpiece of the telephone handset close to the Mac's speaker while HyperCard plays the dialing tones.

The speaker is on the left side of a Mac Plus; the lower front of a Mac SE or SE/30; the lower right front of a Mac II, IIx, or IIfx; and the front of a Mac IIcx or IIci. However, some phones have difficulty picking up sounds from the Mac's speaker. If your phone ends up accidentally dialing the wrong party—for example, an irritable day-sleeper instead of your mother—you can install a HyperDialer between your telephone and its handset and plug it into the Mac sound port. (See the next tip, "Dialer and Speaker.") Or you can plug an amplified speaker, such as the type made for a Sony Walkman, into the Mac.

HyperCard

DIALER AND SPEAKER

DataDesk International's HyperDialer is a reasonably inexpensive and convenient accessory for using HyperCard's telephone dialing capacity. However, connecting it to your Mac's speaker port reroutes all Mac sounds through HyperDialer's tiny, nasal-sounding built-in speaker, and the better sound of the Mac's internal speaker is completely lost.

Plugging anything into the Mac speaker port cuts out the internal speaker unless you open the Mac and rewire the speaker port. If you prefer, you can instead buy a small adapter that doubles the number of speaker port jacks (Radio Shack catalog number 274-310); the cost is less than $2. This adapter lets you attach both a HyperDialer and a small external speaker or a stereo system for a sound that is even better than that of the internal speaker. To silence the HyperDialer's speaker, you must open it and cut or

unsolder either wire from the speaker. The HyperDialer is glued shut, but you can gently pry off the bottom and still close it.

Incidentally, the two-way port adapter is also useful for feeding the Mac's monaural audio output into both the left and right channels of a stereo amplifier.

REMOVING DUPLICATE ADDRESSES

Panorama

You can remove duplicate addresses from a mailing list that you maintain as a Panorama database by using five menu commands. With the database file open, choose Select All from the Search menu to be sure that all records are visible. Then select any cell of the field that you do not want to contain duplicates. For example, you would click your Street Address field if you wanted to eliminate all records having duplicate street addresses. Next, group duplicate records by choosing Sort Up from the Sort menu, and eliminate the duplicates by choosing Unpropagate from the Math menu. Now you can eliminate the duplicate records. Choose Select from the Search menu and, in the data input window immediately below the menu bar, click the ≠ option and press the Return key without typing anything else. Finally, choose Remove Unselected from the Search menu. You can record the procedure as a Panorama macro (as described in the Panorama manual) if you need to use it often.

Looking in only one field might falsely identify unique records as duplicates. A mailing list might contain more than one person at the same address, for example. Determining bona fide duplicates might involve examining more than one field. To facilitate this, make a new text field by adding a new line to the database's design sheet and clicking the New Generation icon (the check mark) in the design window. In any cell of the new field, enter an equation (using the Equation command in the Math menu) that combines all the fields you want to use as criteria. The following example combines six fields for use as a single criterion:

```
Name+Company+Address+City+State+Zip
```

Use your new combination field as the criterion field (by clicking it) in the procedure outlined in the previous paragraph.

COPYING SPECIFIC RECORDS

You can easily copy a group of records from one file to a new file even though Filemaker's Import From command (in the File menu) doesn't let you specify which records you want to import. Follow these steps:

1. Use the Save A Copy command (in the File menu) to make a clone of the source file with no records.
2. In the source file, use the Find command (in the Select menu) to extract the records you want to copy.
3. Open the clone file, and use the Input From command to copy the found records from the original file.

SEARCHING AND SORTING

EASY SEARCH CRITERIA

When finding records in a FileMaker II database, you can specify values you want to search for by selecting them from a scrollable list instead of typing them. Choose Find from the Select menu, and click a field to be searched. To display a list of values used in that field, choose View Index from the Edit menu. Double-click the value you want; FileMaker then pastes it into the search criterion.

FINDING UNRELATED RECORDS, PART 1

How can you find a group of records that have nothing in common? Identify members of the group by tagging them with a common value in a new field. First create a text field with a name such as Group. Then scroll through your database and enter *X* (or some other identifying character) into the new Group field of each record that you want to tag as part of the group. After you've tagged all records that are part of the group, you can find them easily.

FINDING UNRELATED RECORDS, PART 2

You can find a few unrelated records in FileMaker by specifying separate criteria for each record you want found. Each record must contain a value that is not present in any of the records you don't want to find. Follow these steps:

1. Choose Find from the Select menu. In the dialog box that appears, enter criteria that identify one or more of the records you want found.
2. Choose New Request from the Edit menu and enter criteria that identify another record you want found. Repeat this step until you have entered requests for all records you want found.
3. Click the Find button to find the records that match your requests.

CAN'T FIND DATES?

When you try to find dates within a given range in FileMaker, do you sometimes get the correct day and month but the wrong year? The field was probably not defined as a date field. To change it, choose Define from the Select menu, and change the field to a date field.

KEEPING RECORDS SORTED

New records that you add to a sorted FileMaker database are put at the end of the file in the order of entry. Sorting the file lets you view all records in order, but it doesn't actually move the new records from the end of the file. Thus, the records return to their original sequence if you use the Find command, forcing you to re-sort. There is, however, a way to make a sorted sequence permanent (at least until you add more new records). After sorting the records into the permanent order you want them, use the Save A Copy command (in the File menu) to make a clone of the file with no records. Open the clone and use the Input From command (in the File menu) to import the records—in sorted order—from the original file. Repeat this procedure as needed to keep the file permanently sorted.

DESIGN

SIMPLE LAYOUT SWITCHING

The hard way to switch layouts in FileMaker II is to use the Layout command (in the Select menu). You can simplify layout switching by installing a menu item on the Custom menu for each layout you use. First use the Layout command to switch to a layout you want installed. When you can see the layout on the screen, choose Scripts from the Custom menu. In the dialog box that appears, press the New button, type the name under which you want the layout listed in the Custom menu, and set the Switch To The

Layout and the Include In Menu options, as shown in Figure 10-3. Generally, those are the only options you'll want to set. Click OK, and FileMaker installs the item on the Custom menu.

Script Name
General View

When performing this script, automatically:
☒ Switch to the Layout
☐ Restore the Page Setup
☐ Restore the Input Order & Input from a file
☐ Find: ○ Restore the Find Requests & Find
◉ Find All
☐ Sort: ○ Restore the Sort Order & Sort
◉ Unsort
☐ Preview
☐ Restore the Output Order & Output to a file
☐ Print
☐ Switch back to the original layout
☐ Perform another script
☒ Include in menu OK Cancel

FIGURE 10-3. LAYOUT SWITCH SCRIPT.
To install a command on FileMaker's Custom menu that allows you to switch to a layout, select the options shown here for the Scripts command.

QUICK FONT SWITCHING

Both FileMaker and 4th Dimension let you create multiple layouts. You can use this capability to quickly switch fonts for optimum on-screen viewing or for printing on various printers. Fonts with city names such as Geneva and New York look better on the screen than when printed on a LaserWriter, whereas fonts such as Helvetica and Times look lumpy on the screen but look great when printed. Start by creating a layout for the screen. When you finish it, choose Select All from the Edit menu to select all elements of the layout. Copy the selected elements, create a new blank layout, and paste. All the elements from the original layout appear in the second layout, selected and ready to have their fonts changed. After changing the fonts, you might need to adjust spacing slightly because some fonts are more compact than others.

The last step is to set the correct page size for the printer that will print the new layout. Open the Chooser, select the printer, and close the Chooser.

Then switch back to the database program, choose Page Setup from the File menu, and click its OK button. The page boundaries in the new layout now show the area that will print.

FONT FREEDOM

HyperCard

If you are preparing a HyperCard stack for wide distribution, you might think that you can use only the four system fonts (Geneva 9, Geneva 12, Chicago 12, and Monaco 9) because you don't know what other fonts the end user will have installed in his or her system. But you can use any font you want in HyperCard fields. Simply install a copy of the font in your HyperCard stack. Then anyone who views that stack will see the font properly displayed. Note, however, that installing fonts will increase the size of your stack—sometimes substantially.

You can install fonts in many stacks by using the Font/DA Mover program. Normally, that program lets you open only System files and font files. However, if you press the Option key when you click the program's Open button, you'll be able to open and install fonts in stacks (as well as in other documents and programs). The Font/DA Mover will not open stacks or other documents unless they already contain fonts or other resources. If there are no fonts or other resources in the stack, Font/DA Mover advises you that the file you're trying to open could be damaged or in use. In that case, you can use the ResEdit program to copy fonts.

MORE FONT FREEDOM

HyperCard

In HyperCard, when you type text in the card picture or background picture, you can use any available font without worrying whether users of your stack have it installed. Fonts you use when typing text in the card picture or background picture have to be installed only when you create the picture. When you use the text tool from the Tools menu, text in the selected font becomes part of the picture you're creating. The stack user doesn't need to have the fonts installed to see text that you have painted on the background or card.

HyperCard

PLAIN STYLE SHORTCUT

You can quickly change to plain text from any stylized text in HyperCard by clicking the word Style in the Text Style dialog box. To get that dialog box, choose Text Style from the Edit menu (or press Command-T).

HyperCard

REORDERING FIELDS OR BUTTONS

To send a HyperCard field or button behind all other fields and buttons in the same layer (card or background) and thereby set its number to 1, select the object and press Command-Shift-hyphen. To bring a field or button to the front of all other fields and buttons in the same layer and thereby give it the highest number of all similar objects, select the object and press Command-Shift-plus. With these shortcuts, you can reorder objects more easily than with the Bring Closer and Send Farther menu commands.

HyperCard

COPYING PATTERNS

HyperCard offers two ways to copy custom patterns created by using the Edit Pattern command on the Options menu. You can copy the whole pattern palette to a new stack, or you can copy patterns individually. To copy the whole pattern palette, select the Copy Current Background option when you use the New Stack command (in the File menu). If that option is not selected, the new stack gets the standard pattern palette.

To copy individual patterns to another stack, go to the stack that contains the patterns you want to copy, and draw samples of them on one card. Copy the samples, go to the stack where you want the patterns to be copied, and paste. Tear off the pattern palette. Decide which patterns in the palette you want to replace with the new ones. Double-click a pattern you've decided to replace, bringing up the pattern-editing dialog box. Click one of the sample patterns outside the dialog box to pick it up, and then click OK. Repeat the steps in this paragraph for each pattern you want to pick up. Using the script in Figure 10-4 relieves some of the tedium.

```
on mouseUp
  set cursor to 4 -- watch
  doMenu, "New Card"
  --first, draw samples of all patterns in this stack
  choose rectangle tool
  set filled to true
  repeat with n = 1 to 40
    set pattern to n
    put ((n-1) div 10) * 20 + 90 into h
    put ((n-1) mod 10) * 20 + 40 into v
    drag from h,v to h + 20, v + 20
  end repeat
  --second, copy the samples
  choose select tool
  drag from 90,40 to 170,240
  doMenu "Copy Picture"
  doMenu "Delete Card"
  --third, paste into the destination stack
  go to "the destination stack"
  if the result is empty then
    doMenu "New Card"
    doMenu "Paste Picture"
    --fourth, pick up patterns one at a time
    show pattern window at 14, 75
    put "Click a sample to replace this pattern, and then
    click OK"
    repeat with n = 1 to 40
      hide message
      show message at 20, 290
      set pattern to n
      doMenu "Edit Pattern..."
    end repeat
    doMenu "Delete Card"
  end if
  choose browse tool
end mouseUp
```

FIGURE 10-4. PATTERN MENU COPIER.
This button script helps you copy the patterns from the current stack's pattern palette to the pattern palette of any other stack.

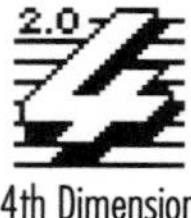
4th Dimension

OBJECT BORDERS

It's easy to create borders around one or more objects in a 4th Dimension layout. With the layout open in the layout editor, select an object or a group of objects and press Command-1 to draw a rectangular border that touches the edge of the selected object or objects. Pressing Command-2 creates a border 1 pixel away from the edge of the selected object, Command-3 creates a border 2 pixels away, and so on. (See Figure 10-5.) The border is drawn with 1-pixel black lines and no fill, but you can change these attributes by using commands in the Object menu. If you press these key combinations multiple times, you create nested borders.

FIGURE 10-5. INSTANT BORDERS.
When editing a 4th Dimension layout, you can draw a border around selected objects by pressing a Command-key combination. These borders were created by pressing Command-9, changing the line width, and then pressing Command-3.

FileMaker

PAGE BORDER

In FileMaker, you can extend a border to the edges of the printable area of the page without sacrificing the number of records you can print. You do this by creating what is essentially a dummy sub-summary. Choose Layout from the Select menu. Drag a new part from the part tool onto the layout.

In the dialog box that appears, select a field on which you never intend to sort for the sub-summary. Drag the sub-summary line down to or beyond the bottom of the page boundary. Draw a big border rectangle for the page, being sure that the top line is located in a Header part. Use the Preview command (in the File menu) to see how the rectangle fits on the page, and adjust the rectangle's size and location as needed.

GRID DEFEAT

To turn off the invisible grid temporarily while editing a FileMaker layout, press the Command key as you drag an object. When you release the Command key, FileMaker reactivates the invisible grid.

SLIDING STOPPED

If some fields you've set to slide to the left in FileMaker stay put, check their alignment with the fields that are sliding. The tops of the fields must line up perfectly or they won't slide as you expect. In FileMaker Pro, use the Alignment command to align currently selected objects. In FileMaker II, use the T-Squares command (in the Gadgets menu). When you drag a field or other object near a T-Square line, the object snaps to the magnetic attraction of the T-Square.

FAKING HIDDEN COLUMNS

You can keep other people from seeing the contents of columns on a Panorama data sheet (well, almost—a telltale, 1-pixel column of seemingly random dots will still be visible) even though you can't actually hide the columns. Follow these steps:

1. Open the design sheet and use the Cut Line and Paste Line tools to move the columns you want concealed to the end.
2. Still in the design sheet, enter *0* as the Width option for all the columns you want concealed.
3. Create a new macro that selects the first column of the next record. The macro script needs to contain only two commands:

```
Column field name
DownRecord
```

4. Return to the design sheet and enter the name of the macro you just created as the Equation option for the last normal-width column.
5. When you finish making changes to the design sheet, use the New Generation tool to have the changes take effect in the data sheet.

RELATIVE LOCATION

How can you specify an object's location relative to the upper left corner of a Panorama layout? Choose Dimensions from the Edit menu, and prefix the upper right and lower left dimension values with a plus sign.

DEALING WITH DOLLARS

If FileMaker's Format Number command (in the Format menu) seems to have no effect—the dollar sign, percent symbol, commas, and so on are missing—you're probably trying to format a text field. FileMaker lets you apply number formats to text fields, but it ignores them. Use the Define command (in the Select menu) to change the field to a numeric field.

COMPLEX LOOKUPS

Although the lookup feature in FileMaker II is used mostly for tasks such as retrieving addresses from a client list for invoices, it can also be used for more complex tasks. Federal withholding tax on a payroll check, for instance, is based on three factors: gross pay, number of deductions, and marital status. These three factors can be combined in one calculation field, which can be used as a lookup index for a federal withholding tax table. The following formula for the calculation field works for any pay amount from $10 through $999.99 and any number of deductions from 0 through 9:

```
if (Gross Pay < 100,Marital Status & No. of deductions & 0
& int (Gross Pay),Marital Status & No. of deductions & int
(Gross Pay))
```

This formula calculates a five-digit index number. The first of the five digits is marital status (1 for single, 2 for married), the next digit is the number of deductions (0 through 9), and the last three digits are the gross pay in even dollars. If the gross pay is less than $100, the formula prefixes it with a 0 so that the resulting amount will have three digits. The Gross Pay field is calculated from the number of hours, which is entered manually, and the hourly pay rate, which FileMaker II looks up in the appropriate employee record. FileMaker II also looks up the Marital Status and No. of deductions fields in that record. It looks up everything and calculates the result as soon as you enter an employee number and a number of hours worked. The index numbers do not have to be displayed.

After it calculates the five-digit index, FileMaker II looks up the index in a file that contains a list of five-digit numbers and corresponding dollar amounts for withholding tax. If FileMaker II can't find an exact match for the index in the table, it uses the next smaller value. For example, the number 11238 (single, one deduction, and $238) isn't in the table, so FileMaker uses 11230. Figure 10-6 shows sample records from the three files involved.

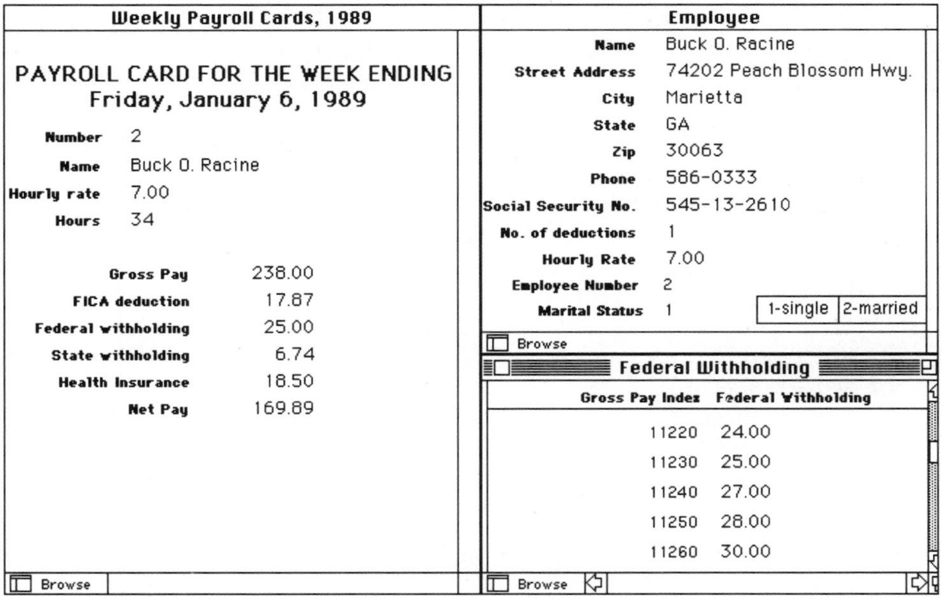

Weekly Payroll Cards, 1989

PAYROLL CARD FOR THE WEEK ENDING
Friday, January 6, 1989

Number	2
Name	Buck O. Racine
Hourly rate	7.00
Hours	34

Gross Pay	238.00
FICA deduction	17.87
Federal withholding	25.00
State withholding	6.74
Health Insurance	18.50
Net Pay	169.89

Browse

Employee

Name	Buck O. Racine
Street Address	74202 Peach Blossom Hwy.
City	Marietta
State	GA
Zip	30063
Phone	586-0333
Social Security No.	545-13-2610
No. of deductions	1
Hourly Rate	7.00
Employee Number	2
Marital Status	1

1-single 2-married

Browse

Federal Withholding

Gross Pay Index	Federal Withholding
11220	24.00
11230	25.00
11240	27.00
11250	28.00
11260	30.00

Browse

FIGURE 10-6. TRIPLE-INDEX LOOKUP.

FileMaker II can look up a value based on a compound index. Here, a formula in an undisplayed field of the Weekly Payroll Cards, 1989 file (left window) combines the marital status, number of deductions, and gross pay to form a triple index.

COMPUTING INCIDENTAL CHARGES

If you use FileMaker for invoices or purchase orders, you might want to list incidental charges such as sales tax and shipping in the same repeating field as deliverable items. (See Figure 10-7.) For aesthetic reasons, don't enter a quantity of 1 for an incidental charge. (Whoever heard of 1 sales tax?) If you leave the quantity blank, however, FileMaker treats it as 0 and computes the total cost of the "item" as 0. (The total cost equals quantity times unit cost.) To avoid the problem, use the following formula to calculate total cost:

```
IF(Item="","",IF(Quantity="",Unit Cost,Quantity*Unit Cost))
```

The formula stipulates that nothing ("") be put in the Total Cost field if there is nothing in the Item field. If there is something in the Item field but nothing in the Quantity field, then the Total Cost field equals the Unit Cost field. If the Quantity field is not empty, then the Total Cost equals the Quantity times the Unit Cost.

Purchase Orders

Order Number: 1001
Deliver To: Coral Springs Technologies
Department: Purchasing
Date Wanted: 12/12/90

Quantity	Item	Unit Cost	Total Cost
2	Overhead Projector	$142.00	$284.00
2	16mm Projector	$254.00	$508.00
4	Compact Disc Player	$158.36	$633.44
	Shipping	$30.00	$30.00
	Tax	$10.00	$10.00
		Total	$1465.44

Browse

FIGURE 10-7. INCIDENTALLY...

If you list tax, shipping, and other incidental charges along with items ordered but you don't enter a quantity for those charges, you need a special formula to compute the total cost.

FIELD NAME REMINDER

When designing a HyperCard stack, it's easy to forget field names or lose track of hidden fields. To refresh your memory, simply choose Print Field from the File menu. (In versions 1.2.5 and earlier, choose Print Report from the File menu.) The field-selection scroll box lists the names of all fields in the current background. Click Cancel after you finish reviewing the names.

NAMES, NOT NUMBERS

Do not assign a number as the name of a button or a field in HyperCard. If you do, when you refer to that button or field by name, HyperCard will look for a button or field whose number is the same as the numeric name. For example, the command Get Field "1492" causes the program to attempt to retrieve the contents of field number 1492, not the field whose name is "1492."

QUICK INFO

In HyperCard 2.0, you can open the stack script, background script, or card script strictly from the keyboard. Press Command-Shift-S for the stack script, Command-Shift-B for the background script, or Command-Shift-C for the card script.

You can also use the keyboard to open the stack info dialog box, background info dialog box, or card info dialog box. Press the S key and then press Return for the stack info, press B and then press Return for the background info, or press C and then press Return for the card info. These three shortcuts won't work unless either the Blind Typing option is set in the Preferences card of the Home stack or the message window is visible.

4-D INVISIBLE POP-UP

You can create an invisible pop-up menu in 4th Dimension. This is useful for placing a pop-up over a graphic so that the menu appears to pop up from the graphic, as shown in Figure 10-8 on the following page. Simply type an exclamation point into the text format area of the object definition dialog box. (See Figure 10-9 on the page after next.)

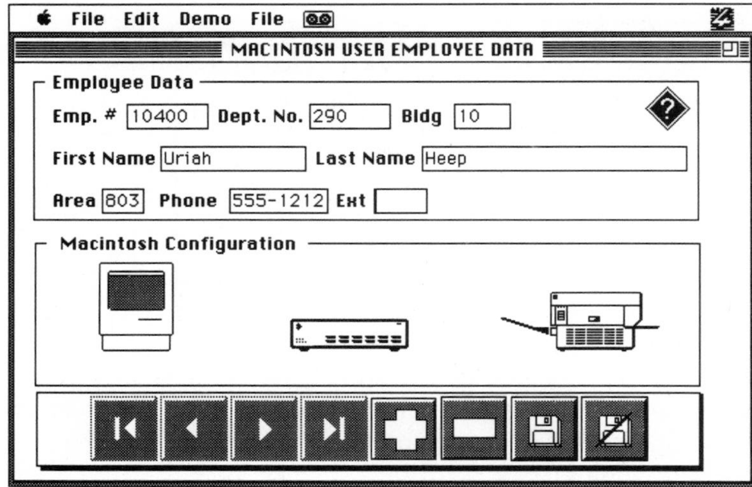

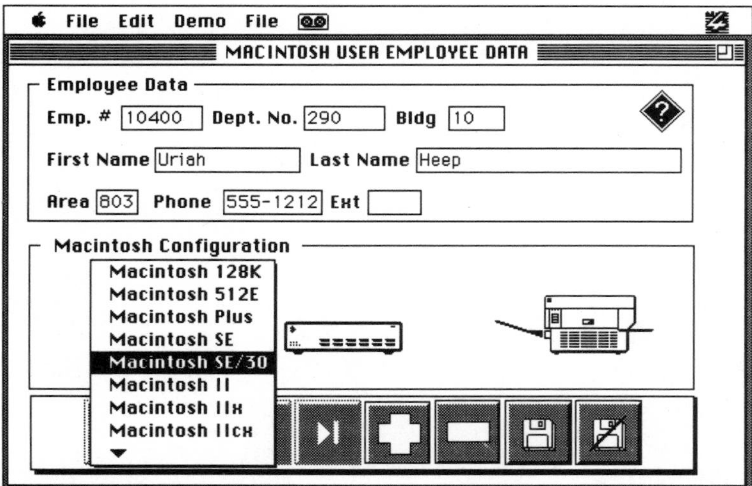

FIGURE 10-8. GRAPHIC POP-UP.

The Macintosh Configuration section of this 4th Dimension data-entry layout contains an invisible pop-up menu behind each of the three pictures—the Mac, the hard disk, and the printer (top). Clicking one of these pictures pops up a corresponding list of model names from which to choose (bottom). In addition, clicking the large question mark in the upper right corner reveals a list of help topics.

Definition
Name: HelpPopUp
Type: Pop-up Menu
Not used. Key...
!
Data Entry
Entry filter:
Choices List...
Required List...
Excluded List...
Text with scroll bar
Minimum:
Maximum:
Default:
Print variable frame
Script... Only if modified
Cancel
OK

FIGURE 10-9. INVISIBLE POP-UP DEFINITION.

Create an invisible pop-up menu in the 4th Dimension Object Definition dialog box by typing an exclamation point in the area labeled Not Used.

LASERWRITER CUSTOM PAPER

FileMaker II's Paper Sizes command (in the File menu) is meant for the ImageWriter, so you can't use it to specify a custom paper size for printing on a LaserWriter. However, you can simulate a custom paper size that's smaller than one of the regular sizes by inserting a blank footer in your layout. The footer should be large enough to make up the difference between the length of the custom paper and that of the standard paper. If you have selected US Letter paper and want to print on 6-by-9-inch paper, use a 2-inch footer. In addition, move your fields horizontally so that they print properly.

REUSING THE LAST TOOL

In 4th Dimension's layout editor, hold down the Command key and drag to simultaneously select and draw with the last tool chosen from the tool palette. If you don't hold down the Command key, the pointer tool (arrow) is selected.

SCRIPTING AND PROGRAMMING

4th Dimension

ROUTINES BY KEY

The procedure editor in 4th Dimension lists all currently defined routines at the lower right corner of the window. You can scroll through the list of routines by typing instead of by using the mouse. Pressing Command-Shift while typing a couple of letters scrolls to routine names that start with those letters. Scrolling by typing forces the routine names to appear in strict alphabetic order rather than in groups, as they are usually displayed. To have them displayed by group again, click the word *Routines* at the top of the list.

HyperCard

SCRIPTING SPECIAL SYMBOLS

You can create the Command-key symbol, a check mark, a solid diamond, or the Apple logo by using HyperCard's NumToChar function with the code numbers 17 (Command-key symbol), 18 (check mark), 19 (solid diamond), and 20 (Apple logo). To create a Command-key character, for example, type the following command in the message window:

```
put numToChar(17)
```

HyperCard immediately replaces your typing with an undefined-character symbol (a small hollow box), which is the best it can do with the Geneva font in the message window. Select the character, copy it, and paste it to a field or another document. Then change the font to Chicago, and it becomes the Command-key symbol.

HyperCard

SAVE THAT SCRIPT

HyperCard doesn't save scripts automatically. You must either use the Save Script command (in the File menu) or close the script window to save the script. Save often. Don't wait until you finish working on a script to save it. It's also a good idea to save a copy of your stack periodically as a backup.

HyperCard

WORKING WITH AUTOHILITE

Clicking a HyperCard button whose AutoHilite property is true deselects text that's selected in a field. If the button's script then tries to get the current text selection, it gets an empty string. As a workaround, have the button's script cycle the button's highlight after getting the selected text. The following script illustrates:

```
on mouseUp
  get the selectedText
  put the selectedChunk into saveSelectedChunk
  set the hilite of me to true
  set the hilite of me to false
  --now do something with the selected text
  put it into the message window
  select saveSelectedChunk
end mouseUp
```

The AutoHilite property behaves as it does to avoid the confusion that could result if two objects were highlighted at the same time.

OBJECT SELF-REFERENCE

HyperCard

How do you get a HyperCard button to refer to itself? Use the Target function, which identifies the object that first received the current message. Try this script:

```
on mouseUp
  go stack short name of the target
end mouseUp
```

AVOIDING SCRIPT DUPLICATION

HyperCard

HyperCard buttons and fields that function alike when you click them probably have identical scripts for handling specific actions. You can remove duplicate copies of script lines from button and field scripts and put one copy in the card, background, or stack script. Where you put script lines determines their purview. If you put them in a card script, they handle events only when that card is open. If you put them in a background script, they handle events when any card of that background is open. If you put script lines in a stack script, the script lines handle events for any card in the stack; the Home stack script handles events for any card in any stack.

If you click a button or field whose script has no handler for that mouse-click action, HyperCard looks elsewhere for a handler. It looks first in the card script, second in the background script, third in the stack script, and fourth in the stack script of the Home card. Before looking in the Home stack, HyperCard 2.0 looks in the stack script of every stack that has been added to the inheritance path with a Start Using command. Centralizing duplicate button scripts and field scripts into card, background, and stack scripts reduces overall stack size and simplifies future script modifications.

The most common action handled in button and field scripts is a mouseUp event. This event occurs as you finish clicking the mouse button. If a card, background, or stack script handles mouseUp events for buttons or fields, the script might need to determine what has been clicked. Otherwise, the script might try to do something impossible such as highlight a card or put text into a button. For example, the following handler does nothing unless the name of the object clicked contains the word *Check*:

```
on mouseUp
  get the short name of the target
  if it contains "Check" then
    if target is empty
    then put "✓" into target
    else put empty into target
  end if
end mouseUp
```

HyperCard

CONDITIONAL MENU BAR

You might want your stack to hide the menu bar on a Mac Plus, Mac SE, or other small-screen Macintosh on which the card completely fills the screen. If the screen is larger than the card window, however, there's no need to hide the menu bar. You can conditionally hide the menu bar by including the following two script lines:

```
if item 4 of the screenRect = height of card window
then hide menuBar
```

HyperCard

SCRIPTED PICTURE COPYING

If you want a script to copy a card picture or background picture from one stack to another, you can use the Copy Picture and Paste Picture commands, like this:

```
set cursor to watch
push card
lock screen
go back -- to previous card
choose select tool
--select the whole card picture
drag from 0,0 to bottomRight of this card
doMenu "Copy Picture"
pop card -- to new card
doMenu "Paste Picture"
doMenu "Transparent"
choose browse tool
```

If you want the areas of the picture that aren't black to be opaque (white) instead of transparent, omit the *doMenu* "Transparent" line. To copy and paste a picture that has both opaque and transparent areas, you must copy and paste the entire card—picture, buttons, fields, field contents, and script. The following stack handler, which you would probably add to the stack script, does this by intercepting the New Card menu command:

```
on doMenu menuItem
  if menuItem is "New Card" then
    lock screen
    doMenu "Copy Card"
    doMenu "Paste Card"
    repeat with n = 1 to the number of cd fields
      put empty into cd field n
    end repeat
    repeat with n = 1 to the number of bg fields
      put empty into bg field n
    end repeat
    unlock screen
    tabKey -- ready to enter first field
  else
    pass doMenu
  end if
end doMenu
```

Note that this handler takes over when you choose New Card from the Edit menu (or press Command-N) as well as when you use a doMenu New Card command.

HyperCard

RANDOM HYPERTALK

To get a random number in a HyperTalk script, use the Random function, as in the following example:

```
put the random of 12 into diceToss
if diceToss is 7 or diceToss is 11
then answer "Craps, you lose!" with "Phooey."
```

HyperCard

SCRIPTED DELETE KEY

If you want a script to press the Delete key (labeled Backspace on Mac Plus keyboards), use the following command:

```
type numToChar(8)
```

The number 8 is the ASCII code for the Backspace character.

HyperCard

STACK MANNERS

Rude HyperCard stacks don't put things back where they found them (a lesson most people learn in kindergarten). Before your stack moves windows, hides them, or changes the user level, it should first put current locations, visibilities, and so forth into global variables. Then, when your stack is closed, it should restore the environment to the state it was in before the stack was opened. The following script illustrates:

```
on openStack
  global saveUserLevel,saveToolWindow,savePatternWindow,saveMessage,
  cardWindowLoc
  --first, remember user preferences
  put the visible of tool window into saveToolWindow
  put the visible of pattern window into savePatternWindow
  put the visible of message into saveMessage
  put the userLevel into saveUserLevel
  put the location of card window into cardWindowLoc
  --then change environment
  if item 4 of the screenRect = height of card window
  then hide menuBar
  hide tool window
  hide pattern window
  hide message window
  set userLevel to 2 -- typing
```

```
  set the topLeft of card window to 0,0
  pass openStack
end openStack
on closeStack
  global saveUserLevel,saveToolWindow,savePatternWindow,
  saveMessage, cardWindowLoc
  --restore to user preferences
  set the userLevel to saveUserLevel
  show menuBar
  set the visible of tool window to saveToolWindow
  set the visible of pattern window to savePatternWindow
  set the visible of message to saveMessage
  set the loc of card window to cardWindowLoc
  pass closeStack
end closeStack
```

Chapter 11

COMMUNICATIONS

Getting two computers to communicate, whether they're connected over phone lines with modems or cabled directly, is not a task for the faint-hearted. Don't let the technical complexity daunt you, however. Look through this chapter for some ideas that will help you get on line successfully. You'll find tips on the following topics:

- Connecting
- Calling
- Using information services
- Using electronic mail
- Transferring files
- Working with transferred files
- Solving problems

CONNECTING

FIRST-TIME SETTINGS

The most common transmission speed and character format settings are 1200 baud, 8 bits per character, no parity, and 1 stop bit (not an option in some communications software). Try them if you don't know what settings to use the first time you call an electronic bulletin board (BBS), information service, or other remote computer. Figure 11-1 illustrates how to set the speed and character format using Smartcom II.

If you're going to receive a text file from another personal computer, you might also need to set an option in your communications software so that it wraps paragraphs. Otherwise, you might receive only the first line of each paragraph. Standard settings usually work for the options XON/XOFF, Wait For Echo, Wait For Prompt, Delay Between Characters, and Delay Between Lines. If the computers have trouble communicating, be sure those options are set the same on both ends.

Speed & Format

Transmission speed (baud):

○ 110 ○ 300 ○ 600 ◉ 1200 ○ 2400 ○ 4800
○ 7200 ○ 9600 ○ 19200 ○ 38400 ○ Maximum

Bits per character: ○ Seven ◉ Eight

Stop bits: ◉ One ○ Two

Parity: ○ Even ○ Odd ○ Mark ○ Space ◉ None

Flow control: ◉ Xon/Xoff ○ Hardware ○ None

[OK] [Cancel]

FIGURE 11-1. STANDARD SPEED AND FORMAT.
These are the most common speed and character format settings.

General Communications

BEST TIME TO CALL

For best performance when communicating with an electronic bulletin board (BBS) or information service, make contact late at night or early in the morning. More people call during daytime and evening hours. The busier the remote computer becomes, the longer it takes to handle your requests and, as a result, the more expensive your communications session will be.

MacTerminal

THE FULL-DISK RISK

When MacTerminal captures (saves) the text of a telecommunications session in a disk file, there is always the risk of running out of disk space while that particular session is in progress, especially with a 400-KB floppy disk. You can minimize the chance of the disk becoming full by clearing the old session with the Clear Lines Off Top command on the Commands menu. Before clearing that session, you might want to use the Save As command to put a copy on a separate disk.

Modems

MODEM TO MOUTHPIECE

Travelers, students, and office workers who want to use their Macs with modems face a common problem if their hotel rooms, dormitories, and offices have telephones without modular connections. All modems that operate at a reasonable speed—1200 baud or faster—require modular

connections. One solution is to connect the modem to the mouthpiece of a standard telephone handset.

If you unscrew the mouthpiece and remove the microphone from the handset of a standard telephone, you see two metal prongs. You can make a cheater cable to connect the prongs in the telephone handset to the modular RJ11 jack on the modem. To make the cable, you need a standard modular telephone cord with RJ11 connectors at each end (not a curly handset cable), two miniature alligator clips, wire strippers or a small knife, a soldering iron, and some solder. First cut the telephone cord into two pieces. Then carefully remove a couple of inches of the outer plastic casing from the cut end of one of the pieces, exposing four colored wires. Strip the insulation from the red and green wires and solder each to an alligator clip. The yellow and black wires are unused.

To use your cheater cord, attach the alligator clips to the handset prongs and plug the modular connector into the modem, as shown in Figure 11-2.

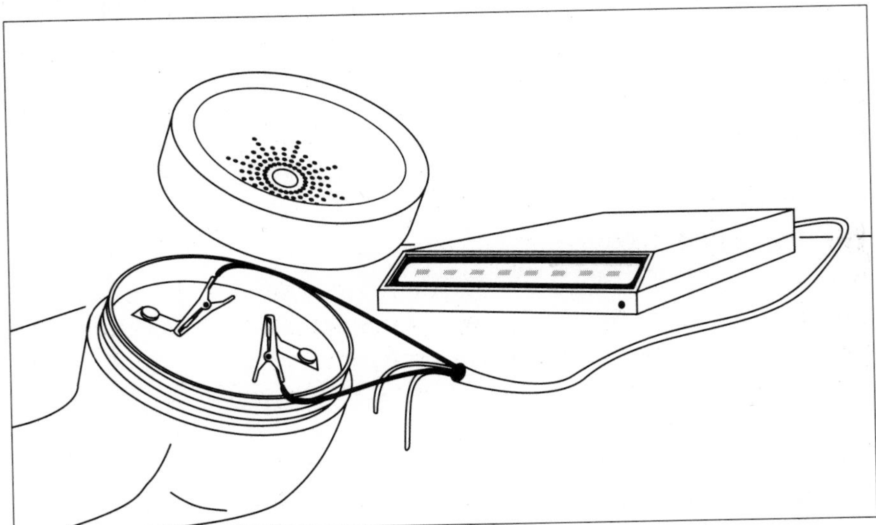

FIGURE 11-2. MODULAR BYPASS.

If you don't have access to a modular wall jack, you can attach the red and green wires of a telephone cord to the prongs inside the mouthpiece of most telephone handsets.

If the phone line is Touch Tone compatible, proceed as if the modem were connected normally to a modular wall jack. The Touch Tone feature might work even if the phone you're tapped into has a rotary dial.

If the phone line requires rotary (pulse) dialing, you must dial the number manually on the telephone. Using communications software that lets you type commands to the modem (MicroPhone, White Knight, FreeTerm, and others), type the command *ATH1* to take the modem off the hook. Be sure to type modem commands in all uppercase letters. Take the phone handset off the cradle and manually dial the number you want to reach. If your modem has a speaker, you will hear it echo the pulse sounds of your dialing. As soon as you hear the carrier tone from the remote computer, type the command *ATO* (the letter O, not a zero) to put your modem on line. You're connected.

When you are dialing manually, the ATH1 command is not always necessary. If you omit it, you can still dial manually with AppleLink, MacNet, and CompuServe Navigator, all of which normally automate the dialing process. Simply set the phone number that the application dials automatically to a capital letter O. In AppleLink, for example, you set the phone number by using the Setup command in the Network menu. Then dial the number manually and immediately initiate the standard connect procedure in the application. In AppleLink, you do this by choosing Connect from the Network menu, typing your password, and clicking the Connect To Network button.

If you don't want to bother with soldering and alligator clips, you can buy a Black Jack connector. It temporarily replaces the mouthpiece with a modular jack so that you can attach a modem using a standard modular telephone cord. Digital Systems claims to have sold more than 23,000 of these connectors worldwide.

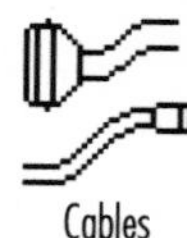

HAYES-COMPATIBLE CABLE

Hayes modems, and most Hayes-compatible modems, can be connected to a Mac with an Apple II Printer-8 cable (Apple part A9C0314 or the equivalent). You can also build your own cable by following the wiring diagram in Figure 11-3.

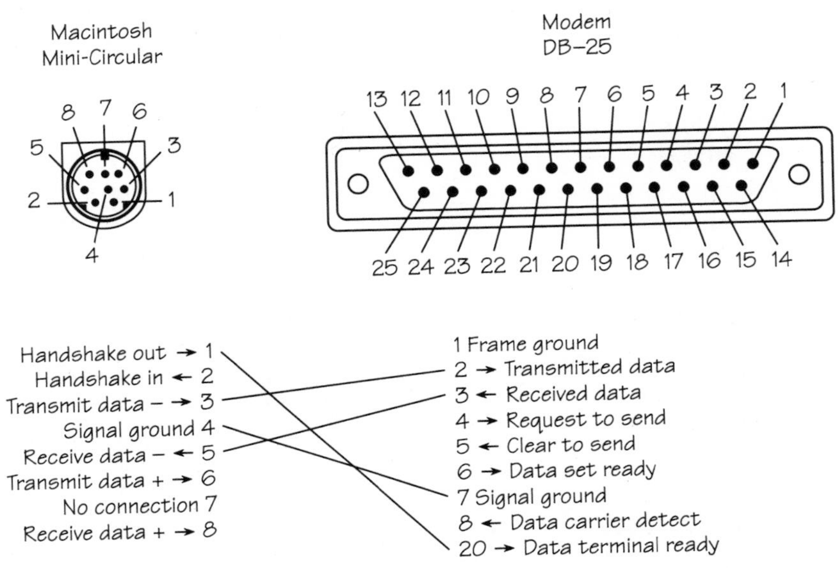

FIGURE 11-3. HEY, HAYES.
A cable wired according to this diagram connects most Hayes-compatible modems to a Macintosh. (The connectors appear as viewed from the back, where connections are made.)

VOLKSMODEM CABLE

It is difficult to find the proper cable connection between a Mac Plus and a modem with a nonstandard connector. To devise a cable for the Volksmodem 12 to the Mac Plus, see Figure 11-4 on the following page.

DIRECT CONNECTION

You can bypass modems and telephone calls by directly connecting the Mac and a nearby computer with a cable. One end of the cable plugs into the Mac's modem port, and the other end plugs into the other computer's serial port. The computers don't see any difference between direct connection and modem connection. You still need communications software on both computers, and both must be set for the same transmission speed and character format. Because you're not limited by modem speed, you can set the fastest transmission speed the software has available.

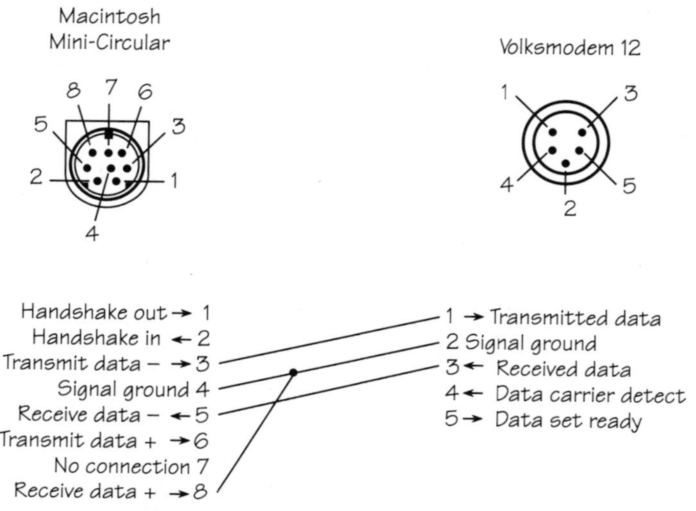

FIGURE 11-4. HELLO, VOLKS.
A cable wired according to this diagram connects a Volksmodem 12 to a Mac. (The connectors appear as viewed from the back, where connections are made.)

A cable that would connect your Mac to an ImageWriter I lets you connect your Mac to most computers whose serial port uses a DB-25 connector, including the following:

- IBM PC–compatible computers
- Tandy (Radio Shack) Model 100 and Model 102
- CP/M computers

You can also wire your own cable. The wiring diagram shown in Figure 11-5 works with most IBM PC compatibles. The diagram in Figure 11-6 works with an IBM PC/AT compatible and with many PC-compatible laptops. If you have a Tandy (Radio Shack) Model 100 or Model 102, use a cable wired as shown in Figure 11-7 on the page after next.

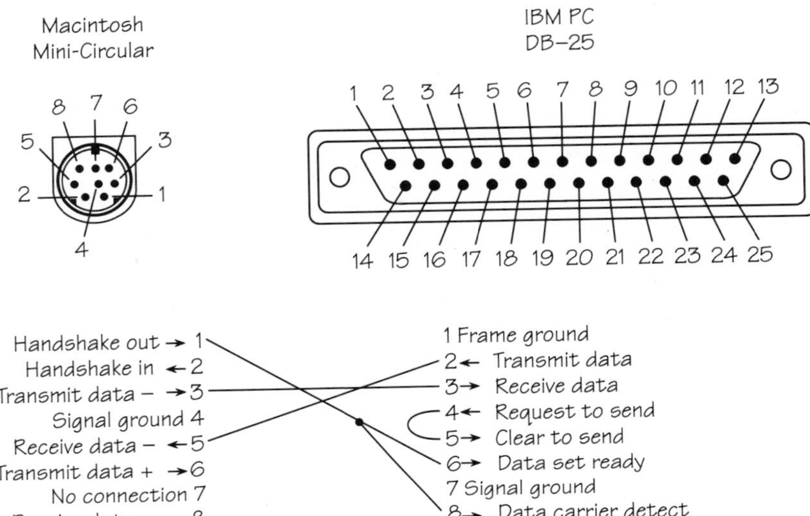

FIGURE 11-5. PC CONNECTION.

A cable wired according to this diagram connects a Mac (except a Mac 512K) to most IBM PC–compatible computers. (The connectors appear as viewed from the back, where connections are made.)

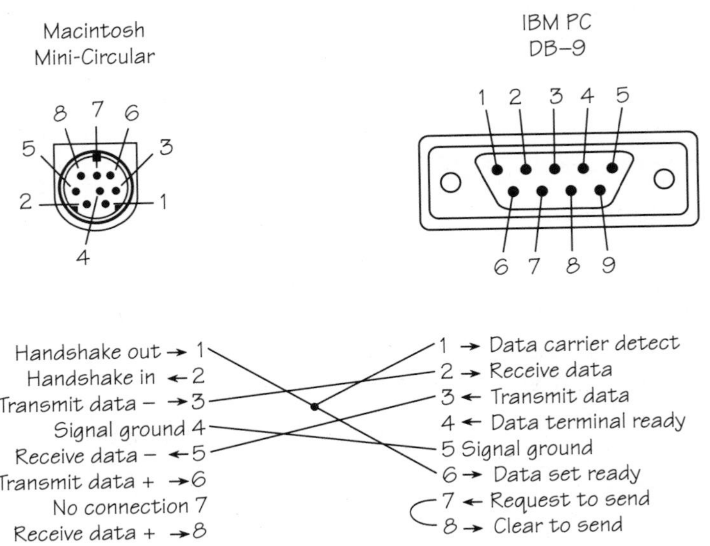

FIGURE 11-6. AT CONNECTION.

A cable wired according to this diagram connects a Mac (except a Mac 512K) to most IBM PC/AT–compatible computers. (The connectors appear as viewed from the back, where connections are made.)

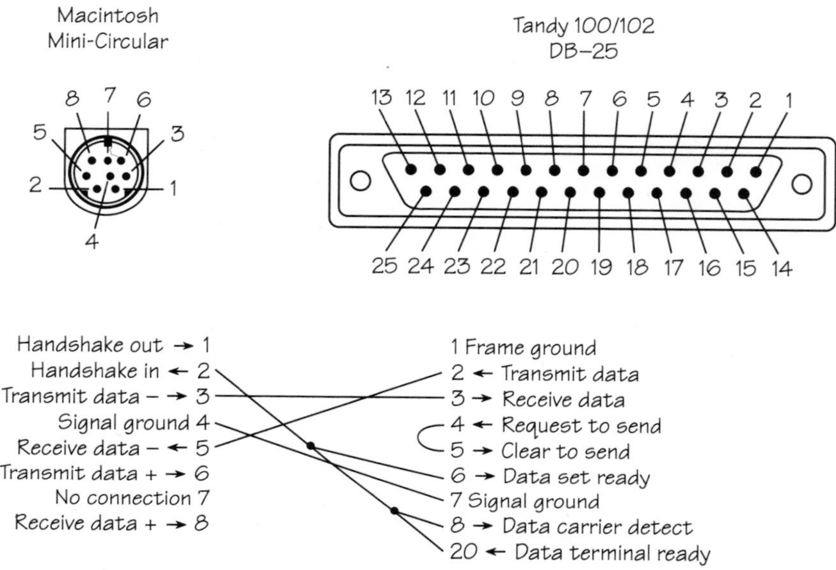

FIGURE 11-7. TANDY CONNECTION.

A cable wired according to this diagram connects a Mac (except a Mac 512K) to a Tandy Model 100 or Model 102 laptop computer. (The connectors appear as viewed from the back, where connections are made.)

MINI-CIRCULAR 8 CONNECTORS

The mini-circular 8 connector you need to make your own cables for the Mac modem port can be difficult to find. If your local electronics parts store can't help you, you can order mini-circular 8 connectors from Electronics Plus in San Rafael, California (800/321-4524 within California). If you have steady hands and good eyes for close work, you may be able to work with the $5 solder-type connectors (part number MD-8P). For a more rewarding cable-fabricating experience, splurge on the $17 connector that comes prewired to a 6-foot cable (part number CA-508).

Standard Macintosh cables are also a source of mini-circular 8 connectors. The Peripheral-8 cable (Apple part number M0196 or equivalent), normally used to connect an ImageWriter II or Apple Personal Modem to a Mac, has a mini-circular 8 on each end. Cutting off and discarding one end leaves a

3-foot cable. Cutting the cable in half leaves two shorter cables. Use an ohmmeter or test lamp to determine which pin each wire connects to. If you cut the cable in half, test each cable separately because the color-coded wires connect to different pins at each plug.

CALLING

INSERTING COMMAS FOR PAUSES

You can instruct any Hayes-compatible modem to pause during dialing. For each 2-second pause required in a dialing sequence, insert one comma. Figure 11-8 illustrates.

Phone Settings

Phone Number

9,555-1212

Dial ◉ Tone ○ Pulse ○ Mixed

Number of Rings Before Answer [0]

Modem ○ Apple 300 ○ Apple 1200 ◉ Other

[OK] [Cancel]

FIGURE 11-8. DIALING PAUSE.

When a Hayes-compatible modem encounters a comma in a phone number, it pauses for 2 seconds before dialing the next digit.

PBX ESCAPE

To dial out of a private branch exchange (PBX), prefix the number you're calling with a 9. If you normally have to wait for a second dial tone before dialing the outside number, insert one or two commas between the 9 and the outside number. Enter the phone number in the following format:

```
9 + ,, + phone number
```

SPECIAL MODEM COMMANDS

Some modems have special dialing commands. For example, the Prometheus ProModem 1200 recognizes the letter W in a dialing sequence as an instruction to wait up to 20 seconds for a second dial tone or an access tone. By using this command, you don't have to estimate how long the wait will be, as you do with commas. Check your modem manual for other commands that can simplify dialing.

CREDIT-CARD CALLS

From most Touch Tone phone lines, your modem can dial all the numbers necessary to complete a credit-card call. (See Figure 11-9.) Use the following phone number format:

```
0 + phone number + ,,, + credit-card number + ,
```

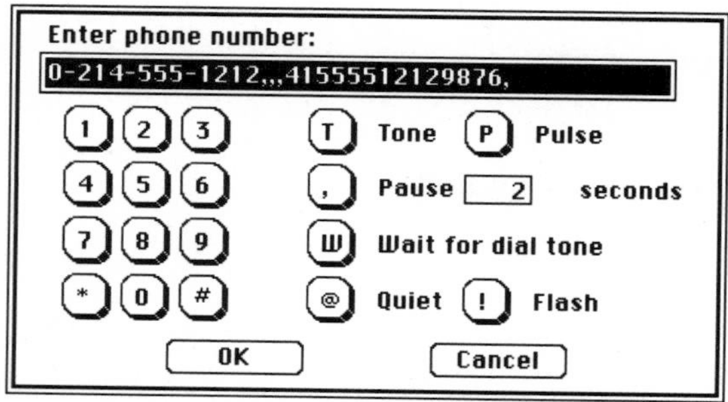

FIGURE 11-9. CREDIT CALL.
This phone number dials the remote computer at 214-555-1212, waits 6 seconds, dials credit-card number 41555512129876, and then waits 2 more seconds before connecting.

ALTERNATE LONG-DISTANCE COMPANIES

Your modem can dial a long-distance number through an alternate long-distance company, as illustrated in Figure 11-10. Enter the phone number in the following format:

```
long-distance company code + ,,, + 0 + phone number + ,
 + credit-card number + ,
```

Phone Settings

Phone Number

950-1022,,,0-214-555-1212,12345678901234,

Dial ◉ Tone ○ Pulse ○ Mixed

Number of Rings Before Answer [0]

Modem ○ Apple 300 ◉ Apple 1200 ○ Other

OK Cancel

FIGURE 11-10. ALTERNATE SERVICE.
This phone number dials 950-1022 (a long-distance company's local-access number), waits 6 seconds, dials the remote computer at 214-555-1212, waits 2 seconds, dials account number 12345678901234, and then waits 2 seconds before connecting.

CALL-WAITING DISRUPTION

The click or beep that announces that a call is waiting on a phone line equipped with the Call Waiting feature wreaks havoc with telecommunications. But in most areas, you can turn off the Call Waiting feature for the duration of the ensuing call by dialing a three-digit or four-digit code, waiting for a second dial tone, and then dialing a regular phone number. Figure 11-11 illustrates.

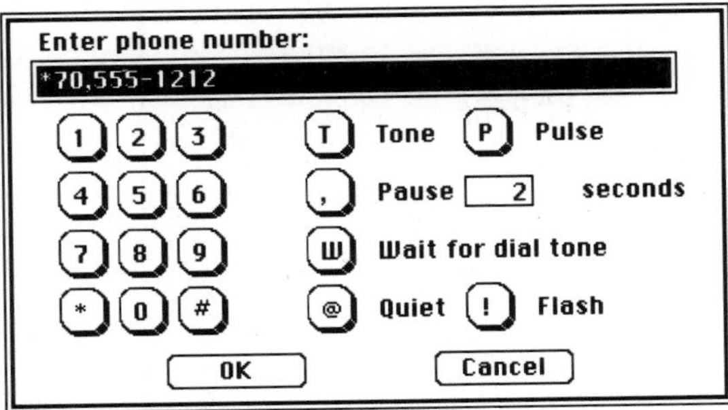

FIGURE 11-11. CANCEL CALL WAITING.
*This phone number dials the code *70 to suspend Call Waiting on a Touch Tone line, waits 2 seconds for a second dial tone, and then dials the remote computer at 555-1212.*

To turn Call Waiting off on a Touch Tone phone line, use the following phone number format:

```
*70 + ,,, + phone number
```

To turn Call Waiting off on a rotary or pulse-dial phone line, enter the phone number in the following format:

```
1170 + ,,, + phone number
```

If you are not able to turn Call Waiting off in your area, it is best to avoid trying telecommunications over a phone line that has this feature.

Modems

STAYING CONNECTED

If your communications software always seems to disconnect shortly after the number you dial is answered, try following the number with two or three commas. Use a phone number format similar to the following:

```
phone number + ,,
```

MacTerminal

BUSY . . . BUSY . . . BUSY

MacTerminal has no special command to redial a busy number. A few seconds after detecting a busy signal, it displays the message "The call was answered, but no computer responded" and waits for you to do something. You could redial by choosing Dial from the Phone menu, but here's a faster redialing method: Assuming the last command you chose was Dial from the Phone menu, type *A/* to redial a busy number. Do not press the Return key or you will cancel this repeat command. You might not see your typing in the MacTerminal window unless you have selected the Terminal command's Local Echo and New Line options. The A/ command tells any modem compatible with the Hayes Smartmodem to repeat the last command it received.

REDIALING CONTINUOUSLY

MacTerminal

Anyone who uses electronic bulletin boards knows that a remote computer can be busy continuously for long periods. At such times, manual redialing becomes tedious. Not all communications software or modems have an automatic redial-on-busy command; certainly MacTerminal and the Apple modems do not. But you can give MacTerminal an unintelligent continuous-redial capability with some preliminary word processing and some temporary changes to MacTerminal's file-transfer settings, as follows:

1. Use MacWrite or another word processor to create a text document containing about 60 lines that each have a capital A followed by a slash (A/, the modem's repeat command).
2. Save the document—in the MacTerminal folder if possible—using the Text Only option. (If the word processor asks whether to put a return character at the end of each paragraph or the end of each line, choose the paragraph option.)
3. Start MacTerminal and dial the number. If the number is busy, MacTerminal will hang up within 1 minute.
4. Choose File Transfer from the Settings menu and note the setting for Delay Between Lines. Then temporarily change it to 1800 (30 seconds). Also note the setting for File Transfer Protocol and then select Text. Click OK.
5. Choose Send File from the File menu, and double-click the name of the redial-command document. MacTerminal starts sending one line of the document, which contains one redial command, every 30 seconds.
6. Listen to the modem speaker. When you hear the remote phone ring, immediately type Command-period to stop MacTerminal from sending any more redial commands. Typing another A/ command causes the modem to hang up!
7. After logging on to the remote computer, restore the Delay Between Lines and Transfer Method settings in the File Transfer Setting dialog box to their states prior to step 4.

If your modem won't respond to the repeated A/ commands, try turning it off and back on again. Then redial the number. If the number is still busy, continue, with step 5.

INTERNATIONAL TEXT TRANSFER

The next time you're tempted to send a fax of a printed text document to an associate in Paris or anywhere else in the world, consider using your modem instead. You'll save money on the phone call because transferring text by 1200-baud modem is at least four times faster than sending it by fax. As a bonus, your associate will have a text file to edit and format instead of 25 sheets of fax paper.

You and your associate can have dissimilar computers, but you must have compatible modems. For example, 1200-baud modems made for the U.S. market use the Bell 212A protocol, whereas French modems use the CCITT V.22 protocol. The two protocols use the same carrier frequencies and modulation schemes but different handshaking (connect sequences). Some American modems are compatible with both protocols; the Hayes Smartmodem 1200 is an example.

Before one modem calls the other, you and your associate must set your communications software for the same speed and format. This topic is discussed in the tip "First-Time Settings," earlier in this chapter.

France and the United States do not restrict or license modem use, but some countries do. Germany, for example, may still require a permit for the use of a communications device. Before you or your associate uses a modem in another country, investigate local regulations concerning modems.

USING INFORMATION SERVICES

THE CONTROL KEY

The Control key can be useful when you're communicating with CompuServe or with certain other information services. For example, pressing Control-S pauses CompuServe, and pressing Control-Q resumes it. Pressing Control-C interrupts CompuServe and lets you continue or do something else. If you press Control-O, CompuServe stops sending text and waits for a command from you as if it had finished. You can use it to interrupt the display of a long menu and immediately type your menu choice.

If your keyboard has no Control key, try using the Command key instead. Most communications software has no Command-key shortcuts for menu commands, in order to allow this use of the Command key.

THE DELETE KEY

When communicating with some remote computers, you might need to press Command-Delete to get the normal effect of pressing Delete. When pressed, the Delete key (labeled Backspace on older Macs) generates what most non-Apple computers consider to be a backspace character, meaning that the character is not erased. With most Macintosh communications software, pressing Command-Delete generates what other computers consider to be a delete character (also called a rubout character).

If you find yourself always using Command-Delete, you might want to have your communications software swap the effect of pressing Delete and Command-Delete. In MicroPhone or Smartcom II, use the Terminal command in the Settings menu.

THE ESC KEY

When communicating with some remote computers, you need to be able to press an Esc key. If your keyboard has no Esc key, try pressing the tilde (~) key. To type a tilde during your session, press Command-Shift-tilde. For a grave accent (`), press Command-tilde.

LINE-LENGTH LIMITS

Electronic bulletin boards and electronic mail systems on some remote computers impose a maximum line length measured in characters. How can you break paragraphs in a message you're writing on your Mac so that each line has no more than a certain number of characters? In your word processor, use a fixed-width font such as Monaco 12 or Courier 12 and adjust the margins or paragraph indentation. For example, a left margin of 1 inch and a right margin of 1.5 inches (line length 6 inches) with Monaco 12 results in a 68-character line. Save the document in text-with-line-breaks file format.

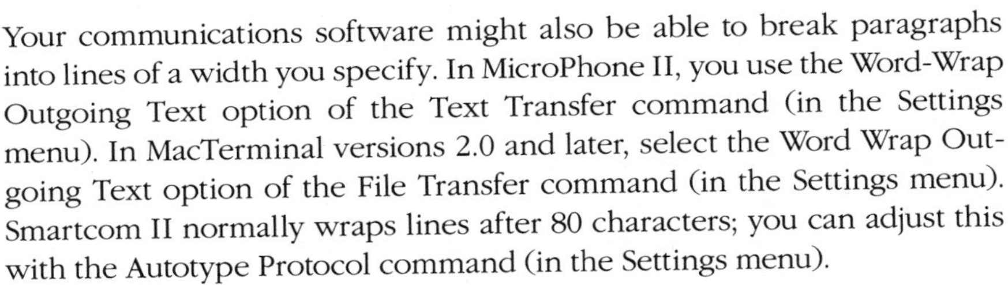

Your communications software might also be able to break paragraphs into lines of a width you specify. In MicroPhone II, you use the Word-Wrap Outgoing Text option of the Text Transfer command (in the Settings menu). In MacTerminal versions 2.0 and later, select the Word Wrap Outgoing Text option of the File Transfer command (in the Settings menu). Smartcom II normally wraps lines after 80 characters; you can adjust this with the Autotype Protocol command (in the Settings menu).

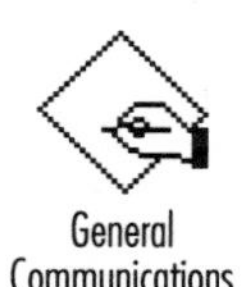

PARAGRAPH BREAKER

The EndLine utility provides a simple method for forcing line breaks in paragraphs of plain text files for electronic bulletin boards and electronic mail systems on remote computers. EndLine breaks the paragraphs of any text file into lines of 70 characters or less and puts a return character at the end of each line. All line breaks occur at spaces, not right on the 70th character. (You can change the line length with the ResEdit utility.)

PREVENTING SCREEN CLEARING

Does CompuServe clear your screen when you have MacTerminal set to Record Lines Off Top? You don't want the screen cleared before the lines have a chance to move off the top, or they'll never be recorded. To prevent unwanted screen clearing in MacTerminal version 2.0 and later, choose File Transfer from the Settings menu and select the Save Screens Before Clearing option. You are now ready to type any standard CompuServe navigational command, such as GO MACPRO to go to CompuServe's Mac Productivity forum, and you can proceed with your communications session with no further screen-clearing problems.

CompuServe

MENU MAZE

If you frequently access a CompuServe forum such as MAUG (Micronetted Apple User Group), its structured menus probably slow you down. You can suppress CompuServe's forum menus by changing a user option. From the main forum menu, enter *OP*. You then see the User Options menu. Enter *UM* and answer the questions to turn off menus, either for the current session only or until you explicitly turn them back on. Turning off menus means you get a one-line prompt instead of a menu. For example, instead of the Forum menu, you get a Forum prompt.

CompuServe

COMPUSERVE DOWNLOADS

Here's how to find and download software from CompuServe's Macintosh forums with MicroPhone or other general-purpose communications software. At the Forum menu, enter *LIB* to see a numbered list of the different software libraries in the forum. (You don't see the list if you've turned off the forum menus.) Each library contains a different category of software and information, such as desk accessories, fonts, hardware, games, art, music, and telecommunications. Choose the library you want by typing its number. If you know the number, you can save time by including it in the LIB command at the Forum menu or Forum prompt. For example, you could enter *LIB1* to go immediately to the Forum Business library.

To see a list of all the files in the library you have chosen, enter *S/DES*. Or, if you want the option of downloading a file after reading its description, enter *BRO* instead. To look for files on a particular topic, enter *S/DES/KEY:* followed by a keyword. For example, *S/DES/KEY:FINDER* shows you the descriptions of files that had the keyword Finder in the current library.

A good place to start is data library 1. There you'll find help files on several topics. You can read a file by entering *R*, a space, and the filename. For example, enter *R FILES.HLP* to read about downloading files from MAUG's data libraries. You can't read all files in the MAUG data libraries because many of them aren't plain text. Those you must download.

After you know the name of a file, you can download it by entering *DOW* at the data library menu or command line. You'll be asked to enter the name of the file you want and to choose a transfer protocol. At 2400 baud and below, choose the Xmodem or the Ymodem protocol.

Many files you download require massaging before they're usable on your Mac. A MAUG file with the suffix .SIT or .PIT actually contains several related Macintosh files packed together. For example, a desk accessory and its instructions might be packed together. You must unpack them after downloading. For type .SIT files, use the application StuffIt (file STUFFI.BIN in LIB8). For type .PIT files, use the application Packit III (file PACKIT.BIN in LIB14) or UnPacker (file UNPACK.BIN in LIB14).

For a complete list of commands you can use in MAUG or any forum, type *GO PRACTICE* at any prompt ending in an exclamation point. That takes you to the practice forum, which you can use for free. At the Practice Forum menu, type *IN*. Then at the Instructions menu, type *10* to get a reference card.

UNSUCCESSFUL XMODEM

General Communications

When an attempt at transferring information to or from an information service is unsuccessful, it could simply mean that the service is too busy. When lots of people are using the service, Xmodem transfer does not work reliably.

MAC TELEX

Using your Mac, you can communicate with over a million and a half telex subscribers worldwide. You need a modem, communications software such as MacTerminal or MicroPhone, and a subscription to the EasyLink service or the MCI Mail service. The subscriptions include complete instructions for sending and receiving telex messages. You do not have to be connected to either service for others to send you a telex.

USING ELECTRONIC MAIL

MAIL MANNERS

Electronic mail is new enough that a set of guidelines for using it is still evolving. Here are some suggestions:

- Keep messages concise. Long messages are hard to read on the screen.
- Focus on one topic. Use a new message to discuss another topic.
- Keep layout clean and simple. Novel text layouts might be fun, but your first goal should be communication, not entertainment.
- Choose a clear, specific, and interesting word or phrase for the subject line of your message. Otherwise, the person receiving your message might postpone reading it.
- Send a copy to people who might be affected by your message or who might have information or suggestions to add. But don't broadcast indiscriminately.
- Assume your messages will be printed and kept forever. Electronic mail might seem as ephemeral as a phone conversation, but it's not.
- Write carefully. Again, you're not talking on the phone. Recipients will have plenty of time to study your messages.
- Don't expect an instant response. People might not check their mail for hours, days, or weeks. If timing is critical, augment or replace electronic mail with a phone call.

LOCAL MESSAGE STORAGE

To send and receive electronic mail efficiently, create In and Out folders on your hard disk (not on a network file server). Start each folder name with a blank space (" In" and " Out") to make them easier to find when using the Open command.

Use the Out folder to store messages you haven't finished composing. Use the In folder to store messages you've received but haven't read. (Remove messages from the mail server after saving them in your In folder.)

Storing your messages in folders on your disk instead of on the mail server disk has several advantages:

- The network operates faster because you're using it less.
- Opening and saving messages is faster from a local hard disk than from the mail server disk.
- The mail server disk has more space available for sending mail.
- You have access to your messages if the mail server is unavailable (such as during backup or routine maintenance).
- The QuickMail desk accessory opens faster because it doesn't have to read a long list of messages—only the new messages since you last got your mail.

LAST NAME FIRST

QuickMail normally displays names with the first name before the last name (George Washington). To display the last name before the first name (Washington, George), enter the entire inverted name as the first name, and don't enter a last name at all. Doing this makes it possible to sort your messages by last name if you want.

MAIL ORDER

What causes the order of messages listed in the QuickMail window to change? Normally, QuickMail sorts messages by the date they were sent. Clicking a column heading in the QuickMail window causes QuickMail to sort your messages by that category, as shown in Figure 11-12 on the following page.

QuickMail™

Version : 2.2.1
User : Zoltan Amadeus Power°
MailCenter : QUICKTIPS

Priority	Subject	Who	Date Sent	
Urgent	Queen waiting in lobby	Cleopatra Kelly	8/22/90	3:56 PM
Importa	WYWO- Buck O. Racine	Babe Rothschild	8/22/90	4:02 PM
Importa	WYWO- Your mother called	Babe Rothschild	8/22/90	3:57 PM
Importa	Expense report	Venus Crooke	8/22/90	3:51 PM
Importa	Encl-Acme Lighting contract	Glory Vasquez	8/22/90	4:00 PM
Normal	Coffee cake in kitchen	Bliss Hashimoto	8/22/90	3:54 PM
Normal	Encl-Sludge Reclamation Rep	Atlas Fang	8/22/90	4:03 PM
Normal	WYWO- Building inspector ca	Babe Rothschild	8/22/90	3:58 PM
Normal	Fish dinner	Venus Crooke	8/22/90	3:49 PM
Normal	Encl-Takeover plan	Achilles de la Cruz	8/22/90	3:53 PM
Normal	QM Serial # Report 8/22/90	QUICKTIPS	8/22/90	2:24 PM
Bulk	TV for sale	Zero McTush	8/22/90	3:56 PM

Public
QM Folder

Welcome to QUICKTIPS

FIGURE 11-12. MESSAGE SORTER.
Click a heading in the QuickMail window to reorganize your messages according to priority, sender, topic, and so on. The underlined heading indicates in which order the messages are sorted.

APPLESHARE AND QUICKMAIL

You can use one Macintosh as an AppleShare file server, AppleShare print server, and QuickMail server. With MultiFinder running, the Print Server software is the active application and the File Server and QuickMail Server programs run in the background. With this configuration, you must run QM Administrator on another Macintosh to handle bridges, dial-in users, and housekeeping. Because QM Administrator must be the active application, you can't run it on the server without deactivating the Print Server software.

QUICKMAIL ADMINISTRATION

If the QM Administrator application isn't running constantly on some Macintosh on your network, you should run the application for at least an hour or two weekly. (Running it overnight will work.) QM Administrator needs this time to perform the following housekeeping chores:

- Send Master Logs of activity at your various mail centers to the Custodians of those mail centers. QM Administrator does this hourly. Even if you set the Disable Master Logs option in the Options screen for an online mail center, the Master Logs aren't totally disabled. Dial-in users still cause entries to be created in the Master Log.
- Remove from online mail centers any public messages that are older than the maximum age you previously specified.

TRANSFERRING FILES

APPLE II DISK ACCESS

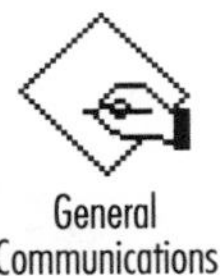

You can directly access 3½-inch Apple II floppy disks on a Macintosh without a problem. All you need is the floppy-disk drive built into all Macs (except an unenhanced Mac 512K) and some software. The Apple File Exchange (AFE) utility that comes with the system software can transfer files to and from 3½-inch ProDOS disks. (See Figure 11-13.) If your Apple II files are on 5¼-inch disks or on disks formatted with DOS 3.3, you must copy them to 3½-inch ProDOS disks with an Apple II before using AFE.

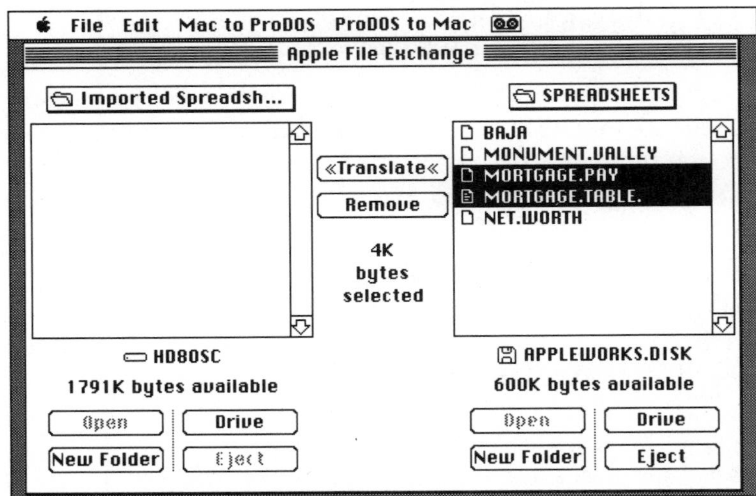

FIGURE 11-13. FILE TRADER.

The Apple File Exchange utility lets you convert Macintosh files to and from Apple II ProDOS files.

Unless you want to copy only plain text, you'll also need a special translator file for AFE, such as Works-Works Transporter. It enables AFE to convert AppleWorks files—from the word processor, spreadsheet, and database—to Microsoft Works files. When you open the converted files in Microsoft Works, they contain all the data of the AppleWorks originals and as much of the formatting as possible.

You can run Apple II software on a Macintosh by using the Apple IIe emulator][In A Mac. On a standard Mac 512K, Plus, or SE, your Apple II software runs at 40 to 50 percent of normal speed, which might not be satisfactory for games.

General Communications

IBM PC (MS-DOS) DISK ACCESS

Your Mac might be able to open and save documents directly on MS-DOS floppy disks. These disks are used by IBM PC–compatible computers. Apple's FDHD floppy disk drive accesses 3½-inch MS-DOS floppy disks and is standard equipment on all Macs built after September 1989 except the Mac Plus. The drive on a Mac II or an older SE can be retrofitted. You can access 5¼-inch MS-DOS floppy disks from a Mac SE or Mac II by using an Apple PC 5.25 Drive with adapter card. Apple's adapter cards are the SE-Bus PC Drive Card and the Mac II PC Drive Card.

In addition to the FDHD or PC 5.25 drive, you need software. You can use Apple File Exchange to transfer files. For more transparent operation, use the DOS Mounter utility. It lets you access an MS-DOS disk as if it were a Mac disk—letting you use the Finder, the Open command, and the Save command.

You can run MS-DOS software on a Mac SE/30 or any Mac II by using the MS-DOS emulator SoftPC from Insignia Solutions. (See Figure 11-14.) On a standard Mac II with 2 MB of memory, your MS-DOS software runs at least 1.2 times faster than it would on an IBM PC/XT.

FIGURE 11-14. SYNTHETIC PC.
SoftPC turns any Mac II or a Mac SE/30 into an IBM PC/XT. Here, Microsoft Flight Simulator runs in the SoftPC window.

IBM PC (MS-DOS) FILE EXCHANGE

You can exchange files with an IBM MS-DOS computer or other MS-DOS computer that's directly cabled to your Mac. The MS-DOS computer does not need communications software; its MODE and COPY commands suffice. The Mac does require communications software, however.

To prepare for an exchange of files, connect the Mac's modem port to the MS-DOS computer's serial port, using a suitable cable. For cable information, see the tip "Direct Connection," earlier in this chapter.

Be sure the MS-DOS computer is waiting for a DOS command. The flashing cursor should be next to a prompt, such as A. Type an appropriate MODE command on the MS-DOS computer to set up the serial port to match the speed and format settings in the communications software on the Mac. For example, the following command sets serial port COM1 for 9600 baud, no parity, 8 data bits per character, and 1 stop bit:

```
MODE COM1:9600,N,8,1
```

To send a file from the MS-DOS computer, prepare the Mac communications software to capture or receive a text file. Then type an appropriate

COPY command on the MS-DOS computer. The following example copies from the file named PCSTUFF.TXT on drive B to the COM1 serial port:

```
COPY B:PCSTUFF.TXT COM1:
```

To receive a file on the MS-DOS computer, type an appropriate COPY command on the MS-DOS computer. Then have the Mac's communications software start sending the file. When the Mac finishes, you usually have to press Command-Z on the Mac to tell the MS-DOS computer that it has received everything. The following COPY command receives a file from serial port COM1 and saves it in a disk file named MACSTUFF.TXT on drive A:

```
COPY COM: A:MACSTUFF.TXT
```

General Communications

MacTerminal

TANDY MODEL 100/102 FILE EXCHANGE

The Tandy (Radio Shack) Model 100 and Model 102 computers are compatible with most Mac communications software. All you need is a cable to connect the two computers. (See the tip "Direct Connection," earlier in this chapter.)

To prepare for file exchange, start the Mac communications software. On the Tandy, place TELECOM in its Term mode. Be sure the communication speed and format are the same on both machines. Try 19,200 baud, 8-bit word length, no parity, 1 stop bit, and XON/XOFF flow control enabled. Set this on the Tandy by setting the status of its built-in communications software, TELECOM, to 98N1E.

To send a file from the Tandy using TELECOM, prepare the Mac communications software to capture or receive a text file. On the Tandy, press the F3 key (Up). When the Tandy prompts "File to Upload?," type the name of the .DO file in memory that you want to transfer to the Mac. At the "Width?" prompt, press the Enter key to keep your paragraphs intact. The Tandy transfers the file to the Mac.

To send a file from the Tandy without using TELECOM, prepare the Mac communications software to capture or receive a text file. Then, from the Tandy menu, select the .DO file you want to send and press F3 (Save). When the Tandy prompts "Save to:," enter *COM:98N1E* to send the file out the serial port at 19,200 baud with an 8-bit word length, no parity, 1 stop bit, and XON/XOFF flow control enabled.

To receive a file on the Tandy using TELECOM, press F2 (Down). When the Tandy prompts "File to Download?," type a valid Tandy filename and press Enter. Then send the file from the Mac. Using this method, you see the text displayed as it comes in, but the transfer rate is slow because of the Tandy's slow screen.

To receive a file on the Tandy without using TELECOM, open a new file and press F2 (Load). When the Tandy asks "Load from:," enter *COM:98N1E* to receive the file through the serial port at 19,200 baud with an 8-bit word length, no parity, 1 stop bit, and XON/XOFF flow control enabled. This method is fast, but you don't see the text as it comes in.

If you're using MacTerminal, you must first perform temporary software surgery on the Tandy. Start the Tandy's built-in BASIC by pressing the Enter key while the main menu is displayed. Type the command *POKE 63066, 255*. Double-check the accuracy of your typing, and backspace to correct if necessary. Press Enter and quit BASIC. This procedure causes the Tandy to send an invisible linefeed character after the return character at the end of each line. Without these characters, MacTerminal tries to display all the text it receives on the same line. The Tandy change stays in effect until you perform a "cold start" or start BASIC and enter the command *POKE 63066,0*.

CP/M FILE EXCHANGE

Any computer that uses the CP/M operating system does not need communications software for simple file transfer when it is connected directly to a Mac. CP/M's STAT and PIP commands do the job. The Mac does require communications software, however. (CP/M computers include Kaypro, Morrow, Osborne, Digital Microsystems, Micromation, Dynabyte, Onyx, Altos, Industrial Micro Systems, Exidy, Vector Graphic, and the Apple II with a CP/M card.)

To prepare for file exchange, connect the Mac's modem port to the serial port of the CP/M computer, using a suitable cable. Set the communications speed and format settings in the Mac communications software to match the standard serial port settings on the CP/M computer. If the manual for the CP/M computer doesn't say what those settings are, try 1200 baud, no parity, and 8 bits per character.

Be sure the CP/M computer is waiting for a CP/M command. The cursor should be right next to a prompt, such as A>. Type the following STAT commands on the CP/M computer to set up the serial port to send and receive files:

```
STAT PUN:=PTP:
STAT RDR:=PTR:
```

To send a file from the CP/M computer, prepare the Mac's communications software to capture or receive a file. Then type an appropriate PIP command on the CP/M computer. The following example copies from the file named CPMSTUFF.TXT on drive B to the serial port:

```
PIP PUN:=B:CPMSTUFF.TXT
```

To receive a file on the CP/M computer, type an appropriate PIP command on the CP/M computer. Then have the Mac's communications software start sending the file. When the Mac finishes, you usually have to press Command-Z on the Mac to tell the CP/M computer that it has received everything. The following PIP command receives a file from the serial port and saves it in a disk file named MACSTUFF.TXT on drive A:

```
PIP A:MACSTUFF.TXT=RDR:
```

WORKING WITH TRANSFERRED FILES

GETTING TABLES FOR SPREADSHEETS

Tables of information that you receive from a remote computer are usually aligned in columns separated by blank spaces. To align the columns of a table with tabs instead of spaces so that you can paste the table into a spreadsheet, you can use a word processor to change multiple spaces to tabs in a downloaded text file. Changing single spaces to tabs does not work. Follow these steps:

1. Count the number of spaces between columns. One way to do this is to click at the beginning of the second column and press the Left arrow key until you reach the end of the first column, counting the number of times you press the Left arrow key.
2. Choose your word processor's find-and-replace command. For the text you want to find, enter as many blank spaces as you counted in

step 1. For the replacement text, specify a tab character. In Microsoft Word or Microsoft Write, you enter the two characters *^t*. In MacWrite, you press Command-Tab. In WriteNow, press Option-Tab.

3. Make the changes throughout the document.

Note that this method does not recognize blank (empty) columns, so sparse tables will not be converted properly.

If your word processor can't replace spaces with tabs, you can use the desk accessory Text Converter. Select its Replace Spaces option.

UNWANTED RETURNS

General Communications

Text documents obtained from other computers might have a return character (paragraph mark) at the end of each line, making each line act like a separate paragraph. Your word processor's search-and-replace feature can probably eliminate extra return characters in a few seconds. It must be able to search for and replace return characters. In Microsoft Word and Microsoft Write, for example, use the two characters *^p* to specify a return character for the Change command. In MacWrite, press Command-Return. In WriteNow, press Option-Return.

First replace the blank line that occurs after every real paragraph with an unusual character. Use something that doesn't appear anywhere else in the document—perhaps ¶. In most documents, you can find blank lines by searching for a pair of return characters (*^p^p* in Word or Write), one return for the end of a paragraph and one for the subsequent blank line. If paragraphs in your document end with a different pattern of characters, such as a return followed by five blank spaces (for indenting the start of the subsequent paragraph), replace that pattern with a unique symbol.

Next replace all the remaining return characters with spaces. This gets rid of the unwanted extra returns at the end of each line. Finally, change the unusual character you used to represent the end of a paragraph back to a return character.

If your word processor can't find and replace return characters, you can use the desk accessory Text Converter. Select its option Remove Line Breaks In Paragraphs.

BOXED IN

How can you get rid of boxes sprinkled throughout a document you received from another computer that is not a Macintosh? (See Figure 11-15.) The Mac puts a box in the text wherever it encounters a character that's missing from the applicable font. Try selecting each box and changing its font to Times, Helvetica, or another LaserWriter font. Any detritus still remaining usually can be removed by a "filter" utility such as CC Filter.

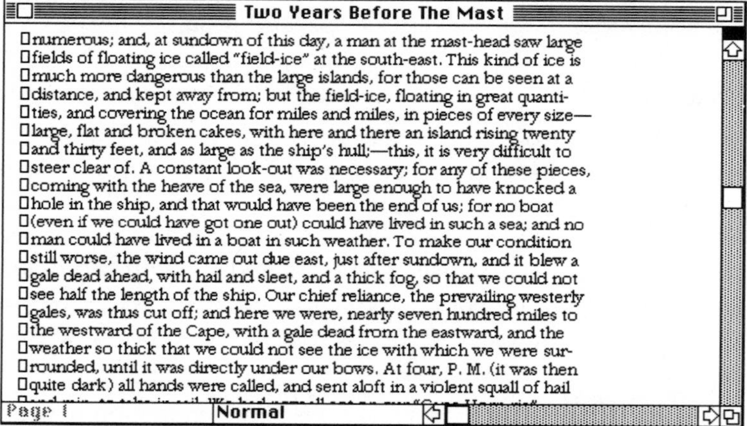

Two Years Before The Mast

□numerous; and, at sundown of this day, a man at the mast-head saw large
□fields of floating ice called "field-ice" at the south-east. This kind of ice is
□much more dangerous than the large islands, for those can be seen at a
□distance, and kept away from; but the field-ice, floating in great quanti-
□ties, and covering the ocean for miles and miles, in pieces of every size—
□large, flat and broken cakes, with here and there an island rising twenty
□and thirty feet, and as large as the ship's hull;—this, it is very difficult to
□steer clear of. A constant look-out was necessary; for any of these pieces,
□coming with the heave of the sea, were large enough to have knocked a
□hole in the ship, and that would have been the end of us; for no boat
□(even if we could have got one out) could have lived in such a sea; and no
□man could have lived in a boat in such weather. To make our condition
□still worse, the wind came out due east, just after sundown, and it blew a
□gale dead ahead, with hail and sleet, and a thick fog, so that we could not
□see half the length of the ship. Our chief reliance, the prevailing westerly
□gales, was thus cut off; and here we were, nearly seven hundred miles to
□the westward of the Cape, with a gale dead from the eastward, and the
□weather so thick that we could not see the ice with which we were sur-
□rounded, until it was directly under our bows. At four, P. M. (it was then
□quite dark) all hands were called, and sent aloft in a violent squall of hail

Page 1 Normal

FIGURE 11-15. BOX INVASION.

Documents from computers other than a Mac might include special characters that show up as boxes on a Mac. Eliminate them using utility software or the find-and-replace command of a word processor.

Alternatively, try the find-and-replace command of your Macintosh word processor. Follow these steps with Microsoft Word (versions 4.0 and later), WriteNow, and FullWrite Professional:

1. Copy the first box to the Clipboard. (Select the box and choose the Copy command.)
2. Choose the find-and-replace command (Change in Microsoft Word, Find/Replace in WriteNow, or Find, Change in FullWrite). Use the Paste command to specify the text to find. Be sure the replacement text is empty. (Drag across the entry box and press the Delete key.)

3. Make the changes throughout the document.
4. If there are still boxes in the document, repeat steps 1 through 3.

MacWrite II and WordPerfect automatically filter out characters they don't recognize when they open a document.

STRANGE CHARACTERS

General Communications

Strange characters appear when one application program encounters formatting codes embedded in a document by another application program. Almost all word processors allow boldface text, variable margins, and page headers, for example, but WordStar accomplishes that formatting one way on an IBM PC, and MacWrite does it another way on a Macintosh. If you simply transfer a WordStar document to the Mac and open it with MacWrite, the document will be full of strange characters—the result of MacWrite's misinterpretation of the WordStar formatting conventions.

To convert document formats, use the Apple File Exchange (AFE) utility with MacLink Plus/Translators, a library of four dozen translators. They translate between MacWrite, Microsoft Word, WordPerfect, OfficeWriter, WordStar, MultiMate, XYWrite, and more. Instead of AFE, you can also use MacLink Plus, which comes with the translators.

CONVERTING TO PLAIN TEXT

General Communications

Sometimes the only way to use a Mac document on another computer, or a non-Mac document on a Mac, is to convert the document to plain text before transferring it. On the Macintosh you do this by selecting the Text Only file format in the Save As dialog box, the form of which may vary depending on the application program. Many programs on other computers have similar options.

SOLVING PROBLEMS

NORMAL GIBBERISH

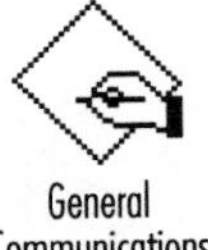
General Communications

It is normal to see gibberish on the screen when you first connect with some information services or electronic bulletin boards. Respond to this sign of life from the remote computer by pressing the Return key once or twice or by pressing Command-C.

EXTRANEOUS CHARACTERS

A bad phone connection creating static on the line is the most likely cause of extraneous characters—such as], {, or }—in the information you receive. Long-distance calls are particularly susceptible to noisy lines. Some long-distance companies have noisier connections than others, but bad connections are possible with any company. Here are some possible solutions:

- Hang up and try again. If you were using an alternate long-distance company (via a local-access number), place the call directly, through your normal long-distance company.
- Try another number for the information service. In major metropolitan areas, you often have a choice of several local numbers for one service.
- Use a slower baud rate (transmission speed). Modems are less sensitive to static at 1200 baud than at 2400 baud.
- Activate XON/XOFF flow control.
- Try a different modem. Some models filter noise better than others.

INVISIBLE TYPING

If what you type doesn't appear on the screen, select your communications software's local echo or half-duplex option. In MacTerminal and MicroPhone, for example, you select the Local Echo option of the Terminal Settings command.

DDOOUUBBLLEE TTYYPPEE

If every letter you type appears doubled, turn off your communications software's local echo or full-duplex option. In MacTerminal and MicroPhone, for example, be sure the Local Echo setting in the Terminal Settings command is not selected.

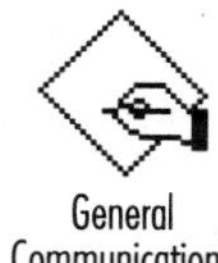

MISSING CHARACTERS

Intermittent missing characters may mean the remote computer is sending information faster than your communications software can receive it. To correct this problem, try one or more of the following:

- Be sure both computers are using the same baud rate; try a slower rate at both ends, such as 1200 or 300 baud.
- See whether activating the XON/XOFF flow control helps.
- Stop capturing or recording incoming information on disk.

APPENDIX

PRODUCT SOURCES

This appendix contains the names, addresses, and phone numbers of the companies that publish, manufacture, or distribute the products mentioned in this book. Most companies will send promotional literature on request. You can also order products directly from most companies, although you might get the product at a better price from a retail dealer or a mail-order company.

PUBLIC EXCHANGE SOFTWARE

Some software is available through user groups or from online information services. User groups charge a nominal amount for disks and shipping. Online information services charge according to the amount of time it takes to transfer the software via modem. Often software from the online information services costs more than the same software from user groups, but for the extra money you get instant delivery by phone. The software itself might be free, or it might be shareware, which means you get it on approval. If you decide to use it, you send payment—usually less than $40—directly to the program author (not to the user group or online information service).

The following two large user groups have worldwide membership and maintain large software libraries:

Berkeley Macintosh User Group (BMUG)
1442A Walnut Street, #62
Berkeley, CA 94709
(415) 549-2684 or (415) 849-2684

Boston Computer Society, Macintosh Users Group (BCS•Mac)
48 Grove Street
Somerville, MA 02144
(617) 625-7080

For the names of user groups in your area, call Apple Computer's referral service at (800) 538-9696, extension 500.

The following online information services have libraries of Macintosh software:

America Online
Quantum Computer Services, Incorporated
8619 Westwood Center Drive
Vienna, VA 22182
(703) 448-8700

CompuServe
CompuServe, Incorporated
5000 Arlington Centre Boulevard
Columbus, OH 43220
(614) 457-0802 or (800) 848-8199

Connect (formerly MacNet)
Connect, Incorporated
10161 Bubb Road
Cupertino, CA 95014
(408) 973-0110 or (800) 262-2638

Delphi
General Videotex Corporation
3 Blackstone Street
Cambridge, MA 02139
(800) 544-4005 or (617) 491-3393

GEnie
General Electric Information Services
401 North Washington Street
Rockville, MD 20850
(301) 340-4000 or (800) 638-9636

PRODUCT LIST

4th Dimension
Acius, Incorporated
10351 Bubb Road
Cupertino, CA 95014
(408) 252-4444

][In A Mac
Computer: Applications, Incorporated
12813 Lindley Drive
Raleigh, NC 27614
(919) 846-1411

A+ Mouse
Mouse Systems Corporation
47505 Seabridge Drive
Fremont, CA 94538
(415) 656-1117

Adobe Illustrator
Adobe Systems, Incorporated
1585 Charleston Road
Mountain View, CA 94039-7900
(415) 961-4400

Adobe Type Manager (ATM)
Adobe Systems, Incorporated
1585 Charleston Road
Mountain View, CA 94039-7900
(415) 961-4400

After Dark
Berkeley Systems
1700 Shattuck Avenue
Berkeley, CA 94709
(415) 540-5536

Alarm Clock
Included with system software from:
Apple Computer, Incorporated
10525 Mariani Avenue
Cupertino, CA 95014
(800) 538-9696, extension 500, for your nearest dealer

AnthroArm
Anthro Corporation
3221 NW Yeon Street
Portland, OR 97210
(503) 241-7113 or (800) 325-3841

Apple File Exchange (AFE)
Included with system software from:
Apple Computer, Incorporated
10525 Mariani Avenue
Cupertino, CA 95014
(800) 538-9696, extension 500, for your nearest dealer

AppleLink
Apple Computer, Incorporated
10525 Mariani Avenue
Cupertino, CA 95014
(800) 538-9696, extension 500, for your nearest dealer

Apple PC 5.25 Drive
Apple Computer, Incorporated
10525 Mariani Avenue
Cupertino, CA 95014
(800) 538-9696, extension 500, for your nearest dealer

AppleShare
Apple Computer, Incorporated
10525 Mariani Avenue
Cupertino, CA 95014
(800) 538-9696, extension 500, for your nearest dealer

AutoMac
Genesis Micro Software
Post Office Box 6236
Bellevue, WA 98008

Black Jack
Digital Systems International
7659 1078th Place NE
Redmond, WA 98952
(206) 881-7544

CacheControl
User groups and online information services or the author:
Jim Hamilton
2914 Aftonshire Way, #13102
Austin, TX 78748

Canvas
Deneba Systems, Incorporated
3305 NW 74th Avenue
Miami, FL 33122
(800) 622-6827

Capture
Mainstay
5311-B Derry Avenue
Agoura Hills, CA 91301
(818) 991-6540

CC Filter
User groups

Chooser
Included with system software from:
Apple Computer, Incorporated
10525 Mariani Avenue
Cupertino, CA 95014
(800) 538-9696, extension 500, for your nearest dealer

Clipper
Solutions International
30 Commerce Street
Williston, VT 05495
(802) 658-5506

CloseView
Included with system software from:
Apple Computer, Incorporated
10525 Mariani Avenue
Cupertino, CA 95014
(800) 538-9696, extension 500, for your nearest dealer

CompuServe Navigator
CompuServe, Incorporated
5000 Arlington Centre Boulevard
Columbus, OH 43220
(614) 457-0802 or (800) 848-8199

Cricket Draw
Computer Associates
711 Stewart Avenue
Garden City, NY 11530-4787
(800) 531-5236

Cricket Graph
Computer Associates
711 Stewart Avenue
Garden City, NY 11530-4787
(800) 531-5236

Curlers
User groups and online information services.

DesignStudio
Letraset USA
40 Eisenhower Drive
Paramus, NJ 07653
(201) 845-6100 or (800) 526-9703

Disk Express
ALSoft Incorporated
Post Office Box 927
Spring, TX 77383
(713) 353-4090

DiskTop
CE Software Incorporated
1854 Fuller Road
Post Office Box 65580
West Des Moines, IA 50265
(800) 523-7638 or (515) 224-1995

DOS Mounter
Dayna Communications
50 South Main, Suite 530
Salt Lake City, UT 84144
(801) 531-0600

Drawing Table
Brøderbund Software
17 Paul Drive
San Rafael, CA 94903-2101
(800) 521-6263 or (415) 492-3200

Drive 2.4
Kennect Technology
120-A Albright Way
Los Gatos, CA 95030
(408) 370-2866 or (800) 555-1232

Easy Access
Included with system software from:
Apple Computer, Incorporated
10525 Mariani Avenue
Cupertino, CA 95014
(800) 538-9696, extension 500, for your nearest dealer

EasyLink
Western Union
1 Lake Street
Upper Saddle River, NJ 07458
(800) 779-1111

EndLine
User groups and online information services

Expressionist
Prescience Corporation
939 Howard Street
San Francisco, CA 94103
(415) 543-2252

Fanny Mac
Mobius Technologies, Incorporated
6020 Adeline Street
Oakland, CA 94608
(415) 654-0556

FDHD SuperDrive
Apple Computer, Incorporated
10525 Mariani Avenue
Cupertino, CA 95014
(800) 538-9696, extension 500, for your nearest dealer

FileMaker
Claris Corporation
5201 Patrick Henry Drive
Post Office Box 58168
Santa Clara, CA 95052-8168
(408) 987-7000

Finder
Included with system software from:
Apple Computer, Incorporated
10525 Mariani Avenue
Cupertino, CA 95014
(800) 538-9696, extension 500, for your nearest dealer

Find File
Included with system software from:
Apple Computer, Incorporated
10525 Mariani Avenue
Cupertino, CA 95014
(800) 538-9696, extension 500, for your nearest dealer

FKey/Sound Mover
ALSoft Incorporated
Post Office Box 927
Spring, TX 77383
(713) 353-4090

Fluent Fonts
Casady & Greene, Incorporated
Post Office Box 223779
Carmel, CA 93922
(408) 624-8716

Font/DA Mover
Included with system software versions earlier than 7.0 from:
Apple Computer, Incorporated
10525 Mariani Avenue
Cupertino, CA 95014
(800) 538-9696, extension 500, for your nearest dealer

Font/DA Utility
Included with MasterJuggler from:
ALSoft Incorporated
Post Office Box 927
Spring, TX 77383
(713) 353-4090

FONTastic and FONTastic Plus
Altsys Corporation
720 Avenue F, Suite 108
Plano, TX 75074
(214) 424-4888

Font Downloader
Included with printer fonts from:
Adobe Systems, Incorporated
1585 Charleston Road
Mountain View, CA 94039-7900
(415) 961-4400

Fonts 4 to 48
User groups

FontSizer
U.S. Microlabs, Incorporated
1611 Headway Circle
Austin, TX 78754
(512) 339-0001

FreeHand
Aldus Corporation
411 First Avenue South
Seattle, WA 98104-2871
(206) 622-5500

FreeTerm
User groups and online information services

Full Impact
Ashton-Tate Corporation
Macintosh Division
6411 Guadalupe Mines Road
San Jose, CA 95120
(408) 370-8902

FullPaint
Ashton-Tate Corporation
Macintosh Division
6411 Guadalupe Mines Road
San Jose, CA 95120
(408) 370-8902

FullWrite Professional
Ashton-Tate Corporation
Macintosh Division
6411 Guadalupe Mines Road
San Jose, CA 95120
(408) 370-8902

Glue
Solutions International
30 Commerce Street
Williston, VT 05495
(802) 658-5506

HeapFixer
CE Software Incorporated
1854 Fuller Road
Post Office Box 65580
West Des Moines, IA 50265
(800) 523-7638

HyperCard
Claris Corporation
5201 Patrick Henry Drive
Post Office Box 58168
Santa Clara, CA 95052-8168
(408) 987-7000

HyperDialer
DataDesk International
9314 Eton Avenue
Chatsworth, CA 91311
(818) 998-4200 or (800) 328-2337

ImageWriter
Apple Computer, Incorporated
10525 Mariani Avenue
Cupertino, CA 95014
(800) 538-9696, extension 500, for your nearest dealer

Installer
Included with the latest system software from:
Apple Computer, Incorporated
10525 Mariani Avenue
Cupertino, CA 95014
(800) 538-9696, extension 500, for your nearest dealer

Key Caps
Included with system software from:
Apple Computer, Incorporated
10525 Mariani Avenue
Cupertino, CA 95014
(800) 538-9696, extension 500, for your nearest dealer

LaserTransliterator
Linguists' Software
925 Hindley Lane
Edmonds, WA 98020
(206) 775-1130

LaserWriter
Apple Computer, Incorporated
10525 Mariani Avenue
Cupertino, CA 95014
(800) 538-9696, extension 500, for your nearest dealer

LaserWriter Font Utility
Apple Computer, Incorporated
10525 Mariani Avenue
Cupertino, CA 95014
(800) 538-9696, extension 500, for your nearest dealer

Layout
User groups and online information services

Long Date
User groups and online information services or the author:
Don Leeper
5181 Fox Hills Avenue
Buena Park, CA 90621

Mac II PC Drive Card
Apple Computer, Incorporated
10525 Mariani Avenue
Cupertino, CA 95014
(800) 538-9696, extension 500, for your nearest dealer

MacBreeze
Levco Sales
6181 Cornerstone Court East, Suite 101
San Diego, CA 92121
(619) 457-2011

MacCalc
Bravo Technologies, Incorporated
Post Office Box 10078
Berkeley, CA 94709-0078
(415) 841-8552

MacCracker
Icon Review
Post Office Box 911, Department CT097
Monterey, CA 93942
(408) 625-0465

MacDraw and MacDraw II
Claris Corporation
5201 Patrick Henry Drive
Post Office Box 58168
Santa Clara, CA 95052-8168
(408) 987-7000

Macify
User groups and online information services or the author:
Eric Celeste
350 North Parkview
Columbus, OH 43209

MacKeymeleon
Avenue Software, Incorporated
2162 Charest Boulevard West
Sainte-Foy, Quebec, Canada G1N 2G3
(418) 682-3088

MacLink Plus
DataViz, Incorporated
35 Corporate Drive
Trumbull, CT 06611
(203) 268-0030

MacLink Plus/Translators
DataViz, Incorporated
35 Corporate Drive
Trumbull, CT 06611
(203) 268-0030

MacNet
Connect, Incorporated
10161 Bubb Road
Cupertino, CA 95014
(408) 973-0110 or (800) 262-2638

MacOpener
Central Products Corporation
Post Office Box 980305
Houston, TX 77098
(713) 529-1080

MacPaint
Claris Corporation
5201 Patrick Henry Drive
Post Office Box 58168
Santa Clara, CA 95052-8168
(408) 987-7000

MacPhonetics
Linguists' Software
925 Hindley Lane
Edmonds, WA 98020
(206) 775-1130

MacroMaker
Included with system software versions between 6.0 and 7.0 from:
Apple Computer, Incorporated
10525 Mariani Avenue
Cupertino, CA 95014
(800) 538-9696, extension 500, for your nearest dealer

MacTerminal
Apple Computer, Incorporated
10525 Mariani Avenue
Cupertino, CA 95014
(800) 538-9696, extension 500, for your nearest dealer

MacWrite and MacWrite II
Claris Corporation
5201 Patrick Henry Drive
Post Office Box 58168
Santa Clara, CA 95052-8168
(408) 987-7000

Map
Included with system software versions 6.0 and later from:
Apple Computer, Incorporated
10525 Mariani Avenue
Cupertino, CA 95014
(800) 538-9696, extension 500, for your nearest dealer

MasterJuggler
ALSoft Incorporated
Post Office Box 927
Spring, TX 77383
(713) 353-4090

MCI Mail
MCI Communications Corporation
1150 17th Street NW, Suite 800
Washington, DC 20036
(202) 833-8484 or (800) 444-6245

MDC II
New Canaan Microcode
136 Beech Road
New Canaan, CT 06840
(800) 942-4008

Microphone and Microphone II
Software Ventures, Incorporated
2907 Claremont Avenue, Suite 220
Berkeley, CA 94705
(415) 644-3232

Microsoft Excel
Microsoft Corporation
One Microsoft Way
Redmond, WA 98052-6399
(206) 882-8080 or (800) 426-9400

Microsoft File
Microsoft Corporation
One Microsoft Way
Redmond, WA 98052-6399
(206) 882-8080 or (800) 426-9400

Microsoft Word
Microsoft Corporation
One Microsoft Way
Redmond, WA 98052-6399
(206) 882-8080 or (800) 426-9400

Microsoft Works
Microsoft Corporation
One Microsoft Way
Redmond, WA 98052-6399
(206) 882-8080 or (800) 426-9400

Microsoft Write
Microsoft Corporation
One Microsoft Way
Redmond, WA 98052-6399
(206) 882-8080 or (800) 426-9400

MindWrite
Delta Point, Incorporated
200-G Heritage Harbor
Monterey, CA 93940
(800) 367-4334 or (408) 648-4000

miniWriter
Maitreya Design
Post Office Box 1480
Goleta, CA 93116

MORE II
Living Videotext, a division of
Symantec Corporation
10201 Torre Avenue
Cupertino, CA 95014
(408) 253-9600

Motorola 68882
Tercom
6900 Roosevelt Way NW, Suite 193
Seattle, WA 98115
(206) 527-1257, (800) 544-9543,
or (800) 669-7555

MouseEase
Tacklind Design, Incorporated
250 Cowper Street
Palo Alto, CA 94301
(415) 322-2257

Mouse Mover
Magnum Software
21115 Devonshire Street, Suite 337
Chatsworth, CA 91311
(818) 700-0510

MultiFinder
Included with system software from:
Apple Computer, Incorporated
10525 Mariani Avenue
Cupertino, CA 95014
(800) 538-9696, extension 500, for your
nearest dealer

Multiplan
Microsoft Corporation
One Microsoft Way
Redmond, WA 98052-6399
(206) 882-8080 or (800) 426-9400

On Cue
ICOM Simulations, Incorporated
648 South Wheeling Road
Wheeling, IL 60090
(312) 520-4440

PageMaker
Aldus Corporation
411 First Avenue South
Seattle, WA 98104-2871
(206) 622-5500

Panorama
ProVUE Development
15180 Transistor Lane
Huntington Beach, CA 92649
(714) 892-8199

PC Tools Deluxe
Central Point Software
15220 NW Greenbrier Parkway,
Suite 200
Beaverton, OR 96007-5764
(503) 690-8090

Persuasion
Aldus Corporation
411 First Avenue South
Seattle, WA 98104-2871
(206) 622-5500

PixelPaint
SuperMac Technology
485 Potrero Avenue
Sunnyvale, CA 94086
(415) 964-8884

PowerPoint
Microsoft Corporation
One Microsoft Way
Redmond, WA 98052-6399
(206) 882-8080 or (800) 426-9400

Print Monitor
Included with system software versions 6.0 and later from:
Apple Computer, Incorporated
10525 Mariani Avenue
Cupertino, CA 95014
(800) 538-9696, extension 500, for your nearest dealer

Print Shop
Brøderbund Software
17 Paul Drive
San Rafael, CA 94903-2101
(800) 521-6263 or (415) 492-3200

QM Administrator
CE Software, Incorporated
1854 Fuller Road
Post Office Box 65580
West Des Moines, IA 50265
(800) 523-7638 or (515) 224-1995

QuarkXPress
Quark, Incorporated
300 South Jackson Street, Suite 100
Denver, CO 80209
(303) 934-2211 or (800) 356-9363

QuicKeys
CE Software, Incorporated
1854 Fuller Road
Post Office Box 65580
West Des Moines, IA 50265
(800) 523-7638 or (515) 224-1995

QuickMail
CE Software, Incorporated
1854 Fuller Road
Post Office Box 65580
West Des Moines, IA 50265
(800) 523-7638 or (515) 224-1995

ReadySetGo
Letraset USA
40 Eisenhower Drive
Paramus, NJ 07653
(201) 845-6100 or (800) 526-9703

ResEdit
Apple Programmers and Developers Association (APDA)
(800) 282-2732 in the U.S., (800) 637-0029 in Canada, (408) 562-3910 elsewhere

Scrapbook
Included with system software from:
Apple Computer, Incorporated
10525 Mariani Avenue
Cupertino, CA 95014
(800) 538-9696, extension 500, for your nearest dealer

SCSI Probe
User groups and online information services such as CompuServe (file SCSI in library 4 of the MACPRO forum) and Connect (file "SCSIProbe cdev" in the file libraries of the Mac Symposium forum)

Sea Breeze II
Computerware
2800 West Bayshore Road
Palo Alto, CA 94303
(415) 496-1000

SE-Bus PC Drive Card
Apple Computer, Incorporated
10525 Mariani Avenue
Cupertino, CA 95014
(800) 538-9696, extension 500, for your nearest dealer

Set File Count
Comes with MasterJuggler from:
ALSoft Incorporated
Post Office Box 927
Spring, TX 77383
(713) 353-4090

Short Date
User groups and online information services or the author:
Don Leeper
5181 Fox Hills Avenue
Buena Park, CA 90621

Smartcom II
Hayes Microcomputer Products, Incorporated
Post Office Box 105203
Atlanta, GA 30348
(404) 449-8791

SmartScrap
Solutions International
30 Commerce Street
Williston, VT 05495
(802) 658-5506

SoftFonts
Bitstream, Incorporated
Athenaeum House
215 First Street
Cambridge, MA 02142
(617) 497-6222 or (800) 522-3668

SoftPC
Insignia Solutions
254 San Geronimo Way
Sunnyvale, CA 94086
(415) 771-7001

Studio/8
Electronic Arts
1820 Gateway Drive
San Mateo, CA 94404
(415) 571-7171

Suitcase II
Fifth Generation
1322 Bell Avenue, Suite 1A
Tustin, CA 92680
(714) 259-0541

SuperCard
Silicon Beach Software
9770 Carroll Center Road, Suite J
Post Office Box 261430
San Diego, CA 92126
(619) 695-6956

SuperLaserSpool
SuperMac Technology
485 Potrero Avenue
Sunnyvale, CA 94086
(415) 964-8884

SuperPaint
Silicon Beach Software, Incorporated
9770 Carroll Center Road, Suite J
Post Office Box 261430
San Diego, CA 92126
(619) 695-6956

SuperSpool
SuperMac Technology
485 Potrero Avenue
Sunnyvale, CA 94086
(415) 964-8884

Swivel 3D
Paracomp
123 Townsend Street, Suite 310
San Francisco, CA 94107
(415) 543-3848

Symantec Utilities for Macintosh (SUM)
Symantec Corporation
10201 Torre Avenue
Cupertino, CA 95014
(408) 253-9600

Tempo II
Affinity Microsystems
1050 Walnut Street, Suite 425
Boulder, CO 80302
(303) 442-4840 or (800) 367-6771

Text Converter
User groups and online information services or the author:
Ronald R. Derynck
Productivity Tools
2423 56th Street NE, #210
Calgary, Alberta, Canada T1Y 2X6

Time
User groups and online information services or the author:
Don Leeper
5181 Fox Hills Avenue
Buena Park, CA 90621

Trapeze
Delta Point, Incorporated
200-G Heritage Harbor
Monterey, CA 93940
(800) 367-4334 or (408) 648-4000

TypeNow
Mainstay
5311-B Derry Avenue
Agoura Hills, CA 91301
(818) 991-6540

Virtual 2.0
Connectix Corporation
125 Constitution Drive
Menlo Park, CA 94025
(415) 324-0727

White Knight
The Freesoft Company
150 Hickory Drive
Beaver Falls, PA 15010
(412) 846-2700

Widgets
CE Software, Incorporated
1854 Fuller Road
Post Office Box 65580
West Des Moines, IA 50265
(515) 224-1995 or (800) 523-7638

Wingz
Informix Software, Incorporated
16011 College Boulevard
Lenexa, KS 66219
(913) 492-3800

WordPerfect
WordPerfect Corporation
1555 North Technology Way
Orem, UT 84057
(801) 225-5000

Works-Works Transporter
Online services such as CompuServe (file WKSAFE.SIT in data library 4 of the MACPRO forum)

WriteFontSize
User groups and online information services

WriteNow
T/Maker Company
1390 Villa Street
Mountain View, CA 94041
(415) 962-0195

TRADEMARKS

Trapeze™ is a trademark of Access Technology, Incorporated.

4th Dimension® and the 4th Dimension logo and screen icon are registered trademarks of ACI and Acius, Incorporated.

Adobe®, Adobe Illustrator®, and PostScript® are registered trademarks of Adobe Systems, Incorporated. Adobe Illustrator, Adobe Photoshop, and Adobe Type Manager screen icons reprinted by permission of Adobe Systems, Incorporated. ©1989–1990 Adobe Systems, Incorporated. All rights reserved.

Aldus®, Aldus FreeHand®, PageMaker®, and Persuasion® are registered trademarks of Aldus Corporation. All rights reserved. Aldus FreeHand, Aldus PageMaker, and Persuasion screen icons reprinted by permission of Aldus Corporation. ©1986–1990 Aldus Corporation.

FDHD™ and Finder™ are trademarks and Apple®, AppleLink®, AppleShare®, HyperCard®, ImageWriter®, LaserWriter®, Mac®, Macintosh®, MacTerminal®, and MultiFinder® are registered trademarks of Apple Computer, Incorporated. Apple screen icons reprinted by permission. ©Apple Computer, Incorporated.

Full Impact™ and FullWrite Professional™ are trademarks and Ashton-Tate® and FullPaint® are registered trademarks of Ashton-Tate Corporation. Full Impact and FullWrite screen icons reprinted by permission of Ashton-Tate Corporation.

Bitstream® is a registered trademark of Bitstream, Incorporated.

MacCalc™ is a trademark of Bravo Technologies, Incorporated. MacCalc icon reprinted by permission of Bravo Technologies.

Brøderbund Software® and The Print Shop® are registered trademarks of Brøderbund Software, Incorporated. The Print Shop screen icon reprinted by permission of Brøderbund Software, Incorporated.

Fluent Fonts™ is a trademark of Casady & Greene, Incorporated.

PC Tools Deluxe™ is a trademark of Central Point Software, Incorporated.

QuickMail™ and the QuickMail logo are trademarks of CE Software, Incorporated.

Claris™ is a trademark and FileMaker®, MacDraw®, MacPaint®, and MacWrite® are registered trademarks of Claris Corporation.

CompuServe® is a registered trademark of CompuServe, Incorporated.

MacLink® is a registered trademark of DataViz, Incorporated.

MindWrite® and Trapeze® are registered trademarks of Delta Point, Incorporated.

Canvas DA® is a registered trademark of Deneba Systems, Incorporated. Canvas screen icon reprinted by permission of Deneba Software. ©Deneba Software.

Super Laser Spool icon reprinted by permission of Fifth Generation Systems, Incorporated.

AutoMac® is a registered trademark of Genesis Micro Software.

Hayes® and Smartcom II® are registered trademarks of Hayes Microcomputer Products, Incorporated.

Wingz™ is a trademark and HyperScript® and Informix® are registered trademarks of Informix Software, Incorporated.

ReadySetGo screen icon reprinted by permission of Letraset Graphic Design Software.

MacNet® is a registered trademark of MacNet Corporation.

MCI MAIL® is a registered servicemark of MCI Communications Corporation.

Microsoft®, Multiplan®, and PowerPoint® are registered trademarks of Microsoft Corporation.

Motorola® is a registered trademark of Motorola, Incorporated.

A+ Mouse and the A+ Mouse icon are copyrights of Mouse Systems Corporation.

Panorama screen icon reprinted by permission of ProVUE Development.

QuarkXPress® is a registered trademark of Quark, Incorporated. The QuarkXPress icon reprinted by permission and is a trademark of Quark, Incorporated. ©1986–1990 Quark, Incorporated. All rights reserved.

Dark Castle™, SuperCard™, and SuperPaint™ are trademarks of Silicon Beach Software, Incorporated. Dark Castle, SuperCard, and SuperPaint screen icons reprinted by permission of Aldus Corporation. ©1986–1990 Silicon Beach Software, Incorporated. All rights reserved.

SmartScrap™ is a trademark of Solutions, Incorporated.

PixelPaint™ is a trademark of SuperMac Software. Pixel Paint screen icon reprinted by permission of SuperMac Software.

More II™ is a trademark of Symantec Corporation.

WriteNow® is a registered trademark of T/Maker Company.

EasyLink℠ is a servicemark of The Western Union Telegraph Company.

WordPerfect® is a registered trademark of WordPerfect Corporation. WordPerfect screen icon reprinted by permission of WordPerfect Corporation.

Swivel 3D™ is a trademark of Young Harvill/VPL Research, Incorporated.

INDEX

G

J

K

L

S

T

U

V

W

Lon Poole began writing about personal computers and their practical applications in 1976, soon after they first appeared. His first book, *Some Common BASIC Programs*, appeared in 1977, followed by several more books on using BASIC for vertical business applications. In 1981, he wrote the now-classic *Apple II User's Guide*, which has sold over half a million copies worldwide.

Lon helped found *MacWorld* magazine in 1983 and has contributed articles regularly since then. Every month he answers readers' questions in his column "Quick Tips." Lon Poole has also authored three Mac books. The first, *MacWork, MacPlay*, is a beginner's workbook for MacWrite, MacPaint, and Multiplan. The second, *Mac Insights*, presents the best tips, shortcuts, and enhancements for Macintosh use drawn from his column and other sources. The third is the *Programmer's Quick Reference Guide to HyperTalk*.

Lon was voted a member of the "Macintosh 100" in 1986 by the readers and editors of *Macintosh Buyer's Guide*.

The manuscript for this book was prepared and submitted to Microsoft Press in electronic form. Text files were processed and formatted using Microsoft Word.

Principal word processors: Debbie Kem and Judith Bloch
Principal proofreader: Jean Zimmer
Principal typographer: Ruth Pettis
Principal illustrators: Rick Bourgoin, Rebecca Geisler-Johnson
Cover designer: Becker Design Associates
Cover color separator: Wescan Color Corporation

Text composition by Microsoft Press in Garamond with display type in Futura Extra Bold Condensed, using the Magna composition system and the Linotronic 300 laser imagesetter.

Printed on recycled paper stock.